Alberta's First Highway Maps

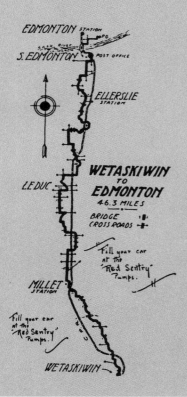

Alberta's first road guide, produced in 1914 by a member of a Calgary auto club, consisted of twelve strip maps with minute directions (including the nearest telephones). Although the guide showed some 440 miles of road, author Leo English minced no words about their state: *"Methods of road construction are crude in the extreme. When a road is newly graded it is all but impassable for months thereafter."*

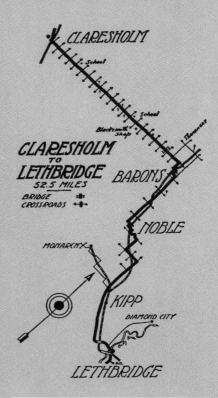

CALGARY TO EDMONTON
Wetaskiwin to Edmonton Section

00.0 WETASKIWIN—(Town)—160.9 miles north of Calgary and 46.1 miles south of Edmonton. Starting at the Post Office, proceed east.
00.1 Turn left, west of railway.
00.4 Curve left; north-west.
01.0 Up 8% grade.
01.5 Turn right.
01.8 Turn left; then right.
02.1 Cross railway.
02.9 Turn left; large slough to left.
03.9 Turn right.
04.7 Down and up 10%, cross culvert.
05.7 Curve left; then right.
06.6 Turn left; road curving north-west.
09.0 Turn right.
09.6 Curve left.
09.9 Turn right.
10.1 Turn left and cross railway, then turn right.
10.2 MILLET—(Station).
10.3 Curve left.
10.6 Curve left, then turn right.
12.5 Direct road north.
15.6 Turn right and cross railway, then turn left.
17.3 Direct road; pass school on right.
18.0 Turn left and cross railway, then turn right.
18.9 Culvert, then curve left.
19.4 Turn left; then right.
21.5 Turn left; then right.
21.9 Ditch bump in road; bad culverts and bumps along here.
22.6 LEDUC—(Town).

Fill up at the "RED SENTRY PUMP"

25.0 Turn right; then left and north.
25.7 Turn right at crossroads.
26.1 Cross railway and turn left.
26.7 Phone in house on right.
28.0 Direct road north.
28.8 Cross railway.
29.2 Culverts and mud in wet weather.

30.0 Turn left; then right.
32.1 Turn right at crossroads. Road very bad in wet weather.
33.0 Curve right; river on left.
33.1 Cross bridge; curving.
33.4 Cross railway.
33.5 Turn left; bad mud hole in wet weather when road a little further east must be taken.
33.8 Turn left and cross railway.
34.2 Curve right and left in north-westerly direction.
34.4 Turn right; road curving.
35.5 Cross bridge.
36.0 Cross bridge; direct road north.
36.2 ELLERSLIE—(Station)—Direct road.
37.0 Curve left.
37.2 Turn right.
37.5 Turn left.
37.9 Turn right; direct road north.
38.3 Direct road.
40.8 Curve right.
40.9 Turn left; direct north.
41.5 Pavement; 106th St. South Edmonton.
42.5 Turn left on 76th Avenue.
42.8 Turn left on Main Street.
43.2 Turn left on Whyte Avenue.
43.3 SOUTH EDMONTON—(Post Office).
43.7 Turn right with car line for bridge.
44.3 Cross bridge; speed six miles.
44.9 Provincial Capital to right; follow car line.
45.4 Turn right on Jasper Avenue.
46.2 Turn left on McDougal Avenue.
46.3 EDMONTON—(Post Office)—(207.2 miles north of Calgary). See index.

CLARESHOLM TO LETHBRIDGE TRAIL

This route is the shortest trail between Calgary and Lethbridge, and the roads are in splendid condition for the greater part of the year. It is also the best route to travel between Calgary and Medicine Hat.

00.0 CLARESHOLM—(Town, 89.2 miles south from Calgary). Starting from Queen's hotel, proceed south.
00.6 Turn left and cross railway.
00.8 Direct road east 20 miles for Lethbridge via Barons; turn right and south for Macleod.
03.8 Telephone on left.
08.5 Telephone on left.
08.8 Telephone on right.
10.8 Telephone on left.
15.4 Blacksmith shop.
21.8 Turn right and south.
22.8 Turn left and east.
23.2 Cross railway and turn right.
23.8 Barons—(Village), turn left and east.
24.4 Turn right; direct south for 7.6 miles.
26.6 Telephone on left.
27.6 Cross railway.
32.0 Turn left and east.
32.2 Jog to right.
32.4 Turn left and cross railway.
32.5 Noble—(P.O. and station), turn right and south.
33.3 Turn left and east.
34.3 Turn right and south.
36.3 Turn left and east.
38.3 Turn left; direct south for 4.3 miles.
42.6 Cross railway and turn left; south-east.
44.0 Kipp—(Station and mining village).
48.9 Turn left and cross bridge over C.P. railway.
49.2 Direct road down 10% grade.
50.1 Cross culvert at bottom.
50.6 Cross steel bridge over Belly river and curve right up 10% grade.
52.2 Cross under railway viaduct and turn left.
52.5 Turn right.
52.6 Lethbridge—(Hotel)—(City, 141.9 miles from Calgary via Claresholm).

ALBERTA IN THE 20TH CENTURY

A JOURNALISTIC HISTORY OF THE PROVINCE IN TWELVE VOLUMES

VOLUME THREE

THE BOOM AND THE BUST

United Western Communications Ltd.
Edmonton
1994

Consultative Committee: Donald M. Graves, a Calgary businessman; Hugh A. Dempsey, curator emeritus of the Glenbow-Alberta Institute in Calgary; Martin Lynch of Kaslo, BC, former chief of the copy desk of the *Globe and Mail*; Richard D. McCallum, president of Quality Color Press Inc., of Edmonton.

Editor: Ted Byfield
Photo Editor: Kathleen Wall

Writers
Ted Byfield
Virginia Byfield
Robert Collins
Michael Dawe
Calvin Demmon
Hugh A. Dempsey
Mary Frances Doucedame
Janet Harvey
Brian Hutchinson
Stephani Keer
Tom McFeely
George Oake
Alan Rayburn
Courtney Tower

Supervisor of Research: Kathleen Wall

Researchers
Robert Butler
Colby Cosh
Jeff Cowley
Janet Harvey
Les Kozma
Paul Kroeker
Jennifer MacKinnon
Michael Peterson
Marc Simao

Proofreader: Gillian Neelands

Page production: Greg Poulin,
Pièce de Résistance Graphics Ltd.
Edmonton

Lithography: Screaming Colour Inc.
Edmonton

Printer: Quality Color Press Inc.
Edmonton

The publisher acknowledges the generous assistance of the Glenbow-Alberta Institute of Calgary, the Provincial Archives of Alberta in Edmonton, the National Archives of Canada, the City of Edmonton Archives, the Red Deer Museum and Archives, the Medicine Hat Museum and Art Gallery, and the Sir Alexander Galt Museum in Lethbridge.

The Boom and the Bust

© Copyright 1994 United Western Communications Ltd.

(Alberta in the 20th Century v.3)
Includes bibliographical references and index
ISBN 0-9695718-2-8

1. Alberta — History — 1905-1945*
2. Alberta — Social conditions — 1905-1945.* I. Byfield, Ted.
II. United Western Communications. III. Series.

FC3672.B66   1994   971.23'02   C94-910373-X
F1078.B66   1994

Alberta in the 20th Century

Table of Contents

Section One THE BOOM

Section Two THE NEW CITIES

Section Three   CRACKS IN THE LIBERAL BASTION

Section Four   THE SOCIAL EXPLOSIONS

Section Five   THE BIG BUST OF 1914-15

The picture on the cover:
This photograph, probably taken near the Canadian Pacific depot in Calgary in mid-decade, strikingly illustrates Alberta's future. In it, the passengers on a colonist train assemble to have their picture taken. The cosmopolitan assortment, which appears to include flannel-clad English gentlemen, an Orthodox priest, and Ukrainian settlers in traditional apparel, represents the kind of population base that would create Alberta in the 20th century.

Foreword

In producing this volume we were compelled to face two crucial and, what seemed, anyway, devastating facts. For one, the title we had provisionally given the volume was historically mistaken. Second, the volume itself, as originally conceived, was a practical impossibility.

The initial plan called for the title, *The Boom, the War and the Bust.* We gave it this name because, in retrospect, the Alberta that emerged from the second decade was far less prosperous than the Alberta of the great boom that preceded the First World War. We assumed, therefore, that the order of events was first the boom, roughly 1900 to 1914, then the war from 1914 to 1918, and finally the bust in 1919 and 1920.

But that, unhappily, is not what happened. The boom came from 1910 to 1913, all right, but the great economic calamity that followed (in which Edmonton alone lost nearly a quarter of its population) actually began in the fall of 1913 and was well advanced when war was declared the following summer. The effect of the war was, in general, to make things worse, but bad times did not begin with the war. Properly, therefore, the book should have been entitled, *The Boom, the Bust and the War.*

Compared with the second realization, however, the inaccuracy in the title was insignificant. As we produced the volume, we became at first suspicious and later appalled. It grew increasingly plain that we could not begin to accommodate even a sparse description of the events of the province's second decade in anything under 600 pages. Such a book would require special binding and a very heavy postage charge. And even at that, the rich heritage of photographs that survives from the era could not be adequately represented.

The reason for this, I should have foreseen. The two great events of the decade — the boom and the war — are each of them too momentous, both in what occurred and in what ensued, to share a single volume. To tell the story of the great boom that produced the Alberta we have known through most of the 20th century, along with the swift economic recession that followed, would in itself require a volume. Similarly, Alberta's role in the Great War — we had more than 50,000 men in arms from a province of roughly 400,000 men, women and children — neither could nor should be encapsulated. There were countless stories of individual Albertans whose raw heroism and dedication to the cause of democracy must be described. To omit them, while pretending to tell the province's story, would belie the whole effort.

We therefore decided to take the decade in two volumes, rather than the one that was originally planned, to vastly exploit the photographic potential of the boom, and both the artistic and photographic heritage left by the war. Thus this Volume III has been entitled *The Boom and the Bust — 1910-1914*, while Volume IV will be called *The Great War and its Consequences — 1914-1920*. Volume IV will appear approximately six months after this one, which is coming out fifteen months after Volume II. We plan to bring out Volume V, covering the 1920s, in early spring of 1995, putting the series back on schedule.

I asked Hugh Dempsey, curator emeritus of the Glenbow-Alberta Institute in Calgary, whether this necessity to proliferate the volumes will now assail us in every decade. He thought not. The only other volume that might be similarly overloaded, he said, would be that which now becomes Volume VII (and was previously Volume VI), covering the Second World War and the Leduc discovery. He said that he too is currently preparing a pictorial history of Calgary, and had precisely the same problem with the 1910-1920 decade.

I should, as I say, have foreseen this flaw in our original plan. The life of the province can no more be divided into a set of equal decades, each with its own equal quota of events, than could the life of an individual be so divided. Things do not befall us in this measured way. There are years when very little happens to us, and other years when many things happen. Our 40s may be largely uneventful and our 50s altogether too full of events. The same is true of our province.

You will notice also that the division between these two current volumes is not strict. Some of the chapters in this one look forward beyond 1914 in order to complete some episode in our history. Some of those in Volume IV will have originated prior to 1914. However, here in general is that which happened to us before the world heard what historian Barbara Tuchman called "the Guns of August." Here are those raucous and zany times in which the man or woman who was not given to optimism must surely be given to treason.

It was all illusion, of course, and by the time the volume ends the bust has begun and the first of our woes have descended upon us. But it was a riotous and wonderful illusion while it lasted. The face of Alberta was young, the eyes bright, and the horizon boundless, as the photographs you'll see herein so eloquently testify.

Ted Byfield,
March 26, 1994.

List of Contributors for Volume III

Ted Byfield is the founder of *Alberta Report, Western Report* and *British Columbia Report* news-magazines. After seventeen years on daily newspapers, he helped found the St. John's Boys' Schools in Manitoba and Alberta where he taught history for ten years. He started *St. John's Edmonton Report*, the ancestor of *Alberta Report*, in 1973.

Virginia Byfield is a senior editor of *Alberta Report* newsmagazine who in a twenty-year career has edited its political, educational, cultural and religious departments.

Robert Collins was raised in rural Saskatchewan and has been staff writer with *Maclean's* and *Reader's Digest*, editor of *Toronto Life* and *Imperial Oil Review*. He has published thirteen books including the best-selling *Butter Down The Well* and the recently completed *Who He?* in his forty years in journalism.

Michael Dawe, a fifth-generation Albertan, is the archivist at the Red Deer and District Archives. He has authored three books on central Alberta history. He is also a freelance writer for the *Red Deer Advocate*.

Calvin Demmon, who served as a writer and later as editor for *Edmonton Report (Alberta Report*'s predecessor) during its first five years, is currently a columnist for the *Monterey Herald* in California.

Hugh Dempsey is a well-known western historian. He is chief curator emeritus of the Glenbow Museum in Calgary and has written several books on Indians and the history of Alberta.

Mary Frances Doucedame is a freelance writer living in Los Angeles who served for five years as a staff writer on *Alberta Report* newsmagazine. Born in Winnipeg, she is a graduate in history from the Sorbonne, Paris.

Janet Harvey holds an MA in history from the University of Alberta and helped perform research for this volume.

Brian Hutchinson, a Calgary freelance writer, was a senior editor at *Alberta Report* magazine until December 1991. He obtained an honours degree in history from Carleton University in 1989.

Stephani Keer was born in Calgary and has lived there most of her life. She is associate editor of the *Calgary Sun*, and writes columns on politics and religion.

Tom McFeely, a native Calgarian, was one of the original staff members of *BC Report* in 1989. He is currently on the *Alberta Report* staff in Calgary.

George R. Oake is a born and bred Albertan. He is the former western bureau chief of the *Toronto Star* and is now retired and enjoying Alberta.

Alan Rayburn is a geographer specializing in place names and a contributor to the *Canadian Geographic*.

Courtney Tower has been a reporter for forty years, since leaving the Saskatchewan homestead. He recently ended thirteen years with *Reader's Digest*, and now freelances with foreign and Canadian magazines.

Section One

THE BOOM

Hundreds of new towns appeared on the Alberta map during the three to four years of the Great Boom, and existing towns like Strathmore suddenly discovered themselves host to scores of settlers and new townspeople. Here, many of the citizenry of Strathmore await the arrival of a Canadian Pacific train from the East in 1910. Notice the CPR colonization office (centre) and irrigation canal billboard (right).
Glenbow Archives, NA-5031-2

CHAPTER ONE

The sun would shine forever on this land of boundless optimism

FOR THREE YEARS OF SEEMINGLY LIMITLESS GROWTH AND OPPORTUNITY
ALBERTA BOOMED AS IT NEVER HAD, AND WOULDN'T AGAIN FOR SIXTY YEARS

by ROBERT COLLINS

The front-page cartoon in the May 13, 1912, Calgary *Albertan* was an apt reflection of the giddy optimism that was Alberta in the opening years of its second decade. There stood "Miss Opportunity" in diaphanous gown, knee-deep in wheat, her arms flung wide in welcome, her tresses crowned with what looked like a dollar sign atop a bowling trophy. Behind her sprawled a panorama of foothills, railway lines, grain elevators, perfect farms, and city factories spewing smoke — which then bespoke progress with the same authority it would later bespeak pollution. Behind it all, an Alberta sun rose king-size in a tranquil sky.

"One day soon," the caption said immodestly, "Alberta's wheat yield will be averaging $2 million per day."

So swaggered the province into the biggest boom its citizenry had ever seen, or would ever see again for sixty years. It was an era of flamboyant boasts, pie-in-the-sky dreams and boundless optimism. Some cities even hired publicists to shout the glad tidings[1], but such flacks were a needless luxury. Politicians, businessmen and editorial writers had all become professional boosters. *Everyone* in the province was either bragging or keeping his mouth tight shut. Naysayers were as popular as smallpox.

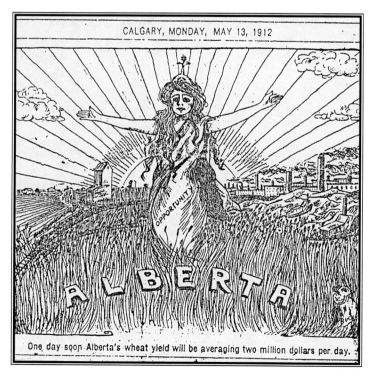

CALGARY, MONDAY, MAY 13, 1912

One day soon Alberta's wheat yield will be averaging two million dollars per day.

"The Knocker is an offspring of failure and envy," warned the editor of the *Magrath Pioneer*. "When you meet a Knocker, hit him where his brains ought to be and kick him where they are."

Thus admonished, Knockers kept their heads down for the first three years of the decade while rhetoric filled the air. Calgary's *Albertan*, for one, greeted 1910 with a special gung-ho edition. It said, "Every new Albertan sunrise spreads its life-giving rays upon a more active and promising province." It published the winners of its booster-poetry contest[2]. It predicted that Alberta would "have a population of five million before some of the people who read this article have gone to their long rest."

Only *five* million? What pikers! Premier A.L. "Little Arthur" Sifton, booster extraordinary, promised *twenty* million people and called Alberta the "wonder child of Canada." A 1910 promotional piece showed the wonder child as a talking head in the shape of the provincial map; its lips (located due west of High River) murmured: "I am the Great Alberta. The Empire of Fulfilment. The land where the opportunities are unlimited and the climate ideal..."

Edmonton, trumpeted the *Journal*, "must inevitably become the largest city in Canada. There is no other way."

Crowds jam Wetaskiwin's main street for the Orangemen's Day parade, July 12, 1912. At every conceivable opportunity, boomtime Albertans staged a parade.

Calgary wasn't buying that; the *Herald* proclaimed its city as "metropolitan" with institutions that "would do credit to the largest city in the Dominion," while the *Albertan* pronounced Calgary "Queen City of the Plains and Mistress of the Gateway to the Great Canadian Rockies." Not to be outdone, the *Medicine Hat News* saw the "Minneapolis of Canada" taking shape at Medicine Hat, while the *Journal* two years earlier had confidently served notice that Edmonton would be greater than Minneapolis and St. Paul combined. The *Lethbridge Herald*, meanwhile, tried for a new kind of distinction. Lethbridge, it said, is "the greatest horse country in the world."

A learned professor, James W. Robertson, informed the world that "hard times will never affect southern Alberta. The interests of this district are now so diversified that there is no possibility of a pronounced depression." Another academic visualized the south with its irrigation becoming "one of dense population accommodated with numerous trolley lines," and Medicine Hat "the greatest alfalfa-producing district on the continent." A Lethbridge farmer, asked by an eastern

Only *five* million? What pikers! Premier A.L. 'Little Arthur' Sifton, booster extraordinary, promised *twenty* million people and called Alberta the 'wonder child of Canada.'

friend how early Albertans started seeding grain, wrote back that there "was not a month in the year" when he couldn't seed if he felt like it.

Children added their tiny voices to this chorus. A schoolgirl won a 1910 Empire Day essay prize with such platitudes as "Sunny Alberta [is] a happy, prosperous land, where living is a pleasure." The boys' prizewinning effort waxed sociological: "It is manifest that a more cosmopolitan population could hardly have been gathered together...to bind together into a strong people united by common aims and ideals."

There was more: the physical director of the Edmonton YMCA (in what the *Journal* called "a singularly suggestive address") pronounced that city's men the most splendid physical specimens

[1] In 1910 the province itself hired PR man Charles H. Hotchkiss, whose American newspaper and magazine background helped him beat the publicity drums at U.S. state fairs.

[2] The second-prize winner (more fulsome than the first) began:

> The brightest and best
> Of the lands of the West,
> Alberta! all-peerless from sea unto sea!
> The finest and fairest,
> The richest and rarest —
> The eyes of the nations are turning to thee!

[3] 'Very rarely does one come across a physical wreck,' proclaimed E.R. Jackson in January 1910. 'I think you'll have to go a long way before you'll find in any city such a remarkably high physical standard as is maintained here.'

he'd seen[3]. Which maybe explained why a 1910 illustration in *The Grain Grower's Guide* portrayed "The Farmer" as a contemporary Atlas, clad in a figleaf, bulging with muscle, holding the rest of Canada on his shoulders.

Viewed from the vantage that eight or nine subsequent decades afford — years of wars, drought, busts, booms, heartbreak and heart's desire — all this talk sounds absurd. In the cocky mood of 1910 to 1913, it did not. Everyone (excepting a few covert Knockers) felt certain the good times would roll forever. Alberta had happy statistics to prove it. Newspapers said "a great tide of English capital" was pouring in: "Millions upon millions have been invested by English financiers and capitalists..." The population was soaring — 374,000 in 1911; nearly half a million by 1914[4]. About 40,000 newcomers were arriving every year[5].

Hundreds waited at Lands Office doors for choice quarter-sections. In 1911, twelve hundred hopefuls lined up in Lethbridge for land in 22 townships eighty miles southwest. Some slept overnight on the sidewalk, covered only in gunnysacks. The Salvation Army serenaded them with such appropriate hymns as *No, We Will Never Give In* and *I Will Not Let Thee Go*.

At times the land rush became a tug-of-war. In Medicine Hat when two sections were opened

Glenbow Archives, NA-3596-14

[4]Sixty percent of the population was male.

[5]So many American settlers came to Alberta — an estimated 30,000 in 1912 alone — that the U.S. secretary of Agriculture was allegedly considering a campaign to stop them.

Lumberyards spread across the province and every sizeable town acquired one. Calgary had sixteen. This is the Beaver Lumber yard at Hanna, about 1913.

to homesteading, the Lands Office doors were shattered in the melée. Settler Isaac Dixon was "considerably bruised," but police restored order and gave him first dibs. In Lethbridge 25 land applicants got into a brawl: "Some bumps were given, all sorts of strangleholds, half-nelsons, scissorholds...C.A. Hunt of Milk River managed to get to the head of the line dragging another man with him, who had his arms around Mr. Hunt's legs and his head between his legs..."

There was also skulduggery. At the Edmonton Lands Office in 1910 the Chandler brothers of Edgerton received a fake telegram saying their father was dying. They left the head of the lineup to rush home. The land agent smelled a rat, discovered no such telegram had been filed and restored the brothers to their place in line.

Land was, of course, the province's heart and soul. By 1914 nearly two-thirds of Albertans were farmers and they'd cultivated 2.5 million acres, almost four times the acreage of 1906.

The population was soaring — 374,000 in 1911; nearly half a million by 1914. About 40,000 newcomers were arriving every year.

Settlement had reached north to the Peace River. Total value of livestock, grains, vegetables and other products sold from Alberta farms in 1911 was about $62.5 million.

True, the grain yield had dropped during dry 1910 — 25 million bushels compared to 32 million in 1909. But the *Lethbridge Herald* put a bright face on it: the yield despite drought simply proved that "Alberta soil can't be beaten." Nobody dared mention aloud that John Palliser had once declared much of southern Alberta too arid for farming.

Wheat was selling for a then-remarkable $1 a bushel. At the time Alberta grain bound for Britain went by rail to the Lakehead, then by rail (or lake boat in season) and ocean overseas. Now Alberta eagerly awaited the Panama Canal (which opened to vessels in 1914) whereby grain shipping costs to Liverpool via Vancouver and the canal would be five to ten cents less a bushel,

The whole province seemed to be under construction

In every town, village, hamlet and city, the banging of hammers, rasping of saws and shouts of team drivers provided the sound track for Alberta's massive construction boom. Housing everywhere was in short supply as settlers poured into the new homesteads and towns burgeoned to meet their needs.

Construction crews were everywhere at work. (Upper left) the big excavation at Seventh Avenue and First Street for Calgary's new Hudson's Bay store in 1911, with Central Methodist Church in background. (Upper right) the Goodridge Block on the northeast corner of 97th Street and Jasper Avenue, Edmonton, 1911. (Above) Strathcona's new post office in 1911. (Lower right) a drugstore being built by J.M. Campbell at Castor in 1910.

Alberta was a business province

City of Edmonton Archives, EA-10-213

Provincial Archives of Alberta, H-564

Real estate was the boom's biggest business with rich and unrich alike speculating in city lots and projected town developments. Gibbs-Dash Co. Ltd. on the southeast corner of Jasper and 101st Street in Edmonton is offering lots at Dunvegan 'City' and Grouard in 1912 (above). Dunvegan was about to vanish, the dreams of Grouard were never fulfilled. Every community had at least one barber shop like Tom Spinks's place (above right) in Bowden in 1912. At right the rapidly arriving settlers provided a brisk business in horse harnesses for this dealer in Killam. Below left, the Union Bank opens in a tarpaper shack at Foremost in 1914, while below right, Dr. Elliott awaits customers at his drugstore at Swalwell in 1912.

Provincial Archives of Alberta, A-2188

City of Lethbridge Archives, P19730137000-GP

Provincial Archives of Alberta, A4964

THE BOOM

depending on the season. This could put an extra 8 1/2 cents a bushel in Alberta farmers' pockets. Based on a low average (at the time) of twenty bushels an acre, the crop from each acre of wheat-land would be worth $1.70 more. This would boost farm land values which, going into 1910, averaged $20.46 an acre.

But as Miss Opportunity had pointed out, this was not merely a province of wheat, oats, horses and cows. Alberta's 154 working coal mines produced three million tons in 1910, and had 86 billion tons in reserve: enough to supply the world for 1,000 years, boosters said; certainly enough to stoke Canada's factories, railway locomotives, home heaters and kitchen ranges for centuries. Natural gas galore lay under the ground around Medicine Hat. Oil was rumoured south of Calgary. Tens of thousands of square miles of forest extended along the east slopes of the Rockies.

At the same time, 700 snorting automobiles shared nearly 30,000 miles of Alberta streets and roads with astonished horses. And by 1910 Alberta Government Telephones had 10,000 subscribers[6]. W.H. Cushing, the minister of Public Works, assured a Regina newspaper that Albertans got more telephone lines and cheaper service for their dollar than any other province[7]. The editor of the *Stony Plain Advertiser*, who also ran the local AGT exchange, begged to differ.

"The old Bell service was none too good but it was 90% better than the present," he grumbled in print. It took about a hundred tries to get a call through to Edmonton, he said, and nearly a day

[6]In 1910 Calgary had 3,179 telephones; Edmonton, 2,264; Lethbridge, 722; Strathcona, 450; Medicine Hat, 409; Macleod, 284; Wetaskiwin, 214; Claresholm, 194; Pincher Creek, 179; Camrose, 169.

[7]Calgarians, for example, paid $20 a month for residential service in 1910; Reginans paid $25.

Stories like this lured the settlers to Alberta
'IN IOWA I HAD TO RENT LAND AND SAVED NOTHING,' SAYS A FARMER, 'BUT HERE I SOON HAD 3,000 ACRES ON WHICH I DON'T OWE A CENT'

"Why did you emigrate from the States?" an *Edmonton Bulletin* reporter asked a farmer in the Westlock district in 1914. The answer was such a masterpiece of boosterism, an Alberta reader of the day would wonder how much came from the farmer and how much from the reporter. But its lure to the would-be immigrant was doubtless compelling.

"I was told that Alberta was a land of opportunity," the farmer is quoted as replying, "and I have found it a poor man's paradise."

He had settled on virgin prairie. Now he was the owner of a landed estate which spread out league upon league of billowing wheat. His stalwart bronzed figure had for impressive background the farm itself, visible embodiment of his labour and achievement — a fine two-storey farm house, a great barn in the midst of a small village of granaries and outhouses, an orchard weighted with fruit; horses, cattle, sheep and hogs in the pastures and on all sides to the horizon wheat, nothing but wheat. (An Alberta reader would have noted there were few orchards on Alberta farms.)

"I farmed on rented land in Iowa," the farmer continued. "I rented because, with land at $100 an acre, I could not buy. I managed to make a living on my rented acres — that was all. Some years were good, some bad, but in general it was hard to keep the wolf away from the door. I was putting nothing away for a rainy day. Old age seemed likely to catch me still penniless, still struggling. My death would have meant poverty for my wife and children.

"I determined to strike for the Canadian frontier where I at least could fight out the battle on land of my own. I came overland behind a mule team. All I owned on earth was in the prairie schooner with my wife and babies. I homesteaded 160 acres. I added to my original purchase from time to time until I now have 3,000 acres. There is no mortgage on any part of it. I owe no man a cent. For some of my land I paid $2 an acre, for some $10. I would not sell it for $50.

"Some of my land paid for itself with the first crop. None of it took longer than three years to pay for itself. If there is any doubt that land in western Canada will pay for itself in three years, it is easily provided. One hundred and sixty acres bought, say, at $15 an acre, costs $2,400. Farm machinery, seed grain, cultivation and harvesting the crop may cost $10 an acre. Say the farmer plants his farm in wheat for three successive years. Say the yield is twenty bushels to the acre. Say, conservatively, he sells his wheat at 75 cents a bushel. Then his crop brings $15 an acre. Subtract $10 an acre for expenses and there is left a profit of $5 an acre a year. For 160 acres that is $800 a year or $2,400 in three years — the cost of the farm.

"I am not going back. Very few settlers from the States ever go back. For the money it takes to buy a 160-acre farm in Iowa, 1,000 acres can be bought in western Canada..."

In a corner of the farmer's yard there was a mound overgrown with weeds and wild flowers.

"What is that? asked the visitor.

"That," said the farmer, "is the ruins of the sod shanty that I called home when I first settled here five years ago."

— *R.C.*

to call long distance. Still, on its good days, AGT was better than sending smoke signals. And in due course the government agency installed copper line between Calgary and Edmonton, after which "not a single call was lost, a condition of affairs which has not occurred in the province for some time past."

Further evidence of the province's civilized state, Alberta in 1911 spent $1.5 million on education and opened 283 new schools. The number of pupils had increased by 50% in three years. School boards were scrambling to keep up; in Edmonton, attendance in 1912 was up 37% over the previous year and a third of the city's 7,000 public and high school students were housed in temporary buildings. Calgary that year spent $1 million on new schools, including eighteen-room and fourteen-room buildings.

In rural areas, where one-room schools went up two to a township, the biggest problem was finding teachers willing to go into those outlying places where, perhaps, few people spoke English and the teacher had to live in a settler's shack and probably share a minuscule bedroom with the children. The best teachers opted for cities or major towns; other schools tended to get the leftovers — the young and inexperienced or the old and jaded.

The facilitators of all this prosperity and progress were the railways. Three major systems

When the king's death was an Alberta 'calamity'

BOB EDWARDS MIGHT SPOOF, BUT ROYALTY WAS DEEPLY REVERED AND KING EDWARD'S PASSING WAS MEMORIALIZED PROVINCE-WIDE

Melting pot of humanity though Alberta was, at least 20% of its people had British roots. To them the Empire was still near and dear. Stout fellows from the Old Land still sprang up on any pretext to toast His Majesty, or to stand stiff as pokers for renditions of *God Save The King*.

front page to stories of the monarch and his successor, and editorialized, "We of the British Empire...had grown to look upon Victoria and her son as institutions that were here when we came and would be here when we departed..."

Other papers printed in delectable detail the names of

The Scouts marched through their hometowns to cheering crowds. They were going overseas to 'celebrate the triumph of peace and the advancement of civilization.'

When King Edward VII died on May 6, 1910, Alberta newspapers mirrored the province's Anglo-Saxon grief. The *Herald* called it a "World-Wide Calamity," devoted the entire

Provincial Archives of Alberta, B-4859

On May 20, 1910, Mounties and soldiers line the edge of the sidewalk on Jasper Avenue in Edmonton while citizens process in mourning for the dead King Edward VII.

the world's royalty attending the May 20 funeral. Lethbridge turned out en masse for a memorial service in Galt Square: Mounties, bands, packs of school children, a fifty-person choir and the city's entire contingent of clerics (eleven). In early June Edmonton's Bijou Theatre proudly announced a three-day film showing (matinée and evening performances) of Edward's funeral, "photographed, developed, printed and now shown in Edmonton, 6,000 miles from the scene, within thirteen days. Imported direct by the Bijou."

A year later there was intense interest in the coronation of George V. When 25 Boy Scouts left Alberta for the event (part of an international jamboree), they too were treated like royalty, although their parents had to ante up $230 for the three-week journey[a]. The Scouts marched through their hometowns to cheering crowds. They were going overseas to "celebrate the triumph of peace and the spread through Alberta with 3,020 miles of steel by 1912 (a 100% increase over the previous three years). They carried people, livestock, building supplies, grain, cattle and coal, the last vital on the shortgrass prairie southeast of Calgary where scarcely a stick of wood could be found.

Canadian Pacific had almost half of the mileage. From its main east-west line through Calgary, a branch ran north to Strathcona with sub-branches east towards the Saskatchewan border. Another branch ran south to Macleod. Paralleling the main line, its Crowsnest Pass line ran west from the Medicine Hat area to Lethbridge and then through the Rockies. The Grand Trunk Pacific's 638 miles of track included the main east-west line running through Edmonton and bound for Prince Rupert, with a Tofield-Calgary branch nearly completed. The GTP planned an extension from Calgary to Lethbridge and into the Crowsnest. Meanwhile the irrepressible William Mackenzie and Donald Mann had pushed their cross-country Canadian Northern through Lloydminster to Edmonton. They were building a Vegreville-Calgary branch, a branch north to Morinville that was to extend to the Athabasca River, and their surveyors were already at work on another line through the Yellowhead Pass to Vancouver. Surveyors were also at work on a line to the Peace River, and the money was being raised, amidst rumour of scandal, for a line from Edmonton to Fort McMurray (Vol. II, Sec. 6, ch. 2).

advancement of civilization," said one farewell speaker.

Bob Edwards of the Calgary *Eye Opener* remained uncaptivated by these events. In March 1911, two months before the coronation, he published etiquette tips for Canadians attending the event. Some excerpts:

Canadians could "get squiffy" at banquets and luncheons before and after the grand affair, "keeping in touch with the spirit of the occasion," but should stay sober on coronation day.

They should "abstain from yelling and screaming in Westminster Hall." They should not "laugh boisterously when the Archbishop of Canterbury is anointing the king with oil."

Calgary's streets are jammed for the memorial parade along Eighth Avenue on May 20, 1910, marking the royal death.

Any untoward accident during the ceremony should not elicit "crude manifestations of astonishment," such as, "Wouldn't that jar you!"

If, afterward, visitors were presented to His Majesty at a garden party, they should avoid jocular remarks about the coronation, such as comparing "the sceptre and orb to a baseball bat and ball."

If by chance the king invited any stray Canadians to the state banquet, they should respond, "I shall be highly honoured, your majesty," — not, "You're on!"

"Canadian representatives attending state banquets are earnestly requested to hit the booze light... Wine should be sipped slowly at decent intervals and not gulped down."

At the colonial banquet given by the Lord Mayor, "loud laughter will be distinctly out of place" so "it is suggested that no reference be made to the Canadian navy... When

their majesties review the Canadian fleet off Spithead, it is suggested that the [cruisers] *Niobe* and *Rainbow* be manoeuvred and turned about and twisted and shot hither and thither with the greatest rapidity, so as to convey the idea of greater numbers"[b].

"Canadian representatives are warned to be careful what they pick up after midnight in the vicinity of Piccadilly Circus."

— *R.C.*

[a]The Scouts, who would be inspected by the new monarch, were instilled with fear of God and king: 'His Majesty...notices everything, and if there is a haversack badly slung or a coat badly rolled, his quick eye will notice it. So Be Prepared, Boys.'

[b]Throughout his career Edwards made sport of the Canadian navy, especially its two pathetic cruisers.

Settlers greeted each new track and chuffing locomotive with unreserved joy. It meant that all the amenities of society would not be far behind. Some farmers deliberately chose poorer land near a village or a railway rather than better soil in the boondocks. In Medicine Hat one man camped seventeen days and nights at the Lands Office to get a quarter-section in a choice location.

The railways and agriculture were, in turn, largely responsible for the incredible metamorphosis of Alberta's major cities. By 1910, Calgary and Edmonton were each spending about $2 million a year constructing houses and business buildings. Between 1906 and 1914, their populations quintupled to 72,561 (Edmonton) and 72,000 (Calgary) while those of Lethbridge and Medicine Hat tripled to more than 9,000 each — or so claimed their boards of trade. The dominion census in 1916 put Edmonton's population at a more probable 53,800, Calgary's at 56,500. Going into 1910, Edmonton and Calgary had 57 and 47 miles respectively of sidewalks, and forty-odd miles each of sewers and water mains; some of those represented 50% increases over three years. Lethbridge and Medicine Hat respectively had seventeen and five miles of sidewalks, eighteen and

In Lethbridge 25 land applicants got into a brawl. Some bumps were given, all sorts of strangleholds, half-nelsons, scissorholds... One man got to the head of the line dragging another man with him, his arms around his legs.

twelve miles of water mains and the beginnings of sewage systems.

Calgary's 1910 bank clearings were $150 million — a 116% gain over three years. This, the city chortled, placed it third in North America behind Vancouver and Atlanta in terms of rapid growth. In the first six months of 1911 Calgary spent $5.8 million more on business and residential construction than in the comparable period of 1910, a gain of 243% which Calgary claimed was light years ahead of any other city in Canada. It didn't bother to even mention Edmonton in its comparative listings.

As always, the two cities were constantly jostling for civic position. Calgary, said the *Albertan* in 1910, "became a big city in a single night" with its new street railway: "The merry hum of the trolley seemed...to stimulate the ambitions of the people and broaden their vision. That was the end of the little man in city life...his small voice was forever drowned in the merry buzz of the electric car." The *Journal* won back the bragging rights a few months later, calling for an underpass to take Edmonton's First Street under the Canadian Northern and Grand Trunk Pacific's station yards. Traffic hazards were something fierce, said the *Journal*, what with a streetcar passing every six minutes, four passenger trains daily crossing at street level, plus assorted freights, switch engines and horseless carriages.

Edmonton also increased its edge with the new Legislative Building, officially opened in 1912. Never mind that it cost $1 million more than the politicians predicted; that somebody forgot to order copper cladding for the dome in time for the grand opening; that the acoustics were so bad one legislator — probably a Knocker — suggested his fellow MLAs be issued with megaphones (Premier Sifton denied this was a government plot to stifle debate). The bitter fact was: Edmonton had the Legislature, Calgary didn't.

This cartoon in the Calgary Albertan shows 'Sunny Alberta' beckoning to a dubious Uncle Sam. The briefcases on the American immigrants are labelled lawyers, capitalists, mayors of cities and farmers to indicate that Americans of distinct accomplishment were Alberta-bound.

A farmer and his wife near the village of Morrin, north of Drumheller, use a home-designed sweep rake and slide to build a haystack. The year is about 1915.

Edmonton also had the site of the "gubernatorial mansion" (the *Journal*'s pretentious label for the lieutenant-governor's residence) in the projected new suburb of Glenora, and the new University of Alberta. Calgary, smarting from the injustice of it all, struck back by establishing its own Mount Royal College and, in 1911, got the regional Canadian Pacific Railway shops. This, crowed the local newspapers, would make it the greatest city between Winnipeg and the west coast.

Edmonton's new Corona Hotel in 1913 was rated "one of the finest and most commodious hostelries in the West" — 128 rooms including suites, each with hot and cold water, each connected to the office by phone. Each table in the attached dining room also had its own telephone. Big deal! Calgary already had the Hotel Alexandra, 140 rooms (48 with bath), two elevators, brass beds, the "best bed spring manufactured in Canada" and, in its dining room, a head waiter with "the smile that never comes off," all for $3.50 a night.

By 1915 Edmonton's Macdonald and Calgary's Palliser hotels had added an eight-storey dimension to the city skylines. Four and five storeys were becoming commonplace[8]. A case in point was Calgary's Underwood Block, a five-storey state-of-the-art business building opened in 1911 at First Street West and 13th Avenue: brick walls, fire-resistant laminated floors, oak-finished interiors, tiled lavatories, elevators to every level. Ground-floor shops were fronted with metal and blue marble. The place was heated with steam and lit with electricity (Calgary Power had dammed the Bow River west of Calgary and began generating power in 1911)[9].

Everywhere, the buying and selling of real estate had become a dizzy dangerous spiral. A 145-acre Edmonton estate that had brought $10 an acre at the turn of the century went for $5,862 an acre in 1912. The same year, a lot at Calgary's Seventh Avenue and Second Street West that had sold for $2,000 in 1905 went for $300,000.

When Strathcona and Edmonton amalgamated in 1912, the city limits embraced about 24 square miles. Subdivisions grew like dandelions. Newcomers kept flocking in. Some of them bedded down in the Granite Curling Club and temporary school buildings but hundreds more camped along the river or outside the city limits.

In Calgary's Riverside subdivision, north of the Bow, business lots that had cost $100 in 1906 now sold for more than $6,000. Residential lots, once worth $100, went for $700 to $2,000. A Chinese laundryman who earlier had managed to buy $5,000 worth of Calgary land was offered $25,000 for it in 1912, then $50,000, then $80,000. He said he'd wait a while longer: "If it's worth $50,000, it's worth $100,000."

It was a bonanza for builders and lumber dealers. In Edmonton, members of the Carpenters

[8] The original Palliser Hotel had eight storeys, and possibly a ninth which was a sunroom or attic. The Macdonald, which opened in 1915, had eight storeys, the topmost of which was an attic.

[9] Calgary was such a bustling place that Sir Max Aitken (the future Lord Beaverbrook), visiting in 1912, got all nostalgic for "the good old days" (his actual words). When he first left Calgary in 1898, Aitken mused, it "was truly a delightful place in which to live. No man was in a hurry, pleasure always took precedence over business and the prevailing motto was 'Never do anything today that can be done tomorrow.' " He hastened to add that he wasn't knocking progress.

As the dome is completed on the Legislature, work proceeds on Edmonton's High Level Bridge which at last carries the Canadian Pacific across the North Saskatchewan River. The year is 1912.

and Joiners Union earned a minimum daily wage of $3 for an eight-hour day (compared to the 25 cents an hour for ordinary labourers)[10]. A year later in Edmonton they were making $4 a day. Calgary by 1912 was the second most important lumber distribution centre (next to Winnipeg) on the prairies, with sixteen lumberyards and several large planing mills.

But the smaller cities and larger towns had lumberyards too, and much more. Red Deer had a couple of major implement dealers, a bookseller, a bicycle shop and — although Calgary and Edmonton were sophisticated venues where tailors and dressmakers could match Paris fashions — a haberdasher's where you could buy a smart suit. Medicine Hat had flour mills, garages, a porcelain factory and a clayworks producing glazed bricks, building blocks, flue lining and pipe.

Lethbridge, like Edmonton and Calgary, had a live theatre. It also had a tree nursery, a tinsmith, a home painting and decorating firm and, to the embarrassment of its burghers, a thriving business in prostitution. In 1911 the Temperance and Moral Reform League, at a meeting led by the militant Rev. Thomas Parker Perry, took Lethbridge's city fathers to task for allowing five houses of ill repute to flourish. The inmates, said Perry, "were of the hardened type, mostly foreigners." The most avid clientele were "the married men of this city." Lethbridge, the *Herald* said sternly, should "lessen the social evil."

Agriculture was still the industry that drove Lethbridge's economy. When the CPR announced that every acre it owned in the area would be turned over to settlers in 1913, meaning an additional 1,000 settlers, the *Herald* effused that it was "like a burst of Alberta sunshine, radiating with hope and driving away the black clouds of pessimism...Now watch Lethbridge grow. Oh, you good old CPR." Jobs for railway gangs, threshers and stookers were going begging in southern Alberta that autumn; at one point employers said they had jobs for 300 men that could not be filled.

But wrinkles were beginning to show in Alberta's happy face. Two Lethbridge ministers did the unthinkable: took a poke at a booster (Tom Richardson, Macleod's public relations man), although earnestly assuring their congregations that they were *not* Knockers. The Rev. J.E. Murrell Wright said he did not "in any way wish to depreciate the work of the Board of Trade but heaven is not a myth nor is Alberta a certainty. Heaven is the certainty and one cannot be sure of Alberta or any other place...Men should not be taught to centre their affections on things of the earth when the teaching of Jesus Christ was and is just the opposite."

The Rev. W.V. McMillen likewise hedged his bets: "Remember, I am not trying to knock anybody. As regards the campaign being carried on by Tom Richardson, I am in accord with much of what he has said...But I can't say that I favour the idea of preaching immigration sermons." The *Herald*, in reporting this, stressed that "Mr. McMillen is not a Knocker."

But already the *Monetary Times* had warned that "the speculation in real estate in western Canada is a menace to the country's prosperity. It is a slap at the maintenance of Canadian credit. It is retarding the proper growth of towns and cities which deserve better treatment...It is putting lands which should be tilled by market gardeners into thoughtless speculators' hands..."

A federal government document in early 1912 noted that "house rents and living expenses have advanced during the past two years fully 50%, and of course the working man and those on fixed salaries are feeling the pressure most."

Foreign financiers were growing wary of Canadian securities. In 1913 unemployed men appeared on Calgary and Edmonton streets — a shocking occurrence. Some had been laid off by the Canadian Northern. Mackenzie and Mann, teetering on bankruptcy, had gone to Ottawa begging the loan of millions, were given quite a few, and a year later were back looking for more.

By the middle of that summer the money markets were collapsing. Alberta companies were hit hard. Major sawmills were left with large inventories of unsold lumber. Crown Lumber, one of the biggest retailers with 52 yards in Alberta, suffered a $171,000 loss and had to close many of its yards in smaller communities.

The 1913 crops were excellent, lulling many into a false sense of security. But that December the *Albertan* fretted about the high cost of living. A month later it used the unthinkable word, "depression." Westerners, it said, "are not so recklessly enthusiastic as they were one year ago today but...they are not despondent over the past year. The experience of depression has been novel but not entirely disappointing. It is true that we were not as well prepared for the strain as the older part of the country and were hit harder by it than if the preparations had been better. However, no great harm has been done...It does seem that we have passed the worst of the depression..."

Alberta in 1911 spent $1.5 million on education and opened 283 new schools. The number of pupils had increased by 50% in three years.

Not so. The *Market Mail*, a British publication, observed in 1914, "People begin to realize that Canada is playing the risky game of keeping solvent by borrowing more with which to pay back, and that only while money is advanced can the country keep straight." Hapless prairie farmers were caught in a bind. They'd sunk their money into expensive machinery. Now the banks refused to extend further credit and threatened to foreclose. Some farmers who not so long before had lined up for land left it in a fruitless search for work in the cities.

As historian James G. MacGregor accurately summed it up decades later: "Everyone in Alberta and everyone in Canada had been swept along beyond his depth in the inflated assessment they had all placed on the value of the West and its ability to yield the daydream riches for which they had all hoped.

"Speculation piled upon speculation had counted too heavily on the vast wealth the West was capable of contributing. Bankers, manufacturers, merchants, western farmers, investors and gamblers from one end of Canada to the other had shared the same fever. Most of them, from the humblest voter to the most embroiled politician, had shut their minds to the risks of the great gamble and, with hands widespread for any passing graft, turned their eyes away."

By January 1914 Edmonton was struggling to provide relief for 4,000 unemployed. And Elizabeth B. Mitchell, a well educated Scot, touring the West in 1913-14, expressed the fear that few dared to voice but many were thinking: "Was all the West one huge horrible bubble, ready now for pricking?"

The answer was no. There was more to the West than a bubble. The great boom of 1910-13 would end, but Alberta would not. And while it lasted, who could deny it was an exhilarating experience, dazzling, delightful and doomed?

[10] At the time, $1 bought ten packs of Player's Navy Cut cigarettes, a year's subscription to the *Lethbridge Herald* or a night in Calgary's Albion Hotel — 'steam heat in every room.'

Bobbie Crump, his wife Ester, and their three children pose in an automobile about 1918 in Edmonton, a city whose Board of Trade was demanding blacks be denied entry to Canada. Bobbie had come to Alberta from Oklahoma about 1912, lived briefly in Calgary and eventually settled in Breton.

Two racial groups were unwelcome in Alberta

Edmonton strove to stop the immigration of black settlers; Chinese were considered drug-prone and a threat to women

It was truly a land of opportunity — if your face was white. The racial prejudice that marked the first decade of Alberta's century was still very much alive in the second. It was aimed particularly at blacks and Chinese whose numbers (about 1,000 and 1,700 respectively) and, especially, skin colour made them prime targets.

By 1911 the estimated 1,000 black settlers had come despite discouragement[a] or outright harassment at the border or on arrival in the province. A group led by Jefferson Davis Edwards, 22, established Amber Valley, a thriving community of (eventually) 350 people east of Athabasca, with school, church, post office and farms.

The Edmonton Board of Trade led the fight to slam Alberta's doors on all future blacks. In April 1910, a board member named Powell, reportedly "a Canadian who has spent a great many years in the southern states where...the principal work of the police courts is in the handling of cases of Negro crime," kindled the flames. Black settlers, he said, were "a serious menace" and Edmonton's one hundred black residents "had a demoralizing effect... Even the best of Negroes are not desirable as citizens since they are unassimilable with whites." Powell urged a $1,000 head tax on all

coloured immigrants. The Board of Trade rejected the proposal (it had no authority to impose taxes anyway) but set up a three-man committee, including Powell, to study the issue. The Board president remarked that some of the finest homestead land was being taken up by Negroes, thus making it "worthless for white settlement."

The *Journal* also rejected the tax idea: "Alberta is a great big country and it scarcely seems reasonable that the arrival of a few Negroes within her borders is going to do any great or irreparable injury." But the editorial seemed less concerned with human decency than whether a head tax on expatriate Americans would anger the United States.

The Board of Trade reflected a sizeable cross-section of Alberta opinion. A Dr. Ella Synge in an inflammatory newspaper interview said "the finger of fate is pointing to lynch law, which will be the ultimate result." A Conservative politician in Lethbridge won applause with a speech berating the federal Liberals for letting blacks into Canada. Blacks were refused service in Calgary hotel bars; the attorney-general said he couldn't force hoteliers to serve anyone.

In Edmonton a black man — "well dressed, in fact stylishly and expensively garbed," said the news report —

entered a busy restaurant with a companion and took the last remaining seats at a communal table occupied by a white family. The latter stalked out in a rage. The proprietor offered to find the whites a private table elsewhere, but the father cried, "Eat in your place with cattle? No, I'll starve first!" Other diners glared, two more left, but the black couple stuck it out and finished their lunch.

Also in 1910, a coloured man in Bassano stabbed a cafe owner. The culprit was arrested two hours later, tried and sentenced an hour after that, put on a train to Calgary and began serving his sentence that evening. The *Albertan* applauded the speedy justice, not reflecting on whether a white suspect would have been as quickly dispatched.

Edmonton kept up the onslaught. In 1911, its Trades and Labour Council passed an anti-black resolution on the grounds that "an unlimited influx of Negroes into the province would invariably lower the standard of living."[b] City council also voted against admitting more coloured people. Alderman James Dundas Hyndman adopted a statesmanlike pose: "I have no animosity towards the Negroes. Because a man is black it should not be held against him...but it is not for the good of the country to have them settle here." The Board of Trade circulated an anti-black petition in downtown banks, hotels and realty offices; 3,400 Edmontonians signed it. The board also pressured its Red Deer counterpart to take up the cause, and Red Deer did. Its secretary, speaking to the anti-black resolution, said they were "an undesirable class of settler and would eventually become a trouble and a burden to the community."

Despite the harassment, a trickle of blacks continued. Alberta was still preferable to the southern United States (the Ku Klux Klan didn't reach western Canada until around 1920). A contingent of 175 Oklahomans arrived in Edmonton in March 1911. A *Journal* reporter met their train. His report was more insulting than hostile:

"Has anyone ever seen a yellow coon?... At the station

Glenbow Archives, NA-3556-3b

THEY ARE FARMERS WILL FARM THERE

They Say That the United States Very Sorry to Have Them Leave

This report from Winnipeg, carried in the Calgary Albertan in 1911, presents a positive picture of black farmers migrating into Canada. The Edmonton Board of Trade did not concur.

one coloured gentleman stoutly declared he had turned yellow. 'I's so sleepy,' said the Oklahoma Negro, 'dat I's a gone yeller in de face.' The reporter to whom the remark was directed, reeled, staggered and, leaning against the station building, felt a little faint at coming on such a revelation. Revived somewhat, he took courage and approached the speaker, but the reflection from the lights dissipated all wonder and the black man was informed that such an affliction had not overtaken him."

There were a few encouraging signs. The Lethbridge Board of Trade refused to be bullied into joining Edmonton's crusade. "If a man has the ability, the honesty and industry to become a good citizen of this country, Canadian justice sees not the colour of his skin," wrote the *Lethbridge Herald*. "Men that will undertake to make a quarter section of bald prairie into a fruitful farm are not the kind of men, whether black or white, that give both races the bad name they have for vice and degradation."

The *Edmonton Journal* in 1911 wished Negro settlers well, providing they adopted the hard-work ethic of Booker T. Washington, the prominent black American educator and leader. And in 1914 when a black man with a $2 reserved seat was barred from a performance of *King Lear* at Calgary's Sherman Grand Theatre, he sued the owners for $1,000. Press reports didn't say how the case turned out. Nevertheless, the relentless campaign slowed Alberta's black immigration almost to a standstill by 1913. It would not resume until some time after the Great War.

Meanwhile, Chinese immigrants suffered their own siege of persecution. Fewer vicious slurs were directed at the Japanese because, in 1911, only 244 were in Alberta, not enough to qualify as a menace. That year the *Calgary Herald* even ran a long feature lauding "industrious Japanese making good in western Canada." The main exhibit was R.B. Nagatany of Cheadle, who had a diploma from Ontario Agricultural College at Guelph and was a large-scale wheat farmer. The writer presented Nagatany as a kind of curiosity: "A dapper little Japanese dressed in modern English or Canadian style. His clothes were well pressed and creased... He spoke better English and acted much more courteously than ten out of every twelve you might chance to meet. But his fine swarthy features, his rather flat face, his gleaming white teeth when he spoke or smiled, marked him as a Jap..."

No such backhanded praise was lavished on the Chinese. There were 1,787 of them in Alberta by 1911, mostly in cities and towns where they operated restaurants, laundries or market gardens. They tended to cluster in "Chinatowns" for friendship and because most of white society shunned them.

In Calgary the Chinese community, having been run out of its previous locale by Canadian Northern Railway

$116.05) it made a headline. If Pat Burns or R.B. Bennett played high-stakes poker, cops and reporters were nowhere in sight.

A trip to an "opium den" inspired news reports of "ten or twelve repulsive-looking Chinamen lounging" or "two fearful looking Mongolians [lying] stupidly on one of the benches." In Coleman the police found "one Celestial hitting the pipe and another Chinaman getting [a pill] ready for heating over a lighted opium lamp." There were numerous tales of raids on two-bit gamblers in the back of Chinese

The churches did not sympathize with Alberta's racism, as this photo taken outside the Chinese YMCA and mission in Calgary evidences. Lethbridge also refused to join the campaign. Any man who can break the Alberta prairie deserves admission, said the Herald, *whatever his colour.*

expansion, pooled its money in 1910 and was about to raise a $20,000 headquarters around Centre Street and Second Avenue. A deputation of angry property owners in the area demanded that city council "segregate" the Chinese. Their spokesman, James Short, KC, said Chinese "should be treated much the same as an infectious disease or an isolation hospital. They live like rabbits in a warren. Thirty of them crowd in where five white people would ordinarily reside."

The press helped perpetuate the campaign. Chinese, billed as "Celestials" or "sons of Confucius," were always good for a lurid story on opium or gambling. When the police raided Loy Dung's store on Calgary's First Street West and arrested thirty men for playing fan-tan (total take:

laundries. The *Lethbridge News* told a "shocking tale of human depravity" about a white woman held in the thrall of cocaine by her Chinese husband, and forced into prostitution.

Little wonder that the populace at large applied the same damning clichés to all Chinese. In Red Deer a speaker addressed the Young Men's Club on "The Yellow Peril" one Sunday just before Christmas 1913. To mark the season of brotherly love he stated that Orientals were "a menace to law and order, to sanitation, to good morals and were hard to assimilate politically, forming a class far too easily bought by unscrupulous politicians."

A few days earlier, two clean-cut Stettler high school students won a debate in Red Deer, taking the affirmative on

Calgarians assemble in a public park to hear speakers protest the city's hiring of 'foreigners' in 1912. Resentment grew worse when jobs became scarce two years later.

"Resolved that the Canadian government should exclude Oriental immigrants." The star debater, speaking with "fine vim and evident sincerity," was unstinting in her abuse: Orientals were degraded, ignorant, untruthful, deceitful, avaricious, vindictive and "apt to brood morbidly over fancied wrongs." They were also conspirators, smugglers and were willing to work "for a mere pittance, and we need to teach the dignity of labour." As her *pièce de résistance* the young student said Orientals "brought in strange diseases such as leprosy."

There were legitimate concerns over the Chinese drug habit. In 1912 the Calgary Children's Aid Society suspected that Chinese sold opium to minors and that a link existed between drug vendors and keepers of "the district of ill-fame." The police raided a few more Chinese establishments and confiscated their drugs and pipes, but there were no reports of widespread corruption of the city's youth. Emily Murphy, a noted Alberta feminist and writer, in a treatise on the drug problem, suggested that the Chinese were not entirely to blame; that politicians in some jurisdictions turned a blind eye to drug peddling, in return for the Oriental vote; and that white women, supposedly lured into drug dependency, might have been wise to keep to their "own reserves."

As if white man's censure were not burden enough, law-abiding Chinese briefly had to contend with their own mafia. In 1911 Edmonton police clamped down on a so-called "highbinders' society," a fifteen-man gang working a protection racket on legitimate Chinese businessmen. Or, as the *Journal* described it, "a gang of lazy Chinks living a life of ease by tyrannizing hard-working Celestials." (These particular thugs either had very modest expectations or were part-time laundrymen. According to testimony, Jim On and Mah Jim Gook threatened to kill storekeeper Hong Tai if he didn't hand over $100, a box of starch and a case of laundry soap.)

Grudgingly, some facets of Alberta society accepted the Chinese. Chinese cooks became a fixture in homes and restaurants, usually with one-word names — "Wong," "Slim," "Looie" — like family pets. Chinese houseboys were prized by the well-to-do. In Medicine Hat, Quon Koy, proprietor of the Empire Reform Association Restaurant, threw a little party for some white folks. Afterward the local *News* rated him "wide awake, public spirited and progressive in his citizenship."

District 18 of the United Mine Workers of America (which embraced all of Alberta) let Orientals into the union in 1909, not necessarily as equals but so they couldn't be hired as strikebreakers. When war broke out the Chinese enjoyed a brief respite. For a while other people (the Germans) were hated more. Alberta even asked the federal government to bring in more Chinese immigrants as badly needed labourers, but Ottawa backed down when the unions loudly protested.

After the war, for most of the hapless "Celestials" and "Chinks," it was back to business — and discrimination — as usual.

— *R.C.*

[a]Some immigration agents, openly racist, tried to scare away blacks with stories of brutal Alberta winters, in which it was 'not physically possible for the coloured race to thrive.' If this failed, Immigration tried to head them off with stringent medical examinations or discourage them with foot-dragging at the border.

[b]In fact, many of the black settlers were well-heeled, averaging $300 each and, in some cases, bringing in as much as $3,500. Many also brought their own tools and implements. 'Canada gets only the best of the coloured immigrants,' observed the *Edmonton Bulletin*, 'for the railways refuse to give them reduced fares. Consequently, none except those that have considerable money make the venture.'

CHAPTER TWO

300 pinpoints of light appeared, each a town, village or hamlet

IN AN AMAZING DECADE ALBERTA'S NEW COMMUNITIES SPRING TO LIFE
AND 'OUR TOWN' BECOMES THE CENTRE OF LIFE IN A BOOM PROVINCE

by **ROBERT COLLINS**

In Alberta's second decade nearly 300 new pinpoints of light, life and commerce sprang up across the province: towns, villages and crossroad hamlets that would become its life's blood. The cities — Edmonton, Calgary, Lethbridge, Medicine Hat, Red Deer and Wetaskiwin[1] — hogged the headlines, but they were a mere 25% of the population. The smaller places, all under 2,000, were far more important than their numbers indicated.

To the rural people, whose agriculture fuelled Alberta's affluence, those little communities

[1]The definitions of 'city,' 'town,' 'village' and 'hamlet' were ever changing and sometimes baffling. As of 1897, a hamlet was any place with five or more occupied dwellings within a half square mile. A village, after 1903, was supposed to have a population of 400 before incorporation as a town — yet in 1906 Vegreville was promoted with only 344 people. Effective 1907, a village had to have a minimum of 25 homes to qualify as such. After 1912, it needed 700 people before graduating to town. (This was supposed to help villages live within their means: as a town it was easier to qualify for loans but village-size tax bases couldn't support town-size debts.) Wetaskiwin won city status in 1906 with a population of only 1,652 — as did Lethbridge and Medicine Hat, with 2,936 and 3,020 respectively. Even by 1920 Wetaskiwin's 2,061 people made it little larger than many towns.

Looking like a western movie set, this was Bow Island about 1909 or 1910. The train is in, on the CPR's Crowsnest line.

were the centre of the universe. In 1912, for example, Airdrie, Cayley and Seven Persons each had populations of 300 but their tributary populations — the surrounding people who depended on them — were 700, 1,000 and 2,000 respectively. Didsbury had 1,000 people that year but it served 5,000. Camrose's population was 1,586 but its tributaries channelled 9,000 into town. That's why surveyor Francois Adam gave it a Main Street as wide as Edmonton's Jasper Avenue.

Their proliferation was phenomenal. In 1905 Alberta had fewer than thirty towns and villages. A year later, there were 49. By 1912 the count was 46 towns and 73 villages. By the end of the decade there were 54 and 119 — plus 167 rural municipalities and 215 "local improvement districts"[2]. There were also at least 160 hamlets (an educated guess, because officialdom didn't bother to include them in its statistics)[3]. Thus, by 1920, there were at least 333 communities below city status.

Many of them followed hot on the heels of the Canadian Pacific, Canadian Northern, Grand Trunk Pacific or Edmonton, Dunvegan & British Columbia railways. Coronation, for one, was born in 1911 (named for the crowning of George V) as a CPR divisional point. When the townsite was sold by auction in September that year, 300 purchasers and speculators arrived by train just two hours after the last spikes were driven. Sometimes the site chosen by the railway had genuine charm. The *Edmonton Bulletin* in 1912 admired Consort (also named after George V's coronation): it perched on the northern slope of a coulee, offering a pretty view. The CPR tracks wound along below, giving local farmers a final downhill run with their wagonloads of grain bound for the four elevators.

Other small huddles of humanity were already in place, waiting impatiently for the steel to catch up and bring them fame, fortune or, at the very least, a grain elevator. One such was Retlaw

[2]Local improvement districts were set up six years before provincehood, to facilitate road construction in sparsely populated areas. They were reorganized in 1903 to encompass three to six townships, with financial decisions made by an elected council. Fifty-five rural municipalities were established in Alberta in 1912, following a torrent of requests for a system similar to Saskatchewan's. (These, and ninety new local improvement districts, were carved from the 227 improvement districts existing in 1911.) RMs — renamed 'municipal districts' in 1918 — were eighteen miles square, required a population of at least one person per square mile, and had five councillors elected for one-year terms.

(Walter spelled backwards, after the governor-general's private secretary), which in 1913 was a huddle of shacks, tents, lumber yards, general store, livery stable and 100 souls, anxiously shuffling their feet until the CPR branch line arrived. (Retlaw, like so many hopeful new communities, ultimately disappeared[4].) Another was Clive which began as a store, post office and livery stable in 1905, got the CPR in 1910, then an elevator and by 1911 was daydreaming of butcher, flour mill, doctor and other tokens of villagedom or, yea, even towndom.

Rosebud and Redland wanted a rail stop so badly that each built a general store just to woo the builders. In the end Canadian Northern gave both a station (although Redland also vanished from the map). Armand Trochu started the town that would bear his name in 1907, hopes buoyed by a CPR survey. Then the railway backed off, leaving Trochu stranded. Finally the GTP built a branch nearby so in 1911 Trochu gladly relocated its site beside the tracks.

Provincial Archives of Alberta, A-6098

The main street of Stettler about 1910. The town claimed among other things the biggest cigar factory in the West.

Pincher Creek, on the other hand, refused to bend its knee to the railway — and suffered for it. Around the turn of the century, when the CPR Crowsnest line went through north of Pincher Creek, the town wouldn't move. Having been there since 1883, Pincher figured the railway should come to it. The railway didn't, and Pincher Station rose in lonely splendour, three miles away.

About a dozen years later Pincher Creek got a second chance when the Western Dominion planned an odd route from the U.S. boundary through Cardston, Pincher Creek, Lundbreck, Calgary, Edmonton and Fort St. John[5]. Track-laying at Pincher began in 1914 at an adjacent racetrack. A jubilant crowd led by the mayor, with brass band and Union Jack, took autos, saddle horses, buggies, buses and bikes to the site. When the first sod came up everyone cheered. When a local politician said the railway would make Pincher Creek second only in importance to Chicago, they cheered harder. They cheered the line's financier and, again, its contractors. A month later, the Great War was on and Pincher's cheers and railway dreams seem to have died with it[6].

If the railways had a choice they ordained that each new community be five to ten miles apart. An analysis (pioneer Alberta had analysts, along with grasshoppers and gophers) concluded that ten miles was the maximum economic distance to elevator for a horse-drawn wagon with grain. Weather, roads and horseflesh permitting, it let the farmer get there and back home in a day.

Provincial Archives of Alberta, Ob-1521

Pincher Creek in 1910 with the Rockies shining beyond.

A Drumheller street scene, 1920.

When the railways named the new village or town, it almost always carried the name of someone with railway connections or, at least, a famous person who might someday scratch the railway's back. Thus Blairmore honours Andrew G. Blair, Laurier's minister of railways (who later quit the cabinet in disgust: Vol. II, p. 111); Chipman was named for Clarence Campbell Chipman, secretary to another such minister, Sir Charles Tupper; Bruce for a former GTP manager, A. Bruce Smith; Chisholm after Thomas Chisholm, a railway tie contractor for the Edmonton, Dunvegan & British Columbia.

Bawlf honoured Nicholas Bawlf, one-time president of the Winnipeg Grain Exchange, and Clive the British architect of Empire in India. Drumheller was named after Samuel Drumheller, an American who jointly owned the townsite with the Canadian Northern Railway. Coutts and Burdett saluted the enormously rich Baroness Burdett-Coutts, a stockholder in the Alberta Railway and Irrigation Company[7].

Once armed with a railway, the little places grew with astonishing speed. In four months Coronation went from a scrabble of tents to a village of 524 people and 141 buildings: six real estate and loan offices, six restaurants and boarding houses, five coal and fuel dealers, four draymen, four pool halls, four lumber yards, three general stores, three hardware stores, three livery barns, three implement dealers, three barber shops, three well drillers, two banks, two drugstores, two butchers, two blacksmiths, two bakeries, one doctor, one print shop producing the *Coronation*

When the first sod came up everyone cheered. When a local politician said the railway would make Pincher Creek second only in importance to Chicago, they cheered harder.

News-Review, a dairy, a laundry, two hotels under construction and $1,500 worth of wooden sidewalks. Castor in 1910, Delburne and Lousana in 1912, and countless others rose to similar size in similar time spans[8].

Every place had at least one grain elevator. After all, grain — along with coal in such mining centres as Drumheller, Lethbridge, the Crowsnest Pass towns and the Coal Branch west of Edmonton — was the reason the railways came. From 1905 onward, the slope-shouldered grain elevators were prairie symbols; landmarks as distinctive as the church spires of Quebec; indicators of a community's place in the pecking order. Didsbury, Daysland and Claresholm with four elevators each in 1912 must have looked down their noses at such two-elevator towns as Airdrie, Bow Island and Ponoka[9].

Alberta had 43 elevators in 1906. By 1912 there were 279: twenty on GTP lines; 35 on the Canadian Northern; 224 on the CPR. They were owned by a great assortment of companies, including the Alberta Farmers' Cooperative Elevator Company, Alberta Grain Company, Alliance

[4]Retlaw, on a CPR branch that went west from the main line at Suffield, was named after Walter Reginald Baker, who from 1874 to 1878 was private secretary to the governor-general, the Earl of Dufferin. Baker later became secretary of the CPR; Retlaw, earlier called Barney, was renamed in 1913.

[5]This line had a curious ancestry. In 1906 the Alberta Oil, Coal and Wheat Railway Company was incorporated to serve this corner of southwestern Alberta. In 1909 it was renamed the Pincher Creek, Cardston and Montana Railway; then the Alberta Pacific Railway which, in 1914, amalgamated with the new Western Dominion under the latter's name.

[6]Train service often revolutionized village life. Consider Acme (pop. 300 or 149, depending if you believed its figures or the government's), which got the CPR in 1910. By 1915 villagers could leave for Calgary at 7 a.m. and return that afternoon at four, any weekday.

[7]Alberta's rich array of place names led to irresistible puns. The *Edmonton Bulletin* in a 1910 story on Castor mused 'if an oil well were struck here it should yield Castor oil...' The name, incidentally, probably came from the French for 'beaver,' which inhabited the local creek.

Irvine proudly boasts three elevators.

It would have been difficult to find a prairie town without its Chinese restaurant, and the Park Restaurant at Crossfield —'fruit, ice cream and soft drinks' — typified hundreds. One customer and his son pose hands on hips for the photo. Mr. Park, the proprietor, seems equally confident.

Grain Company, Gillespie Elevator Company, British American Elevator Company and various milling companies[10].

Yet even with railway and grain elevators, even with its satellite population, how could a place like Coronation support six restaurants? And how on earth could Innisfail — never mind its 1,000 people and tributary of 4,000 — justify four hotels? One possible reason, for the hotels at least, was liquor. You could get a drink in the hotel bar until Prohibition came in 1915[11]. This was a mixed blessing; in the rough tough towns along the Coal Branch west of Edmonton, where there wasn't much to do except work, fight and drink, wife abuse became a serious problem.

But the main justification for so many hotels, restaurants, banks and other amenities in these smaller centres (compared to their relative absence in such towns by the century's end) was simply this: the neighbourhood town or village was a lifeline and social centre. Most Albertans still travelled by horse and buggy or wagon. Automobiles, although increasing in numbers, still moved at moderate speeds with limited range, even when the awful roads were passable. People couldn't race to a city and back in a day.

So farm folk rattled into town on train days to collect mail, groceries and gossip; go to the bank, blacksmith or lumber yard. Humane farmers (not necessarily in the majority) stabled their horses in the livery stable, then took their own unkempt heads to, say, Sam Creighton's barber shop in Rocky Mountain House ("first class hair and whisker artist"). Or in Czar they could — if their religion did not equate billiards with original sin — mosey over to Abel's Pool Hall for a cigar, a shave or a game of snooker. Czar had only 70 people by 1920, but a pool hall was *de rigeur* if a community expected to hold its head high.

Women, if in Fort Saskatchewan, could buy the latest in "Shapes, Flowers, Ribbons and Trimmings" at Bentley's millinery, and a full range of drugs and magazines in Dr. Aylen's drugstore (Doc was a former RNWMP surgeon). In Sedgewick, a town of only 400, intellectuals found the only Aberdeen Library in Alberta with "750 volumes of the best literature"[12].

On a Friday or Saturday night towngoers might stay over for a little treat. Almost everywhere, they could dine in the equivalent of Killam's City Cafe, run by the genial Pon Moon Get, who served meals day and night and spent "much of his time in studying the English language." Wainwright visitors could attend the Elite theatre where a silent movie, dance, lecture or live show with visiting artists was on every night. People in Gadsby's orbit could, in 1915, catch six

Hughenden's buggies and cars, 1912.

Barrhead's citizenry pose for the camera.

acts of vaudeville at the local Pantages theatre or "a sensational musical comedy success" with a cast of 55 at the Empire, starring "the flashing prima donna Zoe Barnett."

But the people of 1910-1920 were perfectly content with simpler pastimes: whist drive, box social, dance. Consider the sweetly innocent goings-on in Irricana, one night in January 1910, as reported in the Calgary *Albertan*. A man named Davis, "popular ranchman who kept the stopping house on the Carbon trail," had moved his big barn and house into town (thereby bringing Irricana's building count to 37). To celebrate he threw a dance for the whole village. Fifty people came:

Dancing was the order until midnight, when refreshments were served by the ladies and after singing several very appropriate songs the dancing started again and it was in the wee small hours of the morning when the tired, but happy, dancers departed for their homes. Music was furnished by Mr. Fred Putman. All who were there voted Mr. Davis was an ideal host and a jolly good fellow.

From 1905 onward, the slope-shouldered grain elevators were prairie symbols; landmarks as distinctive as the church spires of Quebec; indicators of a community's place in the pecking order.

If weather and roads were uncommonly bad and no hungry livestock were waiting back home, country folk might stop overnight in a hotel. But mostly the hotels catered to travelling salesmen who flocked off the train, bedded down in a place such as the Windsor in Hughenden, right across from the station, lugged their sample cases around to local merchants or showed their wares in the hotel. That's why the 47-room Alberta Hotel in Vegreville lauded its "excellent sample rooms for displaying goods." And why Viking on the GTP boasted that its King Edward — solid brick, 34 rooms, bathrooms, toilets and a thirty-foot bar — was known to travelling salesmen as "one of the most comfortable hostelries in the West"[13].

The most unlikely places had "hostelries." Halkirk, with only 97 people in 1916 according to the census, had a three-storey hotel, "every room steam heated and electric lighted." Gadsby, population 153, had that and more in its Oxford Hotel: "... bedrooms elegantly furnished with white iron beds and the finest felt mattresses, mission oak chiffonniers and dressers, writing tables, rich rugs and the windows are all curtained with lace curtains."

The Hotel Diamond in Diamond City near Lethbridge operated under a slight handicap. Built by the Diamond Coal Company, which in turn was controlled by staunch Baptists, it was strictly teetotal. Hence the Diamond had to make up in luxury what it lacked in booze. Four of its 26 bed-

[8]No churches were listed among Coronation's first clutch of banks, restaurants and pool halls, but nearly every community had one. Castor's pioneer worshippers attended a sod church long before lumber arrived. By 1910, for example, little Killam (pop. 197) had three churches, Lacombe had four and Innisfail five. By mid-decade Camrose and Didsbury had six apiece.

[9]Three grain elevators — as in Cayley, Leduc, Stavely and Strathmore, for instance — were a respectable average in 1912. Stavely had one that held 90,000 bushels which, it said, was the largest of any town in western Canada.

[10]Around 1912, the Taylor Milling & Elevator Company of Lethbridge produced its own brand of flour: 'Mother's Favorite.'

[11]Innisfail, among others, covered all the bases with two licensed hotels and two temperance establishments for those who refused to patronize licensed premises.

[12]Lady Aberdeen (1857-1939), wife of the 1893-98 governor-general, kept herself busy with projects — the National Council of Women (founded 1893), the Victorian Order of Nurses (1897) and the Aberdeen Association (1898), whose function was the shipping of books and papers to settlers on the prairies. The Canadian government agreed to pay the postage charges.

Leduc's open for business, probably about 1908.

[13] Builders of the day, facing incredible obstacles, moved faster than many a 1990s construction gang. Work on Viking's second hotel began in December 1908. The ground being frozen hard, a hole was dynamited for the stone foundations, which were then laid despite temperatures as low as -50° C. A blizzard filled the hole with snow; they cleaned it out; it filled up to ground level again; they cleaned it out. Brick came from Edmonton via the GTP. The furnishings came from Vegreville on the CNR (a week getting through because of heavy snow). The Viking House opened in April 1909 at a cost of $30,000.

[14] Tiny Alix was one of a few communities that also had a thriving polo club.

[15] The *Edmonton Journal*, in a 1915 puff-piece about Bawlf, issued an unabashed endorsement: 'The *Journal* representative has found in reviewing the towns of Alberta that from a financial standpoint the happiest located towns are those in which there is a branch of the Canadian Bank of Commerce.' Which certainly made Bawlf bank manager M.R. Complin's day.

rooms had private baths and all were finished in "spotless white" with furniture in "early English" style and leather upholstered chairs. The ground floor, finished in oak, had fireplaces in the sitting room, writing room, rotunda and ladies' parlour. A water and sewage system was planned for 1915. As the management said starchily, in veiled rebuke of liquor-lovers, the hotel was "one that requires no apologies."

Why did some towns grow and others fail? The *Red Deer Advocate* addressed that very question in 1910. It attributed success to "men of push and energy who are not afraid to spend their time and money to boom their town" — writing about it, talking about it, boosting it. Many a small town had a slogan or a gimmick, something, anything, to make it stand out from the ruck. Bassano, with a new irrigation dam, was "Best in the West by a Damsite." Edson termed itself "the Calgary of the North" and "the Pittsburgh of Canada." Entwistle flatly claimed "more natural resources than any other town in the province."

Redcliff had the "finest and largest brickyard in Canada." Wainwright was blessed with "the world's biggest buffalo herd" in the federal park established in 1909. Cardston rejoiced in its million-dollar Mormon Temple. Stettler claimed one of the biggest cigar factories in the West. Vegreville lit its main street with natural gas from a local well. Hardisty had a jeweller other towns would have killed for: he was a watch inspector for the CPR. Alix, with only 267 people, had Alberta's 1910 amateur baseball champion team[14].

Slogans, gimmicks and even a railway were not enough in themselves. The strengths of any small place were its natural resources and its movers and shakers. A handful of people were usually catalysts for the entire community: mayor or reeve, banker[15], postmaster, doctor, notary public. Some wore several hats. In 1915, Holden's Dr. S.J. Farrell was also its drugstore proprietor, postmaster and mayor. Bawlf's J.C. Paulson doubled as druggist and town councillor. Morinville's mayor Omar St. Germain was the local lawyer. Ryley's hardware merchant, J.D. McNaughton, served stints as manager of the local hockey team and vice-president of the board of trade.

Alberta was still a patriarchal society, although by 1916 males in the prairie provinces outnumbered females by only 55% to 45%. But under Alberta's Town Act of 1912 the councils, consisting of mayor and six councillors, had to be male and owners of freehold estate over $500.

Nevertheless, farm wives were the pillars of the farm homes, and thousands of other unsung heroines, the rural and urban teachers, taught a generation of children to read and write better than their counterparts did seventy to eighty years later. Women were also showing up in so-called men's activities. Pincher Creek in 1915 had women's hockey teams that played to earn electric lights for the local hospital. Mabel Mahaffey, whose Tofield shop sold china and school supplies, was rated "an industrious and energetic young woman" by the press. Lamont in 1918 had Mrs. A.E. Archer on village council, which the *Edmonton Bulletin* said was "rather unique."

For man or woman, the thankless task of town council or rural school board was almost a

Glenbow Archives, NC-6-663

Viking, looking north, probably about 1909.

General view of Lacombe, 1908.

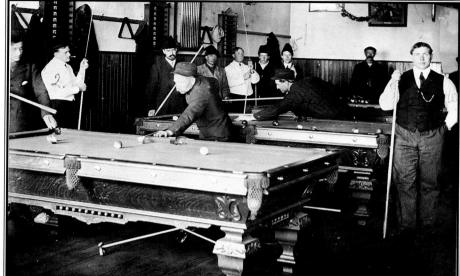

guarantee of strife. Passions ran high; jealousies raged; feuds, over real or imagined slights, simmered for years. But there was comic relief in such incidents as the Case of the Occasional Cop.

In 1913 Coronation reprimanded its chief constable, W. Abbott, for brandishing firearms in a local brothel. (Council's minutes did not say whether he was there on business or

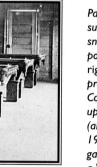

Patrons (above left) look on suspiciously as a photographer snaps the scene at a Wainwright pool hall. A pool hall was de rigueur in any community pretending significance. Coronation had four. Patrons line up outside a Big Valley pool hall (above) to be photographed in 1912. But if pool was a man's game nobody told these ladies in a Whitecourt pool hall (left) in 1913.

pleasure.) Abbott resigned. The town hired a new chief named Stoesser. Seven months later Abbott asked for and got his job back, and Stoesser was out. Two weeks later Abbott was charged with extortion. A month later, found guilty, he was fired, Stoesser was back and Coronation's head was spinning.

Mayors, cops and councillors came and went but the real bulwarks of rural Alberta were the farmers. City, town and village newspapers were packed with agricultural achievement:

Main street of Camrose, about 1910.

Suddenly Banff had a rival of awesome beauty

NOT UNTIL THE PARKS CHIEF MOVED TO EDMONTON DID WORD LEAK OUT, BUT JASPER BEGAN AS A ROWDY CAMP PLAGUED BY LIQUOR AND WOMEN

To make the wild places of the land sacred, keeping the streams pure, and planting fresh blooms along their edges; to preserve the air crystalline and without taint — sparing all living creatures as far as possible rather than destroying them — to do all this in singleness of heart were indeed to open up riches for mankind of which few dream.

— Edward Carpenter

With this quotation from English author Edward Carpenter, a government document writer named M.B. Williams began a hymn of praise to Jasper National Park, years after it was established. His point: that the object of a national park is to keep some of those wild places "sacred."

But at the start of the province's second decade, the name "Jasper" meant nothing to most Albertans. Banff had been queen of the parks for a quarter of a century (Vol. II, Sect. 3, ch. 4). "Jewel of the Canadian Rockies," effused the *Lethbridge Herald* in 1910. "Best and most beautiful holiday resort in the whole of western Canada," declared W.H. Kidner, editor of the *Banff Crag and Canyon*. A decent road now permitted motorists to sputter from Calgary to Banff and back in a day[a]. The famous summer resort would soon be an equally renowned winter resort, predicted the *Albertan*.

But now, suddenly, there was an upstart rival to the north. The first inkling most Albertans had of it came in September 1910, when Howard Douglas, commissioner of Dominion Parks, moved his longtime headquarters from Banff to Edmonton. Banff was "in good running shape," he said. Now he would concentrate his efforts on "the new national park in the Yellowhead Pass, to be known as Jasper, work upon which has already been started."

In fact, a 1907 order-in-council had reserved an enor-

Glenbow Archives, NA-1328-1988

In 1912 Jasper was a tent town and here the residents trudge along the Grand Trunk Pacific's main line, which served as the main street.

mous tract along the future Grand Trunk Pacific right-of-way, following the valleys of the Athabasca and Miette rivers. As Alberta newspapers subsequently gloated, the new park would be bigger than many European countries. Explorers, missionaries, fur traders, even the artist Paul Kane, had traversed the pass and followed the Athabasca River for a century or more.

Already a few homesteaders (Ottawa called them "squatters") were ensconced in the Athabasca Valley. The federal government made its peace with all but one, an American, Lewis J. Swift, who had homesteaded on 160 acres in 1892. When Swift rejected the government's terms the government tried to seduce him with a title: acting game warden. Swift didn't budge so they removed the title, but Swift and his family stayed on for years.

The Grand Trunk Pacific began creeping toward the park site after contracts were awarded in late 1909. It was tough going. Materials were laboriously hauled in via tote road or lake scows. Fifty construction camps went up, with 4,000 workers at peak times.

The camps were as rough as the terrain. J. Burgon Bickersteth, Oxford soccer player and member of a family of Anglican clerics, trekked along the line in 1910. As historian Frank Anderson wrote in *Frontier Guide to Mystic Jasper and the Yellowhead Pass*, the clergyman was "no panty-waist. [He won the Military Cross and bar in the Great War with the Royal Dragoons]...and [was] ready to mix with men under all conditions." But even Bickersteth was shocked by what he found. "Every other log shanty or tent is either a gambling joint, drinking saloon, brothel or pool room," he wrote. "The women make large sums of money and they are constantly going to Edmonton to cash regular stacks of cheques. Some of them make $200 to $300 a month."

A Grand Trunk Pacific construction camp near Jasper in 1910. At the peak of the construction boom 4,000 men were at work in 50 camps.

Loose women, illicit whiskey and food were about the only pleasures the workmen had. Historian Anderson told of one who ate twelve hard-boiled eggs as an *hors d'oeuvres*, then tucked into a full meal, and of another who gobbled 27 sausages at a sitting and ended up in hospital.

Out of these lusty beginnings, however, came an exquisite mountain preserve. As with most other things in early Alberta, the catalyst was the railway. In August 1911 steel reached the divisional point of Fitzhugh (named after E.H. Fitzhugh, a GTP director). Later it was renamed Jasper after Jasper House, an early 19th-century trading post on Brulé Lake run by Jasper Hawse, a North West Company clerk. The first park headquarters was a log cabin. Regular train service began in 1912.

In 1911 Jasper was reduced from its original 5,000 square miles to a mere thousand. This excluded some of the finest big-game territory and such superb scenery as Medicine and Maligne lakes and Mount Edith Cavell. Railway companies and mountain climbers raised such an outcry that the government in 1914 enlarged the park again to 4,000 square miles[b].

The first permanent superintendent, Lt.-Col. Samuel Maynard Rogers, had fought in the Boer War and been an undertaker in Ottawa, things that were somehow seen to qualify him to run the country's biggest national park. The first official tourist came in 1912 when Banff guide Fred Brewster led Samuel Prescott Fry in from Lake Louise.

Fry and the millions who followed (Jasper tourism would not begin to hit its stride until the 1920s) found what the newspapers aptly called a "primeval wilderness." But it fell to the government writer Williams to give Jasper its poetic due:

"A region of superb mountain grandeur where peak after peak lifts its frosty head above the clouds, where the remnants of the last great Ice Age still lie in thick fields upon the shoulders of the mountains and flow down in slow frozen rivers or leaping green streams to the valleys below; a region of tremendous distances, of high waterfalls, deep canyons, and black upsoaring cliffs; yet a region, too, of green loveliness, of grassy valleys and thick pine forests, of emerald alplands bright with flowers, of lakes pure and brilliant in colour as precious gems..."

— R.C.

[a]Until 1916 the good people of Banff, assuming rightly that the automobile was an evil device that would desecrate their mountain playground, forced motorists to check their cars at the police barracks and go it on foot.

[b]Jasper Park was extended again in 1927 to embrace the Columbia Icefield; this area was later transferred to Banff. For a time Jasper was Canada's largest national park. By the century's end, with 10,878 square kilometres, it was fifth — after Wood Buffalo, Ellesmere, Kluane and Auyuittuq.

Forestburg has three creameries; the average yield of oats around Olds is sixty bushels to the acre; the sugar beet industry is a "great source of wealth" around Raymond (where beet farmers allegedly netted $45 an acre); "Wheat Bigger Crop Per Acre Than Ever" (Cardston, 1911).

Although grain farms were nipping into ranchland, the export of horses and cattle going into the decade ran about $9 million a year. Portraits of sturdy bulls and noble horses adorned the news pages.

Farmer success stories abounded. "D.A. Kennedy [Vegreville] paid $12 an acre for his land and could get $40 an acre for it today...He keeps 16 horses, 25 cattle and 100 hogs..." T.C. Gorrell and family [fifty miles east of Stettler] from Yakima, Wash., had in three years "established a comfort-

A Grand Trunk Pacific locomotive pulls the first train into Trochu in 1911, five years after Armand Trochu founded the place.

able home[16] and fine farm and would not go back on any account." William Sherwood went from London, England, to Vermilion with $5 in his pocket and no experience. Ten years later, in 1914, he had 100 acres, thirty cattle, 130 sheep, sixty hogs and 100 chickens.

Farming was becoming more of a science. Long before the turn of the century the federal government and CPR were jittery over western Canada's Palliser Triangle, an enormous swath of the Canadian prairie taking in much of southern Alberta and Saskatchewan and a corner of southwestern Manitoba which Captain John Palliser had declared unfit for agriculture (Vol. I, p. 231). But very soon the industrious Mormons around Cardston proved that irrigation worked.

Ottawa began drafting a western water policy. One plan, the North Saskatchewan Diversion Scheme, would have carried water into dry southern Alberta through a network of great canals, but would have cost $100 million. The politicians decided drought was just a passing thing and Alberta's wonderful soil would withstand the occasional dry year. (Farmers did not know that its wonders were being rapidly eroded; the words "soil conservation" were not yet in their lexicon.)

But the droughts did not go away. Now even the CPR got involved. In taking up its remaining land grants in the West, the railway accepted certain blocks on the understanding that they would be improved through irrigation. One such was an area of about fifty by 125 miles, east of Calgary. By 1911 the CPR had laid some 2,500 miles of canals and ditches, taking water from the Bow River at Calgary and a holding reservoir at Chestermere Lake. Around the same time it built a dam near Bassano.

Didsbury viewed from the CPR line, 1911.

The main street of Sedgewick, 1910-12.

It was a moderate success: crops improved; more settlers came. But farmers began complaining that their land was too sandy to hold water, or too high for gravity flow, or had a clay base that caused alkaline salt to form at ground level. Much of the land was reclassified as non-irrigable, and the CPR lost heavily. Still, it deserved marks for effort.

Meanwhile, on the good-husbandry front, the federal government opened "demonstration farms" at Medicine Hat, Claresholm, Olds, Sedgewick, Vermilion, Stony Plain and Athabasca Landing; the CPR had one at Strathmore. There were

(Right) Charles S. Noble, the genius of dryland farming, who began as an impoverished farm boy. (Above) the Noble family's Grandview Farm east of Nobleford. Noble farmed twenty sections and had forty men working for him.

Dominion Experimental Farms at Lethbridge and Lacombe and experimental stations at Fort Simpson and Fort Smith. Charles S. Noble of Noble (later Nobleford) — a modest immigrant from Iowa who started out near Claresholm walking barefoot behind a plough pulled by oxen — was establishing himself as a genius in dryland farming, with evolving techniques on weed control, summerfallowing, and tilling the land to retain maximum moisture. In 1916 Noble owned twenty sections (12,800 acres) and formed the Noble Foundation, a profit-sharing organization for his forty workers. That same year he set a world record for wheat yield on 1,000 acres: 54,395 bushels (averaging more than 54 to the acre), compared to the 51,210 bushels raised by the previous record-holder in Washington state. By 1920 Noble had 56 sections, ran 61 binders, 600 horses and mules and some powerful tractors, and was rated the biggest wheat farmer in the British Empire[17].

Albertans won most of the prizes in the autumn of 1910 at the International Dry Farming Congress in Spokane. A year later the province won the Sweepstakes Cup[18] at the Congress in Colorado Springs and took home a quarter of the prizes[19]. All over the province farmers were clamouring for the new "miracle" wheat, Marquis, developed by Charles Saunders of the Ottawa experimental farm, which ripened several days earlier than the conventional Red Fife (Vol. I, p. 248).

In moments of reality, Albertans admitted through clenched teeth that farming was not always profitable or idyllic. The *Lethbridge Herald*, reporting on Magrath's progress for 1911, acknowledged in gentlest terms what seems to have been a catastrophic year: "It must be remembered that all over the West the wheat yield has been somewhat of a disappointment, the season being the most unsettled in many years. Magrath did not escape these unfavourable factors and suffered with the

[16]Homes weren't so shabby in the small cities either. Prince Edward Islander Hugh John Montgomery went to Wetaskiwin as a store clerk in 1898 and ended up buying the store and employing eighteen people. He became an MLA in 1914. His home included a library, a parlour clad in green Oriental carpet, a dining room with 'exquisite plate rail and fine furniture,' a wrap-around verandah and grounds designed and maintained by professional gardeners.

[17]Years later Noble invented a revolutionary cultivator blade to kill weeds while leaving a trash cover on parched soil.

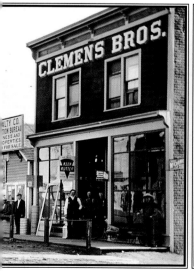

Rosebud at the end of the province's second decade, 1920.

[18]The Sweepstakes Cup was awarded for best state exhibit, and was received by the Honourable Duncan Marshall on behalf of the province.

[19]When the Congress was held in Alberta in 1912, the U.S. railroads insisted that American farmers have a return ticket — for fear they'd defect.

rest. The Magrath farmer encountered first the high winds which blew out his seed, often twice, and then in succession the dry spell, excessive rain, the early frost and snowstorms which deterred threshing, and lastly the car shortage..."

Similarly, some little towns didn't measure up, despite great expectations. Duhamel, about ten miles southwest of Camrose, in advertising its building lots in 1910, proclaimed that it "simply cannot help becoming one of the most important marketing centres in central Alberta." In fact, it never grew beyond a hamlet and eventually dwindled away.

Lille in the Crowsnest Pass had high hopes in 1910 with a hotel, general store, post office, telephone system, RNWMP detachment and school for forty pupils. But its star was tied to West Canadian Collieries. The miners went on strike in 1911. The population nosedived from nearly 1,000 to around 300. In 1912 the company shut down the local mines and coke ovens. Lille died.

Suffield, like old soldiers, just faded away. In 1909 British entrepreneurs launched Canada Wheat Lands Ltd. with £1 million capitalization and 64,000 acres west and north of the Suffield whistlestop. By 1910 the place had blossomed with hotels, business blocks, homes, banks and a

---

The main justification for so many hotels, restaurants, banks and other amenities in these smaller centres was simply this: the neighbourhood town or village was a lifeline and social centre.

---

two-storey school. One hotel, the Alamo, had 32 rooms with hot and cold water, "square" flush toilets, brass beds, eiderdown comforters, mahogany furniture, Brussels carpets on maple floors. Its forty-foot mahogany bar, backed with splendid mirrors and exquisite small windows, was dressed in soothing colours. The three-storey Alamo, named after the place in Texas, was a thing of beauty.

But it was not to be a joy forever. The company's first crops in 1912 and 1913 were only average. By then the ambitious Brits had broken more than 20,000 acres using steam engines, gasoline tractors and oxen with Doukhobor drivers. But 1914's crop was a total failure. At the same time, British capital suddenly was diverted to the war in Europe. Prohibition in 1915 dealt a death blow to the Alamo and other non-temperance hotels. Canada Wheat Lands collapsed. Another company promised irrigation but failed to deliver. The lands were eventually turned back to grazing. The town dissolved.

Today a hamlet remains on the one-time headquarters of the biggest commercial grain farming endeavour in Alberta — mute testimony to the broken dreams that went hand in hand with extravagant success in the decade that saw those hundreds of pinpoints of light appear on the map of Alberta.

Provincial Archives of Alberta, A-5077

Provincial Archives of Alberta, IR-128

Dennis Avenue, Fort Saskatchewan, 1915.

Carstairs street scene about 1906.

The shout that terrified any town: 'FIRE!'

IF THE ONLY PROTECTION WAS VOLUNTEERS FORMING BUCKET BRIGADES
A CARELESSLY THROWN MATCH COULD DESTROY MUCH OF THE COMMUNITY

Fire that started in the Palace Pool Room threatened much of Wainwright in 1911. The buildings were replaced within four months.

"FIRE!"

All over Alberta that terrifying cry brought people bolt upright in their beds and running into the streets. They knew their community might be wiped out in two or three hours — and often there was little they could do about it.

Fire was a prairie plague. The cause was usually peculiar to the times. It sprang up from carelessly dropped matches in the dry hay and straw of livery stables, or among the cans of gasoline or kerosene in general stores. It raced swiftly among frame buildings, tinder boxes almost begging for the burning. The local fire department, if any — sometimes motorized, sometimes not — was usually outmatched by the blaze. The firefighters might consist entirely of valiant citizens manning bucket brigades.

In this catalogue of a few of the decade's fires, it's worth remembering that the financial losses were far more significant than they would seem in the dollar values of the century's end. A $10,000 building in 1910 might be equivalent to a $200,000 structure eight or nine decades later.[a]

1910

APRIL: Volunteer firemen, the RNWMP and "practically every ablebodied citizen" join to save Fort Saskatchewan from total destruction by a galloping prairie blaze, with their carefully set back-fires and ploughed fireguards.

JUNE: Livery stable fire in Irvine kills 41 horses, then guts a hotel.

1911

JANUARY: A defective flue in a Ryley butcher shop starts a blaze that destroys the shop, two hardware stores, two general stores, and damages others. Bucket brigade can't prevent $21,000 loss. In another fire, Stony Plain is described as "burned out." In another, overheated furnace pipes cause loss of Lacombe tailor shop, restaurant, implement dealer and butcher shop. Other premises are damaged. Lacombe had boasted of its "expert and enthusiastic" volunteer fire department with pumper truck, gasoline engine, hook and ladder, and 1,300 feet of hose. Its firemen had won three trophies in a firefighters' competition in Calgary.

1912

JANUARY: $60,500 loss in Gleichen; whole town seems doomed until a store's brick wall stops the spreading flames.

MARCH: Suspected arson almost wipes Acme off the map. Losses: $125,000 (bank, hotel, general store, pool hall, bowling alley, dance hall, lodge room and two implement sheds). Entire town turns out to fight but a strong north wind and insufficient water beats them.

JUNE: A $10,000 fire takes out Sedgewick's lodge hall, chopping mill, stables and a private home. Sedgewick was proud of its new concrete fire hall, chemical engines, manual pump and hook and ladder. Unfortunately, the volunteer fire brigade was at a sports day in Killam that afternoon.

1913

MARCH: "Edson Fire Loss $150,000; Business Section A Charred Ruin." Cause: gasoline explosion. Three men injured when firefighters dynamite buildings to prevent spread of fire.

Townspeople rescued what meat they could when fire destroyed Gamble's butcher shop at Didsbury, Jan. 1, 1914. Looting was almost unknown when such tragedy struck.

APRIL: One carelessly tossed cigarette, and down goes Langdon's livery stable, then a hotel, then flames jump the street to other buildings.

AUGUST: A half-million-dollar fire sweeps the entire business district of Athabasca Landing — which has no firefighters or equipment. The citizens make "a brave struggle to stay the progress of the flames but their efforts were puny compared to the odds against which they had to contend." More than thirty businesses are wiped out. A relief committee is formed to help 100 destitute people. One businessman loses $200,000 worth of buildings, all uninsured.

SEPTEMBER: A $25,000 blaze destroys a business block in Brooks. The fire, originating in a laundry, becomes so fierce that Brooks telegraphs Medicine Hat for help. The request is cancelled when the wind changes, saving what's left of the town.

NOVEMBER: Much of Pincher Creek's business section is

A gasoline explosion in a hardware store started a fire that nearly wiped out Alderson in 1919.

lost after fire causes a blowout of combustible materials in the Hudson's Bay store. Local fire brigade and citizen volunteers finally beat it down. Damage: $33,000.

1914

JANUARY: A $250,000 fire, originating in a movie theatre at 3:30 a.m. on New Year's Day, takes out business in Didsbury. Local fire department tries hard but a strong west wind whips flames through flimsy wooden buildings.

FEBRUARY: Fire damages Banff's King Edward Hotel and other buildings; local brigade hampered because hydrants are frozen. At Seven Persons, a fire destroys the central block of the main street.

1917

DECEMBER: A chimney fire destroys the *Edson Herald* building.

1918

APRIL: A $500,000 fire in Vermilion. One firefighter is overcome with smoke, another is cut by falling glass.

MAY: Most of Entwistle business section lost in $40,000 fire.

1919

MAY: Large part of Hanna's business section destroyed. A forest fire wipes out much of Lac la Biche; $200,000 damage

The Edson volunteer fire brigade, 1913. Pumps and hoses made it well equipped. Some towns had only buckets.

Fire on Fifth Street South

The Balmoral Hotel fire on Fifth Street South, Lethbridge, on March 7, 1911. Fire Chief Thomas Kilkenny died from injuries received fighting it.

leaves entire population short of food and clothing.

AUGUST: $75,000 fire in Alderson; gasoline explosion in hardware store blows out plate glass that severely cuts two men.

However, even this litany of terror and subsequent misery had its up side. Like most other kinds of adversity, it tended to bring out the grit, resilience and innate neighbourliness in pioneers.

Less than ten hours after Athabasca Landing was levelled — embers still smouldering, smoke heavy in the air — a dozen local businessmen were off to Edmonton to replenish lost goods and to order new building materials. Four days later the druggist reopened in temporary quarters with new stock. Within two weeks the bank and other offices were rebuilding.

It was the same in Didsbury, and in Wainwright (where most of the buildings lost in a 1912 fire were replaced within four months). Often the new structures were brick and relatively fireproof. In Vermilion, for example, the replacements for most of its 23 lost buildings were "bigger and better than ever."

In a Canadian city at the century's end fire-ravaged buildings might be looted by roving gangs of thugs. Not so in these Alberta towns. In Didsbury, as the Calgary *Albertan*

reported, "men, women and children went at [the] salvage with desperate vigour. They would rush into a store, all who could crowd in, and in an incredibly short time practically everything that was loose would be piled up in the street in comparative safety. They seemed to realize that the town was doomed, and were determined to cheat the hungry flames of what they could. It was good work, in which neighbour helped neighbour... Thousands of dollars of valuable goods were saved."

In fifteen minutes the salvagers retrieved all the furniture from a hotel, plus the bar and its mirror. They filled a vacant lot with goods saved from a general store, covered them with tarpaulins and ringed them with the store's counters. Later that day, the store owner got out his cash register and "was actually doing a mercantile business *al fresco* with the blue sky as the roof of his business establishment..."

Fire be damned; these were Albertans.

— *R.C.*

[a]Statistics Canada's inflation index goes back only to 1914, and indicates costs have gone up about fifteen-fold since that time. However inflation was also at work between 1910 and 1914, which this rough calculation allows for.

Manufactured by Redcliff Motors Co. Ltd.

The Redcliff, manufactured by Redcliff Motors Co. Ltd. in that centre, enjoyed a brief existence, giving Alberta a short-lived truck manufacturing industry.

CHAPTER THREE

With dust, joy, mud and anguish the car transformed Alberta

THEY APPEARED LIKE FLIES IN THE SPRING ALL OVER THE PROVINCE;
ONE CAR LOOKED LIKE A HEARSE, A TRUCK LIKE A HUGE ROLLERSKATE

by **ROBERT COLLINS**

It was the best of times and the worst of times — depending on whether you loved automobiles or hated their mechanical guts. Although only 699 Albertans actually owned a car in 1910,[1] everyone had strong opinions.

"Macleod is Auto Crazy," exulted a headline in May of that year; in a single month the local car population had jumped from one to twenty. But in Lacombe the sceptical Rev. F.W. Locke warned his flock to keep the Sabbath holy, not spend it all taking "a spin in a motor car."

"It is the poetry of motion, the ideal mode of travelling," enthused the *Calgary Herald*. Not to Bob Edwards, it wasn't. Ban automobiles from St. George's Island park on Wednesdays, Saturdays and Sundays, thundered the crotchety editor of the *Eye Opener*, so that women and children would not "have their humble pleasures spoiled by the selfishness and arrogance of automobile fatheads."

Early in 1912 Lethbridge's police chief, upon getting a new "chug wagon,"[2] was reportedly "as pleased as a boy with a new rocking horse." Two weeks later, near Calgary, a couple of gun-toting car-hating cowpokes rode up to an unarmed automobile around midnight and shot it right through the hood. Then, cackling derisively as the car's occupants huddled in fright, they galloped into the night.

So it went, pro and con. Automobiles killed people, terrified horses and drove provincial and city officials into a frenzied quest for better roads and laws to curb speeders, car thieves and reckless drivers. They also brought new jobs to communities; eased the work of firemen, ambulances and police, and gave men a new plaything[3].

The hazards of inter-town travel near Hanna. The car is a Model T Ford which, after it appeared in 1908, proliferated all over North America. No car, however, was equal to the conditions routinely imposed by the Alberta prairie.

[1]One of them was Carl Beny, the International Harvester agent at Irvine. He drove an IHC High-Wheeler, licence #299. He subsequently launched a car dealership dynasty: first at Brooks, then Medicine Hat, then Lethbridge, where his grandson Milton was president of Beny Chevrolet Oldsmobile Cadillac later in the century.

[2]The auto was also dubbed 'benzene buggy,' 'benzene perambulator' and 'joy-cart.' Its proper name came from the Greek *autos* (self) and the Latin *mobilis* (moving).

Like it or loathe it, nearly everyone agreed the thing was here to stay. Alberta's first Automobile Act in 1906 set the licence fee at three dollars. In 1911 the fee rose to ten dollars plus one dollar for a set of plates, but it didn't quench enthusiasm. The driver population soared: 1,700 in 1911, 2,500 in 1912, 3,733 in 1913, 4,728 in 1914. City people quickly became auto fanatics: roughly half of the 1911 permit holders were in Calgary (475), Edmonton (210), Lethbridge (90), Medicine Hat (88) and Wetaskiwin (19).

Farmers and ranchers were the main dissenters, with reason. Motorists thought nothing of taking shortcuts through farmers' wheatfields or ranchers' pastures, flattening crops and sending livestock into fits, or into barbed-wire fences. A High River rancher drove off one carload of motorists at gunpoint. Some farmers nurtured mudholes near their property, appearing fortu-

Near Calgary, a couple of gun-toting, car-hating cowpokes rode up to an unarmed automobile around midnight and shot it right through the hood while the occupants huddled in fright.

itously with horses to haul out bogged-down cars for, say, five dollars (which in 1911 bought you a cord of wood or five bags of potatoes).

By law, drivers (also called chauffeurs or autoists) were supposed to slow down when approaching or passing a horse-drawn vehicle and take "every reasonable precaution" to avoid frightening horses. Some didn't, but farmers could be equally to blame. A motoring party near Medicine Hat one Sunday met a cursing farmer with wagon who refused to relinquish half the road; being late for church, they backed up to a crossroad. Near Diamond City another driver and passengers were stalled by a rural roadhog on a steep hill, toppled into a ravine and had to jump for their lives. Soon after, it became obligatory to yield half the road.

Gradually farmers discovered that the automobile served them too: speeding them to town for mail, groceries or machinery parts; easing neighbourhood visiting; reducing rural isolation. Nor did the car's mechanized relatives immediately supplant the farm horse. In 1911 the president of the Alberta Horse Breeders' Association told a Calgary audience that automobiles were reducing the

William Dobbie of Pincher Creek sits proudly beside the driver of his Alberta-made car, the Glover, whose fifth wheel was designed to drag it out of prairie mud. It didn't, and the Glover soon vanished from the market.

Glenbow Archives, NA-138-1

The automobile brought to Alberta a new phenomenon, the auto parade, and a new kind of local businessman, the automobile dealer.

An automobile parade in Leduc, probably May 24, 1915.

The Edmonton Garage opened for business in 1914 at 10119-121 Street. On display are five Overlands (three on the left and two on the right) and a Chalmers (third from right).

New cars parade down Calgary's Seventh Avenue in 1915.

New Oakland cars parade in Medicine Hat, 1912.

Model Ts on parade in Hardisty, 1914.

First delivery of Model Ts to Castor, 1912.

4This probably explains why
there was no decline in blacksmiths
during the decade (Calgary and
Edmonton together had three
more blacksmiths in 1920 than in
1910). They still hammered out
ploughshares and horseshoes.
Some — like Charles Edwards of
Rocky Mountain House, who
enlarged his shop and stocked auto
tires and parts — became automobile mechanics. Livery stable
owners were harder hit, although
some of them also went into the
garage business.

numbers of light horses (for buggies or riding) but draft horses still did most rural pulling[4]. As late as 1926 there was only one tractor to every six Alberta farms, and only one motor truck to every 48 farms.

Many truck advertisements were aimed at urban buyers. Models were strictly utilitarian. The Gramm, with chain-driven rear wheels and blunt ugly body, looked like a tank. A Calgary dealer sold Chase "motor wagons" in 1911 — a three-quarter-ton model for $1,300 and a one-ton panel model that resembled a hearse for $2,000 — and in 1919 a more modern-looking Maxwell for $1,550 (f.o.b. Windsor). Nash sold one-ton ($2,410) and two-ton ($3,100) trucks plus something called the Nash Quad Chassis for $4,775. Medicine Hat's Central Garage offered a Ford one-ton chassis that looked like an oversize roller-skate. It sold for $750 but the buyer had to supply his own truck-box.

In contrast, Albertans could choose from a wide array of reasonably attractive automobiles. In July 1911, 29 members of the Calgary auto club drove to Banff (as venturesome then as a modern trip to Ulan Bator). Among them were two Cadillacs, two Regals and one each of Reo, Winton,

'Come with me, Elaine, in my Whiskey-6 with chain'

MORE MODELS WERE ON SALE IN ALBERTA IN 1910 THAN IN THE '90s, A 'GRAY DORT' IN CALGARY COST $910, A 'TUDHOPE' WAS $1,625

Along with the popular Model T Ford, Russell and McLaughlin-Buick, numerous other models were available in Alberta — many more than would be available by the century's end. This sampling is from 1910-1920 advertisements.

Briscoe: An American design, built in Brockville, Ontario. In 1916 a four-cylinder touring model or roadster[a] sold for $975; an eight-cylinder for $1,185. The Briscoe Four, claiming 32 miles to the gallon, was the Canadian army's choice for a light car in France.

Cadillac: The innovator; introduced electric headlights in 1911, self-starter in 1912, left-hand drive and a V8 engine in 1915; $2,700 (U.S.).

Chalmers: Popular in the U.S. during this decade. A six-cylinder, 54-horsepower model sold in Medicine Hat for $3,250 in 1913.

Chevrolet: First made in the U.S. in 1911; manufacturing in Canada began about 1915. The next spring a touring model sold at Baalim Motor Company in Lethbridge or Michener Brothers in Red Deer for $750, including electric horn and starter, speedometer and a "clear vision ventilating windshield" (the top half swivelled out). Michener sold 48 Chevs in 1916.

Dodge: Launched in 1914; by 1917 it sold in Medicine

Hat and Lethbridge for $835 (touring) and $1,265 (sedan).

Dominion: Canadian car from Walkerville, Ontario. The four-cylinder 35-horsepower model did 50 mph; in 1910 sold in Edmonton for $1,850. Company folded in 1911.

EMF — with its companion, the **Flanders**: Detroit tourers marketed by Studebaker. Available in Edmonton, Lethbridge, Mannville and Vegreville in 1911-12 at $1,000 to $1,250. The top, windshield and speedometer were $105-$110 extra.

Franklin: Allegedly the most successful air-cooled car before the Volkswagen (hence no frozen radiators). Medicine Hat Garage and Calgary's Chapin Company sold four-cylinder and six-cylinder models.

Gray-Dort: Made in Chatham, Ontario, by the Gray family (associated with Dort in the U.S.). A 1916 version with Canadian-made components sold at MacTavish Brothers in Calgary for $910.

Hudson: The 1914 Hudson, a solid boxy-looking seven-passenger vehicle sold in Edmonton and at Dominion Motor in Medicine Hat for $2,250 (f.o.b. Detroit).

Kissel Kar: This six-cylinder tourer originally appeared under an equally unfortunate name, Badger.

Maxwell: American car immortalized by comedian Jack

1915 Dodge
$835 at the Hat and Lethbridge.

1914 Maxwell Model 15-4
$890 and up at Medicine Hat.

1910 Hudson.
The later 1914 'Six' cost $2,250.

1915 Metz roadster
At Lethbridge for $800.

Haynes, Napier, Stoddart-Dayton and Maxwell. All except the Regal[5] were U.S. imports.

But five members drove the Canadian-made Russell which, until the Great War, was one of the most popular in this country. Built in Toronto between 1905-1915 by the Canada Cycle and Motor Company (famous for CCM bicycles), it featured a gearshift mounted on the steering column (years ahead of most others) along with throttle and spark controls. It had two kerosene headlights plus an additional driving light adjustable to any angle. The handbrake, when applied, automatically disengaged the transmission even when the car was in gear. The Russell, in ultramarine blue with leather upholstery, sold in 1910 for $1,550 to $4,500.

Another strong contender was the McLaughlin-Buick from Oshawa, Ontario (where resident genius Sam McLaughlin would become Canada's only true automobile tycoon and an originator of General Motors of Canada). The thirty-horsepower Model 27 came on the market in 1910 at $1,500. There were sixteen other McLaughlin-Buick models in several shapes and colours (including a dazzling cherry red). Lethbridge distributors Hyde & Saunders reported "speed to burn and a corker to climb hills."

[5]The Regal was made in Walkerville, Ontario; four-cylinder, thirty horsepower, in three colours (brown, park lake and regal blue). Slogan: 'The Car That Satisfies.'

Benny. Touring, roadster, cabriolet and sedan models sold in Medicine Hat for $890 to $1,400 in 1917 (wooing Alberta drivers with an "all-weather" metal top)[b].

Metz: A roadster, with speeds up to 30 mph; could be bought on the Metz Plan, meaning fourteen separate packages of parts for home assembly. In 1910 Howard Case & Co. of Lethbridge offered it assembled for $800 or "knocked down" for $675.

Mitchell: Made in Wisconsin; by 1910 produced a 50-horsepower six-cylinder touring car. Sold in Calgary for $1,950 to $3,400.

Oldsmobile: The six-cylinder 70-mph model with four-speed gearbox sold in 1912 for a pricy $5,000 (U.S.); even the four-cylinder was $3,000 (U.S.).

Overland: Made by Willys in the U.S.; a four-passenger 35-horsepower touring model sold for $965 at Edmonton Garage Ltd. in 1916; a roadster, for $935. It included electric starting and lighting and electric control buttons on the steering column. Lethbridge dealer D.S. Williamson sold seventeen in the spring of 1916.

Paige: A Detroit car introduced to Alberta in 1917. Eight models ranged from a six-cylinder coupe at $3,400 to the six-cylinder Dartmoor roadster at $1,825.

Rambler: Forerunner of what would later become American Motors; 1912 model, guaranteed for 10,000 miles, could be ordered through E.L. Becker in Medicine Hat. It cost $2,150 (U.S.) but a folding top ($105), windshield ($45), spare tire and tools ($10) and self-starter ($65) were extra.

Studebaker: Model 25 ($1,050), Model 35 ($1,500) or the Studebaker Six ($1,800) were sold in 1913 at Western Auto in Lethbridge, Tanner Brothers in Medicine Hat or Alfred Pelter in Pincher Creek. The Stude Six offered electric starter, lights and horn; curtains; some models had a flower holder.

(To certain citizens with shifty eyes and hat brims as wide as beach umbrellas, the Stude's flower holder was less prized than its ability, with back seat removed, to carry fifty-gallon jugs of illicit booze up to 80 mph on country roads. After Prohibition the "Whiskey-6" was fitted with two spare tires, a spotlight for shining in pursuers' eyes and a thirty-foot chain which, when dragged behind, threw dust in cops' faces.)

Tudhope: The Tudhopes of Orillia, Ontario, in 1911 produced an all-Canadian five-passenger model — "The Car Ahead — Just One Step Ahead of the Horse." It was ahead too: in 1913 it offered shock absorbers, a gasoline gauge (many autos still used a dipstick), brass-trimmed plate-glass windshield, electric starter and electric lights, all as standard equipment. It sold that year in Medicine Hat for $1,625.

— *R.C.*

[a]A 'touring' car was open with seats for four or more passengers. Early versions had a fold-up roof but no side protection; later models had detachable side screens. 'Runabout' and 'roadster' were light two-seaters.

[b]The folks in Fort Smith, just across Alberta's northern border in the Northwest Territories, couldn't have cared less about winterized cars; they had Dasher and Dancer. In 1911 the Alberta government imported for them, as an experiment, a herd of reindeer from Labrador which, said the *Calgary Herald*, meant that 'winter travel in the Canadian North will be robbed of its dangers entirely and a good deal of its hardship.'

1915 Cadillac Eight $2,700 U.S. in Alberta.

1916 Franklin two-door air-cooled 4- and 6-cylinder models at Calgary.

1915 EMF Six $1,000-$1,250, speedometer extra.

1915 Chevrolet 48 sold at Red Deer in 1916.

A gory crossing smash-up showed what was to come

ALBERTANS READ OF THE EVENING-GOWN-CLAD WOMEN UNDER THE TRAIN AND THEY KNEW THAT THE AUTOMOBILE WAS MORE THAN A PLAYTHING

The "most terrible automobile disaster in the history of Edmonton," said the newspapers, was a two-person fatality one October evening in 1913 when a car ran into the Canadian Northern express at the Namayo Avenue (97th St.) level crossing. Passengers Dorothy Gifford and Constance Lines died instantly. Passenger F.R. Cochrane was badly injured. Driver Laurie Jellett was unhurt.

These were not the city's first motoring deaths but the *Bulletin* gave the story a banner headline; it was gory, and its victims were members of Edmonton's upper-crust. Mrs. Lines, wife of a local brewery manager, and Miss Gifford were "prominent in local society." Cochrane was a bank manager. Jellett, in his early 20s, was the son of a well known realtor.

The four, in evening dress, had come from "a merry little dinner party" in the Empire Hotel and were headed for a charity ball. Jellett ploughed into the slow-moving train at about 35 mph (20 mph above the limit). Both women were flung under the locomotive; the *Bulletin* gave explicit details of severed limbs and mangled bodies. Jellett was arrested, charged with "driving an automobile furiously along the streets to the danger of the public" and let out on $10,000 bail.

By now Albertans realized that the automobile for all its charms could be a lethal weapon in the hands of careless, drunken or inexperienced drivers. Newspapers teemed with accident stories. Car mishaps were still a novelty and every incident was reported, even the poor wretch in Red Deer who ran into a telephone pole, spraining his wife's ankle.

"Two people were knocked down by an automobile on Sunday," editorialized the *Bulletin* in June 1912. "One was killed on Monday, four were struck on Tuesday: an average of rather more than two a day. The question is becoming simply: Who next?"

The earliest accidents most often involved cars and horse-drawn vehicles. In 1910 seven people in a Ford tried to pass a buggy south of Lethbridge. The frightened horse jumped in front of the car, the driver swerved, the Ford rolled over and one passenger broke an arm and dislocated an elbow.

City of Edmonton Archives, EA-10-1218

Smash-up at Edmonton's 87th Avenue and 104th Street, about 1918. In Calgary, the police chief warned it was time to enforce the new traffic laws 'without mercy.'

That same month in Edmonton a speeding car scared a wagon team; a 14-year-old girl fell off, was knocked unconscious but recovered. Near Lacombe a year later a driver — braking sharply to avoid a farmer and team ambling out of the bush onto the highway — flipped the car over, injuring two passengers.

Probably the worst car-horse crash was in Calgary when a car ran head-first into a street-watering wagon. A horse was cut and bruised, two motorists died and three more were badly injured. The most bizarre accident was in 1917 on Calgary's Macleod Trail when a runaway horse, crazed with fright, jumped *into* an oncoming car and killed a passenger, Mrs. O.M. Pope from Blackie[a]. The horse broke a leg and was shot.

Imperfect vehicles accounted for some of the crashes; bad roads and worse drivers did the rest. Most automobiles had wooden frames and bodies without heavy-duty metal supports; they cracked and buckled easily on impact. Two Medicine Hat men ended up in hospital and their red Hupmobile was wrecked when the steering gear failed. High-slung auto bodies (the better to navigate deep ruts) were unstable, always teetering into ditches or rolling upside down.

One man was killed and four more were hurt when, speeding at midnight, they skidded off a bridge and down forty feet into Edmonton's Latta Ravine (located at Jasper Ave. just east of 92nd St.). Two frolicsome carloads from Red Deer — passing and repassing each other on the way home from Sylvan Lake — came to grief when one missed a sharp bend in the road. A Lethbridge child died when her father's car tumbled into an irrigation ditch. He said he didn't know the ditch was there.

Alberta Premier Charles Stewart got off with scratches and bruises when, blinded by dust, he ran into a bridge near Gleichen; the impact bounced the premier up to the roof. In one particularly grisly turn of events, a Lethbridge man was pinned under a vehicle in a ravine, bruised, cut and scalded with boiling water from the radiator. He died four days later.

Pedestrians were frequent victims. In 1912, nine-year-old Edmonton newsboy Teddy Schmaltz was run over and killed at Jasper and First Street (101st). In Lethbridge a man standing beside a parked car was knocked down and dragged twenty feet[b]. The wife of Alberta's education minister took a corner too fast and first hit a real estate man, then an 11-year-old boy. In Medicine Hat a brand-new driver lost control as he turned a corner, crashed into the sidewalk and, as the Calgary *Albertan* delicately put it, "collided with J. Hewitt, hardware merchant, who was walking in the same direction." J.J. Hewitt went to hospital.

A prevailing joke reflected the pedestrians' bitter mood:

First motorist: "Does running over a pedestrian upset you?"
Second motorist: "No, I've never run over one that big."

Conversely, motorists began demanding that jay-walkers be fined. As the *Edmonton Bulletin* acknowledged in a 1912 editorial, motorists had rights too.

By decade's end, public and officialdom were getting tired of the mayhem. Calgary police chief David Ritchie reported that of the city's 1,290 street accidents in 1919, more than a thousand were caused by automobiles. Speeders in earlier years were habitually fined $15 to $20. Ritchie suggested they be fined *and* get "a mark" on their licence (anticipating the points system that came to Canada

Boys stare in fascination at the crumpled remains of a car that plunged into Edmonton's Latta Ravine at Jasper Avenue, just east of 92nd Street on Feb. 5, 1918. One man was killed and four injured.

warnings of the crossing guard on duty. Yet the jury did not recommend prosecution, and in police court he received only a $20 fine.

Seven years later, a Czar farmer crashed into a speeding train — he was trying to beat it over a level crossing west of

---

Alberta Premier Charles Stewart got off with scratches and bruises when, blinded by dust, he ran into a bridge near Gleichen; the impact bounced the premier up to the roof.

---

much later). He warned he would in future enforce the law "without mercy. I am not an enemy of motorists, but I am an enemy of some men who are handling cars here."

Others were likewise taking a sterner view of bad driving. In 1917 a Lethbridge miner ran down a nun, a few hours after he bought his car and got his licence. The nun, Sister Mary from Sacred Heart convent, wasn't seriously hurt but the miner was locked up. Having spent all his money on the car, he couldn't make bail.

Back in 1913, the coroner's inquest into the death of the two Edmonton socialites found that young Laurie Jellett had driven at an excessive rate of speed and had ignored the

Strathmore — killing two of his passengers and seriously injuring the third. He was charged with manslaughter.

Albertans were serving notice on reckless drivers — but the problem would endure many generations after them.

— *R.C.*

[a]A few days earlier the Pope family, tenant farmers, had been burnt out. Mrs. Pope had come to Calgary to buy new clothing for her five children.

[b]The motorist claimed he didn't know he'd hit a pedestrian; just thought he'd grazed the other car — so why stop for that? He was fined $5 and costs for driving without lights.

Neither the time, place, nor persons involved in the above motoring humiliation is known. It is somewhere in the Medicine Hat area. The car would one day prevail over the horse, though this luckless driver may not have thought so.

The joys of a drive in the country

By the 1930s, the idea of a Sunday afternoon 'drive' would become one of life's pleasures for thousands of Albertans and the 'Sunday driver,' noted for dawdling inattention, would become one of driving's greater hazards. Early in the century, however, going for a 'drive' was a risky adventure which often wound up in a ditch or mudhole with a long hike to the nearest farmhouse.

As women watch sceptically, four men heave hard to free a Model T from mud in the Edmonton area about 1913.

There was even an Alberta-made car. William Dobbie of Pincher Creek, with a mechanic and $8,000 worth of parts from Chicago, built one wagon-like vehicle with steps leading up the back. He called it the Glover. It had big buggy wheels and a *fifth* chain-driven wheel which, when lowered, was supposed to pull the car from mudholes. Like most fifth wheels it was superfluous; it simply dug a deeper hole. The Glover soon disappeared. So too did the Redcliff, a truck manufactured by Redcliff Motors Co. Ltd. in that centre.

Loaded for a camping trip at Macleod, about 1918. Eight years earlier the local editor declared the town 'auto crazy.'

By mid-decade the hands-down favourite all over North America was the Model T Ford. It was a legend almost from the moment Henry Ford built it in 1908: the epitome of standardization and mass production — yet owners swore that each T had a distinct and usually weird personality[6]. It was variously known as the Tin Lizzie and Mechanical Cockroach. From a distance it resembled a top hat on wheels. Whole joke books were written about it[7]. It added the word "flivver" to our language, derived from the claim that a rattling ride in a Model T was good "for the liver."

From the beginning it was manufactured in Windsor as well as the U.S. In 1914, 38% of the cars sold in this country were Fords; by 1917 there were more Fords in Canada than all other models combined. The Model T weighed 1,200 pounds, had a four-cylinder twenty-horsepower

[6]**A Lewis Carroll parody went:** *Speak harshly to your little Ford, And kick it when it freezes; It does it only to annoy, Because it knows it teases.*

[7]**Sample joke: 'I hear Henry's painting all his Model Ts yellow.' 'How come?' 'He's gonna sell 'em in bunches, like bananas!'**

[8]**For a while British Columbia and the Maritimes drove on the left.**

Motorists thought nothing of taking shortcuts through farmers' wheatfields or ranchers' pastures, flattening crops and sending livestock into fits, or into barbed-wire fences.

---

motor and could manage forty miles per hour. Fuel feed was by gravity from a tank under the seat; when gas was low a driver had to back up steep hills to keep it flowing. In 1911 the touring Model T sold for $975 and the basic runabout for $875.

The Hudson's Bay Company in Calgary bought a fleet. Drumheller coal miners, striving to fill wartime orders, swore by the "three Ms": men, mules and Model Ts. The little Ford could scramble up the valley's steep hills where other vehicles floundered. John S. McKellar, government road inspector working out of Fort Saskatchewan, who had driven his Ford for eight years over 200,000 miles of awful road, said of the model in general, "I don't think there is a car of any make that has covered as many miles in Alberta."

Be it Glover, McLaughlin, Russell or Ford, every car early in the decade had the steering wheel on the right. This British legacy made no sense in Alberta, or other provinces where driving on the right side of the road was law[8]. But North American manufacturers had decreed that drivers should sit on the right to keep an eye on the ditch. Besides, where else would you put gearshift, brake lever and horn (which were then positioned outside the right-hand door, with the spare tire and tool box)?

When left-hand drive came (around mid-decade; the Model T was one of the first to change) car-makers discovered that controls fitted nicely inside and spare parts went in the trunk. Until then, right-hand drive was simply one more headache for Alberta's beleaguered drivers: they could never see around the vehicle ahead to pass and their passengers had to disembark in the middle of the road or street.

Picnicking was one of the uncertain joys of motoring and this group near Edmonton in 1913 appears successful, though they're not yet home.

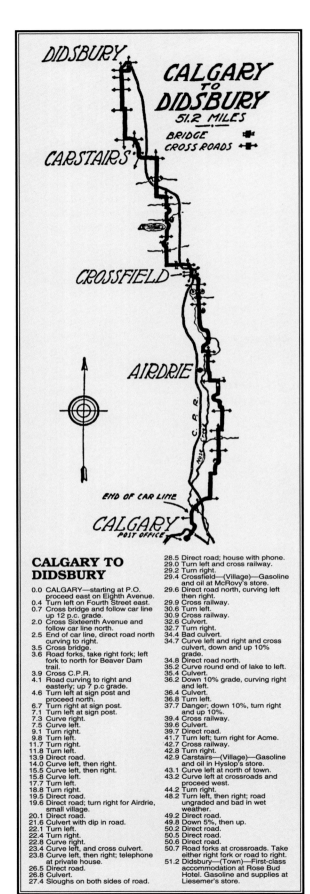

CALGARY TO DIDSBURY

0.0 CALGARY—starting at P.O. proceed east on Eighth Avenue.
0.4 Turn left on Fourth Street east.
0.7 Cross bridge and follow car line up 12 p.c. grade.
2.0 Cross Sixteenth Avenue and follow car line north.
2.5 End of car line, direct road north curving to right.
3.5 Cross bridge.
3.6 Road forks, take right fork; left fork to north for Beaver Dam trail.
3.9 Cross C.P.R.
4.1 Road curving to right and easterly; up 7 p.c grade.
4.6 Turn left at sign post and proceed north.
6.7 Turn right at sign post.
7.1 Turn left at sign post.
7.3 Curve right.
7.5 Curve left.
9.1 Turn right.
9.8 Turn left.
11.7 Turn right.
11.8 Turn left.
13.9 Direct road.
14.0 Curve left, then right.
15.5 Curve left, then right.
15.8 Curve left.
17.7 Turn right.
18.8 Turn right.
19.5 Direct road.
19.6 Direct road; turn right for Airdrie, small village.
20.1 Direct road.
21.6 Culvert with dip in road.
22.1 Turn left.
22.4 Turn right.
22.8 Curve right.
23.4 Curve left, and cross culvert.
23.8 Curve left, then right; telephone at private house.
26.5 Direct road.
26.8 Culvert.
27.4 Sloughs on both sides of road.
28.5 Direct road; house with phone.
29.0 Turn left and cross railway.
29.2 Turn right.
29.4 Crossfield—(Village)—Gasoline and oil at McRovy's store.
29.6 Direct road north, curving left then right.
29.9 Cross railway.
30.6 Turn left.
30.9 Cross railway.
32.6 Culvert.
32.7 Turn right.
34.4 Bad culvert.
34.7 Curve left and right and cross culvert, down and up 10% grade.
34.8 Direct road north.
35.2 Curve round end of lake to left.
35.4 Culvert.
36.2 Down 10% grade, curving right and left.
36.4 Culvert.
36.8 Turn left.
37.7 Danger; down 10%, turn right and up 10%.
39.4 Cross railway.
39.6 Culvert.
39.7 Direct road.
41.7 Turn left; turn right for Acme.
42.7 Cross railway.
42.8 Turn right.
42.9 Carstairs—(Village)—Gasoline and oil in Hyslop's store.
43.1 Curve left at north of town.
43.2 Curve left at crossroads and proceed west.
44.2 Turn right.
48.2 Turn left, then right; road ungraded and bad in wet weather.
49.2 Direct road.
49.8 Down 5%, then up.
50.2 Direct road.
50.5 Direct road.
50.6 Direct road.
50.7 Road forks at crossroads. Take either right fork or road to right.
51.2 Didsbury—(Town)—First-class accommodation at Rose Bud Hotel. Gasoline and supplies at Liesemer's store.

There were other problems, such as how to start a car with the hand-turned crank without it kicking back (with pressure of up to eighty pounds per square inch) and breaking your arm. So many North American drivers sprained or broke wrists and forearms that a surgeon wrote a paper about "chauffeur's fracture" for the *Medical Record*. (Cadillac introduced the electric self-starter in 1912. By 1914 Albertans could buy, for $32.50, the "Perfection Auto Starter" for Fords: "eliminates the risk of your wife or one of your family sustaining a broken wrist.")[9]

Next dilemma: how to drive? There were few reputable driving schools. In 1912 two swift operators started the Edmonton Auto Exchange and Livery, offering to teach young men how to repair and operate automobiles for fifty dollars. Fifty suckers signed up. One second-hand "training" car appeared briefly on the premises. A lecturer with several mythical university degrees, known as Prof. Whiffenpuffer, "didn't know whether an exhaust was a disease or a new variety of washing machine." Eventually the two shysters took a fast train and a blonde woman to the U.S., one jump ahead of the law.

Most people learned to drive from friends, a car salesman or by trial and error. Some yelled "Whoa" when the car wouldn't stop. Daily newspapers had columns of questions and answers for motorists. "The most difficult task for the driving novice to master is gear shifting," said the *Lethbridge Herald*. "The disengagement of the clutch together with the speed lever movement is quite as difficult at first as patting the head with one hand and rubbing the chest with the other."

A trip to the country — called "touring" — required a day's prepara-

In 1912 two swift operators started the Edmonton Auto Exchange and Livery, offering to teach young men how to repair and operate automobiles for fifty dollars. Fifty suckers signed up.

tion. The tourer checked and refilled the car's grease cups, loaded a spare tire or two, a half-dozen inner tubes plus pump, jack, rawhide tire bandage (to wrap around bruised casing), chains, tire repair kit[10] and a set of nail pullers. The last, attached to the rear mudguards, were supposed to peel off horseshoe nails before they pierced an inner tube.

Optional equipment included tow rope, block and tackle[11], lantern, crowbar for prying rocks off the road, seat covers, headlamp covers for daytime driving and a canvas to spread underneath the vehicle where the motorist could expect to spend several hours.

Wise drivers also took along spare fuel, water and oil. The average car, with its inferior piston rings, could use thirteen litres of oil over 2,000 miles. Garages and hardware stores in larger cities[12] sold gasoline but in the country, early in the decade, fuel was scarce and might cost double the normal price (which in Calgary and Edmonton ranged from 29 cents a gallon in 1914 to 52 cents in 1920)[13].

Canada's first gasoline station — an Imperial Oil tank hooked to a kitchen hose in Vancouver — didn't appear until 1908. Filling stations were more plentiful by the beginning of the Great War. One of Alberta's earliest may have been Imperial's Ioco station at 125 - 12th Avenue West, Calgary, in mid-decade. Calgarians could also buy Imperial products at six other places, including J.H. Ashdown Hardware and Hillhurst Hardware[14].

Touring men habitually wore leather cap, goggles, jacket, duster (like a butcher's cloth coat) and gauntlets. Raincoats, rubber boots and dust masks were optional. The women anchored their straw hats with cheesecloth veils (which also kept flying mud out of their mouths), long-sleeved gloves and ankle-length dusters. If two couples travelled together the men usually sat in front, tight-lipped, while the women huddled stoically in back. Ideally, all were blessed with strong kidneys. It was a long distance between comfort stations.

Those elaborate preparations were essential. Of the 29 cars that toured from Calgary to Banff in July 1911, only 25 arrived — because the road was wet and some drivers forgot to take tire chains. The *Calgary Herald* wasted no sympathy on them: "An auto that starts on a trip like the one to Banff should never attempt it without proper equipment," the *Herald* admonished[15]. A year later the auto club said the Banff road was now so good drivers could make the (then) 85-mile trip in five hours if they didn't dally[16]. In 1913 four men drove a Cadillac from Calgary via Lethbridge to Medicine Hat and back: 517 miles in eighteen hours, 24 minutes. The *Albertan* made a news item of it.

Auto clubs became the nuclei of the Alberta Motor League in 1917. Their members, usually led by a road-wise "pathfinder," travelled in packs, visiting other cities, sizing up roads and roadside facilities and campaigning for better ones. They posted 350 warning and directional signs around Calgary, including 100 along the Banff road; twelve-foot white posts bearing rectangular yellow placards with black lettering: "Slow!" "Danger!" "Blow Horn!" and the like. Other signs endeavoured to lead the befuddled motorist out of the wilderness: "R" for right turn, "L" for left, and "X" for a railway crossing.

A Calgary club member produced in 1914 Alberta's first road guide — twelve strip maps with minute directions (including the nearest telephones). For instance, it led drivers out of Wetaskiwin toward Edmonton in fractions of miles:

00.0 Starting at the Post Office, proceed east. At .1, turn left west of railway. At .4, curve left north-west. At 1.0, ascend 8-foot grade. At 1.5, turn right...

[9]In December 1916 an anguished motorist wrote to the *Medicine Hat News*, 'Please advise if there is any way known to the mind of man to put a self-starter on a Ford car, which will not need a starter to start the starter?'

[10]Motorist Gordon Seale of Edmonton once patched and re-patched the same flat eleven times in one afternoon.

[11]In 1913 M.C. Huff of Bowden patented and marketed his International Auto Extractor for $45. It was a cable-and-anchor, connected to front or rear wheels, and supposedly plucked a car from mudholes under its own power.

[12]Calgary had a 'garage' in 1906: the Calgary Novelty Works. It advertised 'automobile and type-writer repairs a specialty.'

[13]In 1922 Alberta levied a two-cent sales tax on gasoline, the first in Canada.

When driving might entail a race with the antelopes
AN ALBERTA VISITOR TELLS HOW A HERD OUTRAN HIS CAR ACROSS THE PRAIRIE

In September 1920 H.B. McKinnon of the Toronto Globe *drove around southern Alberta. His dispatch says the rest.*

Lethbridge, Alta., Sept. 10 — Driving by car across the Bow-slope country on a recent occasion we raised a herd of antelope. The graceful animals, some twelve or fourteen of them, suddenly appeared on the left of the trail we were following and after a brief survey of the oncoming motor decided upon evacuation of the territory upon which they had been browsing. Hurriedly gathering into mass formation, with the buck guiding their manoeuvres, they headed directly across our track and toward a low rolling terrain on the right horizon.

At the moment of their discovery we were on a particularly fine piece of prairie trail, smooth and hard, with a straight stretch ahead of a dozen miles or more. As the antelope crossed our path in a wide safe circle, and the buck laid his course for the shelter of the hills, our driver gave chase — merely in the hope of securing a closer view of the quarry. The heavy car shot ahead at forty — a pretty fast pace among badger holes — and for a moment seemed to gain on the startled animals, now running shoulder to shoulder, the buck well in the lead.

But only for a moment! As the seconds passed the race became more uneven. We saw the pack begin to draw away; slowly but surely they widened the gap between us. At constant urging the driver "stepped on her" and the speedometer steadily climbed to forty-five — our outside limit of safety. Then we saw real speed! As if sensing our fragmentary gain upon his mates, the buck settled himself into serious running. He was being challenged by the noisy contraption of man! Imperceptibly his gait quickened. This was the signal his following awaited. Slowly, deliberately, beautifully — no other word fits so well — the graceful creatures got down to their stride. The level backs bowed ever so slightly; necks lengthened; white bellies swept the waving grasses; dainty hoofs spurned more than a fleeting touch of earth. We were hopelessly outclassed! We might have been standing still on that prairie trail. In far less time than it takes to tell it, the antelope gained the sunset and, without pausing a backward glance upon their unworthy adversaries, dropped below the horizon into the hidden valleys of the Bow-slope hills.

The automobile as status symbol

THE CAR CAME TO ALBERTA FIRST AS A TOY, THEN AS A TOOL, AND FINALLY AS A STATUS SYMBOL, A ROLE IT WOULD PLAY THROUGHOUT THE CENTURY. THESE SCENES SHOW THAT BY THE PROVINCE'S SECOND DECADE IT WAS ALREADY DEFINING WHO WAS WHO.

Gottfried Ruch and friends at Medicine Hat about 1911-12. The scenic canvas behind them suggests the car may have been a prop in a photographer's studio.

F.L. Whitney, D.J. Whitney and Doug Stickley are shown in a Cadillac on Fifth Street South, Lethbridge, about 1910.

Albert Chevigny leans on the fender of the first car in Plamondon in 1920, staring confidently at the camera. His exhausted friend has obviously been struggling with the crank.

An Edmontonian identified as 'Jack McNeil's son' drives a car bearing Alberta licence No. 1779. Note the right-hand steering in many of these cars. Left-hand steering did not become standard in Alberta until about 1915.

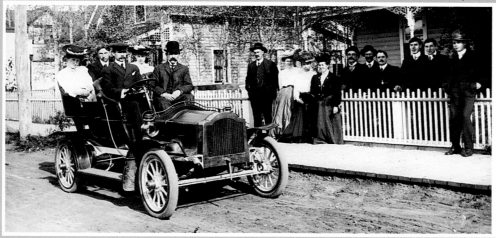

A car identified as belonging to James W. Clements of Edmonton attracts a host of admirers in this undated photograph. The peaked hat on the driver suggests he's a chauffeur.

Provincial Archives of Alberta, A-20131

Provincial Archives of Alberta, B-5820

Here is the famous six-cylinder Studebaker which boasted a flower vase in the rear seat, though it was better known as the Whiskey-6 because bootleggers used it to outrun police. Sometimes the front bumper was filled with concrete to knock down roadblocks. Posing with it is a man identified as Glyn Lewis, though there's no reason to believe he's a bootlegger. He's more probably an oil promoter.

The woman driver was never a new phenomenon in Alberta where women took up driving as soon as men did. This Edmonton lady is not identified; she seems utterly confident behind the wheel.

City of Lethbridge Archives, P19891068087-GP

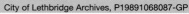

This driver, both hands firmly on the wheel, seems equally self-assured, though the older woman behind her may have some doubts for the safety of the seven passengers. The people are not identified, though the house behind is that of Thomas J. and Martha Kirkham on 13 Street South, Lethbridge.

[14] By 1916 Imperial sold gas under its 'Red Ball' sign in 29 smaller Alberta cities and towns, from Bassano and Beiseker to Vulcan and Youngstown. Alberta's first self-serve station was probably Northern Hardware's 'Gasoteria' in Edmonton in 1920. It sold Imperial's 'Premier' gasoline at four or five cents less per gallon than conventional stations.

[15] One driver's used car conked out before the motorcade left Calgary, yet he arrived in Banff before the others. He took the train.

[16] Until mid-decade, autos weren't allowed beyond Banff's outskirts and were *fined* if they arrived after six p.m.

[17] Most of Alberta's main highways were not kept open year-round until the mid-1930s.

[18] Alberta had no numbered highways until the late 1920s.

[19] In 1918 the first experiment with tractor-drawn twin graders took place near Coaldale.

The cheapness of the bicycle as a mode of travel was demonstrated years ago, and war conditions have revived its popularity. Many men are admitting a feeling of relief at the prospect of economy and convenience in the substitution of a bicycle for larger machines, much more expensive to keep up and awkward to handle for short trips on city streets. The total upkeep of a bicycle for one season is scarcely more than the cost of gasoline for a car for one day.

**– Medicine Hat News
March 31, 1916**

Although the guide showed some 440 miles of road in the Calgary-Lethbridge area alone, its author, Leo English, minced no words about their state: "Methods of road construction are crude in the extreme. When a road is newly graded it is all but impassable for months thereafter." A visitor from eastern Canada confirmed that Alberta roads were "nothing more or less than old trails, with two rather deep ruts into which the wheels of the car fit very nicely." There was little the auto clubs could do about that.

Most roads were impassable in winter. Country people put the car up on blocks until spring[17]. Main highways were known by their old-fashioned names — Macleod Trail, Calgary or Edmonton Trail — and colour coded with markers on poles and trees. Calgary-Banff was the Blue Route; Calgary-Edmonton was the Black Route; the Trans-Canada, which later passed through Medicine Hat, Lethbridge and Macleod, became the Red Route[18].

The highways wandered back and forth — the Edmonton-Calgary road was a series of switchbacks — and towns and villages weren't identified on their approach roads. Without Leo English's strip maps, it was easy to get lost. The first provincial road map didn't appear until the mid-1920s.

Alberta's Department of Public Works, which inherited "highways" in 1905, devoted its limited resources over the first few years to grading routes between major cities and building some corduroy roads in the North. In 1913, the province created a highways branch within Public Works. It spent $643,937 on roads that year but the results were trifling. Road work for the most part meant dragging the dirt surface with horse-drawn scrapers[19]. Farmers sometimes did it to work off back taxes, but only when the farm didn't demand their time.

Highways were usually just wide enough to accommodate two cars. As late as 1918 a ministry spokesman warned communities against grandiose plans: "Narrow up your roads if you expect to get results. You cannot make a New York Broadway out of prairie mud... A road with sixteen feet from shoulder to shoulder is as wide as should be attempted in this country..."

Most people learned to drive from friends, a car salesman or by trial and error. Some yelled 'Whoa' when the car wouldn't stop.

A year earlier the *Lethbridge Herald* wrote optimistically of experiments in mixing bitumen (from the Athabasca tar sands) with clay to make waterproof roads. But the highways spokesman put a damper on that too. "For many years to come, 95% of our roads will be classed as earth roads," he cautioned. "There may be a limited amount of top-dressing with gravel or other suitable material... The average cost of an eighteen-foot strip of paved road extending into the outlying portions of Edmonton exceeded $30,000 per mile." Which was too rich for the ministry's budget.

As late as May 1920 a Lethbridge grocer, The Good Company, ran this newspaper advertisement:

> All Deliveries Discontinued Until Roads Dry Up
> Owing to the condition of the roads at present we find it almost impossible to get through in a great many places without running a great risk of either getting stuck or else breaking the car, so we have decided for the time being to stop delivering goods. We will again deliver as soon as the roads dry up...

While province and rural municipalities strove for decent roads, cities experimented with street surfacing: oil-on-dirt, macadam (gravel and tar), brick (too expensive) and asphalt. (Calgary laid one small slab on Eighth Avenue in 1911.)

But the sudden flurry of traffic violations was more pressing. The Motor Vehicles Act of 1906 (revised in 1911-12) required every vehicle to carry a "proper alarm bell, gong or horn" and a lighted lamp or lamps "in a conspicuous position," with the permit (licence) number clearly displayed on the lamp. Now police courts overflowed with motorists charged with not having a licence, not displaying a licence number, failing to have headlights, failing to sound a horn at a railway crossing, running with the "cut-out open" (meaning, presumably, an unmuffled motor), making illegal left turns, failing to stop for passengers disembarking from streetcars. It was always

good fun when a high official was nabbed — as were an Edmonton magistrate and the city's medical health officer for not having their licence numbers painted five inches high on their headlamps.

Suddenly, too, cars were cluttering streets. Medicine Hat prohibited street parking in the city business section for more than thirty minutes; in Calgary, it was twenty minutes. Boards of trade and visiting farmers resented these restrictions (although there seems to have been no limit on side-street parking). "A business street filled with autos gives a most favourable impression to visitors," editorialized the *Medicine Hat News* in 1920, also urging that diagonal parking replace parallel parking so it would be easier to move one's benzene buggy away from the curb. At decade's end, Edmonton planned to introduce painted parking slots on the streets, to keep motorists from hogging two spaces.

Speeding and "joyriding" (a polite term for theft) were by far the biggest concerns. The 1906 speed limit — 10 mph in the city and 20 mph in the country — was modified in 1911. City speed limits now ranged from 6 mph to 20 mph, depending on location and situation; 15 mph seemed to be the norm. Highway limits were, somewhat ambiguously, "a rate of speed greater than is reasonable and proper, having regard to the traffic and use of the highway or so as to endanger or be likely to endanger the life or limb of any person or the safety of any property."

Ten miles per hour, or even 20, was too tame for drivers with cars capable of 40, 50 or (in the parlance of the day) "goin' like 60." More speeders appeared in court; here, too, the mighty sometimes fell, to brighten the little man's day. A Medicine Hat alderman, who had helped frame the local speeding bylaw, paid a $1 fine for doing 17 mph in a 10-mph zone. An Edmonton alderman paid $20 for breaking the limit.

Calgary and Medicine Hat appointed police patrols to control traffic (which, Medicine Hat claimed, was getting "more like little old New York every day"). An Edmonton magistrate warned in 1912 that he was going to get tough with speeders, fining them the maximum $20 for a first offence instead of the "paltry $10 minimum." Edmonton's police chief suggested jail, with no options, for third offenders. Bob Edwards of the *Eye Opener* said speeders "should be stood up against a wall at sunrise."

In 1911 the *Calgary Herald* noted that "borrowing automobiles without leave" was becoming common. Two drunken youths and a girl pinched a Cadillac from the owner's garage, drove it all night and dumped it over an embankment near Midnapore. The men left the woman beside the wreck while they went to find other transport. She was there, sleeping off a monumental hangover, when police arrived in the morning.

The conflict between ranchers and motorists could become bitter. Some ranchers drove motorists off their land at gunpoint. Farmers were known to dig holes in the road, then charge $5 to pull cars out of them. Where in southern Alberta this encounter occurred is not recorded.

Joyriding led to Alberta's first high-speed chase. In August 1915, 21-year-old Edmontonian James Ferris enlisted in the army, then celebrated by stealing a car. The police were quickly after him in a cloud of dust. At speeds up to 50 mph he headed for an embankment and jumped free. Police found him hiding in a potato patch. He was fined $100 and costs.

The Great War brought a shortage of new cars, a brief revival of bicycling in Calgary, a plea to Lethbridge motorists to avoid Sunday driving to save gasoline, and a desultory search for other fuels, such as kerosene. Used cars were advertised: Albertans could get a year-old Ford five-seater for $400, a 1917 Studebaker Six for $1,095 or a Maxwell truck for $350.

Two new industries: road construction and car repairs

The corduroy wagon roads continued to serve the car. This one (left) led to the Alberta Provincial Police detachment office near Sturgeon Lake. Municipalities were warned not to try building "Broadway" highways in Alberta.

Right, road-building in the Edson area in 1910. This photo was taken near Wolf Creek where the Grand Trunk Pacific construction crews built the original townsite, later moved to Edson.

The first gasoline retailers were hardware stores, like this Northern Hardware in Edmonton (below). Filling stations began appearing just before the Great War.

One interesting side-effect of early motoring was its wary recognition of women as people, after a bad start. The 1911 Traffic Act was flat-out discriminatory, allowing males to drive at the age of 16 but females only at 18. Bruce Watson, solicitor for the Calgary Auto Club, felt it was justified because the city had "too many show-off girls who simply haven't strength enough to stop a car quickly."

But women prevailed. In 1913 the *Albertan* reported that many "own cars built especially for their private use, and not a few of these handle a car with the skill of an expert." One was Mrs. James A. Lougheed (who as owner of Calgary's first large automobile was hardly typical): "Mrs.

One of Alberta's first repair garages, 1912-13. Austin Vickery Motors was located on Seventh Avenue, Calgary, west of Centre Street.

Medicine Hat's Central Garage (left) about 1918. It offered a Ford one-ton truck chassis for $750.

[20]As further evidence of Lethbridge's passion for cars: in 1917, dealer A.G. Baalim contracted for $1 million worth of vehicles over the ensuing fourteen months, including 1,000 Chevrolets.

Lougheed is very fond of motoring and one of her pet luxuries is her garage and her motor-driven equipages. Her cars are probably the finest in this province."

In 1917 Mark Drumm, Calgary Ford dealer, supporter of the women's franchise and "a strong advocate of woman having her place both in politics and in business," hired Alberta's first female automobile salesperson. The *Calgary Herald* somewhat spoiled the moment with phraseology that would cause a modern feminist's gorge to rise: "The individual chosen for this important innovation is Miss Bertha Clark, one of Calgary's best-known business girls, who for a girl of her age has had a wide experience in business and whose friends confidently predict for her a most successful career as a salesman."

Women manned gas stations during the war, and some stayed on afterward. When Imperial Oil opened a $100,000 state-of-the-art service station (three pumps, rest rooms) at Calgary's Sixth Avenue and Second Street West in 1919, it featured "smart young lady attendants" in khaki riding breeches, white blouses and military forage caps.

"The automobile has brought greater contentment into the lives of women than any other thing in recent years," the *Lethbridge Herald* floridly concluded in 1918. "It has shattered the shackles of customs which kept women in the narrow confines of the home, entirely dependent upon men, and has opened up a new world for them — a world of better health, wholesome recreation, self-confidence, convenience, independence, joy, pleasure and contentment."

As the decade wound down there were more gadgets and improvements. A "spark intensifier," a "compensating vapour plug" and something called "gastine" all promised to put more oomph in a motor. A gas-line lock would thwart joyriders. A "Non-Freeze" potion for radiators ($2.25 a can)

Of the 29 cars that toured from Calgary to Banff in July 1911, only 25 arrived — because the road was wet and some drivers forgot to take tire chains. 'An auto that starts on a trip like the one to Banff should never attempt it without proper equipment,' the *Herald* admonished.

---

promised carefree winters. A Prest-O-Lite storage battery would use "less than one four-hundredth of its power for a single start." Dominion Tires had six models with varying types of tread, guaranteed for 5,000 miles. Goodrich guaranteed its best tire for 8,000. Auto insurance was available after 1917.

By 1919 Alberta placed third in Canada in use of automobiles (after Ontario and Saskatchewan). In 1920 it had 38,015 licensed vehicles and the government took in more than $682,000 in fees. Civic governments, fire departments and ambulance firms were motorized. The fee scale, which had moved from a flat rate to fifty cents per unit of horsepower, was now based on wheelbase, ranging from $15 to $22.50. A 1918 amendment to the Motor Vehicles Act stiffened up on drunken drivers: first offences drew a fine of $20 to $50, but upon a second conviction the driver lost his licence. Another amendment provided twelve months in jail and/or a $50 fine for joyriding, and seven years' imprisonment for outright theft.

Automobiles improved realty values, by fostering suburban living, and stimulated city economies. For example, the auto industry (dealerships, garages, suppliers) was Lethbridge's third largest, a $1 million investment employing 350 people[20].

And yet, the *Medicine Hat News* in a melancholy editorial of October 1920 viewed the automobile as a mixed blessing. It aided business — and crime; increased mortality while improving the general health of the country; saved time and caused people to waste time.

"It demands constant attention. It breeds a desire for speed and converts a desire to go somewhere into a desire to go fast, but the faster the driver goes, the less mind he has for anything else than going.

"No more the friendly nod to the passing stranger which was the inviolable demand of courtesy in all rural districts when horses had their day. What is the use of nodding when the man you nod to is half a mile back before he can nod in return?"

Motoring was making the road a less friendly place, the writer concluded.

He didn't know the half of it.

The ups and downs of Alberta's first aviators

1911 SAW PERILOUS FLYING EXHIBITIONS IN THREE ALBERTA CITIES, CALGARY'S WAS AN EMBARRASSMENT AND EDMONTON'S SOURED THE HERO

by HUGH DEMPSEY

The year 1911 marked the beginning of aviation in Alberta. Prior to that time, the province had seen a few balloon flights and had heard plenty of ideas about new inventions,[a] but the first actual heavier-than-air flight did not occur until April of 1911 and by the time the year was finished, Edmonton, Calgary, and Lethbridge had all experienced the thrill of seeing a man aloft in a flimsy aircraft.

Edmonton was the first city to host an aeroplane flight. Arranged by the *Edmonton Journal* and real estate interests, a Curtiss-type plane was brought to the city to fly as an added attraction to the city's first horse show. C.W. Shaffer, a former actor who used the stage name of R.C. "Lucky Bob" St. Henry, was the owner and Hugh Armstrong Robinson the pilot.

On April 28, the first day of the show, between 600 and 700 people paid their way into the exhibition grounds to see the flight, while hundreds more gathered outside the fence, hoping for a glimpse of it. At 3 p.m., despite heavy winds, Robinson taxied his aircraft to the east fence inside the racetrack oval, sped across the grass, and when within a hundred feet of the west fence, the biplane rose gracefully into the air. He then climbed to about two hundred feet and circled the racetrack three times before returning to earth. After half an hour, he took the plane up again and made two further loops around the grounds.

On the following day the weather was so unsettled that Robinson had to fly in wide circles, providing a free show for the hundreds of sightseers outside the fence. At one point, the winds were so fierce he was forced to swoop low over the heads of the excited viewers. He was supposed to fly to Strathcona and back but the weather was too rough. Instead, he collected his fee of $3,000 and dismantled his machine. Edmontonians, he decided, did not appreciate how momentous was the event. He was "not much impressed" with their "aviation enthusi-

asm," he observed upon departure.

Not to be outdone, Calgary planned its own aviation meet less than three months later when international aviation promoter Charles J. Strobel was brought to the Calgary Exhibition with an aeroplane which resembled a Curtiss machine. The first time pilot Howard Le Van tried to take off from the Exhibition Grounds on July 1, he was forced to abort because of engine trouble. Two days later, the carburetor adjusted, he made a couple of dashes across in front of the grandstand before he finally got enough power to be airborne. According to press reports, Le Van "flew from the oval within the racetrack, circled about the city east of the fairgrounds for a few minutes and returned, alighting on the spot from whence he had arisen. The grandstand was filled with spectators who went wild with excitement."

On the following day, Le Van made another attempt, but he was only fifteen feet in the air when the aeroplane dipped and crashed into the racetrack fence. The pilot was not hurt but the craft's wheels were broken, its fabric damaged, and it was out of commission for the rest of the exhibition. That ended Calgary's "air show."

Two weeks later, a noted American pilot, Eugene Burton Ely, put on Alberta's best performance of the year at the Lethbridge Fair. He was an employee of the Glenn H. Curtiss Exhibition Company of Hammondsport, N.Y., and was offered $2,000 by the Lethbridge Agricultural Society for his services. Ely was one of the most famous fliers of his day. He was the first pilot to land on the deck of a battleship, first to fly from a cruiser to shore, and the first to ascend to an altitude of 13,000 feet.

Ely and the aircraft were the centre of attention for all of southern Alberta, with special trains bringing spectators from as far away as Medicine Hat and Crowsnest Pass. Visitors were impressed by his tiny eight-cylinder Curtiss biplane which was almost as famous as the pilot. It had more air

Glenbow Archives, NA-1180-1

—GREAT AVIATION EXHIBITION—

EUGENE ELY

The world famous Anglo-American Aviator and hero of several world-wide sensation creating flights with his

CURTISS AEROPLANE

Aviation is the most modern and fascinating of the Sciences and the Aeroplane the most ingenious and wonderful contrivance ever designed by man's mind or fashioned by man's hand. Ely will give flights at

HENDERSON PARK, LETHBRIDGE

FRIDAY NEXT, JULY 14

Commencing at 1.30 p.m. and continuing throughout the afternoon. This is positively the first exhibition in Western Canada of a flying machine operated by an experienced and expert aviator. Ely will be seen in his famous

SPIRAL GLIDE AND OCEAN DIP

Two of the most daring and difficult feats ever performed by any airman

Weather conditions permitting, a

WELL KNOWN LOCAL YOUNG LADY

Will make a flight seated in Ely's biplane

ELY DAY IN LETHBRIDGE will be one of the Biggest Events ever pulled off in Southern Alberta

ADMISSION 75 Cents Children under 12 years and accompanied by their parents will be admitted free

Opening the splendid new $30,000 Main Exhibition Building

—WATCH FOR RAILROAD EXCURSION RATES—

Hugh Robinson's pusher-type Curtiss aeroplane is wheeled into position for its Edmonton take-off. Robinson felt that Edmontonians didn't appreciate such a momentous occasion.

time than any other aeroplane in existence and had set a record speed of 85 miles an hour. "The frailty of the aeroplane was what seemed the most peculiar thing about it," said a reporter, "as outside of the engine and the two heavy pieces of wood which form the main central part of the frame, there was nothing at all heavy or cumbersome about it."

On July 14 the aircraft soared northward over the entrance to the fairgrounds and circled back towards the field, maintaining a steady altitude of four hundred feet. Ely stayed in the air for seven minutes and skilfully landed, coming to a full stop in almost the exact spot from which the plane had left the ground. It was, in the view of the reporter, "one of the most successful aeroplane flights ever witnessed in Canada, and the first really successful one ever staged in Alberta." In the afternoon, a second flight lasted for thirteen minutes at the speed of "that made by the ordinary passenger train."

Lethbridge people immediately fell in love with the daring pilot who had brought aviation to their city.

'Lucky Bob' St. Henry poses at the controls of Robinson's aircraft.

Three months later they learned with shock that Ely had been killed in a flying accident in Georgia.

Realizing the enthusiasm of Albertans for aviation, two of Calgary's daily newspapers constantly competed for public attention by featuring both international and local aviation stories. In the autumn of 1911, the *Calgary News-Telegram* offered a reward of $5,000 for the first person making a record-breaking flight from Vancouver to Calgary. A man named George M. Ellis announced that he would compete for the purse as soon as his aircraft was ready but he left town and never returned. There were no other takers.

The *Calgary Herald* responded by sponsoring an air show in the latter part of October. Like the Edmonton demonstration, it consisted of one aeroplane. Besides putting on flying demonstrations, it was supposed to make a non-stop flight from Calgary to Edmonton. If successful, it would establish a North American record.

The pilot was a Frenchman named Didier Masson. His Curtiss-type aeroplane was powered by a Gnome seven-cylinder air-cooled engine and could be fitted with a six-gallon gasoline tank for short flights or a forty-gallon model for the Calgary-Edmonton trip. Masson was supposed to provide two days of aerial demonstrations and then make the flight to Edmonton. He set up a temporary airstrip in a field near the Macleod Trail and on October 17 he made a successful test flight, circling east Calgary for about four minutes. But from that time onward, he had nothing but trouble and the air show became an acute embarrassment for the *Herald*. The newspaper had booked the grandstand at the Exhibition Grounds for two days and sold tickets at 50 cents for admission to the grounds, 50 cents for reserved seats, and $1 for automobiles.

On the afternoon of the

grandstand, "alighting as gracefully as a lazy black crow."

After refuelling, Masson made a second flight and rose to the unbelievable height of 2,000 feet — a mere speck of canvas in the autumn sky. He flew to the downtown area, circled the Calgary Herald Building, and returned safely to the grounds. He also flew on the following day in spite of high winds and prepared for his Edmonton flight. "I have not the least fear that I will be unable to fly there," he told the press.

On the morning of October 26, everything was in readiness for the flight. Masson was at his tent camp on the Macleod Trail and a specially-chartered train was fully loaded with spectators and waiting at the station. Twice the pilot tried to take off but his large gas tank proved to be too heavy. Finally he decided to use the smaller tank and make a refuelling stop at Lacombe. However, after a quick change, Masson took off and was airborne when the gas tank shook loose, struck the pilot on the head and knocked him out. While still in a daze, he made a forced landing but his only

More than 600 people paid to see Robinson circle gracefully over the field. The next day, unsettled weather forced him to fly higher and share the show with non-paying spectators outside the fence. Inset is Didier Masson whose projected Calgary-Edmonton flight was defeated when his gas tank blew off.

17th, Masson took off from his private strip and reached an altitude of 25 feet when his motor failed. He landed, tried again, but this time struck a bundle of baling wire which smashed his propeller. Disappointed spectators were issued "wind checks" and the *Herald* explained that "Rome was not built in a day. Air flight exhibitions cannot yet be organized to take place on a schedule."

The next day was too windy to fly and on the third day Masson broke his propeller in an attempted takeoff. By this time, many people began seeking refunds instead of "wind checks." Finally, on October 20 — the day he was supposed to leave for Edmonton — Masson gave his first public demonstration. He flew to the Exhibition Grounds, circling the city as far as 14th Street, to let the public know he was finally airborne. Then as a small crowd watched from the Exhibition Grounds, he flew over Victoria Park at 400 feet, climbed to 1,000 feet, and swooped down in front of the

propeller was shattered. The air show was over; the dream of a Calgary-Edmonton flight was dead.

"Aviation as a sport has not yet reached the precision of croquet," said the *Herald* philosophically. "It is, in fact, as unstable as the winds of sunny Alberta. Such is the experience of the *Herald* in endeavouring to produce for the benefit of its public a real exhibition of flying." Bad luck continued to follow Didier Masson; two years later, while flying for Pancho Villa in Mexico, he was captured by Federalists and executed.

— *R.C.*

[a]**Elmer, George and John Underwood of Stettler in 1908 and Alfred Lauder and J. Earl Young of Calgary in 1909 invented kite-like planes, but did not have powerful enough motors to fly them. Also, Reginald Hunt of Edmonton and A.F. Baden of Calgary claimed to have invented and flown planes in 1909 and 1910, but both of these claims were fraudulent.**

Entertainment in rural Alberta was of necessity home-grown, and dancing was the highlight of it, though some clergy deplored such a 'demoralizing' influence. At this July 1 sports day dance at Lesser Slave Lake, circa 1910, natives and whites join in the festivities. City folk had sports days too, featuring everything from dances to biscuit races, singing competitions to tug-of-wars.

CHAPTER FOUR

The arts: enter the professional

IN THE COUNTRY, ENTERTAINMENT REMAINED ALMOST WHOLLY HOME-MADE,
BUT CITY AUDIENCES MADE POSSIBLE THE FIRST SYMPHONY ORCHESTRA

by CALVIN DEMMON

In Alberta's rural communities before the advent
of radio and television, entertainment was largely home-grown, often consisting of music
performed on instruments that were home-made. Families and friends would gather, when the
gruelling work of carving a living from the land was done and there was time to spare, for picnics,
dances, weddings, church socials — events that depended for their success upon the direct participation of those in attendance. The performing arts, on the other hand, depended for their

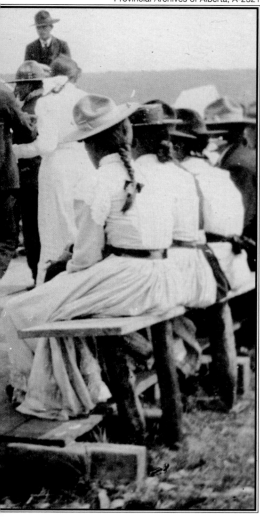

existence upon an audience large enough to support the performers, or at least to pay the bills, and for the most part such audiences were much easier to attract in the cities. It was in the cities that the great theatres were built and in which symphonies and lecture halls and libraries sprang up, and it was therefore in the cities that Alberta's popular culture took its shape.

Not that there were no picnics, pageants, banquets, parades, festivals and other such gatherings for city dwellers. The five-church Presbyterian picnic held in Fort Saskatchewan on Labour Day, 1910, for example, drew members of Edmonton Sunday schools to the garrison town, where athletic events were run, tables were laden with good things to eat, and after-dinner speeches were delivered by the visiting clergymen and the ensign of the Salvation Army. In the same year the Canadian Northern Railway's men's picnic at St. Albert featured a tug-of-war, a beauty contest, singing competitions, and such perennial picnic favourites as the biscuit race, the sack race, the fat men's race and the egg and spoon race. Also in 1910, a thousand Lethbridge citizens filled a heavy steam train for an excursion to the Crowsnest Pass, where they picnicked, played baseball, and explored the mountain paths. On other days in other years there were horse shows and dog shows and historical pageants, including, in Calgary in 1920, a three-mile-long parade marking 250 years of history for the Hudson's Bay Company, with trappers and traders in costume and a float depicting fur-bearing animals common to the Canadian North.

But it was in the production of events to which an audience arrived, was seated, and watched or listened, that the cities excelled. These were by no means limited to theatrical or musical productions. The Chautauqua, an outgrowth of the annual Methodist Episcopal camp meetings in Chautauqua, NY[1], was reorganized in 1912 as a commercial event, a summer program that was part revival meeting and part touring vaudeville show, with a troupe of lecturers and entertainers making a circuit of cities that included, in 1917, both Edmonton and Lethbridge. That was the first year for the Chautauqua in Lethbridge, which welcomed 2,000 people to a week-long program of entertainment. Included were an appearance by impersonator S. Platt Jones, a performance by the Waikiki Hawaiian Quintette, a lecture by J. Sherman Wallace entitled "The World's Greatest Need," the recital of humorous stories by Miss Ada L. Ward of England, and a 45-minute program by a quartet of women known as the Treble Clef Club who offered a combination of song and elocution.

For those who preferred their hilarity unadulterated by uplifting speeches and recitations, there was vaudeville, a form of entertainment that included just about any attraction that could be carried out on stage before a mixed audience. At the Lyceum Theatre in Lethbridge[2] on the evening of April 13, 1910, the program featured a trained dog act (two bull terriers who put on a punching bag exhibition), a trick bicycle rider (handicapped, according to an account in the *Lethbridge Herald*, by the size and height of the stage), the singing and dancing Tyrell children, and a ventriloquist ("his work didn't come up to the standard and manager Brown closed his act").

Edmonton's Empire Theatre[3], built specifically for vaudeville shows but also capable of showing motion pictures, opened in September 1912, with what was called "the best vaudeville west of Chicago," thanks to its connection with the Orpheum circuit, which also added Calgary to its tour that year. A 1914 advertisement for the Empire Theatre called attention to the upcoming

[1] The Chautauquas would become a standard feature of prairie life. The last one was held in Alberta in 1933 as part of a circuit that included towns in northern Alberta and Saskatchewan. The company went out of business in 1935, destroyed, it was generally agreed, by the increasing popularity of movies.

[2] The Lyceum Theatre (330-5th St. S.) became the Starland in 1911 and remained as a theatre until 1925, when it was converted to other uses.

[3] The Empire Theatre was located at 101 Avenue and 103 Street. In 1946 it was renovated as the Trocadero Dance Hall.

Dancing was not the only anathema to urban moralizers. Cards were equally doubtful. But like dancing, cards flourished in the country. Enjoying a game in a Calmar district home, circa 1912-15, are (l to r) host Matt Olson, a guest identified only as Wickstrom, Signe Olson, Lottie Erickson and Fred Erickson.

[4]Orpheum was the name of a theatrical production house which enfranchised privately owned theatres around the country, all of which bore the name Orpheum. The company later became part of RKO, Radio Keith Orpheum.

[5]The Pantages Theatre chain leased the Lyric Theatre in 1910. Shortly after, Alexander Pantages, who had run saloons in Dawson City during the gold rush, built the Metropolitan Theatre with partner George Brown of Edmonton. In 1931 it became the Strand Movie Theatre and from 1936-40 was used by 'Bible Bill' Aberhart for his Sunday radio broadcasts. Despite having been proclaimed a historic site by the provincial government in 1976, it was demolished three years later.

three-day run of a show headlined by Marie Lloyd, who was said to be both "England's Idol" and the "Queen of Comedy Song"; she would be joined by six other performing individuals or groups including Eva Taylor and Co., Billy Rogers, and Binns, Binns and Binns.

However, in October of 1914 the Orpheum circuit withdrew from western Canada, citing plummeting revenues caused by the war and the resultant economic depression. Manager Thomas Becker of the Orpheum Theatre in Calgary[4] said the circuit enjoyed excellent business until the war broke out, but "from the commencement of hostilities we began to feel the strain of decreased revenue. People who have sent their relatives away to the war have little heart to enjoy the lighter things of life, and our business has suffered accordingly. In ordinary times, this is what is known as a good town for amusements." It was only a year later, though, with the war still raging, that the Orpheum circuit returned to Calgary for a show that included the battle-axe juggling of the Tuscano brothers and aerial stunts by Miss Leitzel, direct from her appearances at the Ringling Brothers Circus.

Vaudeville was an on-again off-again affair for the next ten to fifteen years, as the continually improving quality of motion pictures steadily eroded the vaudeville audience. Most of the theatres built for vaudeville eventually became movie houses, their dressing rooms turned over to storage and their marquees advertising filmed performances by the likes of Buster Keaton and Will Rogers, both of whom had performed live at the Pantages Theatre in Edmonton[5] during vaudeville's days of prosperity.

Vaudeville was not the only theatrical entertainment available in Alberta, however. Plays, both locally produced and imported from the East and from the United States, enjoyed continued popularity despite the advent of the movies. Local producers were accused in 1912 of mounting plagiarized plays; plagiarism of American plays was quite prevalent in western Canada, admitted W.B. Sherman, manager of Calgary's Grand Theatre[6], who said it was necessary so that theatres could remain open. "Of course if I did this across the line I would be in jail the same night, but this is not the United States and I am within my rights." But not all the staged material was plagiarized. On Jan. 13, 1913, "a red-letter day in the theatrical history of Edmonton," according to the *Edmonton Bulletin*, Sarah Bernhardt, declared to be the world's greatest actress, appeared at Edmonton's Empire. Her performance in the play *La Dame aux Camélias*, although delivered in French, moved many in the audience to tears. In 1918 she returned to the West, performing in Calgary.

As for music, the young province never lacked for that either. The third annual Alberta Music Festival, held in Edmonton in May 1910, opened the decade with a three-day program that included a forty-piece orchestra and a 250-voice choir along with bands, quartets, and soloists. Three years later the festival's sixth appearance brought competitors up from Calgary for the first time; Edmonton's city fathers regarded the festival as so meritorious they awarded it a $1,000 grant that year. Both touring and local musicians performed in Calgary and Edmonton to appreciative audiences. A local operatic society presented *Tom Jones* to an enchanted Medicine Hat audience in 1916. Calgary's Cabaret Garden featured what an advertisement called "Jaz" music in 1917, with an appearance by L.B. Morgan, a black pianist and baritone. And in 1919 John Philip Sousa, America's most famous bandmaster (and also a leading trapshooter) brought his world-

renowned band to Edmonton.

In 1913, a group of Calgary citizens met to discuss their intent to confer the benefits of a resident symphony orchestra upon their city. By September a fund-raising effort, aimed at generating $25,000, was in full swing, and on November 10 the Calgary Symphony Orchestra, believed the first ever organized in a city of under 200,000 population in either Canada or the United States, gave its first performance. The new orchestra visited Edmonton in January 1914, prompting some jealous Edmontonians to suggest that a similar organization be set up in the capital city. However, there was no need for that, according to an editorial in the *Edmonton Journal*. Even Calgary could not maintain a professional body such as the symphony with its own resources, the *Journal* said — witness the symphony's trip to Edmonton in search of an audience. "There is no reason why Edmonton should not have several visits from the orchestra in the course of the year." Creating a similar symphony in Edmonton would be "a waste of effort." Anyway, the *Journal* continued, Edmonton had "already accomplished big things in a choral way, and if we are wise, we shall confine our energies mainly, for some years at least, to activity along this line. A great Edmonton choral society acting in co-operation with the Calgary orchestra would put the cause of music on so good a basis in Alberta as to affect in a most profound manner the whole of our provincial life"[7].

Dancing was a favourite pastime in the rural areas, but when it reached the cities, leaving behind in large measure the social fabric that gave barn dances and other rural gatherings their unique flavour, it was viewed as trouble. President Edwin J. Wood of the Alberta Stake of the Church of Jesus Christ of Latter-day Saints, the Mormons, vowed at a gathering in Cardston in February 1914 to ban Mormons from public dances that went beyond 10 p.m. "Girls fairly dance their limbs off," Wood declared, claiming that the functions of body in the maternity period of young motherhood were thereby seriously hampered. In the following month, the Medicine Hat

Theatre gained rapid popularity all over the province, both amateur and professional. Here is the cast of the play, Mohawk Crossing, *as staged by the Ladies Aid of Wesley Methodist Church, Lethbridge, about 1914.*

The pride of Calgary was its symphony orchestra, founded in 1913 after a public fund-raising effort. Edmontonians did some soul-searching when it performed in the capital in January 1914. Should they try to match it? No, said the Journal — 'Edmonton had already accomplished big things in a choral way' and should concentrate on that.

CHAUTAUQUA WEEK
JULY 23RD TO 29TH, 1918
On the Grounds on 102nd Street, The Old Thistle Rink Site

THE programs of Chautauqua Week are devoted to PATRIOTIC SERVICES. Splendid LECTURERS are coming with stirring patriotic messages, prominent MUSICIANS and ENTERTAINERS bring splendid diversion to relieve the war-time tension of mind.

A FEW FEATURES OF THE WEEK

Sergt. Gibbons
Member of the first Canadian Expeditionary Force. Wounded at Ypres, captured and held prisoner in Germany for seven months. The most thrilling war lecturer on the platform.

J. C. Herbsman
Direct from the International Conference in Washington, D.C. His lecture, "Carry On," presents the vital war problems. One of the most stirring patriotic appeals ever presented.

Y. Minakuchi
Japanese scholar and orator, lectures on the fourth afternoon on "The War and the Anglo-Japanese Alliance." Answers with authority the questions in every person's mind about the Oriental Chess-Board.

Chicago Ladies' Orchestra
Two full concerts by this splendid Chicago musical organization, featuring stirring martial and patriotic airs. Estelle Hays, American soprano, appears as soloist.

EDMONTON CHAUTAUQUA ASSOCIATION

The following public-spirited citizens have made your Chautauqua possible. They have personally pledged themselves for the sale of season tickets. They are bringing "the world to your door." They are bringing great lecturers to present the national problems at home and abroad. They are bringing splendid inspiring music and clean, wholesome entertainment. They are doing this without the hope of one cent of financial gain. They are doing it solely to upbuild this community and make it a better place in which to live. They are doing this as much for YOU as for themselves. You owe them your support.

J. E. BROWN	J. F. McLEAN	M. J. HUTCHINSON	J. B. BROOKBANK	J. E. LOWRY	GEORGE H. EATON	MRS. CLYDE MacDONALD	NELLIE L. McCLUNG
A. M. FRITH	A. W. CLELAND	JAMES A. COLLINS	E. L. HILL	PERCY W. ABBOTT	E. M. SHILDRICK	E. J. CASE	JOHN R. LAVELL
EUGENE C. DAVIS	W. R. BLOOM	MATHEW ESDALE	JAMES RAMSEY	H. H. CRAWFORD	R. B. DOUGLAS	W. G. CARPENTER	H. MILTON MARTIN
J. A. MacGREGOR	L. G. MAFFIE	W. W. HUTTON	D. M. DUGGAN	R. B. BUCHANAN			A. C. RUTHERFORD

TOMORROW—FRIDAY—WILL BE THE DAY OF THE BIG TICKET DRIVE

Season Tickets are on sale by committee until noon of the opening day at $2.50 — War tax extra. After that time they advance to $3.00. They are transferable only within the owner's immediate family.

The Chautauqua shows were becoming another summer highlight in many cities and towns, and the automobile made it possible for more people to attend, as the lineup (right) at the Chautauqua in Vulcan in the late teens attests. Below, the Chautauqua tent at Medicine Hat later in the decade.

school board voted to eliminate dancing from all school social events because it "frequently became the chief centre of amusement at the function to the shutting out of everything else" and had no educational value whatever. In June 1915 the Rev. C.C. McLaurin, addressing a Baptist convention in Edmonton, decried the West as "dance crazy" and said that such worldliness and pleasure-seeking were "a curse to the community." None of which stopped very many people from dancing, of course, and especially in the rural communities dancing continued as a means of wholesome entertainment available to all. Kathleen Strange, in her autobiographical book *With the West in Her Eyes,* described one such event, a 1920 square dance held in her home in the community of Fenn south of Stettler to the accompaniment of fiddle and guitar:

"When the big living-room was jammed with people, the orchestra started to play. One of the crowd appointed himself a sort of master of ceremonies and shouted out the various numbers, which, as usual, followed each other in breathtaking succession. The floor soon began to heave so alarmingly that we had to dash down into the basement, find a substantial post and prop up the floor for safety. In less time than it takes to tell, the entire surface was gone from my carefully polished wood, and many hours of hard labour had been completely undone."

Provincial Archives of Alberta, IR-51

Edmonton Journal, Jan. 24, 1919

Glenbow Archives, NA 1328-2124

Vaudeville was the principal form of live entertainment throughout the decade, though as the movies became better, it gradually declined. Amateur nights often took the place of the vaudeville acts, promoted with the kind of hoopla shown above. At right, Edmonton's Pantages Theatre presents 'Imperial Russian Violinist Alexander Kaminsky (His Equal Is Not In Vaudeville)' and the crowd spills out over Jasper Avenue. Other vaudeville attractions included performing dogs, trick bicyclists and battle-axe jugglers.

The 'movies' brought joy, thrills and many new problems

Scenes portraying blood, boozing, drugs were all censored, Nellie McClung demanded that Alberta ban all crime films

During the decade that produced the Great War, Albertans turned increasingly to one form of popular entertainment: the moving picture, a marvel of technology that began as a novelty and quickly assumed a position of prominence in everyday life, eventually driving the live-performance variety shows of vaudeville out of the theatres altogether.

Motion pictures made their appearance in the province in 1898, when audiences in Edmonton and Calgary watched flickering films of Queen Victoria's Diamond Jubilee. By 1903 the Edmonton Opera House[a] presented a Canadian travelogue with full orchestral accompaniment.

So rapid was the growth of film exhibition that by 1910 theatres dedicated solely to motion pictures were spread through cities big and small, offering filmed presentations of current events as well as drama. An advertisement in the *Edmonton Bulletin* on June 2, 1910, invited the citizenry to the Bijou Theatre[b] to see moving pictures of the funeral of King Edward, "photographed, developed, printed and now shown in Edmonton, 6,000 miles from the scenes, within thirteen days." In 1912 the *Edmonton Journal* reported that "movies" (the newspapers generally preferred the term "motion pictures," but the shorter "movies" appeared occasionally in headlines) were attracting 26,000 Edmontonians every week, year round.

There were six motion picture theatres in operation by then in Edmonton: two Bijous, the Garland, the Dreamland at Jasper Avenue and 96 Street, the Monarch at 100 Street and Jasper, and the Orpheum, each with a seating capacity of from 300 to 600 persons; two additional "picture houses" were under construction.

'Bijou' was a popular theatre name and Alberta had several. This magnificently ornate specimen, at 127 - Eighth Avenue East in Calgary, was showing a Universal picture, The Beggar Prince of India, *probably about the mid-teens.*

"The reasons for the popularity of the motion picture houses are many," the *Journal* said. "First may be mentioned the price, a nickel up to 15 cents for the best seats in the house. For that nominal admission fee a varied program of comedy, drama and tragedy may be seen and in most cases an illustrated song is on the programme to round out an afternoon or evening of entertainment."

The Princess Theatre, ventilated by electric fans, decorated with gold leaf, and "modern in every respect," opened on south Edmonton's Whyte Avenue in March 1915 as the war rained destruction on Europe, and the *Journal* noted that the new playhouse "stands as a splendid tribute to the greatness of an invention dedicated solely to the purpose of peace."

Reaction to the phenomenal growth of motion picture entertainment, however, was not always receptive. For every new theatre constructed, a new cry for the regulation of "bad shows" went up. In September 1910 the *Journal* urged parents to "find out what their children see upon the screen — or better still, to find out beforehand what the children will see if they are taken or allowed to go." If a theatre manager persisted in exhibiting offensive films, "he must be prevented doing what he ought not to do," the paper said.

That October, the Edmonton Council of Women urged the city council to appoint a censor to prohibit pictures that "should never be viewed by impressionable youth." In Calgary, too, concern was raised. "My private opinion is that all moving pictures depicting murder or other scenes of crime should not be allowed...in the city," Mayor Rueben R. Jamieson said, in observing that Calgary would soon have more than half a dozen moving picture shows. Similarly, the *Medicine Hat News* observed in January 1912 that while the

Movies were immensely popular, not least because fifteen cents would buy the best seat in the house, but what's entertainment without imaginative advertising? Edmonton's Monarch Theatre boosts a three-reel feature in 1913. Complaints about film improprieties soon arose, and in 1915 Alberta's first censor was appointed: R.B. Chadwick (at right), late of the Neglected Children Department. That year, he banned the world championship boxing match.

educational value of motion pictures was fully recognized, the danger of abuses was also well known, and the chief of police at Medicine Hat recommended that children under sixteen not be admitted to evening shows unless accompanied by adults.

Thus the appointment of film censors became inevitable, and by 1915 Alberta had its first: one R.B. Chadwick, who also served as head of the provincial Neglected Children's Department. Chadwick ruled in February of that year that moving pictures of the Welsh-Ritchie world's championship boxing match could not be legally shown in the province. "Alberta fans will lose a chance to see something exceptionally good," the *Edmonton Bulletin* sighed wistfully.

By January 1916 Alberta boasted a total of 100 motion picture theatres, 54 of them divided among Edmonton, Calgary, Medicine Hat and Lethbridge, and 46 in smaller towns. Mr. Chadwick having died, the province also had a

new chief censor, Howard Douglas, assisted by a former New York penitentiary warden named Frank Cole. Cole brought to the job his own views on censorship. It was unfair, he thought, to snip objectionable sections from a motion picture, as had been Chadwick's practice. Instead, if part of a picture was not fit for the public the whole thing was unfit and should be dispatched immediately to its manufacturers.

Alberta's motion picture theatre owners were said to be delighted with Cole's all-or-nothing practice because it put film producers on notice that Alberta wanted respectable motion pictures. Cole added a new wrinkle, however, when he ruled that an occasional film could be exhibited with deletions — and that the exhibitors themselves should make the cuts, submitting the excised sections to him for storage in what became known as Alberta's Celluloid Morgue, which

Edmonton's Portola Theatre. Alberta's censorship was considered the most liberal in Canada.

by 1921 contained 10,000 feet of censored film.

The provincial censor's written standards prohibited pictures portraying white slavery ("unless a true moral lesson is conveyed") as well as scenes involving gruesome bloodshed or corpses, offensive drunkenness, exploitation of notorious characters, drug addiction, poisoning, robbery, pickpocketing, the use of ether or chloroform, counterfeiting, brutal treatment of children or animals, the ridicule of races or classes, irreverent or sacrilegious treatment of religious bodies, comedies burlesqueing morgues or funerals or insane asylums, immodest dancing, needless exhibition of women in nightdresses and lingerie, sensual kissing and lovemaking, titles or subtitles employing profanity, and vampire scenes.

Despite the list, Alberta's censorship, according to the *Journal*, was considered the most liberal in Canada, largely because most films that came into the country were first censored in Ontario and Quebec, and "the Alberta censors take it for granted that when the excellent Ontario board passes a film it must be proper for exhibition here or it would not be shown in the East. So these films are promptly passed here without preliminary exhibition."

Not everyone was

convinced, however, that the Department of Censorship performed its protective mission satisfactorily. Speaking in March 1917 to the Edmonton Council of Women, Nellie McClung urged that women be added to the censorship board, which she said should be expanded to keep an eye on vaudeville performances as well as motion pictures. "There are many children in our city now whose fathers are away, fighting for our ideals of civilization, and it seems more than ever the duty of women to protect these children from anything that would harm them," she said.

In the same year, the Rev. Father Reynolds of St. Joachim's Catholic Church in Edmonton condemned, in a Sunday sermon, what he said was the part that motion pictures played in the delinquency of young girls. Reynolds observed that Charlie Chaplin often seemed in his pictures to be drunk — a sad lesson to children — and that in *Vampire* Theda Bara took three men away from their wives, while in *Hell's Hinges* three men were killed. Worse, in Reynolds' view, darkened theatres offered unprincipled boys the chance to make advances to girls sitting next to them. He said parents and priests should discourage children from attending all but clean, educational pictures, thereby sending a message to the producers.

In all of this, of course, elected officials saw potential profit for their own causes as well. In April 1916 the Alberta government enacted a one-cent tax per movie admission; the tax was paid by purchasing a special ticket at the theatre.

— *C.D.*

[a]The Edmonton Opera House became the Lyceum Theatre in 1910, but was closed permanently in 1914.

[b]The Bijou Theatre was located at 10134 - 101 St. In 1912 its name changed to New Bijou, and later the Rialto.

The Edmonton Bijou, far less pretentious than Calgary's Bijou, could nevertheless boast its electric projection system and its staff of eleven.

Not so lively as vaudeville or public dancing, but not without their own controversies, were the public libraries, the development of which began before the war. Andrew Carnegie, the steel king, had a soft spot in his heart for public libraries and was in the habit of donating substantial sums of money to cities that would agree to build libraries and name them in his behalf. Edmontonians were excited in 1910 by the prospect of a donation from Carnegie and the library that would result. A public library board was formed and began to work on selection of a site.

At first the board recommended purchase of a lot at the corner of Rice and Howard (later 100A Ave. and 100A St.), at a price of $33,000, but opponents to the location were many, including the *Edmonton Journal*, which warned that a library in an area primarily filled with wholesale and commercial buildings would be isolated and out of place — buried, in fact. The *Journal* interviewed prominent citizens, most of whom agreed that the recommended site was unsuitable. That argument, however, took a back seat to one that was far more crucial. In August 1912 the board sent word to Carnegie that it would need more money than the $60,000 he had offered if a library bearing his name were to be built. According to the board's calculations, based on figures from the Edmonton Board of Trade, the city's population was more than 50,000. Carnegie, taking his numbers from the dominion census, called the population 38,000 and based his grant on that figure. The board was so enraged that it rejected Carnegie's money altogether. "'Take Back Your Gold,' Sings Library Board to Yankee Ironmaster," a headline in the *Journal* declared. Their decision

Calgary, first with a symphony, was first with a library too (below), opening it in January 1912 with an initial stock of 5,500 books. Strathcona followed in 1913 with the fine building at right. Edmonton, which spurned philanthropist Andrew Carnegie's proffered grant as too small, remained library-less until the 1920s.

Picnics, often combined with other events such as the Sylvan Lake Regatta in 1920 (right), were the joy of every summer. Some went on for two or three days while families in attendance camped at them. The big event below is a picnic at Three Hills in 1916.

meant that Edmonton would wait ten more years for a public library. The City of Strathcona accepted a grant from Carnegie, and in 1913 opened the Strathcona Public Library.

Calgary, which had been first with a symphony, was first with a public library as well, funded by a Carnegie grant. The Calgary library opened its doors on Jan. 2, 1912, with 5,500 books on its shelves. "Though the volume of books is limited, the quality is excellent," said the *Albertan*. The grand opening was followed two weeks later by the reassuring announcement that any library books found in any house placed in quarantine would be fumigated, and that library privileges would be suspended for any occupant of a house under quarantine. "This arrangement will effectually prevent the spread of infectious diseases through the medium of books distributed on loan throughout the city," the *Calgary Herald* explained.

Bob Edwards, the iconoclastic publisher of the *Eye Opener*, had the last word on libraries. "Certain quarters," he noted, had forced the library to close on Sundays. "This is the day above all others when the doors of this institution should be open. Those who work during the week are unable to avail themselves of the opportunities for mental recreation and useful self-instruction that the library affords and for which purpose it was erected. Calgary surely does not need to follow Toronto in everything. Calgary's library is like the Banff Hot Sulphur Baths in that it closes its door tight on the only day the workaday people have leisure to patronize it."

A 1913 photograph of the Edmonton Daily Capital's editorial department finds its staff in a serious and sombre mood. Was the news sparse that day? Had somebody been badly 'scooped' on a major story? Or did they have a premonition of personal economic disaster? Competition in the newspaper business was ferocious. Within a year the Capital, which had been launched in 1909, would go down under the onslaught of the Bulletin and the Journal.

Corporatism takes over the newspapers

FRANK OLIVER STILL HAD THE *BULLETIN* AND EDWARDS THE *EYE OPENER* BUT WHEN EDWARDS GOT MARRIED, THAT MEANT THINGS MUST BE CHANGING

Calgary citizens by the thousands flocked to the Herald Building[a] early in the evening of Sept. 21, 1911, eager to learn the outcome of the federal election that had been held that day. The returns came in from eastern Canada by telegraph and when they arrived at the *Herald*'s offices they were posted for public viewing on an elaborate system of outdoor bulletin boards, with every riding in the country represented. Other announcements about the election were flashed on a large screen, and results were also shouted by megaphone to what was said to have been the largest crowd ever assembled in Calgary.

Although snow was falling, the gathering continued to grow until by 6 p.m. it became impossible to walk along Centre Street in front of the Herald Building, and the specta-

tors had spilled onto Seventh Avenue, blocking it as well. Enthusiastic cheers and patriotic songs greeted each announcement from the East.

Meanwhile, the *Herald* rushed into print continually updated editions carrying the latest election figures, peddling them in the streets to news-hungry readers who snapped up more than 5,000 extra copies of the paper before the outcome was clear and the crowds finally began to dissipate. It was a glorious day for the *Herald*, and it was a scene that was to be repeated throughout the decade, particularly during the years of the Great War, when Albertans turned their attention outwards and newspapers grew in circulation and influence.

Newspapers in Alberta, as elsewhere, had begun for the

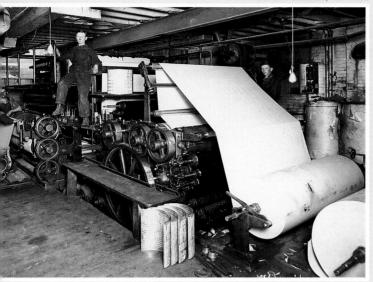

New technology was making the newspaper business a more efficient — and more expensive — proposition by the time this photograph of the Edmonton Journal *rotary press was taken, probably about 1912.*

most part as soap-boxes for strongly opinionated editors and publishers with an entrepreneurial and often contrary spirit. But in the years before the war the larger papers had already taken on personalities that were more corporate than individual. In this they were aided by new technologies and new approaches to building and maintaining readership.

In March 1912, the *Edmonton Journal* announced that it was now fully hooked up, over a leased wire, to the Associated Press, the Canadian Press Association, and the Reuters cable news service. The following year the *Journal* published its first full-page funnies, a cartoon feature called

Newspaper circulation drives offered prizes as alluring as Reo and Ford automobiles, to salesmen who signed up the most subscribers. Above, an Edmonton Journal *promotional bicycle race gets under way early in the decade. At right, very important foot soldiers in the journalistic army, two* Calgary Herald *newsboys pose, circa 1913.*

"Brick Bodkins' Pa." "Mutt and Jeff," the first daily cartoon besides the editorial page's political offerings, appeared in the *Journal* in November 1914. The *Edmonton Bulletin* added a daily strip called "The Inventor" in March 1916. In July 1917 the *Medicine Hat News* proudly described its acquisition of a new Duplex printing press that would cut the paper's daily production time from nine hours down to forty minutes, "its installation having become a necessity in order to meet the insistent demand for an earlier delivery of the paper to the reading public." A plate-glass window was installed in the front of the News Building to allow the curious to examine the new press. And in October 1919 the *Edmonton Journal*, headquartered in the Tegler block at 101st Street and 102nd Avenue, secured a site at the corner of 101st Street and Macdonald Drive, where it began constructing a new home whose 22,500 square feet would give the paper what it called "the largest, brightest, most modern graphic arts building in the city, and one of the best of its kind in Canada."

Financing such improvements required increasingly large sums of money. The *Calgary Herald* and the *Edmonton Journal* had the advantage, financially at least, of having been purchased by William Southam, whose Ontario-based family

built itself a powerful newspaper chain by purchasing existing newspapers from the often idiosyncratic men who had been their founders[b].

For the Southam chain and most other publishers, circulation boosting became an important goal, with gimmicks of all sorts employed to attract new subscribers. A *Journal* circulation campaign in March 1911 offered two Reo 30 five-passenger automobiles, valued at $1,800 apiece, as first prizes for those who signed up the most new subscribers. Later that year the *Medicine Hat News* announced "the greatest subscription campaign ever attempted in a city the size of Medicine Hat," with $2,500 in prizes including a $1,100 Model T Ford.

Whether the contests helped or not, circulation grew. In January 1910 the *Journal* published the results of an outside audit verifying that the average number of copies circulated daily was 3,454, morning and evening combined. By May 1919 the *Journal*'s average daily circulation had risen to 19,269, making its proposed new headquarters building a necessity.

Soul-searching within the offices of the newspapers was inevitable as their influence expanded. The *Edmonton Bulletin* took pains, in a lengthy editorial on July 5, 1910, to explain why it had decided to publish the results of the Jeffries-Johnson prize fight even though it condemned the sport of boxing. "Newspapers do not exclude reports of everything of which they do not approve," the editorial said. "If they did so there would be a wonderful shrinkage in the size of the ordinary paper, and a wonderful mortality among newspapers as well...It is to be remembered, too, that the best way to remedy a social ill is to let the public know about it...If the report of the prize fight presents in disgusting detail the brutality of the performance to thousands of people who [otherwise] would not know its nature, or perhaps would not even know that a fight had occurred, this surely is making for the cultivation of public opinion which will put the ban on this relic of barbarism."

Charges that news coverage had been

A Medicine Hat News *cartoon early in the century deplores the Southams' expanding Alberta empire. The* News *itself would one day become part of that empire.*

influenced by the strategic application of large sums of money were heard occasionally. In a front-page box on Aug. 29, 1911, William Buchanan, a Liberal MP and managing director of the *Lethbridge Herald*, rejected claims that his paper had received payment from a Liberal "slush" fund raised in New York. The charge had been levelled by Dan McGillicuddy, former editor of the *Calgary News*, along with an accusation that Frank Oliver, founder of the *Edmonton Bulletin* and minister of the Interior, had $50,000 placed to his credit from the same source. "The *Herald* was financed on money raised by its shareholders who are all local men," Buchanan wrote, adding that "Mr. Oliver has denied every charge that Mr. McGillicuddy has made and I think that the people who know Mr. Oliver will believe what he says while those who know Mr. McGillicuddy always take what he says with a grain of salt."

Governmental attempts to direct the daily flow of news generally failed. In March 1914, after the *Edmonton Bulletin* published an editorial accusing the city council of "spending in the quietest season of the year at the rate of a half-million per month," Mayor William J. McNamara decided it was time to protect himself and his colleagues by starting a newspaper he could control. It would be called the *Edmonton Municipal Gazette*, and it would be published weekly, at a cost in its first year of $18,790. "I do not think this is very much to spend to give the citizens of Edmonton complete, fair, uncoloured, unbiased reports, without comment, of what is taking place in the city," the mayor said. The council approved the venture on a 6 to 5 vote.

Four months later the *Bulletin* gleefully pronounced the *Municipal Gazette* a flop, after the mayor suggested that the paper switch from a weekly to a monthly. "Evidently Mayor McNamara has come to the conclusion that the people of this city will persist in reading the newspaper reports of what the council do in preference to the extensive and expensive reports furnished the ratepayers in the official gazette," the *Bulletin* chortled.

Bob Edwards' marriage late in life shocked the province.

After the Edmonton Capital *folded, the war heated up between the* Journal *and the* Bulletin. *By 1914, both were using motorized equipment. The war would continue until the* Bulletin *finally lost it in 1951.*

What the *Calgary Herald* characterized as "a marriage of very considerable interest" took place in July 1917, when Bob Edwards, by now 53, the bachelor-proprietor of the

The Herald *occupied this magnificent new building in 1913. Gargoyles, peering down from the roof, depicted publisher, editor, printers and other denizens of the newspaper industry.*

fortnightly *Eye Opener*, married Kate Penman, an employee of the Calgary Land Titles office. Edwards' paper circulated widely outside Calgary as well as within the city, and he enjoyed his national reputation as an irascible, deeply opinionated man who skewered crooked politicians and empty-headed socialites with dry humour and great enthusiasm; his marriage, which lasted until his death in 1924, was greeted with bewilderment.

It was Edwards, after all, who had writ-

ten in the *Eye Opener* that "the saddest and funniest thing on earth is to hear two people promising at the altar with perfectly straight faces to feel, think and believe for the rest of their lives exactly as they do at that minute."

Edwards' highly personal style stood in sharp contrast to that of the dailies, which by the end of the decade had grown in size and influence by offering a broadened package that included such innovations as features, comics, contests, and wire stories from abroad. Radio and television, which would pose a greater risk to the newspapers than anything they could do to themselves, were as yet undeveloped. In the meantime, if an Albertan wanted to find out immediately how an election was going or what was happening on the battlefronts of the war, he headed down to the local newspaper office to read the bulletins posted there, and more often than not he returned home with a copy of the paper tucked under his arm as well.

— C.D.

[a]By 1911, the *Herald* outgrew its old rented quarters at Centre Street and Seventh Avenue. So in October 1911, Southam's bought two corners at Seventh Avenue and First Street SW. On the Lougheed corner (NE) they began excavation in August 1912 and moved the *Herald* into the ten-storey Herald Building in December 1913. Meanwhile Southam's began construction on a six-storey building on the Revillon corner (NW) to lease to the Calgary Furniture Company. The furniture company moved into the new store in the Southam Building early in 1914. The Southam Building had a checkered life, housing a number of businesses until the Calgary Post Office moved in and stayed until 1932 when the *Herald* itself took up residence and the two buildings switched names.

[b]Two Ontario men, Tom Braden and Andrews Armour, started the *Calgary Herald* in 1883; subsequent owners sold it to the Southam empire in 1908. In 1903, Manitoba newspapermen John Cunningham, John MacPherson and Arthur Moore established the *Edmonton Journal*, which Southam acquired in 1912. Southam had begun in 1877 when William Southam and William Carey purchased the *Hamilton Spectator* with the aim of restoring the Tories to power.

CHAPTER FIVE

Luther McCarty reeled and fell and boxing went down with him

FROM ALL OVER THE CONTINENT SPORTS WRITERS SWARMED TO CALGARY
FOR A BOUT THAT SAW THE CHALLENGER CHARGED WITH MANSLAUGHTER

by BRIAN HUTCHINSON

It was billed as the fight of the decade, a ten-round, $10,000 slugfest with nothing less on the line than the white heavyweight boxing championship of the world. The air in Calgary's Manchester Arena was thick with cigar smoke and body odour that morning of May 24, 1913, as 5,600 fans squeezed inside to witness boxing history. On one side sat the supporters of Luther McCarty, the half-Indian "white" champion of the world, undefeated in his last fifteen bouts. On the other sat those betting on Arthur Pelkey, the young challenger facing the second fight of his career.

The eyes of the boxing world were on Calgary that night. Newsmen from across North America were in town to witness the bout. Those eyes were likewise on Tommy Burns, the ex-prize fighter, clothing store operator and sometime fight promoter, who had put the match together and expected it to propel him to the top of the fight promotion world. It was also to make Calgary the undisputed "hub of the boxing universe."

General admission cost $2, ringside went for $5, and box seats cost $6. Tickets sold out within a week of going on sale at Burns' Eighth Avenue clothing store, which that week just happened to be offering a special on men's suits. Burns had opened his shop in 1910, the year he moved to Calgary after a spectacular career in the ring. Born Noah Brusso, the native of Hanover, Ontario, stood just five feet seven inches and weighed less than 170 pounds, but he had been a relentless puncher and had beaten some of the best heavyweights in the world. In 1906, he knocked down Marvin Hart during a championship fight in Los Angeles, and successfully defended his world heavyweight title ten times in two and a half years. One fight, against Irish contender Jem Roche,

The caption scratched onto this old photograph indicates it was a lineup for tickets for the big fight. More probably it was the lineup to get into the Manchester Arena, which mysteriously burned down the next day. The Stampeder Hotel was later built on the site.

netted Burns $30,000, the largest payout in boxing history.

He had finally lost his belt to Negro Jack Johnson after a bloody prize fight in Melbourne, Australia. Burns broke three of his opponent's ribs that night, but took several vicious jabs to the head. By the 14th round he was bleeding so profusely that police stopped the fight. Burns wanted to continue but the championship was awarded to Johnson.

Burns had returned to Canada, defeated but by no means forgotten. He was still a Canadian hero, and Calgarians rejoiced when he announced he was moving to their booming metropolis,

where boxing enjoyed enormous popularity. A brass band and a crowd of 2,000 had welcomed him at the Canadian Pacific station when he arrived in 1910. He'd bought a cozy house on the banks of the Elbow River[1], opened his clothing store, and plotted his revenge on Johnson. He sparred a few exhibition rounds in city gymnasiums, and started promoting local bouts. This soon became his primary occupation. Calgary attracted a steady stream of professional pugilists, even though city council had banned all boxing matches where admission was charged.

On the advice of Attorney-General Charles W. Cross, Burns avoided breaking the law by building a $5,000 stadium just outside the city limits on Calgary's

Luther McCarty (right) had only a few minutes left to live when this photo was taken at Calgary's Manchester Arena on May 24, 1913. One heavy punch from Arthur Pelkey (left) took him to the floor. He died soon after on the lawn outside the arena where doctors had carried him. Here in the ring, Pelkey smiles confidently; McCarty's expression could be said to betray fear.

[1] The Henderson's Calgary City Directory for 1914 lists Burns as living at 319 - 40th Avenue W., in Elbow Park.

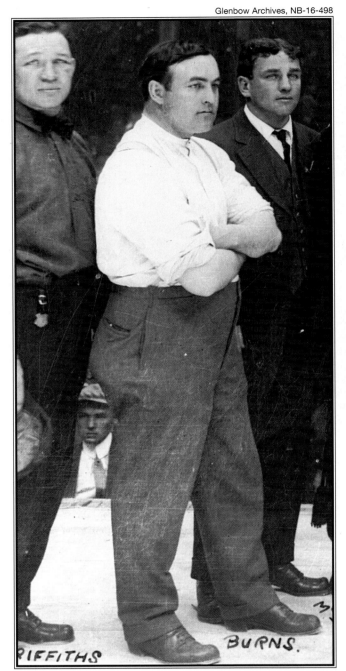

RIFFITHS · BURNS.

Tommy Burns, fighter turned fight-promoter, had come to Calgary in 1910 and opened a clothing store on Eighth Avenue. After the tragedy when boxing was prohibited in Alberta, Burns left Calgary. Eventually he became a Christian evangelist.

[2]The Elbow View Hotel was located at Fourth St. W., on the corner of 26th Avenue facing Mission Bridge.

southern fringe in the summer of 1912 near Mission Hill Road and the Macleod Trail. Conveniently located near the end of the street-car line, the Manchester Arena soon became western Canada's premier boxing venue, hosting a string of well-attended bouts that made Burns all but forget climbing back into the ring himself.

Though only 31 years old, Burns was in no shape to consider a comeback, according to the *Edmonton Bulletin*: "There is a soft look in his cheeks which makes one think that they would be easily cut. A hard blow would rip them open." Realizing he was no match for the new breed of young fighters moving through the ranks, Burns decided to hang up his gloves for good and find a protégé capable of exacting his revenge on Jack Johnson.

This led him to Arthur Pelkey. He was an unknown French-speaking lumberjack from the woods of eastern Ontario when Burns first spotted him. But at six feet two inches and weighing 205 pounds, he had decent size and possessed remarkable strength. Just

---

Calgary attracted a steady stream of professional pugilists, even though city council had banned all boxing matches where admission was charged. On the advice of Attorney-General Charles W. Cross, Burns avoided breaking the law by building a $5,000 stadium just outside the city limits.

---

as important, he was white. The boxing world was still reeling over the fact that a black man had taken the heavyweight title and promoters were desperate for a "great white hope" to step up and regain the championship. Burns figured that all the 23-year-old giant needed for a shot at Johnson were a few well publicized bouts and some headlines in the major papers. In May 1913 Pelkey moved to Calgary and took up residence at the Elbow View Hotel[2], near the exhibition grounds. It took his manager less than a week to line up Pelkey's first big shot: a fifteen-round prize fight with Boston heavyweight Andy Morris on May 1, 1913. Pelkey knocked him out in eight rounds, and prepared to meet his next victim: Luther "Lute" McCarty, a curly-headed ranch hand from Lincoln, Nebraska.

McCarty was no stranger to Calgary; his first professional bout was held there in 1910, when he knocked out Joe Grim in the fourth round. Although his mother was an Indian, McCarty was considered the "white" champion of the world, having rendered unconscious the fifteen opponents he'd met in the past two years. His latest victim, the top-ranked Frank Moran, had hit the canvas just two weeks earlier, in New York City. Some pundits argued that McCarty was the only man alive capable of beating Johnson, but his manager, Billy McCarney, vowed that the 21-year-old scrapper would "never meet a Negro," a position that likely had more to do with fear than bigotry[3].

McCarty and his small entourage checked into the National Hotel in east Calgary[4] a week before the Victoria Day bout with Pelkey. A doctor examined the fighter and gave him a clean bill of health, even though McCarty was bothered by a running sore in his right ear, a leftover from his scrap with Moran. He also complained of an upset stomach and was given medication for it. Five days later, he was bucked off a horse and injured his neck. The accident was kept quiet, although Charles McLennan, sports reporter for the *Lethbridge Herald*, remarked that the mighty halfbreed "did not appear to be enjoying his customary healthy colour."

Bettors initially gave McCarty a five-to-one edge over his less experienced opponent. But

Pelkey's muscular frame and quick left jab impressed everyone who visited his training camp, and with 24 hours left before the bell sounded, the odds were almost even. "Pelkey has a chance, and a mighty good one," observed the *Calgary News-Telegram*. "Some of his followers are going so far as to predict that he will win by a knockout." Pelkey himself was confident. "I never felt better in my life," he avowed. "I'm quite sure that I'm McCarty's master."

The big day finally arrived, and by nine o'clock in the morning the vicinity of the arena was swarming with fight fans, "all heading to see what many considered to be the most important bout ever staged in Calgary," writes William McLennan in his book *Sport in Early Calgary*. Ever the entrepreneur, Burns leased eight City of Calgary streetcars and shuttled patrons from the Victoria Park exhibition grounds to his remote wooden grandstand, for 25 cents a head, five times the regular fare. Once at the site, ticket-holders were surrounded by peddlers hawking everything from scrambled egg sandwiches to hand-rolled cigars. By eleven o'clock, the largest boxing crowd in Calgary's history had filed into Manchester Arena. "Swarms of young boys hung around the entrances," writes William McClennan, "hoping for a free ticket or waiting for the ticket taker to turn his back so that they might skip in."

There were three preliminary bouts. Jimmy Potts, a slow-footed, plodding middleweight from Minnesota, fell in the third round to Young Leppo, much to the crowd's delight[5]. Buster Brown won a six-round decision over Dick Phillips, Alberta's bantamweight champ. Then Roy George and Zeno Casey clashed in a classic seesaw battle, with George, the local favourite, coming out on top after four rounds. McCarty sat down at the press bench during the third preliminary and chatted with reporters. He seemed very loose, even jolly, playfully grabbing an usher's white cap and putting it on his head. His mood changed by the last preliminary bout, however; McCarty stopped talking and stared sullenly at the ring. "Every other person at ringside was showing the deepest interest," observed one reporter, "but Luther had a stolid look on his face and was seeing nothing, apparently." His manager, McCarney, watched from across the ring, a mysterious worry etching his face.

Finally, the main event. McCarty snapped out of his trance and jumped into the pit, still wearing the usher's cap. A

Glenbow Archives, NB-16-496

Glenbow Archives, NB-16-495

(Left) Burns with Pelkey in training. (Right) McCarty works out at Calgary, about a week before his death.

great cheer greeted him as he smiled and bowed to the crowd. Pelkey appeared a minute later to an even louder roar. The fighters received their instructions from the referee, Ed Smith, a sports editor of the *Chicago American*. "No clinching," he told them. "When I say break, you break." After posing for pictures, the two fighters adjourned to their respective corners and had their hands taped before slipping them into their blood-red eight-ounce gloves.

At that point, Burns introduced the Rev. William Walker of St. Augustine's Anglican Church. The preacher, dressed completely in black, was lifted into the ring and proceeded to deliver a grim sermon. "Do not forget in your chase of fame that you have a Creator," he said. "The Great Referee watches over you, all powerful. Prepare to meet him." The warning was to prove chillingly apt.

When the gong struck at 12:57, the two men exchanged smiles, touched gloves, and started circling. After a few seconds of light outside sparring, McCarty stepped up and delivered a left jab

[3] The champ's father, Aaron McCarty, was an Irishman who ran a travelling Indian medicine show and was nicknamed White Eagle. His Indian mother died when he was two. As a teenager, McCarty held a variety of jobs — cutting corn in Kansas, delivering messages for Western Union, and travelling to South America and the Orient as a seaman. In 1910, he found himself engaged as a 'human punching bag' for a boxer training in Culbertson, Montana, but showed such promise that he decided to strike out on his own.

[4] Located at 1042 - 10th Ave. E., the National Hotel was still standing in the 1990s.

[5]Calgarians had not forgotten that three years earlier, after being forced to fight outdoors in the month of November, Potts had dismissed their city as a frozen village run by misers. 'James avers that the Canuck sportsman is a tightwad of a tightness, rivalled by the snugness with which a boa constrictor coils around a spring crop goat,' reported the *Minneapolis Tribune*.

Pelkey shakes McCarty's hand in this formal photo before the bout begins. Between them is referee Smith. By now the cocky, jocular demeanour of McCarty is gone and the distant, glazed look that some noticed about him has taken its place.

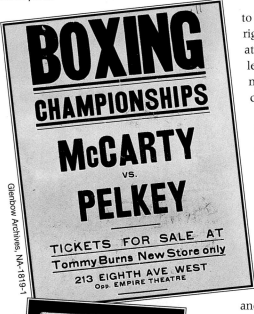

A poster advertises tickets for the fight which could be purchased only at Burns' store on Eighth Avenue which just happened to have a special on men's suits that week. One fan kept this ticket stub, now on file at the Glenbow.

to his opponent's head. He came up a foot short, and Pelkey countered with a quick right to the kidneys. Still grinning, McCarty came back with a wild uppercut aimed at Pelkey's jaw, but again he missed the mark. When Pelkey connected with a sharp left jab to McCarty's forehead, the crowd cheered wildly, and the champ's smile narrowed. The fighters clinched, broke, and traded a few more short punches at close quarters.

McCarty skipped back and lunged. Pelkey stepped around him and hammered him with a huge roundhouse, the hardest blow of the evening, right on the face. McCarty responded with a stiff blow to the ribs. The two boxers clinched again, McCarty shoved the other man back, but took a wallop on the chin. Pelkey followed with a stiff right jab to McCarty's chest, putting all his weight behind it. "The big lad seemed rather stupefied at first," recounted Charles McLennan, who was sitting ringside. "A queer look passed over his face. His eyes seemed to change their hue and his smile disappeared completely." McCarty paused, raised his fists in the classic boxing pose, and winked at his cornermen. Then he turned halfway around, dropped his arms to his side, and fell to the mat with a heavy thud. There was a minute and fifteen seconds left in the first round.

The arena erupted in cheers. Referee Smith stood over the stricken fighter and started the ten-count: "One, two, three," he barked, the crowd chanting along with him. McCarty lay on his back, almost motionless, his mouth open wide, lungs gasping for air. "Eight, nine...he's out!" Smith could sense something was wrong. Instead of marching over to the challenger's corner and hoisting Pelkey's right arm in the victory salute, the referee made a frantic gesture to the timekeeper and covered his mouth in horror. Billy McCarney was the first to jump into the ring. He rushed to McCarty's side and tried desperately to rouse him before crying out for help. "My God," he yelled. "A doctor! A doctor, quick!"

Pandemonium broke loose in the arena. Dozens of onlookers scrambled into the ring for a better look. The mob trampled over the press table, sending a row of telephones crashing to the floor. Some shouted. Some waved their arms. A path was cleared and a team of doctors crowded around the fallen fighter. All their attempts to revive him failed, so they decided to move him. As his still body was carried from the fighting area, the mob inside the stadium hushed. "Thousands of heads were bared," reported the *Calgary Herald*. "Thousands of hearts fluttered and pulsated with fear and excitement."

The champ was laid out on the ground outside the arena. Three mounted police officers kept the crowd at bay, as doctors tried every device they knew to rouse him to consciousness. Morphine was injected into his right arm, and a shot of brandy forced down his throat, all to no avail: McCarty's face darkened, his eyes gazed skyward, and then he died, there on the grass. Billy

THE CALGARY NEWS-TELEGRAM

FIRST SECTION

CALGARY, ALBERTA — MONDAY, MAY 26, 1913.

...VENTH YEAR—No. 49

12 O'CLOCK EDITION

SIXTEEN PAGES

CHAMPION McCARTY DIES AT ARENA

MURDER, IS CHARGE OF PREACHER

Rev. J. C. Sycamore Severe in Comments on Prize Ring Tragedy—Rev. S. E. Marshall Compares Fighting in Calgary with Cruelties of Ancient Rome—Many of Leading Pastors of City Join in Condemning Arena Battles as Detrimental to Morals of Citizens.

THE CALGARY DAILY HERALD

5 p. m. City   5 p. m. City

CALGARY, ALBERTA, THURSDAY, JUNE 19, 1913

THIRTIETH YEAR, No. 3234   16 PAGES

ARTHUR PELKEY ON TRIAL FOR MANSLAUGHTER

McCarney knelt over him and wept.

Pelkey and Burns retreated to the Elbow View Hotel, unaware that McCarty had been pronounced dead. Pelkey took a bath and changed into a clean set of clothes. When he saw the undertaker's wagon pass by his window, he turned to his manager and said in a low voice, "I pray to God it isn't McCarty." An hour later, a Royal North-West Mounted Police officer came to his room and arrested him for manslaughter. Pelkey broke down and cried like a child. He was later escorted to the courthouse downtown and released on $10,000 bail. The next evening, the Manchester Arena burned mysteriously to the ground[6].

A coroner's inquest was held the following Tuesday, and while a jury found that McCarty's death had been accidentally caused by a brain haemorrhage, Pelkey was told to remain in Calgary until his trial. Meanwhile, McCarty's body was shipped to his father's home in Ohio. Before leaving Calgary to attend the funeral, his manager McCarney vowed to "never have anything to do with boxing again"[7].

Pelkey's trial lasted four days inside a packed courtroom. The bulky fighter could barely fit in the prisoner's box and was allowed to sit in a special chair. He appeared calm at first, occasionally leaning over to confer with Burns and his lawyers, A.L. Smith and M.S. McCarthy[8]. No one expected the jury to render a guilty verdict; the whole affair was considered a formality. But the prosecutor, James Short, played it tough, making Burns look like a heedless profiteer, and Pelkey his hairy-knuckled stooge. He argued that McCarty had been in perfect health before entering the ring, and laid blame for his death directly on the man sitting across the courtroom.

When it came time for the final arguments, Smith rose and faced the jury with memorable words:

DOCTORS NOT AGREED AS TO CAUSE OF McCARTY'S DEATH; MOSHIER & MERRITT DIFFER

This Morning's Session of Pelkey Trial Devoted to Taking of Medical Testimony—Much Technical Evidence Given by Witnesses—Public Interest In Case as Great as Ever—Courtroom Crowded Again

TAKING OF EVIDENCE IN PELKEY TRIAL CONCLUDED; ADDRESSES THIS AFTERNOON

ALBERTA DEBENTURES

Canadian Associated Press. LONDON, June 22.—Latest quotations in Canadian funds show Alberta 10-year debentures, 1922, at 95 and British Columbia registered stock, 1941, three percents at 79-81.

G.T.P. A FACTOR IN MOVING THE

Large Number of Medical Witnesses Called by Defence This Morning—Testimony Given by Them Differs From That For Prosecution

OGDEN BLACKSMITH SAYS McCARTY WAS IN HIS SHOP AND HELD HIS BACK WITH HAND AS IF IN PAIN

Dr. Moshier Recalled But Refuses To Go Back on His Previous Evidence—Addresses of Counsel Started Directly After Luncheon

GREAT CROWD APPLAUDS AS ARTHUR PELKEY IS SET FREE BY JURY MONDAY AFTERNOON

Jury Declares Bout Was a Prize Fight, But That Accused Was Not Responsible For the Death of McCarty—Elimination of Boxing Recommended

What is of supreme importance is that fourteen people have been called in this court and each has told you that in their experience in boxing or medical science they did not see any blows struck that would have killed McCarty. I submit if there is any fairness, if our system of justice is what we pride ourselves it is, I trust you will say to this man, take back your reputation and live your life, you have done nothing wrong. I submit to you by the blood that flows through your veins as Anglo-Saxon, that spoke in Wellington, in Nelson, in Drake, in our brothers to the south of us, I submit, then, that is all he is asking from you today.

The twelve jurymen were moved to tears by the speech. Before retiring to their chamber, they

[6] The cause of the Manchester Arena fire was never determined. Police suspected angry churchgoers, opposed enough to boxing to commit arson. McCarty's death had come on a Saturday. The next morning, the tragedy was denounced from almost every pulpit. 'Christians should rise up and put this fight game out of business,' urged the Rev. Alex Esler, of Grace Presbyterian Church.

[7]It is not clear whether McCarty's manager lived up to his word and quit boxing. He arrived in Ohio with McCarty's body, and was called back to Calgary to appear as a witness at Pelkey's trial. Then he disappeared. McCarty's estranged wife, a saloon worker in Fargo, North Dakota, was left a $20,000 estate.

[8]Maitland S. McCarthy, one of Pelkey's lawyers, had been Tory MP for Calgary during the city's unsuccessful bid to have itself made capital of Alberta (Vol. 2, p. 75).

were given a final address by Chief Justice Horace Harvey, who told them that in order to find the accused guilty of manslaughter, they would have to decide whether McCarty died during an illegal prize fight. The jury left the courtroom. Pelkey sat and chatted with Burns. Short must have expected a long deliberation, for he left the building and was still absent an hour later when the jury returned.

Lawrence Clarke, clerk of the Supreme Court of Alberta, stood and addressed the twelve men: "Have you reached a verdict? If so, say by your foreman."

Foreman F.W. Mapson rose. "We have."

"What say you, do you find the prisoner guilty or not guilty of the offence charged against him?"

"We find that the contest held at the Burns arena on May 24 was a prize fight, but that Arthur Pelkey is not guilty of causing the death of Luther McCarty."

Pelkey leapt to his feet and shook hands with each juror before being surrounded by a happy throng of admirers. "The pent-up feelings of the crowd burst forth," recounted the *Calgary Herald*. "They clapped as an audience might have applauded in a theatre when a prima donna had rendered her final effort." Four days later, Alberta's deputy attorney-general, L.F. Clarry, announced that professional boxing would no longer be tolerated anywhere in Alberta. Burns sold his clothing store and took his young protégé on a promotional tour along the west coast, where prize fighting was still legal.

But Pelkey's heart wasn't in it. Tormented by the memory of having killed a man in the ring, he appeared indifferent and lackadaisical during the tour. In September, he shocked his followers by announcing that Burns had "fixed" an earlier bout leading up to the McCarty showdown. In Portland, Pelkey told the *Oregonian* that his manager "lured him from Ontario and forced him into a 'fixed' match and staged nightly rehearsals of the battle in a garret." Burns vehemently denied the allegation, but his relationship with the young franco-Ontarian was finished. So too was his dream of exacting revenge on Jack Johnson.

After splitting up with Burns, Pelkey fought a few more times and lost every bout. He died Feb. 18, 1921, of what was described by reporters as "sleeping sickness."

Out of luck and desperate for money, Burns was forced to climb back into the ring. In 1918, he beat Tex Foster in Prince Rupert, B.C. A year later, at the age of 39, he was knocked out by British champion Joe Beckett, in London. It was the first time Burns had ever hit the canvas and stayed there. He hung up his gloves for good after that bout and moved to Manchester, where he opened a pub. He later moved to New York, and operated a popular speakeasy. Burns continued to perform on the vaudeville circuit, shadow-boxing and skipping rope in front of appreciative audiences. Eventually he was slowed down by arthritis and moved to California, where he suddenly "found religion" and became a fire-breathing evangelist. He died of a heart attack in 1955 while in Vancouver on church business, and was buried there.

Early baseball drew great crowds at Edmonton, but when they shouted, 'Kill the umpire,' there was reason to believe they meant it.

The raucous short-lived history of the brawling WCBL

DESPITE FIGHTS, GRUDGES, PLOTS, BOOZE, BRIBES AND BANKRUPTCY ALBERTA WAS BASEBALL COUNTRY, AND UMPS GOT POLICE PROTECTION

When the home-town Regina Bonecrushers of the Western Canada Baseball League lost a nail-biter to the Edmonton Eskimos in July 1910, people shouted, "Kill the umpire!" Only this crowd wasn't kidding, and the life of the umpire, a man named Houston, whom they accused of accepting a bribe, was in imminent danger. The hapless official had to be escorted to his hotel by a group of truncheon-swinging policemen.

However, in the tumultuous heyday of the WCBL, incidents like this came to be expected. The league had lived in chaos since its inception in 1907. One rung below "class C" ball, the eight-team outfit attracted the dregs of the minor leagues — raw-boned rookies, washed-up veterans, boozy managers, and wild, unruly fans. WCBL games were heated, brawl-filled affairs, full of conspiracy and intrigue. Every team accused the other of cheating, and every umpire was supposedly on the "take." Whether or not it was baseball, it was a spectacularly entertaining product.

Financially, the league's history was a saga of disaster. Teams came and went with alarming regularity; the $1,200 monthly salary cap was openly flaunted. While most teams averaged around 700 paid customers a game, any potential profits were eaten up by imported "ringers" who bolstered each line-up.

At the end of the 1909 season, the Calgary Bronks were the only club to report a surplus and there was talk of disbanding the league. The remaining Alberta entries — the Edmonton Eskimos, the Lethbridge Coal Barons, and the championship squad from Medicine Hat, the Hatters — all lost between $1,000 to $3,500. The other franchises, based in Moose Jaw, Regina, Brandon and Winnipeg, fared just as poorly. But changes were made to the 1910 schedule limiting the amount of travel each club would have to endure, and the league looked forward to another year.

The Hatters, pennant winners in 1908 and 1909, were the popular pick to repeat again in 1910. Their championship roster remained intact save for pitcher "Betsy" Campbell, who defected to Spokane of the Northwestern League. "Billy Hamilton is again wielding the managerial baton," noted the *Medicine Hat News*, "and has plenty of money behind him to strengthen up the weak spots as they develop."

Lethbridge, led by its inimitable manager Eugene (Chesty) Cox[a], was expected to mount a strong challenge, even though the team's directors insisted that "every man who is in their service must be a fellow of good respectable character, immaterial of his playing ability." The Eskimos, "cellar champions" the previous year, promised a "10,000 percent" improvement in 1910.

The Bronks were the league's most stable franchise, having sold $10,000 worth of season tickets. They were also the most hated. Their third baseman, Frank Smith, was on every opponent's "get" list, thanks to his foul mouth and carefully sharpened cleats. In May, after a victory over the hometown Eskimos, Smith was cornered on McDougall Avenue (100th Street) by a mob of angry fans. The Calgary newspapers reported he was beaten to a pulp. The *Edmonton Bulletin* insisted the episode had been "wildly exaggerated," and that Smith had been merely the victim of some "verbal abuse."

Even the Edmonton papers recognized that some "loose-tongued and thoughtless" spectators seemed to attend games for the sole purpose of heaping scorn upon members of the visiting teams. "People do not go to ball games to hear profanity and obscenity," expounded the *Edmonton Bulletin* piously. "A little ginger on the part of the police would correct this defect."

Things as usual ended on a sour note that year. The Bronks, regular season champions, refused any playoff games in Edmonton. The Eskimos swore they would not travel south to Calgary. Edmonton owner and manager Deacon White said he would refuse the pennant if it was offered under such circumstances. Unhandicapped by such

This trio, all unidentified, date from the WCBL's bawdy days before the Great War. Taken at Edmonton's Diamond Park in 1914, it probably consists of two management people from the Eskimos and a referee, all three in starched collars and ties.

niceties as vanity and pride, the Bronks accepted the prize.

The 1911 season was a calamity even before it began. Lethbridge and Moose Jaw could not overcome their fiscal shortfalls and pulled out before the first pitch was thrown. Winnipeg folded with just three weeks left in the season. Brandon won the championship and then withdrew under a staggering debt. By the following spring, the WCBL was reduced to four teams, all from Alberta: Calgary, Edmonton, Red Deer and Bassano. Thanks to poor crowds, Red Deer could not meet its payroll obligations. The players went on strike, and by the end of July it looked as if the "Deers" would be the next failure. But the club bounced back and finished the season, only to lose to the Bronks in the finals. Thus ended Red Deer's venture into pro ball. The Bassano franchise folded when, in a desperate attempt to pay creditors, team officials dismantled their stadium and sold off the lumber.

The WCBL struggled along for two more years. Things seemed to be looking up in 1913, when four additional teams joined the fold.

The Medicine Hat squad, revived later in the decade and posing for this official photo, plainly did not shy from their reputation as the 'Dirty Monarchs.'

At practice about 1913, Edmonton's Eskimos seem to be affecting a kind of hoodlum look. Calgarians would have said it wasn't an affectation.

Attendance suddenly jumped; Edmonton drew 2,500 fans to its home opener against the Bronks, and managed a small profit at the end of the season. The new entries from Saskatoon and Moose Jaw shocked everyone by landing in the black. But the relative peace was shattered when league president Frank Gray suspended three managers — Ray Whisman from Edmonton, Bill Hurley from Saskatoon, and

terrible year, losing all but 37 of its 118 games. Thanks largely to its strong line-up of pitchers, Saskatoon's Quakers ended up with the championship.

It was the last WCBL pennant ever awarded. When it came time to prepare for the 1915 season, Canada was at war. The league's directors decided to suspend operations, and teams sold their rosters to clubs in more senior leagues.

The Bassano franchise folded when, in a desperate attempt to pay creditors, team officials dismantled their stadium and sold off the lumber.

Billy Hulen from Regina — for exceeding the salary limit. Hurley was given an extra $15 fine for insulting an umpire. The three were eventually reinstated after a long, well publicized power struggle, but the incident divided the league into warring factions.

In 1914, the salary limit was raised to $1,800 a month, and a new, full-time president was appointed. For the first time, every team that survived the previous season was back for another crack at the pennant. Once again, Edmontonians turned out magnificently to watch their Eskimos — 5,000 for the opener against Saskatoon's Quakers. The Eskimos boasted two of the league's finest outfielders, Eddie Lemieux and Dean Crum. Medicine Hat led the league in batting. Calgary, meanwhile, had a

Some players made it to the bigs, including Art Buckles of Medicine Hat who went to the Chicago Cubs, and Bill Williams of the Eskimos who was picked up by the Chicago White Sox. Some simply drifted through the minors, playing for room and board and a little spare change. Others ended up fighting for keeps with a different kind of enemy, on a harsh, foreign field.

The WCBL was resurrected after the war and carried into the 1920s, though never with quite the bawdy reputation it gained in the teens.

— *B.H.*

[a]Coal Barons manager Chesty Cox moonlighted as an actor. In 1908 he wrote, directed, and starred in a play candidly called, *Chesty Cox — Idol of Fans*. The performance drew mixed reviews after its premiere in La Crosse, Wisconsin.

The Calgary Bronks were both financially secure and cordially hated everywhere else. They posed for this photo in 1910.

The game Albertans called rugby football began on a purely amateur basis as a curious combination of soccer and rugger and achieved immediate popularity. Here are the Calgary Tigers in action at home. The date is unknown, as is the opposition team.

As the pros went sour, Alberta turned to amateur sport

Curling, bowling and football gained popularity rapidly, though women liked a clean sport, wrestling for instance

By 1910, professional sport was on the wane in Alberta. People still embraced their "home" teams, but there was a growing sense that corruption was making sports a mockery. Boxing was riddled with fakers and fixers. Baseball and hockey teams bought players from other leagues and paid them under the table. Newspapers ran accounts of referees accepting bribes. True or not, such stories soon gained more attention than anything that occurred on the field or rink[a].

At the same time, amateur sport was discovering a new popularity. Volunteer bodies like the Young Men's Christian Association, dedicated among other things to the preservation of fair play, saw their ranks swell between 1910 and 1920. The Alberta Amateur Athletic Union, an umbrella organization, quadrupled its membership.

By 1913, Calgary boasted seven amateur baseball leagues; Edmonton had five. The Alberta Amateur Hockey Association grew from nine teams in its inaugural 1907-08 season to more than thirty by 1914, attracting crowds in excess of 3,500.

Wrestling enjoyed a remarkable boom, attracting a particular interest among women. In 1911, the *Lethbridge Herald* reported that "a large number of ladies" turned out for an exhibition series in southern Alberta — proof, wrote one enthusiast, that, unlike boxing, "wrestling is a clean game and need not be necessarily vulgar or brutal. It is merely a display of strength and agility and knowledge of a scientific art."

Curling, Canada's "roaring game," continued to grow, especially in rural Alberta. In urban centres, five-pin bowling emerged as a popular activity. In December 1911 a "long-distance bowling match" took place, featuring teams from Calgary, Edmonton and Winnipeg. Scores were relayed by telegraph. The four-man team from Calgary won the tourney. A few weeks later, the city proclaimed itself the "bowling capital of the world." That was after Ole Christenson and Kit Carson combined for a world-record, three-game total of 1,427 points, down at the Exchange Alleys on Second Street and Ninth Avenue W.

"Canadian-style" football attracted a large following after the Calgary Tigers beat the Winnipeg Rowing Club

Ladies dressed in the Edwardian fashion with flannel-clad gentlemen shown at the Strathcona tennis courts on the future 103rd Street about 1910. Tea was served at the courts on Saturdays and on holidays a refreshment tent was set up. There were two grass courts and a cinder one. Provincial Archives of Alberta, A-10,286

and captured the 1911 Western Canadian championship. A curious hybrid of British rugby and American football, the new game caught on quickly, replacing lacrosse as Alberta's favourite rough-and-tumble outdoor sport. In 1913, almost 4,000 Edmontonians witnessed a contest between the Tigers and the hometown Eskimos at Diamond Park (First St. and Hardisty).

"The crowd filled the grandstand and bleachers and lined the ropes seven or eight deep," reported the *Edmonton Bulletin*. "Outside the fence on house tops, telegraph poles, mounds of earth and other points of vantage, hundreds of people followed the progress of the game."[b]

Rules protecting the amateur game were at first strictly enforced. Individuals or teams found guilty of accepting payment were severely disciplined. Even associating with professionals was considered an offence. In August 1913 the Calgary *Albertan* reported "the biggest scandal in the history of amateur sports" when six Calgary senior league baseball players were suspended for playing in a picnic tournament that featured a couple of pros.

The Alberta Amateur Hockey Association adopted a

presenting the AAAU with a new problem when the war ended. Many of the returning veterans who wanted to rejoin their old amateur teams were considered professional, since they had played with, against, or as professionals while in the service. In May 1919, the AAAU decided to relax its standards and offer amateur status to any athlete, regardless of prior affiliation. It also permitted some games between professionals and amateurs, and allowed professionals from

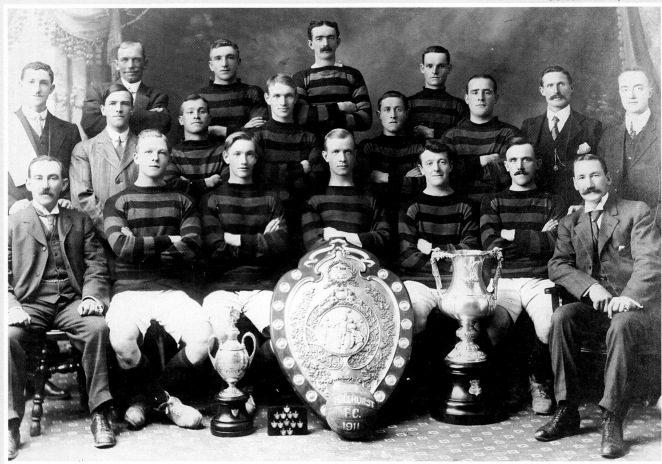

Calgary-Hillhurst Football Club, Canadian champion team, 1910-11. This game would become known as soccer, while 'rugby football' would take over the name football. A huge crowd of Calgarians saw this team off for Toronto in a private railway car. There, they defeated the hometown Toronto Thistles 3-0 in the semi-finals, then went on to a 1-1 tie with Hamilton, necessitating another final game. It wound up with a scoreless tie. With three minutes to go in an overtime period, Hamilton posted a 2-1 lead. As the clock ran down Archie Stewart (second from right, front row) scored a tying goal. With a minute to go, the player identified as B. Baldwin (second from left) scored the winner and won the 'People's Trophy.' Calgary went crazy over the club, and the Toronto press called it the most exciting game in Canadian soccer history.

tough "residence rule," stipulating that a player had to be a "*bona fide* resident of the city or town in which he is playing." This didn't sit well with Fred Gravelle, manager of the Calgary Athletic Club. In 1911 Gravelle formed the Southern Alberta Hockey League, which gave teams unfettered access to players from around the province[c].

By 1916 the war in Europe had seriously depleted Alberta's stock of male athletes over the age of 18,

one sport to play as amateurs in another.

While the AAAU's new rules drew the wrath of Canada's other provincial athletic unions, most Albertans argued they

*Back row, left to right: F. Foster, patron; Alex Melville, George Boss, Jack Ross. **Middle row:** trainer J. Melville, secretary-treasurer H.J. Ford, William Melville, captain Art Wakelyn, F. McEwen, D. Jenkyn, manager Robert Mills, patron S. Jackson. **Front row:** Mayor and patron J.W. Mitchell, B. Baldwin, S. Wakelyn, W. Dyke, G. Johnson, vice-captain Archie Stewart, vice-president F.R. Riley.

STUDENTS CLASS, 08, Y. M. C. A.

A gymnastics class at the YMCA in Olds, 1908. During the decade membership in the YMCA soared, largely because of its emphasis on fair play.

merely reflected reality. The *Bulletin* admitted that the changes were "radical" but insisted it was the correct decision: "Alberta is absolutely sick of the camouflage amateurism of eastern Canada, Manitoba included, and can run its own athletics without any advice from the East." For the first time, Albertans seemed to accept that their amateur athletes would have to share the playing fields with professionals. It was an uneasy compromise, one that would continue to trouble the sporting world for decades.

Nevertheless, by the end of the 1920s, most athletic unions had adopted similar measures. By 1931, notes Donald Wetherell, in his book *Useful Pleasures: The Shaping of Leisure in Alberta,* "the majority of people no longer equated the ideal sportsman with amateur status... This significant shift accepted that a professional was capable of fair play."

— *B.H.*

[a]While the Edmonton Eskimos' second successive Stanley Cup challenge in January 1910 drew wide interest, many locals complained the team was really a collection of highly paid foreigners. Of the eight players, only one, Harold Deeton, was originally from Edmonton. After the Eskimos lost their two-game series with the Ottawa Senators, six chose to sign up with eastern Canadian teams and collect bigger pay cheques.

[b]The Western Canada Rugby Football Union, formed in 1911, joined the Canadian Rugby Union in 1921 and began competing for the Grey Cup. The Eskimos were the first western-based team to compete for the cup, but lost to the Toronto Argonauts 23-0. Ten years later, the CRU approved the forward pass. In 1958, the organization was renamed the Canadian Football League.

[c]The SAHL folded after its first year of operation, but amateur hockey in Alberta was soon plagued with charges of corruption. Tommy Thompson, a forward with the Calgary Shermans of the AAHA, was suspended after he admitted to having played professional hockey in the East. A year later, in 1913, the Taber Chefs were kicked out after it was revealed that their star forward, Lloyd Cook, had once played with a semipro team in Fernie, B.C.

The Athabasca Landing Curling Club in 1911. The 'roaring game' grew all through the teen years.

Section Two
THE NEW CITIES

Work crews pause for a portrait during the building of Calgary's
Centre Street Bridge over the Bow River. All Alberta in those
boom years seemed like one vast construction camp.
Glenbow Archives, NA-4443-1

CHAPTER ONE

5,000 to 75,000 in 12 years — that's how Calgary came to be

Most of it happened in those dazzling 36 months of 1910 to 1912; whole districts appeared monthly, and optimism was a civic duty

by BRIAN HUTCHINSON

In 1912 the London publishing house of Hodder & Stoughton produced an anonymously penned, 84-page panegyric to "the bouquet" of the Canadian prairies. Those unfamiliar with Calgary would undoubtedly have been fascinated to learn it was "one of the most significant cities of our twentieth century," where men "labour so cheerfully at their appointed tasks, and the climate is so bracing, that nobody is heard to grumble, and everyone seems to have sufficient at hand to keep him profitably employed for the term of his natural life... He who goes to such a town becomes at once a citizen of no mean city; he is captain of his own fate, the master of his own soul."

Such exaggeration of the city's quality, potential and accomplishments was not only encouraged, but a virtual requirement of citizenship. Residents were urged to write to distant friends and relatives, listing reasons why they should move to "the City of Business and Bustle by the Bow," or to "Calgary the Phenomenal".[1]

The population figure was constantly embellished, though it was hardly necessary. In 1900 it stood at 5,000, a decade later at over 40,000, and after 1910 newcomers were pouring in at the rate of 1,000 a month. By the end of 1912 it was edging 75,000 and promoters talked of a half-million by the 1930s. Every day, carpenters, bricklayers and surveyors stepped off the train with families in tow. Meanwhile, land speculation was the city's biggest industry. *Henderson's Directory* for 1913 listed 358 real estate agents against 166 grocery stores, 17 banks and 27 hardware stores. It was like a hive, wrote Australian journalist Desmond Byre. "The town was humming...huge, prosperous and contented. Everybody seemed to have a chance and to be conscious of it."

No one better epitomized all this than Fred Charles Lowes (he never listed his name as Frederick) who had come to Calgary from his Ontario birthplace in 1902 with the $400 he'd saved after six years in the life insurance business. In six months he and his younger brother Bertrand had converted this into $65,000 by acquiring properties and selling them. To Calgarians Freddie Lowes was "Mister Boom," the man everyone wished to emulate, as he whizzed by in one of his shiny Pierce-Arrow motor cars.

In six years the value of Lowes' holdings in southwest Calgary alone rose to $2 million[2]. He had offices in five Alberta cities, British Columbia and Saskatchewan, London and New York. By 1913 he had some 400 employees and had opened the Calgary suburbs of Elbow Park, Glencoe,

---

[1] Newspaper editors joined in the orgy of boosterism unrestrained. Plaudits paid the city by visitors were given marked prominence. The Allan Line christened a 17,515-ton North Atlantic liner the *Calgarian* in 1912. The name of the city, exulted the *Herald*, will be 'on the lips of thousands of people each day.'

[2] Real estate didn't provide the only excitement. In 1912, a grizzled prospector named Terrence Brady rushed into town claiming he had struck gold on the Ghost River near Morley. A hundred people headed out to the area, but came back discouraged. Brady's claim produced metal all right, but it was iron pyrites — fool's gold.

THE NEW CITIES

Britannia and Roxborough and sold the suburb of Ogden for $750,000. (He wanted to call Ogden "Ceepeear" to recognize its dependency on the railway, but the old name persisted.) The Roxborough development was made possible by an engineering feat. Backfill was washed down from Mission Hill area above it to raise the elevation of the land below. In Edmonton Lowes is reputed to have handled the largest land deal in the city's history. When the Canadian Northern required a route into Calgary, Lowes got the contract to acquire the property. He made extensive use of advertising, spending an unheard-of $12,000 on it in 1909 alone. He would bring prospective investors west by chartered railway car, and made skilful use of newspaper publicity.

In his personal life Lowes was similarly flamboyant. In *Calgary, An Illustrated History*, Max Foran and Heather MacEwan tell how he once spent $25,000 on a shopping spree in New York. He was an avid sportsman. His fine horses were considered some of the best in the country, and he claimed the record for the best driving time from High River to Calgary. He was an amateur boxer as well, and was said to have provided the land for Tommy Burns' Manchester Arena (Sect. 1, ch. 5).

A traffic policeman is silhouetted against the profile of downtown Calgary, about 1912. In less than a decade the city has been transformed from frontier town into a modern metropolis.
Provincial Archives of Alberta, P-3971

But Lowes was by no means the city's only developer. Seemingly every month a new residential district would be added to the city's treeless outskirts. Development began in Tuxedo Park in 1910, in Mount Pleasant in 1912. Capitol Hill was annexed in 1910 and a few houses appeared, though most development there would not occur until the 1950s. The developments were often financed from eastern Canada or Britain. Local agents subdivided the properties and auctioned them, often grading the streets, paving sidewalks and erecting street lighting before putting the lots on the market.

As the boom gained momentum, lots were increasingly bought and sold by speculators — "flipped" as it would be called in a later boom — without any development occurring. Grant MacEwan, in his history of the city, *Calgary Cavalcade*, tells how 2,000 dealers bought and sold property, usually at huge markups. When the Canadian Pacific offered 150 lots at the foot of its prestigious Mount Royal district at $500 to $600 each in 1910, they were snapped up in twenty minutes, speculators immediately selling them at double the CPR price. Downtown property that sold for $2,000 in 1905 was commanding $300,000 six or seven years later.

Contractors worked twelve-hour days building houses, store fronts and office blocks. There were five stone quarries and six brickyards; thirty men toiled in the Mission yards alone, turning out 22,000 bricks a day. Construction permits totalled $5.5 million in 1910, up 130% from the previous year, the greatest increase in Canada and a satisfying four times the level of activity in Edmonton. Two years later, building permits totalled $20 million. Twenty chartered banks handled the fifth largest volume of business in the Dominion, over $200 million in 1911. Still, the *Calgary Herald* advised its readers to "put your money in real estate, not in the bank."

There was a wild, unfinished feeling about the place. Downtown was noisy and crowded, filled with the smells and sounds of industry, and shrouded in dust and soot.

Mounds of horse manure piled up in alleyways behind the fifteen livery stables that competed for business. Blacksmith shops belched smoke. At the end of each day, workmen caked with dirt and sawdust retired to the hotels that lined Ninth Avenue from Third Street East to First Street West. Known as Whiskey Row, the strip featured cheap rooms and ten lively watering holes with hard liquor at fifteen cents a shot. When the city jailkeeper freed nine drunks in honour of the King's birthday one year, Calgary's reputation as a good "wet town" spread across the Dominion.

Not everyone rejoiced in this brawling bush camp atmosphere. Rev. John Clark, a Presbyterian minister, launched an intense beautification campaign in 1911, exhorting people to pick garbage off the streets and voluntarily remove horse droppings. Clark was especially offended by cigar and liquor advertisements, but any billboard seemed to disgust him. "The man with an aesthetic eye who walks the streets of Calgary is offended by these huge, unsightly billboards covered with hideous pictures and advertising," he wrote to the *Herald*.

A horticultural society was formed to plant trees and dig flower beds. Fines were handed out for failure to remove noxious weeds from vacant lots. In 1913 the city introduced a spate of bylaws which, it was hoped, would lend an air of refinement to the downtown; therefore it became an offence to "expectorate, spit, or otherwise deposit saliva on any sidewalk in the city of Calgary, or in any public building." Horn-blowing, bell-ringing, singing, shouting and loitering were all prohibited. Sidewalk preaching was permitted, however, as were church bells.

Some of Calgary's finest private landmarks appeared at the beginning of the new decade. Huge brick and sandstone fortresses stared down at the hustle and bustle from the lofty heights of Mount Royal, locale of the *nouveaux riches*, where the first streets developed were Amherst, Durham, Sydenham and Dorchester. First known as American Hill, owing to the number of wealthy American immigrants living there, the neighbourhood featured

Provincial Archives of Alberta, A-20097

Calgary never hears the truth about herself. Even though she did she wouldn't listen. The great trouble with the West is that it is never told the truth. Men are afraid to open their mouths... The average citizen is too infatuated with his own little Tin Pot Concerns to contemplate the future with discrimination and breadth of vision.
— *The Eye Opener, Aug. 24, 1912*

Picturesquely situated so as to be within easy reach of the brewery, Calgary extends right and left, north and south, up and down, in and out, expanding as she goes, swelling in her pride, puffing in her might, blowing in her majesty and revolving in eccentric orbits round a couple of dozen large bars which close promptly at 11:30 right or wrong.
— *The Eye Opener, March 9, 1918*

THE NEW CITIES

Freddie Lowes: a spectacular operator in spectacular times

Sportsman-developer Lowes stands (at left) below Mission Hill, which provided backfill for the swampland that became Roxborough. (The spelling was later contracted to Roxboro.) Above is one of his Elbow Park road crews; at right is his own modest Elbow Drive home; and the aerial photo below shows Roxborough as Lowes laid it out.

93

A fountain graces the hillside in then sparsely treed Mount Royal (above). Its grandeur notwithstanding, Mount Royal was the habitat of the nouveaux riches. The 'old money' still resided much closer to the city centre, but south of the railway and west of Centre Street. Below is a 1913 sketch of the block-long, 57-suite Devenish apartment building at Eighth Street and 17th Avenue, on which O.G. Devenish spent $80,000.

large, treed lots, winding asphalt lanes, and cement sidewalks.[3] The most impressive residence belonged to Eugene Coste, an Ontario geologist who came west in 1908 and made a huge gas strike near Bow Island, 35 miles southwest of Medicine Hat. Coste's Canadian Western Natural Gas, Light, Heat, and Power Company provided both Calgary and Lethbridge with a "practically inexhaustible" supply of energy, via 171 miles of pipeline, and provided him the means to build his $75,000, 28-room mansion[4].

In 1911, eighteen teams of horses created an enormous excavation at the corner of First Street and Ninth Avenue S.W., and that November the foundation was laid for what would long remain the pride of the city, the Canadian Pacific Railway's hotel. It would be a lavish, eight-storey affair, costing $1.5 million, by far the city's largest and most expensive status symbol, featuring 315 guest suites. Just before the hotel opened in 1914, it was named "The Palliser," after Captain John Palliser, the 19th-century British explorer of the Canadian West (Vol. 1, p. 229). This raised a few eyebrows, as Palliser once referred to the region east of Calgary as an "extension of the Great

American Desert," a place fit for Indians, perhaps, but not Europeans. But the hotel was as tranquil and lush an oasis as could be found anywhere in western Canada, with dark oak panelling, marble floors and columns, and exotic carpets.

The Hudson's Bay Company unveiled its new department store, immediately hailed as a "splendid pile of steel and tile" by the Calgary *Albertan*. Festooned with pretty tapestries and fresh flowers, the $1-million edifice looked "like a fairyland." The Canada Life Building (six storeys plus a mezzanine, later raised to twelve), opened three months later on Eighth Avenue at Third Street W. and was, said the *Albertan*, "another splendid assurance of the confidence of the largest business and financial houses of Canada in the solidity of Calgary." Glazed terracotta covered the exterior, while mahogany, birch and marble lent the interior a satisfying air of elegance and sophistication[5].

Middle-income earners sought shelter in the suburbs, where

new houses cost an average of $3,000. To supply comfortable rental accommodation close to downtown, O.G. Devenish spent $80,000 on a 57-suite building at Eighth Street and 17th Avenue, "the finest and most up to date structure" of its kind. The block-long, crenelated Devenish was built of red brick with sandstone trim. Its three-room apartments featured "murphy beds"[6], so that at night the living rooms could be converted into bedrooms. (By the end of the century it was still there.)

Calgary's municipal services were soon over-strained by the population explosion, so the city embarked on a wild spending spree. Between 1907 and 1913 it spent some $10 million on new public facilities and improvements. The waterworks system was extended to 2,000 new homes in outlying areas, and a 20-million-gallon reservoir was excavated on the Elbow River, just west of the Golf and Country Club. The work cost over $500,000, yet barely satisfied the city's growing need for water.

The school system meanwhile was forced to build frantically to accommodate legions of new pupils. By the time the Great War broke out in 1914, nine primary schools had been built: Riverside, Mount Royal, Hillhurst, Earl Grey, King George, King Edward, Stanley Jones, Colonel Walker and Victoria, which was opened in January 1914 to teach industrial arts. Crescent Heights School was moved from its original location on Main Street to First Street W. and 16th Avenue. Between 1910 and 1920 six separate schools appeared: St. Mary's, St. Ann's, Sacred Heart, St. Joseph's, Holy Angels and Bridgeland.

Two independent schools were founded. St. Hilda's College occupied a collection of small buildings on a site purchased by Anglican Bishop W. Cyprian Pinkham, at 12th Avenue and Eighth Street. The school struggled through the bust of 1914, the Great Depression, and two world wars before folding in 1947. Western Canada College was founded in 1903 on 17th Avenue at Fifth, on twenty acres of property donated by the Canadian Pacific. Some of the property was sold to finance the building program. The college sent many graduates to the Great War, but foundered in 1926 after a secretary-treasurer absconded with the funds. It was sold to the public system and became Western Canada High School.

In 1910 six elegant new streetcars, purchased with part of the $31,000 profit the system had

Eugene Coste's natural gas strike near Bow Island made his Canadian Western Natural Gas, Light, Heat, and Power the supplier of both Calgary and Lethbridge and provided Coste himself (above) with the wherewithal to build this $75,000, 28-room home at 2208 Amherst Street in Mount Royal, the most opulent in an exceedingly opulent district. The house survived for the century.

earned in its first year of service, were added to the city fleet. The eleven original cars, with their coarse wooden benches and smelly coal-fed heaters, simply wouldn't do for a city as prosperous and ambitious as Calgary. "Did you see that streetcar with the smokestack sticking out the top?" huffed an indignant Simon John Clarke, one of the city's most outspoken commissioners. "Why, it looks like an old CPR boarding car. I call it a disgrace to this city." The new Preston cars, painted dark green, had fashionable frosted windows, corrugated iron steps, cherry woodwork inside, cane seats and, of course, electric heaters. By 1911, the system covered 38 miles and had carried over six million passengers[7].

Almost 1,500 Calgarians turned out to view the new, four-storey General Hospital when it opened in February 1910 on the north side of the Bow River in the Riverside district. The imposing brick building cost the city $150,000. Its state-of-the-art equipment included vacuum-pressured air purification and ventilation systems, inter-communicating telephones, and two operating rooms complete with etherizing and X-ray chambers. There were beds for 200 patients. The private ward was so well furnished, according to the *Albertan*, that it was "enough to make a person with a penchant for luxurious surroundings envy the sick." Dean E.C. Paget, chairman of the hospital building committee,

was only half joking when he said, "If you want to enjoy poor health, this is the place to come."

Few expenses were spared with the new city hall either. Three thousand saw it opened in June 1911, a brass band playing marching songs beneath an array of red, white and blue bunting. A dozen police officers stepped out into the bright sunshine and formed a solid line behind Mayor John W. Mitchell. Then Robert L. Borden, national leader of the Conservative Party, who would become prime minister a few months later, pushed open the two oak doors at the entrance, turned, waved, and stepped over the threshold.

Built in the Romanesque revival style, the city hall featured brilliant yellow sandstone, polished white maple floors, and a shiny copper roof. The rafters were

Provincial Archives of Alberta, P-4101

Provincial Archives of Alberta, P-10718

Expansion, it seemed, would never end — but end it did

In a 1917 cityscape (above) workmen are cleaning up the site of the newly completed Centre Street Bridge. The Eau Claire area beyond is still residential, as it would remain for thirty years. Small houses on 25-foot lots, as shown at left in southeast Calgary, would long be the 'working class' standard. On the opposite page, two shots of Stephens Avenue (Eighth) illustrate the economic halt. Except for the departure of horse-drawn vehicles, the scene scarcely changes between 1920 (above) near the peak of the boom, and 1912 (below). The same would be true for the next three decades, until the oil boom would initiate a new surge.

[3]Toole Pete & Company handled the development of Mount Royal and succeeded in enforcing a building code, making it Calgary's first exclusively luxury subdivision, with residents guarding its building code through the Mount Royal Improvement Association.

[4]The Coste house (2208 Amherst St.) would remain for the century as one of Calgary's most luxurious private residences.

[5]Both the Hudson's Bay store and the Canada Life Building would survive for the century.

[6]Press beds, or in-a-door beds, were constructed to fold up and fit against the wall behind cupboard doors. They are referred to in print as early as 1755. In North America they became known as 'murphy beds' after those manufactured by the Murphy Door Bed Co. of San Francisco, established in 1909.

[7]Calgary was expected to become an electric railway centre when a group of investors announced plans to build a new line extending from Banff to Medicine Hat with a network of connecting lines to Lethbridge, Macleod and Montana. The Alberta Electric Railway Company went so far as to seek incorporation. It changed its name in 1911 to the Alberta Interurban Railway Company, but the dream crashed with the end of the boom in 1914.

finished with bronze. An electric elevator, furnished with leather seats, was of "the best grilled polished antique open design," according to its builder. Ceramic tile was "laid in the best manner, neat and workmanlike and first class in all respects."

A glass dome fifteen feet in diameter crowned the building, providing a halo of natural light inside. So rarefied was the atmosphere that people spoke in hushed tones upon entering. Visitors and workers alike were forbidden to smoke cigars, reported the *Calgary News-Telegram*. "Neither must they chew tobacco. If they do, the action will have to be concealed so that the movement of the facial muscles may not be detected. Also, they will have to swallow the juice."

Glenbow Archives, NA-2399-181

Preparing to lay watermains during the city's big boom is this crew, posed with their Waterworks Department truck (at right). City water service was extended to 2,000 new homes in the outlying areas during the boom period.

Trolleys were profitable — but accidents did happen

City and transit dignitaries pose in 1911 (below) with the first streetcar to cover the Crescent Heights route. The system made a $31,000 profit in its first year. At right, trolleys pass on First Street West. On the opposite page a less happy occasion is depicted. In December 1919, this car skidded out of control down icy 14th Street Hill and crashed disastrously into a drugstore.

A handsome imported clock adorned the seventy-foot tower at the front of the building. It cost $3,657 and ran a few minutes slow. In a final burst of exuberant affluence, more than 200 palm trees were imported from the tropics and planted on the grounds. Only one survived the first couple of winters, and it was moved indoors, where it clung to life for two more decades.

The entire extravaganza cost taxpayers over $300,000, twice the original estimate, and helped send the tax rate soaring by 14.5 mills. Landowners felt they were being taxed to death; Senator James Lougheed said the assessment on his vast property holdings had increased over 100% since 1910. Sheriff Isaac S.G. Van Wart complained that even his horse and buggies had been taxed. "My children seem to be the only articles about the house immune from taxation," he noted.

Unsurprisingly, municipal politicians became targets for all manner of criticism, and aldermen were often showered with verbal abuse. When some council members were discovered riding the streetcars free, a fury ensued. Mitchell, a dry goods and later lumber dealer, who was elected alderman in 1905 and mayor in 1910 at the age of 38, had promised to hold the line on spending. But the city found itself $2.5 million in debt at the end of his tumultuous two-year regime. Moreover, petty squabbles and

Thousands of workers were attracted to Calgary, like this crew (at left) photographed during construction of the public library, circa 1911. The Glenbow has identities for only three: Peter Mooney, second from left, back row; John Hardie, seventh from left, centre row; and Robert McGregor, second from left, front row.

101

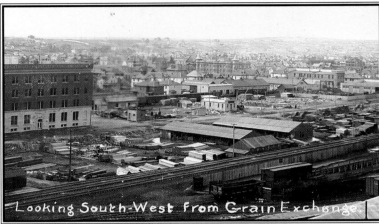

Calgary as the boom began. This series of photos was taken in 1910 by the Progress Photo Company from the Grain Exchange Building at 815 - First Street W., for a city booster pamphlet. Three years later many of these scenes would have changed dramatically after the city went through its astonishing surge of growth.

8Sinnott's bid to clamp down on municipal spending forced a group of Calgarians to abandon plans for a city zoo. Since no appropriation was made for the construction of cages, most of the animals in its collection, including a bear and a coyote, were shot.

9The Centre Street Bridge, completed in 1917, would remain an architectural showpiece for the century. An enormous cut had to be made through the river's bank to accommodate the northern approach to the 1,300-foot upper deck. A lower deck took traffic to and from Memorial Boulevard at river level. Kiosks at the north and south approaches, with the rose of England, the thistle of Scotland, the shamrock of Ireland and the maple leaf of Canada, symbolized the British connection. Thirteen-foot concrete lions topped the kiosks. The bridge was designed by engineers G.W. Craig, J. Bernard Richards and Lt. Frank Lawson, who was killed in action in 1916.

bickering had plagued his administration. Fistfights were not unheard of inside city hall. On one occasion a building inspector named Harrison landed a series of well-aimed punches on Alderman A.J. Samis, in full view of the mayor. As a matter of fact, reported the *Herald,* Mitchell was "standing up, taking a very lively interest in the one-sided match." After Harrison had delivered his final blow, he ran out the door. Samis, meanwhile, "abandoned his crouching pose and looked up smiling. 'Never touched me,' he said."

Samis had had this trouble before. In 1911, running for alderman, he was attacked by a taxpayer named Conrad Pohl. Samis accused him of tearing down his posters. Infuriated, Pohl grabbed Samis and punched him twice about the head. Pohl later claimed Samis had hit him first.

By 1912, Mitchell was under pressure to resign. "He has allowed city hall to run itself until it is in a horrible jungle of disorganization," the *Albertan* editorialized. "His time is up." Apparently Mitchell agreed; he resigned. His successor, Herbert Sinnott, promised to make city hall more accountable to taxpayers by offering a series of spending plebiscites[8]. The citizenry, as it turned out, were just as spendthrift as the aldermen. In 1913, Calgarians voted to build a stockyard, a tubercular hospital, and a $100,000 bridge over the Bow on Centre Street, which was intended to spur development of the new luxury neighbourhood of Tuxedo Park. It didn't work, however, and Calgary north of the Bow throughout the century never did embrace a district to rival those south of the river. The ratepayers defeated proposals for five more river crossings[9], and a plan to increase the number of commissioners was likewise soundly defeated.

Sinnott's efforts at frugality assuaged the critics only briefly. Then came the Minchin Affair. Charles Henry Minchin, a former alderman, assistant city treasurer, and candidate for commissioner, was charged with embezzling $5,000 in civic funds by doctoring the books with a penknife and some glue. At his trial the shortcomings in the city's fiscal management became painfully evident. No one seemed to keep track of revenues and expenses. When one department faced a shortfall, money was simply taken out of another. It took the jury just 25 minutes to render a

guilty verdict. "I do not think," said Mr. Justice William Walsh, "that any language of mine can be too strong as to the disgraceful state of affairs in the city hall which the evidence shows existed." Minchin was sentenced to a five-year term in the Edmonton penitentiary.

Minchin, however, was no more than a symptom of the boom, a time when Calgary became home to what historian James Gray calls a motley assortment of "con-men, pickpockets, pimps, and other vermin preying on incoming immigrants and visiting settlers." The city jail was a frightening, overcrowded corner of the old municipal building on Drinkwater Street (Second St. S.E.), a ramshackle frame firetrap erected in 1887. However, the prospect of a few nights there didn't seem to deter the criminally inclined, who knew that the city's 26-man police force was largely occupied chasing drunks down back alleys.

Calgary's police chief at the peak of the boom was aging Thomas English, whose eye to certain criminal activity seemed blind, particularly to prostitution, a business that flourished on many downtown street corners. As Judy Bedford notes in a 1981 article in *Alberta History* entitled *Prostitution in Calgary, 1910-1914*, it "was not a city which provided much opportunity for the employment of women." Most of the city's hookers were American immigrants, many of them black, she says, followed closely by women from central Canada and a few from Britain. The majority listed their occupations as either housekeepers or domestics.

Every night, lonely tradesmen and construction workers loped off to the Nose Creek bordellos, pay cheques in hand and songs on their lips. "We could hear them coming a mile away," said one neighbouring resident. "I can remember how mad my father used to get. 'We'll get no sleep tonight, I can promise you that!' he used to say as we went to bed." But none of this troubled Chief English. "There may be houses of prostitution in Calgary," he once said, "but I do not know of them."

Pressure from the Prohibition movement eventually forced English's retirement after eighteen years as chief. His successor was Thomas Mackie, a grim-faced Scot who had worked under English for almost a decade. Riding the wave of reform, he was able to considerably expand the size of the force. His men, however, disliked him intensely. Mackie was a stern disciplinarian, and determined to rid the department of its slovenly reputation. In March 1910 he charged five of his officers with various offences, including public drunkenness and "failing to report promptly to the chief of police." Two months later the *Herald* disclosed that a revolt was brewing against him. "The

The new city hall is decked with flags, possibly in preparation for its official opening. With brass bands and before a crowd of 3,000, Conservative leader Robert L. Borden opened the building in June 1911, shortly before he became prime minister.

A renowned planner blueprints Paris on the Bow

APPALLED BY CALGARY'S WEEDY CHAOS, THOMAS H. MAWSON WAS HIRED TO DO THINGS RIGHT, BUT HAD TROUBLE EVEN COLLECTING HIS FEE

So consumed with the urge to build were Calgarians that the face of their city kept changing, not always for the better. No coherent strategy directed the growth; scarcely any zoning laws controlled it. Ten-storey "skyscrapers" competed for downtown space with modest wood-frame houses. Factories sprouted in the middle of new residential subdivisions. Lumber yards and garbage dumps cluttered the banks of the Bow and Elbow rivers. By 1911, writes historian Max Foran,

This would have been Calgary as conceived by Thomas Mawson, who was no fly-by-night flake but a widely recognized city planner.

Glenbow Archives, NA-2018-2

Calgary looked "as wild as the dandelions, lamb's quarter and fireweed which adorned the few city parks."

Most residents were too busy to notice any of this until a flamboyant landscape architect from England stepped off the train in 1912. Thomas Mawson saw opportunity the moment he arrived. He bluntly informed Calgarians that their city was headed for disaster. He did not share the local view of "Calgary the Phenomenal." Rather, he saw a place overwhelmed by its sudden prosperity, and utterly lacking in intelligent design.

The people in charge of managing the city's expansion were obviously incompetent, he declared. "You expect men who have no claim either temperamentally or scholastically to be regarded as artists to interpret Nature, and give you a beautiful composition," he told the city's Canadian Club. If something wasn't done, visitors would soon come to view Calgary as a blight upon the beautiful prairie soil. Edmonton had a plan, he taunted. Why not Calgary?

Such a denunciation from Thomas H. Mawson could not be lightly dismissed. Born in 1861, he was a landscape architect and town planner of wide recognition, who maintained offices in Lancaster (his home) and in London, Vancouver

and New York. He had been commissioned to design a number of private gardens in England, Scotland and Wales, and he made speeches across Canada and in the United States on the need for civic planning. In Canada he would work on plans for the University of British Columbia campus in Vancouver, draw up a design for a new bridge at Banff, and formulate a comprehensive design for the city of Regina.

His apocalyptic forecast sent the city's dormant planning commission into action. Made up of fifty prominent citizens, including, not by accident, a large proportion of real estate agents and building contractors, the commission set about raising funds to invest in a comprehensive report on Calgary's "present and future needs." The call went out for an "expert town planner" and dozens of applications came pouring in from all over North America. But there was never any doubt who would get the job. Thomas Mawson had promised, given a few months, that he could turn the city into a gleaming monument to prosperity, civility, and order.

In January 1913 the planning commission recommended the city hire Mawson. Council agreed, setting his salary at $6,000. Mawson expressed some disappointment at the figure, saying he needed $25,000 to create a proper model. But he took the job anyway, perhaps thinking he could reap bigger rewards if his report was implemented, and spent the next fifteen months designing the "new" city of Calgary.

No one seemed prepared for the final product. Mawson's

vision of the future looked suspiciously like something from the past, the distant past — ancient Greece, to be precise. "Calgary: A Preliminary Scheme for Controlling the Economic Growth of the City" seemed to many like a work of whimsy, complete with grand diagonal roadways leading into sweeping public squares, boulevards festooned with sparkling marble fountains, and a magnificent downtown marketplace surrounded by row upon row of perfectly uniform office buildings.

Mawson decided the working class should be moved into industrial-style row houses, nestled in compact "garden suburbs" a stone's throw from the factories. Wealthier Calgarians would live closer to the centre, in symmetrical apartment blocks, thus putting an end to that vulgar North American obsession with separate lots. Mawson wanted to make even more changes to the landscape, but noted that "since so much is already fixed and unalterable in your city, an ideal lay-out is quite impossible."

Reaction to the plan was mixed. The *Albertan* declared that "if followed, Calgary would be the most beautiful inland city in all Canada." The principal of Mount Royal College, George Kerby, said the report was "one of the best investments the city has ever made," and that steps should be taken to implement its recommendations. Others called it an extravagant piece of nonsense. Commissioner Arthur Graves said it would cost the city at least $8 million to follow Mawson's advice, an impossible expenditure considering Calgary was already $2.1 million in debt.

Meanwhile Mawson was having financial troubles of his own. The onset of war had virtually eliminated the demand for town planning back home in England, so he was desperate for Calgary to adopt his project. He told the commission it would be "suicidal" not to carry

Calgary's ornate civic centre (above) according to the Mawson design. The photo below shows Thomas H. Mawson at right and his son E. Prentice Mawson (left) at their head office in Lancaster, England.

things forward. "This is how Paris has been made so beautiful," he argued, "and there is no doubt Calgary can do it too." Commission members should use their "influence with the local press" to muster public support, he exhorted. "Is this scheme merely a paper one made for the purpose of gaining a little cheap publicity? Or are [Calgarians] really enlightened above their fellows? And are they determined to put a stop to haphazard and selfish lines of development and really and truly grapple with the problems which confront them if they are to break away from the universal grid-iron system of planning, and arrange their roads, their streets, and their open spaces on intelligent and up-to-date lines?"

But the city was so cash-strapped it couldn't even manage to pay Mawson his fee on time. The publishing company that printed 1,000 hardcover copies of the plan was also forced to wait for payment. "Things could not possibly have turned out worse for us," explained the planning commission's treasurer. "The report reached us when the full weight of the financial depression was upon us and this has been greatly accentuated by the war." Three months later the planning commission disbanded, and the Mawson Plan became just a curious reminder of boom-town notions.

Although neither his Calgary nor Regina design was acted upon, many years later the Saskatchewan capital would incorporate some of Mawson's Regina proposals into its Wascana Centre. The firm of Thomas H. Mawson & Sons (he had four sons, as well as four daughters) maintained its base in Lancaster, the county town of Lancashire. Mawson died in 1933.

— *B.H.*

But instead of striking, the disgruntled force simply began to defy the chief's orders. When one sergeant was discovered cavorting in a brothel, Mackie realized that ordinary measures wouldn't win the battle against prostitution. So he hired a private detective to infiltrate the most notorious district, Nose Creek. This, too, failed. The women invariably discovered when Mackie's agent was bound for Nose Creek, and chased their clients away. When a brothel was shut down, the permanent residents moved across the Bow River to another stroll, known as South Coulee. Soon a citizens' movement was being organized against Mackie, led, of course, by retired chief English. In 1912 Mackie resigned in disgust. He wanted "to live in peace," he said, and the search began for his replacement. It ended in Toronto, where a crack crime-fighter named Alfred Cuddy was rounding out a remarkable career.

"Cuddy Unravelled Many Mysteries — Nearly Killed by Desperadoes," recounted the *Albertan* after the appointment of the celebrated inspector was announced, further describing him as a top-notch manhunter and "the handsomest officer" on the Toronto force. After his appointment, Chief Cuddy increased the department to 100 men and moved it into new headquarters, with a sixteen-cell jail that could accommodate, if pressed, as many as sixty prisoners.

[10]Cuddy endorsed the contention of Bob Edwards, publisher of the *Eye-Opener*, that if beer were five cents a glass instead of fifteen, 'the dinner pail man would take more of his money home to his family.' Since whiskey was also fifteen cents, the customers preferred it and became much drunker.

Calgary's first attempt to found a university comes to a sad end

WAR AND POLITICS FOIL THE EFFORT TO MATCH THE U OF A IN THE SOUTH

Calgarians were still livid with their Edmonton rivals for having (as they saw it) stolen both the provincial capital and the provincial university (Vol. II, Sec. 1, ch. 4). They could do nothing about the first outrage, the capital. It would take a civil war to dislodge the northern city as the political centre. Calgary would have to be content with its status as Alberta's financial hub. About the second, however, a remedy was definitely possible. Whatever the obstacles, Calgary must have its own university.

Dr. Thomas Blow, a Calgary physician and booster extraordinaire, started the campaign with the slogan, "Give Me Land and I'll Build a University." W.J. Tregillus, a cattleman and owner of a clayworks, responded by donating 160 acres on the city's western flank, near the Bow River[a]. He even managed to persuade his neighbours to join in, and Blow ended up with a 480-acre site. In 1910 Calgary council voted unanimously to give $150,000 to the proposed institution, and almost a million dollars was raised privately.

There were, of course, some nay-sayers. "The people of Calgary are prepared to spend thousands of dollars just for the satisfaction of delivering a hard blow at us," complained an Edmonton editorialist. Even in Calgary some pointed out that British Columbia, which had had provincial status for

more than 35 years, still lacked a university.[b] Alberta was now proposing to have two. All this pessimism, however, was waved aside, and by the summer of 1910, Dr. Blow was ready to proceed and classes were scheduled for that fall. He reported he had 25 students lined up, and was working on a curriculum. There remained a single hurdle: the school needed legislative authority to grant degrees and compete head-on with the capital city's University of Alberta. How could this be extracted from a Liberal government dominated by Edmontonians?

Dr. T.H. Blow

Opposition leader R.B. Bennett introduced a draft bill to the assembly in December 1910. Alexander Cameron Rutherford, the first premier and founder of the U of A, had

He then flew into action against crime. Three months into his regime he had uncovered drug dens, gambling joints, and a host of "blind pigs" where booze was sold illegally. The biggest bust came in April 1912, when Cuddy raided Chinatown's notorious Canton Block. Nine pounds of opium and 22 cases of illegal spirits were discovered, "ranging from the exquisite liqueurs of sunny France to the unintelligible labelled concoctions of China". Forty-four Chinese were arrested. "The police state that this is only one of a series of raids in pursuance to the design of the new chief to clean the city up," reported the *Albertan*[10].

In October Cuddy swooped down on the South Coulee bordellos, arresting 56 prostitutes. Like his predecessors, however, he failed to solve this problem. As Judy Bedford notes, the

Students enjoy the spring weather at St. Hilda's College in 1912. The school, at 12th Avenue and Eighth Street, survived the Great Depression and two world wars, then folded in 1947.

by now been driven from office, a plus for the bill, but it nevertheless became rapidly clear Bennett's proposal was going nowhere. So he struck the word "university" from the motion, making the "Calgary University Bill" into the "Calgary College Bill." Much to his constituents' dismay, he even removed all reference to degree-conferring powers. The bill was defeated regardless. The official explanation was that the province could not afford to fund another post-sec-

appointed dean and acting president. Dr. Blow was chairman.

One more attempt to win degree-conferring status was launched in 1913. Again the bill was defeated. This time, the chief opponent was John Boyle, a Liberal member from Sturgeon near Edmonton. Alexandra's Alwyn Bramley-Moore also opposed the bill. The college should quit putting "University of Calgary" on its letterhead, he said. "Probably many of the students were secured under false pretences."

There remained a single hurdle: the school needed legislative authority to grant degrees and compete head-on with the capital city's University of Alberta. How could this be extracted from a Liberal government dominated by Edmontonians?

ondary institution, though Blow had assured the legislators that his school would be self-sustaining.

The proposal was advanced again at the 1911 session and the 1912 with the same result. The resistance was no mystery to Bob Edwards of the Calgary *Eye Opener*. Premier Arthur Sifton "has passed most of his adult life in Calgary," wrote Edwards, but "he sees that there is no longer any chance of a Liberal being returned in Calgary and has decided to cast his lot with the Edmonton bunch."

Dr. Blow pressed on undeterred. Using private funds, including a $25,000 gift from Lord Strathcona, he opened his college in October 1912 with 160 students. It would not be able to grant degrees, but everyone called it the University of Calgary anyway. Operating out of the Central Park public library, it offered courses in English, history, politics, law, chemistry, physics and mathematics. The following year, enrolment jumped to 168, and philosophy, classics, and economics were added. Frank Macdougall, a graduate of Queen's University and the University of Leipzig, was

By 1914, the college was showing signs of distress. Enrolment went down, thanks chiefly to the war. Blow was forced to sell some of the property, at bargain prices. Taxpayers were forced to pick up the wages for six professors. In 1915, a federal commission on higher education concluded there was absolutely no need for another university in Alberta. Blow finally gave up hope, and the college shut its doors at the end of the spring term, 1915. A technical institute was established a year later, but the U of A remained the only degree-granting institution in Alberta until the University of Calgary came into being in 1966.

— *B.H.*

[a]William John Tregillus moved to Alberta in 1902 and ranched on the western edge of Calgary. Born in England in 1859, he had been a flour miller and importer in Southampton before heading to Canada. He was vice-president of the United Farmers of Alberta, chairman of the West Calgary School Board, and president of the Direct Legislation League. The property was the NE quarter of Section 14 in Township 24, Range 2, an area later known as Strathcona Park.

[b]UBC was chartered in 1908, but did not begin operations until 1915.

When the Burns plant burned the fire raged for two days

The blaze that broke out in a wooden warehouse at the Burns plant on a January night in 1913 was Calgary's worst yet, entirely destroying the plant. Pat Burns' vast plans to replace it with a whole new city to be known as 'Burnstown' that would rival Calgary itself were demolished by the outbreak of the Great War the following year. Photographs at right and below show the ferocity of the blaze. The fire department, whose equipment is on proud display above, could only keep it from spreading to the rest of the city.

THE NEW CITIES

Once a fire got started, the best hope was to save the adjoining buildings

Until fire-fighting equipment and construction standards improved, the fire menace was a ubiquitous one. Wooden structures like the Sherman Roller Rink at 17th Avenue and Centre Street, used for many other activities including dance classes and concerts, were usually doomed. It burned spectacularly in 1915 (above). The brick Empire Hotel, gutted in 1920 (lower left), fared little better. And there was no saving frame tenements like those at left, home of scores of Calgary Chinese, in October 1912.

Reform mayor Herbert Sinnott (centre) poses in his shirt sleeves with other senior city officials for this publicity photo emphasizing his determination to cut back on city spending. Sinnott tried to do this by giving ratepayers a vote on major city projects, but the boom-minded ratepayers proved as spendthrift as the city council. Left to right: city engineer G.W. Craig, commissioner A.J. Samis, Mayor Sinnott, commissioner Arthur G. Graves, and Andrew Melon, the city's advertising agent. Samis, when an alderman, had been engaged in at least one city hall fistfight.

11 The Queen's was not exactly on Ninth Avenue's Whiskey Row. It stood on the south side of Eighth Avenue between Second and Third Streets, probably backing on Ninth.

The Bow ran high enough in 1914 that it threatened to swamp the bridge to St. George's Island, but not high enough to frighten away these curious spectators.

business continued to flourish in massage parlours, Turkish baths, and even restaurants. The Queen's Hotel accommodated several of these women and was considered one of the finer establishments on Whiskey Row[11], at least until an explosion blew it apart in December 1912. At four o'clock in the morning George Burke, a hotel porter, and Glenn Merrill, a bellboy, were in the basement looking for a ladder. The room was dark, so they lit a match, unaware of an insidious gas leak.

The ensuing blast was heard for half a mile. The two hotel workers were hurled across the room and Merrill was knocked unconscious. Burke managed to escape through an opening and ran outside, screaming with pain, his clothes on fire. A bystander tackled him on the street and tore the burning clothes from his body. Merrill came to and staggered upstairs, engulfed in flames. An alert night clerk grabbed a fire extinguisher and doused his colleague.

Police Chief Thomas Mackie (at right) retired in disgust in 1912 after his efforts to clean up the department resulted in a general rebellion in the force. His much-heralded successor Alfred Cuddy (below), launched an all-out crackdown on booze, gambling and prostitution. Above, five members of the mounted patrol pose for the camera.

The guests meanwhile were in a state of panic, running outside into the snow wearing nightclothes or wrapped in blankets, some under the impression there had been an earthquake. No one was killed, and the fire department responded quickly and managed to harness the blaze. Damage to the building was extensive, however, estimated between $5,000 and $10,000; the rear wall had collapsed and several rooms were destroyed. Although the hotel was restored, it never regained its former distinction.

A month later, the worst fire in the city's history to that time claimed the big Burns meat-packing plant in east Calgary[12]. It too started in a basement, but the cause was never discovered. A nightwatchman found flames in the cellar of the plant's old wooden warehouse and sounded the alarm. Trucks from Stations 1 and 3 were dispatched, but most hydrants in the area were frozen and the ten-inch main alongside the plant provided only a trickle of water. Although the department's new Webb motor pump, working furiously, sucked water out of the Bow River, the fire spread quickly, moving over to the stockyards and cold storage building. It was obvious that more help was needed, so a general alarm was sounded and every piece of equipment in the city converged on the scene.

The Burns fire raged almost two days, while hundreds of Calgarians, including most of the plant's 300 workers, watched the disaster unfold. Between 12,000 and 14,000 animal carcasses were destroyed, and losses were estimated at $2 million.

Owner Patrick Burns was in Toronto. But instead of cursing his misfortune, he saw only an opportunity; by the time he arrived home, he had already hatched a plan. Insurance would cover most of the damages, of course, and a new plant would go up on the old site. Then he would build an entire city around it, populated by eager new immigrants and dotted with factories. No one doubted he would succeed. After all, Burns had started out with almost nothing and had built up Canada's largest meat-packing operation (Vol. 2, p. 264). The *Albertan* even predicted that the new community of "Burnstown" would rival Calgary itself.

By the summer of 1913, the new plant was taking shape. Yet there was no more talk of endless growth and instant cities. Europe was in turmoil, and immigration slowed to a trickle. Grand schemes like Burnstown were put on hold or forgotten. The boom had turned, almost overnight, into a bust that halted growth across the West. However Calgary was spared most of its depredations because of something that occurred the very next spring at a place called Turner Valley.

[12]The original Burns plant lay west of the Canadian Pacific tracks in what would later be known as Inglewood. It was rebuilt at 21st Avenue and Ogden Road and torn down in 1986.

THE NEW CITIES

*Eighty thousand spectators watched the 1912 Stampede parade (at left); the native contingent was already its most spectacular feature. Above, some of the Stampede's early backers are caught in a 1912 photograph in the Glenbow collection.**

A great idea paid off and the Stampede was born

'YOU'RE TWO YEARS TOO SOON,' THE CPR AGENT TOLD GUY WEADICK;
HE WAS BACK IN THREE, AND CALGARY'S 'BIG FOUR' RISKED $100,000

The boom may have transformed Calgary from a dusty prairie outpost to a centre of commerce and industry, but the city clung fast to its cowboy roots. Livestock exhibits still drew big crowds, and people flocked to see the Wild West pageants that swung through town every year with their staged cowboy-and-Indian shootouts. But the greatest of spectacles was the Stampede, a week-long extravaganza that did more than merely entertain the masses. It put Calgary on the map.

* Among those present are the famed Big Four — Burns, Cross, Lane and McLean — whose guarantee against losses made the event possible. From left to right are: White Headed Chief, an unidentified cigar smoker, a Mr. Galbraith who was a friend of rancher George Lane, RNWMP Inspector James Spalding, George Lane, a man unidentified peering over Lane's shoulder, Mrs. Charlie Russell, Medicine Hat lawyer G.M. Blackstock (in bow tie), Provincial Secretary (and Big Four member) Hon. Archie McLean, Alex Newton, Pat Burns, Montana artist Charlie Russell, an unidentified man, A.E. Cross, another unidentified man, and Edward Borein, an American artist who illustrated the Stampede's promotional literature.

In 1908 an American trick roper named Guy Weadick whistled into town with the Miller Brothers' 101 Ranch Show. The crowd's overwhelming response to his equestrian circus act got Weadick thinking. Why not give them the real thing, a frontier celebration featuring genuine cowboys and herds of savage, snorting livestock? He ran his scheme past Harry McMullen, the general livestock agent with the Canadian Pacific. "It's a fine idea," McMullen told him, "only two years too soon."

In fact, McMullen waited three years before sending for Weadick. The summons came while the lanky entertainer was touring the vaudeville halls of Europe with his wife, a trick rider professionally known as Flores LaDue. Four months later, Weadick arrived in Calgary. With McMullen's help he tried to drum up financial support for his venture.

At first the pair found little interest. Calgary already hosted Alberta's biggest exhibition every summer. But in

March 1912 Weadick managed to convince a group of cattlemen that he could recreate the old pioneer days, "devoid of circus tinsel and far-fetched fiction." Not only that, the show would attract visitors and generate publicity from around the continent, even beyond. George Lane, Pat Burns, A.E. Cross and Archie McLean — the "Big Four" — agreed to guarantee up to $100,000 against losses, with one condition: "Make it the greatest thing of its kind in the world."

The Stampede was to run seven days, beginning Labour Day, and offer the usual exhibition fare: trick roping, fancy riding, historical exhibits, and an Indian village. But the main feature would be rodeo, a new sport that was attracting thousands of fans across the West. A few years earlier, someone had the idea of transforming workaday ranch jobs like horse breaking and steer wrestling into breakneck duels between man and beast. Soon folks all over cattle country were paying for the privilege of watching wiry cowboys risk their lives taming wild animals. The possibility of serious injury, even death, was part of the appeal.

Stampede promoter Guy Weadick and his wife, performer Flores LaDue, in a photo taken about the time of the 1912 Stampede. When the Calgary Exhibition and Stampede was created in 1923, Weadick became manager.

Working out of his cramped headquarters on Eighth Avenue, Weadick set about organizing the Stampede. With $20,000 to offer in prize money he had no trouble lining up the best rodeo cowboys on the continent, from Cardston to Cheyenne. A.P. Day, the arena director, supplied the horses, 300 of the meanest bucking broncs around, while Gordon, Ironside & Fares promised to round up 200 Mexican longhorns for the roping and steer-wrestling events.

John McDougall played an important, if controversial, role in the first Stampede. The Methodist missionary delivered 2,000 Indians for the opening day parade, and was paid $390 for the service. But some didn't like the idea of bringing "savages" to the fairgrounds.

McDougall assured the critics that the Indians would be well behaved, however, and would lend colour to the event. In fact, they were the highlight of that first Stampede, which opened on Labour Day 1912. Eighty thousand people watched in fascination as the "savages" led the inaugural parade down Eighth Avenue. "The Crees, Blackfeet, Bloods, Stonies, Sarcees and Peigans were all out in full strength, donned in their finest regalia and paint," reported the *Calgary Herald*. "They reflected great credit on their race."

Two days later the governor-general, the Duke of Connaught, arrived in Calgary with the duchess and their daughter, Princess Patricia. They were captivated by the Indians, even stopping by their village during a tour of the grounds and taking photographs.

Tom Three Persons, a young Blood from Cardston, stole the spotlight in the rodeo arena too, winning the bronc-busting competition with a spectacular ride on a rank black horse called Cyclone. It was the first time the animal had been successfully ridden in 129 attempts.[a]

Three Persons' performance "was a marvel of horsemanship, the crowning of the Stampede," wrote the *Lethbridge Herald*. "Cyclone bucked viciously, and resorted to all his vicious tricks, including the most dangerous one of rearing up straight, twisting his body and then jumping sideways.

Tom having mastered Cyclone came before the Royal Box on his own horse," doffed his hat and bowed. He was $1,000 richer, and won a $500 saddle and a gold-mounted championship belt.

The Stampede too was a resounding success, "undoubtedly the very biggest public stunt ever undertaken in this country," proclaimed the *Eye Opener*. Heavy rains couldn't dampen the enthusiasm; in four days almost 100,000 people passed through the gates. The Big Four netted a small profit and donated this windfall to charity. But plans to hold a sequel in 1915 were shelved when war broke out in Europe, so the Weadicks returned to the vaudeville circuit.

Other towns tried to copy Calgary's magic formula, much to the chagrin of the agricultural exhibitors, who suspected that fair-goers would rather watch rodeo than examine their prize-winning wheat. When Raymond added a rodeo to its annual fair in 1915, "the sports, bucking, roping and racing were so good that the people had little time to look at the exhibits," said a Department of Agriculture report. The Big Gap Stampede attracted 25,000 people to the Neutral Hills of eastern Alberta[b]. "Warring Indian tribes and vast herds of buffalo" complemented the action in the rodeo arena.

In 1919, with the war over, the Big Four invited Weadick back to Calgary, and he set about organizing a "Victory Stampede." Though not nearly as successful as the inaugural one, attracting only 57,000 spectators, it at least broke even. The Big Four became more determined than ever to supplant Calgary's annual agricultural exhibition, which was losing money yearly by the end of the decade. In 1923 the Stampede idea was added to the exhibition to form the annual Calgary Exhibition and Stampede,

and Weadick was named manager. Nine years later he retired to his High River spread, having succeeded in creating a "true replica of the days that were." Some people think he even fulfilled his other promise, to build "the greatest outdoor show on earth."

— *B.H.*

[a]The *Albertan* made the story even more remarkable by reporting that the rider had spent the previous week in jail for whiskey trading and that a magistrate in Macleod took pity on the accused and allowed a wealthy cattleman to bail him out in time for the Stampede. It turned out, however, that the reporter had invented the story and the paper had to print an apology and retraction.

[b]The 'Big Gap' is a natural amphitheatre located in the Neutral Hills, about eight miles east and 20 miles north of Consort. A native legend attaches to the name. The Great Spirit, wearied by the constant warfare between the Blackfoot and the Crees, one night caused the Neutral Hills to spring up between them. The warriors on both sides were awestruck when they beheld the hills in the morning, and realized their fighting had displeased the Great Spirit. Spotting the gap, they met there and smoked the peace pipe.

The 1912 Stampede triggered many imitators, like the one at Big Gap, a natural amphitheatre in the Neutral Hills, which one year attracted 25,000 people.

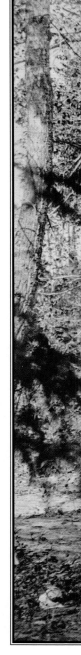

CHAPTER TWO

In the bust the smallest city took the hardest hit

WITH THE USUAL HEEDLESS OPTIMISM RED DEER GAINED CITY STATUS, BUT SOON THE BANK CUT THEM OFF AND PAYROLLS COULDN'T BE MET

by STEPHANI KEER

Red Deer became the sixth city in Alberta on March 25, 1913. Clearly the residents feared nothing ominous in the number thirteen. However, if they could have foreseen what the next six years were to bring they might have been more superstitious. No city in the province would suffer so dramatically from the recession that came with the onset of the Great War as did Red Deer. None would come closer to bankruptcy or to total collapse.

In terms of population Red Deer was being presumptuous in calling itself a city at all. In 1911 it boasted 2,118 residents, not even 1% of the total population of the province, recorded as 374,663 in the 1911 census. By 1921 Red Deer's population would rise by 210 people to 2,328, and that was only four-tenths of 1% of the province. This decline in its relative standing would continue until the Second World War[1].

In the boundless optimism of 1911 Alberta, however, limitless growth and therefore city status seemed irrefutable. The lumber business was booming, homesteaders and new railways were arriving, automobiles were coming in such numbers the town imposed a ten-mile-an-hour speed limit. The *Red Deer Advocate* abounded in stories of new companies, schools, railway stations, bridges, roads, churches, even new concrete sidewalks. Even the Calgary *Albertan* had rhapsodized for four full pages on Red Deer's economy, natural beauty and cultural advantages. The *Edmonton Bulletin* had called Red Deer's development "unequalled in the West." How much reassurance could you ask?

There was more. In 1912 the town celebrated the greatest building year in its history. Building permits for the first ten months hit $355,000, up more than $100,000 over 1911, another banner year. Publicity commissioner J.R. Davison listed the town's businesses: Manufacturers — clay products, coal development, flour and cereals, foundry, boots and shoes, harness, gauntlets, robes, coats, pulp and paper, boxes and caskets, shirts and overalls, stone quarries, biscuits and confectionery. Wholesale — groceries, dry goods, hardware, fruits, produce, machinery, pumps, seeds, books, paper, rubber goods.

Then too there were more exotic things: a gold strike in 1912 in the Red Deer River valley in which 72 claims were filed. Only three made money, true enough, but the hope was still there. That same year, 1913, oil was reported found near Content (about 35 miles northeast of Red Deer) and 200 oil claims were filed. And the city publicity commissioner produced a promotion pamphlet that even the bullish council couldn't swallow. It depicted Red Deer as about to build a street railway and ready to welcome a fourth railway, the Grand Trunk Pacific, into town, neither of which was true, and confident of a population of 25,000, twelve times its level at the time.

In other ways, however, the city's booster advertising made a curious aesthetic appeal, at least sixty years ahead of its time. Red Deer was portrayed as "the prettiest town in Alberta...a place of homes, a highly desirable city in which to live." It is "the educational centre of Alberta, not because of its numbers but because of the high intelligence of its citizenship." One ad stresses the

[1] In the year of Red Deer's incorporation as a city, Medicine Hat's population stood at 15,000, making it the third city behind Calgary and Edmonton and seven times as big as Red Deer. Lethbridge, at just over 10,000, was the fourth city, and nearly five times as big as Red Deer. The new city did not include the village of North Red Deer, which would not join it until 1947. The fifth was Wetaskiwin, incorporated as a city May 9, 1906, whose population in 1911 was 2,411. Strathcona had become a city in 1907, but merged with Edmonton in 1912. This made Red Deer the sixth city.

"variety, quality, selection, delivery, personal touch, convenience, price and value" in buying a Red Deer home. It continues: "The personal relationship, the mutual interests of the community of buyer and seller, give to home trading a responsibility and value which is lost when the citizen ignores these mutual relations and for an occasional bargain breaks the tie of community promotion." Another ad concludes:

> Today Red Deer is the fifth city in Alberta,
> Red Deer will hold her position.
> Red Deer is safe, sound and healthy.
> Red Deer is good.

Yet even as city status was proclaimed there crept into the city's promotion material an unusual note of concern: "Despite the stringency in finance in some lines, Red Deer never had so

Red Deer boosterism emphasized lifestyle aesthetics sixty years before such claims became fashionable. It was 'a highly desirable city in which to live,' said the ads. Residents were honest, highly intelligent and community-minded, and Red Deer was, moreover, 'the prettiest town in Alberta.' High among municipal amenities was Gaetz Park, where some of the citizens are depicted above, on a leisurely drive in 1912.

Ode to Red Deer

The optimism of Red Deer in 1912 is shown no more clearly than in a poem that ran in the *Red Deer Advocate* of May 24 of that year. Entitled "Bonnie Red Deer" and signed only "A.M., Red Deer, May 15, 1912," it reads:

Oh Red Deer, dear Red Deer, thou hast stood the test
Among the new towns in the flourishing West,
Hard times they have pressed you, but you held your own,
Now one of the finest in Alberta has grown.

Your streets are remodelled, your sidewalks cement,
Giving pleasure and comfort, showing money well spent;
Your council for years has sure done their best;
To make you, Red Deer, the pride of the West.

In and around you are autos in scores,
Never without them at real estate doors,
At baseball and football they're a wild pack,
My, scarcely a horseman is safe on the track.

And now cops you have, men without fear,
With their Chief Georgie Bell who was wounded last year,
By a .44 bullet from Kelly, you know,
While rescuing Grant and tailor Munro.[a]

Three railways you have, bringing souls from afar,
The CP, the CN, and the fine ACR
Two of them racing towards the Brazeau,
Where coal in abundance is bedded all through.

Ye that are men in positions of trust
Stand shoulder to shoulder and do what is just,
Welcome the stranger, then never fear,
There's a future in waiting for Bonnie Red Deer.

[a]For the full story of Chief Bell's rescue, see sidebar.

A town develops its assets

These photos (c. 1910-20) show the bridge and power house (opposite page); the landscaped station (below); Ross Street looking west past the intersection of Gaetz Avenue to the depot in 1912 (above left); and hikers on the Hogsback in the canyon east of town.

much promise of permanency as at present. Even the money stringency has been due to some extent to the fact that many of the Red Deer people have so much faith in their city and district that they have tried to spread their investment over too extensive an area and the money shortage caught them... But the financial conditions are due to causes beyond our control and just as soon as the causes, whatever they are, are modified or removed, then Red Deer has the permanent basis with which to shoot ahead."

But the causes were not modified and within a few months the grim consequences of the little city's lavish fiscal policies began to become evident. In the surge of enthusiasm, the city — already $177,000 in debt by 1910 (based on an assessment of $1.46 million) — spent more money, taking the municipal debt to $440,000 by 1914. The assessment had then risen to $4.229 million and the millrate had dropped from 22 to sixteen.

That year, 1914, the boom collapsed. Red Deer was caught with a debt load which, in relative terms, exceeded that of other municipalities. As the population began to decline, speculators simply refused to pay taxes on the hundreds of lots they had hoped to sell at a profit. The *Red Deer Advocate* of Jan. 23, 1914, started what was to become a regular feature: a list of lands being sold by the city for back taxes. Tax arrears for 1913-15 amounted to $122,000. Suddenly the treasury was empty. The city even owed $2,800 to Western General Electric Co. Ltd. for power and street lighting and couldn't pay the bill.

The response of city councillors was to plunge in deeper still. In September 1915 they offered to buy Western General Electric's power plant and assets for $200,000, a move that would have increased the debt from $124 to $207 per capita, claiming dubiously that they had taxpayer

The schizo career of Red Deer promoter John T. Moore

A SUBURBAN TORONTO ALDERMAN BECAME A PRAIRIE INDUSTRIALIST BUT WHEN THE BUST CAME, BACK HE WENT TO HIS ONTARIO ROSES

By Janet Harvey

Of all the people who contributed to the growth of early Red Deer, one of the most problematic — but no less significant on that account — was John T. Moore. He was a man with a schizophrenic political and business career, half in Alberta, half in Toronto, and when the bust began thumping Alberta, it was to Toronto that his final loyalties adhered. Nevertheless, although Moore actually lived in Red Deer for a relatively short time, he managed to play a significant if somewhat chaotic role in its development.

Born in Markham, Ontario, in 1844 to Irish parents, Moore began his erratic public career as deputy-registrar of the County of Waterloo. He became councillor and then reeve in the Toronto suburb of Yorkville and later a Toronto alderman, was an active temperance campaigner, and supported union of the Protestant churches.

However, the *Red Deer Advocate* once suggested, Moore's "genius was creative, and the East hampered him." He came west in 1881 and became managing director of the Saskatchewan Land and Homestead Company, travelling by buckboard to select land for the enterprise. With the agricultural depression of the 1880s the rosy expectations of the settlers began to fade, however. The company failed and Moore, who had originally planned to take over all of its lands, lost them in a legal struggle with a financial backer.

He nevertheless remained fascinated with Red Deer, and carried on undaunted in the promotion of other schemes. In 1902 he incorporated the Western Telephone Company, and was granted a 25-year franchise by the town council, only to be beaten by the Bell Telephone Company in the race to provide the town with its first long distance service.

So Moore reorganized his enterprise as the Western General Electric Company and supplied Red Deer with its first electricity in 1904. Later he promoted the first central-energy telephone system in Alberta. Before long, however, he seemingly lost his competitive ambitions for private ownership of utilities. He became an advocate of the government-owned telephone system that bought out Bell. In 1926 Western General Electric was sold to the city of Red Deer.

Another big Moore venture was the Alberta Central Railway (Vol. II, Sect. 3, ch. 4). This line was chartered in 1901 to run from the Delburne area to Rocky Mountain House, part of the intention being to supply a rail link for the Saskatchewan Land and Homestead Company properties around Red Deer. The charter was renewed in 1903, 1905, and 1907. Work finally began in the spring of 1910, with no less a personage than Prime Minister Wilfrid Laurier on hand in August of that year to drive the first spike, on Red Deer's South Hill near Gaetz Avenue. But delay followed delay, high hopes and optimism for the line gradually dwindled, support. The offer was rejected, much to the relief of the Bank of Montreal, which had the city account.

Meanwhile, the fiscal crisis hit the school board. It discovered abruptly that it could not pay the teachers. It was stuck with a model system, one that had been a Red Deer boast. The board had even hired a musician, Mrs. John Quigg, to give special lessons in music through the schools, a first for Alberta. By 1913 teachers' salaries had risen dramatically, with a principal receiving $1,900 and the highest-paid assistant $1,200, with no teacher receiving less than $900 annually.

Even as early as June 1913 there had been signs of trouble. The trustees asked city council to pay them the school's share of the weekly taxes as collected, so they could meet operating costs. Later that year, teachers offered to take a 5% pay cut in their 1914 salaries. Ultimately, they lost far more than that, with the result that by 1917 educational costs for Red Deer were $6,000 less per year than they had been in 1913.

The teachers weren't the only civic employees to suffer. In 1914 when the *Red Deer News* announced "the most terrible war since the fall of the Roman Empire," city council reacted by redoubling a program of financial restraint. City staff accepted pay cuts of between 20% and 40%, and some were laid off.

Even nature changed. In June of 1915, torrential rains caused the Red Deer River to rise by nearly twenty feet, the highest level in recorded history. Roads were washed away and Western General Electric's power plant was flooded. In North Red Deer, the Great West Lumber Company's dam and millpond were damaged and the Canadian Northern rail bed was badly eroded, providing yet another setback to on-again, off-again plans to extend the Canadian Northern line into the

and in January 1912 the axe fell. The Alberta Central Railway went into bankruptcy. The CPR took over construction of the line and completed it to Rocky Mountain House in 1914.

Meanwhile, in 1905, Moore had rekindled his political career in the West. Originally attempting to run as an independent for a provincial seat in the newly formed Red Deer constituency, he swung to the Liberal side when he realized his chances as an unaligned candidate were slight indeed. Some Liberals doubted his conversion, and actually nominated a second candidate, but Moore secured a narrow victory to become Red Deer's first MLA. One of his early aspirations was to have Red Deer made capital of Alberta in 1906 (Vol. II, Sect. 1, ch. 4). He spoke eloquently in the Legislature, lauding its central location and modern amenities, and comparing it to the smaller American state capitals.

Unfortunately Charles A. Stuart, the member for Gleichen, who had seconded the motion, immediately negated the effect of this rhetoric by stating that he did not agree with it. He only wanted to be "able to give the House the opportunity to hear the masterly oration of the member for Red Deer." Moore withdrew his motion and cast his vote for Calgary instead. He ran again in 1909,

John T. Moore had an oddly chequered business and political career, and as many failures as successes, but he made a vital contribution. Red Deer & District Archives

this time using the promise of his railroad to drum up support, but was defeated by Edward Michener, the Conservative candidate.

With his railroad bankrupt and his political career over, John T. Moore returned to Toronto in 1912. He settled in Moore Park, a district named after himself as president of the short-lived Belt Line Railway running through part of that area, and attempted to turn Toronto into a "City of Roses." To that end he imported rose stock from the British Isles, along with a gardener, for his Moore Park estate. That the man who once left the stifling confines of Ontario suburbia for the expanse of the West should end up back in Toronto, devoting himself to gardening, provides just one more ironic twist.

Moore maintained various business interests in Red Deer, however, and his son, William, remained to manage them. John T. died in June 1917 at the age of 73. Notorious though he was for passing his ambitious schemes on to others, or losing interest altogether, the fact is that most of them eventually prospered. Furthermore, it was he who drew the attention of Leonard Gaetz (a director of his first failure, the homestead enterprise) to Red Deer — thereby bequeathing the town its founding family.

Booming North Red Deer's odorific pièce de résistance

A TOWN WITH SUCH HIGH POTENTIAL JUST HAD TO HAVE A HONEY WAGON

In 1913, two years after its incorporation as a village, North Red Deer decided to get serious about its sanitation facilities. Up to then it had used the time-honoured method of outhouses that straddled pits dug in the ground. When the pit was filled the outhouse was moved.

But when the village of North Red Deer acquired its first medical health officer, he decided that this arrangement was unworthy of a community with such a promising future[a]. So the village council devised a plan whereby large containers of 100-gallon capacity — immediately dubbed honey pails by the public — would be sold at cost to the residents and placed in pits, one in each backyard.

The village would then hire a "scavenger" to collect these containers as often as should prove necessary, take them to the local dump, empty and return them. He would be paid thirty cents a pail a month. The city bought a wagon for the job. The scavenger himself had to supply the horses, and also a sleigh for winter. He would get an additional $100 to clean out and enlarge the existing 120 privy pits and get the program underway.

The residents were a good deal less enthusiastic about the new arrangement than the council. Some indeed regarded the whole project as a frightful invasion of personal privacy. The council found it necessary to impose a $5 fine for violation of the new bylaw.

Welcome or unwelcome, the scavenger and his unsavoury wagon became part of village life until a better idea emerged in the next decade. The better idea was called a sewer system.

North Red Deer had other things municipal to boast about during the boom years: 7,500 feet of solid six-foot plank sidewalks, for example, a bridge over to Red Deer, and a Roman Catholic convent, church and school. It also had several industries that included the Great West Lumber Company, the Freytag Tannery, and railway construction headquarters. As soon as it became a village, it borrowed $4 million to lease a municipal building, build a dog pound and create a works storage area.

No sooner did North Red Deer become a village than discussion started about whether to amalgamate with Red Deer, with petitions repeatedly circulated to this effect. Not until 1947, however, would it be absorbed by the city.

— S.K.

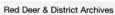

The Great West Lumber Company in North Red Deer employed some 400 men when these photographs were taken in 1911-13. Its future was not to be so bright. The company's dam and millpond were damaged when the Red Deer River rose nearly twenty feet in June 1915, and by 1916 it was running out of timber limits and — on account of the economic downturn — customers.

[a]North Red Deer was on the northwest bank of the Red Deer River, just upstream from the Canadian Pacific crossing. It was bounded by what would later become Gaetz Avenue to the east and 58 Street to the south.

[2]The Red Deer Board of Trade, in a desperate attempt to open the snow-clogged street system to cars, considered the ingenious if impractical possibility of having sleigh runners set the same width apart as the wheels of a car in order that automobiles could drive along the hard-packed strips of snow formed by the sleighs.

city. However, the rain did provide one bright light: combined with hot, dry weather in late summer and fall, it led to the largest grain crop in the history of central Alberta.

The following winter, 1915-16, snow conditions were so severe roads were closed to automobile traffic[2]. In the spring of 1916 the Bank of Montreal cut off the city's credit. The province came to the rescue by allowing cities the power to issue treasury bills secured by the amount of taxes in arrears. The idea was that the amount raised — some $55,000 — would tide the city over until property values returned to normal. Unfortunately, in the minds of the politicians, "normal" meant the over-inflated values of the land frenzy of 1911-13.

Red Deer was caught with a debt load which, in relative terms, exceeded that of other municipalities. As the population began to decline, speculators simply refused to pay taxes. Suddenly the treasury was empty. The city even owed $2,800 for power and street lighting and couldn't pay the bill.

The economy continued down. The eleven-year-old Great West Lumber Company sawmill, which employed up to 400 men in 1912, ran out of both timber limits and customers and closed down. Two of the city's three hotels, deprived of their booze sales through Prohibition, did likewise in 1916. The Great War halted the tide of new homesteaders. And in any event, by 1914, the land in the immediate area of Red Deer had all been taken up, and future settlers who did come

An earlier industrial idea becomes an unhappy failure

BUT ONE DAY THE CANNED MILK PROJECT WILL BECOME A RED DEER SUCCESS

Diversification of industry, an economic ambition in every prairie province and city since the first prairie sod was broken, had its advocates in Red Deer as it had everywhere else. But in Red Deer in 1910, a very hopeful diversified industry appeared.

It was called the Laurentia Milk Company and it was financed largely with local capital. Laurentia opened a factory to produce canned milk which, the promoters claimed, even connoisseurs would be unable to distinguish from fresh milk.

People foresaw a great boom in dairying, because the sale of whole milk to the factory would bring the farmers a steady cash income greater than they could hope to receive from cream alone. In 1912 enthusiasm was still high for the product, which the company described in a publicity release as being homogenized and sterilized so it would "keep good for any length of time."

At first the company was successful, but by the start of the Great War in 1914 it was in serious financial difficulty.

Customers found some of the milk spoiled as soon as the bottles were opened, and word spread quickly. This soon destroyed the company, and its failure added another item to the general woe of the economic collapse.

However, in a sense Laurentia was a forerunner. Years later, in 1936, Central Alberta Dairy Pool built a milk condensery in Red Deer, marketing its products over a wide area, first under the Alpine name, then renaming it Alpha in the late 1930s.

— *S.K.*

Red Deer & District Archives

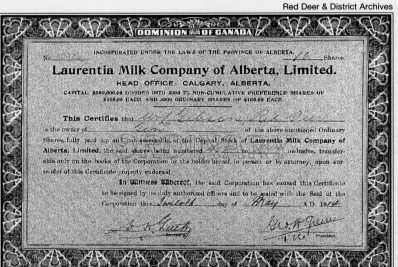

When W.L. Gibson bought his ten shares in 1914 his company was already in trouble — but two decades later the idea would be made to work.

Hopes soared with the ACR but it, too, went under when the big bust came

The much-heralded Alberta Central Railway gets under way as Prime Minister Wilfrid Laurier (above) drives the first spike in August 1910. At top are depicted some of the grade crews and their teams. At right a steam digger works along the edge of North Hill, and below right is the ACR trestle bridge across the Red Deer River, c. 1912. But when the bust came, vast plans to take it to the Pacific collapsed. The ACR ran west 65 miles and stopped.

An enterprising photographer managed to capture almost the entire city when things were going well in 1912, in this panorama shot copyrighted by a Chicago firm.

moved west into the Eckville and Rocky Mountain House areas. In this vicinity, the vast plans for the Alberta Central Railway, previously envisioned as bound for the Pacific through Howse Pass, came to an end. The track went west 65 miles from Red Deer and stopped.

Uncollected taxes for 1917 reached $48,000 and the city defaulted on some bond payments. City bankers cut off all credit and teachers' salaries were paid by the school board only after private individuals took out notes in their own name. The city, however, found a new banker — which imposed strict overdraft limits — and sold $30,000 in new treasury bills. Because of earlier cutbacks and rising costs fuelled by the war, the city was forced to provide its employees with a $10-a-month inflation allowance.

Not all the news was bad. In 1916, farmers received outstanding prices for grain and livestock and they spent a lot of that money in Red Deer. Alberta Pacific Grain Co. and Kenny Farm Agency built new grain elevators. Sales of farmland were good and, despite the shutdown of the Great West Lumber operation, Manning-Sutherland Lumber Co. opened a yard on the south side of Red Deer in 1918, adding to the city's status as a retail and distribution centre. Nor, it was noted, did the recession stop residents from buying cars at a dramatic rate, necessitating the construction of two new garages and causing the editor of the *Advocate* to opine that reckless driving was "keeping some citizens in terror of their lives."

Even so, by 1918 the assessment had dropped to $2.621 million, the millrate had risen to 25 (it went as high as 65 in 1922) and there was no appreciable decline in the debt load. That debt, combined with failing industry, a sharp decline in homesteaders and virtually no growth in population, effectively plunged Red Deer into the Great Depression of the 1930s more than a decade ahead of the rest of the province.

Debt, failing industry, a sharp decline in homesteaders and virtually no growth in population, effectively plunged Red Deer into the Great Depression more than a decade ahead of the rest of the province.

As soldiers returned from war the situation in Red Deer became more gloomy. There was little money for residential housing. Schools were overcrowded and the city had no money to build new ones. Returned servicemen could find nowhere to live and nowhere to work. Rampant inflation was diminishing the value of people's savings and incomes. The situation in early autumn of 1919 was so bad that the local Patriotic Fund committee was empowered by the federal government to distribute emergency relief to incapacitated or unemployed veterans. By spring of 1920, after a killer winter, more than $27,000 had been paid out, the veterans' administration had spent more than $1,000 on relief payments and the city itself handed out several hundred dollars to non-veterans.

The resultant labour unrest was inevitable. Red Deer was largely a non-union community, but it was beset by strikes and disruptions organized by province-wide groups such as the rail workers'

As the police chief lay shot, scouts tracked the gunman

BEHIND RED DEER'S FIRST BIG CRIME LAY A TRANSIENT'S UNHAPPY STORY

By Michael Dawe

Bustling Red Deer in 1911 was full of railroad construction workers and transients looking for work, which was how Police Chief George Bell came to grief on the evening of June 1.

At around 11:30 p.m. two local citizens, H.G. Munro and W.L. Grant, were crossing a field south of 48 Street when a bandit, armed and masked, appeared out of the darkness. "Stick 'em up!" he commanded, and relieved them of the few dollars they had in their pockets.

When Chief Bell, who happened to be nearby, saw what was happening and rushed to their rescue, the masked stranger fired two shots into Bell's stomach. The chief, as he collapsed, managed to sound an alarm by blowing his whistle. Help arrived promptly. Bell was rushed to hospital for emergency surgery and the town siren sounded to rouse the community. Five parties of policemen, firemen and volunteers began a search for the assailant.

He was actually found next morning by a troop of Boy Scouts. He was still armed and hiding in a clump of trees near the Exhibition Grounds. Some of the boys ran for help; others tracked the fleeing robber. Fire Chief Horace Meeres, covered by police with shotguns, subdued the now desperate fugitive.

The Scouts became instant heroes, and more than $500 was raised by public subscription to reward them. Scouts Phil Galbraith and Donald Chadsey were sent to England to attend a special King's Rally, the rest got a dollar apiece, and the troop got fifty dollars.

The villain turned out to be a young transient, Arthur Kelly, who had been sent from England as a young boy. Badly treated by the Canadian family he was assigned to, he had run away and ended up wandering through Montana

Red Deer & District Archives

The transient who shot Police Chief George Bell in the stomach that June night in 1911 later asked the chief to forgive him.

and Alberta. Ironically, a few days earlier the kindly chief had loaned Kelly a dollar.

Convicted of attempted murder and sentenced to seven years in Edmonton Penitentiary, Kelly later wrote Chief Bell, saying in part, "Please forgive me for the trick I have done to you. Hope to see you soon." But fate was not finished with him. Working in the penitentiary coal mine, he fell down the shaft and was badly crippled. But he reportedly was also taught a trade there, and possibly fared better after he had served his sentence.

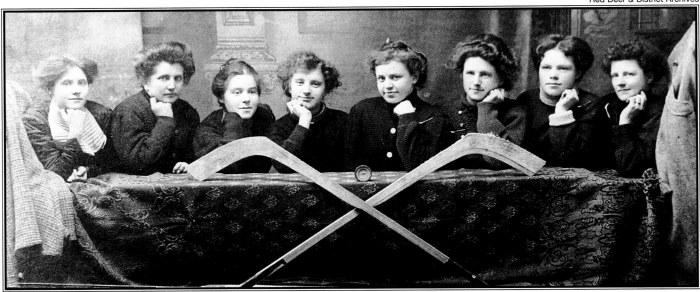

unions. In January 1920 the staff at the Soldiers' Sanatorium, formerly the women's college, went on a wildcat strike over the firing of a worker. A few weeks later retail store employees organized. City employees, while not formally organized, banded together to push for higher salaries.

Council reluctantly coughed up the money, despite a growing litany of financial woes. Tax arrears were continuing to grow. The city raised the millrate and business tax, but the money simply did not come in. An effort to sell $90,000 worth of ten-year treasury bills failed; not a single bid was received for six months. Finally, the mayor went to eastern Canada and sold half the bills, but it was not enough to cover maturing bonds, continuing expenses and a growing bank overdraft.

In mid-1920 came a glimmer of hope when Alberta Government Telephones bought out Western General Electric's telephone system for $85,000 and built a new brick exchange building on Ross Street. Piper's Brickyard contracted to supply the bricks, leading to an expectation the struggling company would recover. That did not happen. It was the 28-year-old company's last job.

The eleven-year-old Great West Lumber Company sawmill, which employed up to 400 men, ran out of both timber limits and customers and closed down. Two of the city's three hotels, deprived of their booze sales through Prohibition, did likewise.

And then in the fall of 1920, another hope: it was announced that the newly organized Canadian National Railways would at last bring the old Canadian Northern line into the city to a new station at Ross Street and Third Avenue E. (47th Avenue). Rock ballasting on the new line would begin immediately, and on the new station and yards very soon.

Instantly, the town's boosters regained their former optimism. "Red Deer people have reason to be thankful that their lot is cast in such pleasant places," lyricized the *Advocate*. "With a bright, beautifully situated town, and every modern municipal service efficiently conducted; with such charming summer resorts as Sylvan Lake, 15 miles, and Pine Lake, 25 miles, within easy reach; and with a mixed farming and dairying district which has never known a crop failure, the people of the district and town of Red Deer may well greet the incoming of the Canadian National Railway with the expectation that the steady growth of the district and town will be continued, and life made larger and happier, despite some ups and downs, for all who reside therein."

But for Red Deer there were to be no ups, just downs. Within months work on the railway was halted as farm prices slumped. North America was proceeding into the Roaring Twenties, but not Red Deer. It was already sliding into the century's worst economic disaster. Elsewhere that depression was a decade away. In Red Deer it had already begun.

The Gaetz-Cornett Drug & Book Co. Ltd. of this city have with characteristic enterprise, demonstrated their ability to keep well abreast of the times by connecting themselves with the largest druggists' co-operative in America. The men connected with this enterprise do a yearly business aggregating over $15,000,000, which well emphasizes its soundness and magnitude. Gaetz-Cornett Drug & Book Co. Ltd. are so well and favorably known for their sterling honesty and square dealing that one can predict a great success for them with the Rexall Remedies, and they are to be heartily congratulated in bringing this great and modern business enterprise to Red Deer.

– Red Deer Advocate
Jan. 6, 1911.

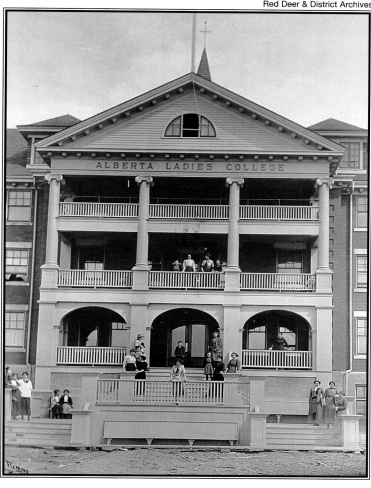

Above right, students gather at the Red Deer Ladies' College. In the 1917 graduating class photograph at Red Deer High School (above), future governor-general Roland Michener is standing in the back row on the right. On the opposite page a ladies' hockey team poses with sticks symbolically arrayed. Below, a crowd watches a baseball game in 1912.

CHAPTER THREE

The Hat was a boom town until the CPR shops went to Calgary

THAT DECISION BEGAN A DOWNTURN THAT WOULD SEE THE CITY LOSE A QUARTER OF ITS PEOPLE; THEN THE LONG, HARD STRUGGLE BEGAN

by STEPHANI KEER

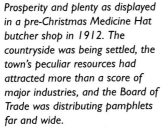

Prosperity and plenty as displayed in a pre-Christmas Medicine Hat butcher shop in 1912. The countryside was being settled, the town's peculiar resources had attracted more than a score of major industries, and the Board of Trade was distributing pamphlets far and wide.

Rudyard Kipling, popular bard of the British Empire, called it "the town that was born lucky." Few in the burgeoning years that opened Medicine Hat's second decade of the 20th century would have disagreed. On every hand was promise. The settlers, arriving by hundreds, promised prosperity. The soaring population, the vast visions of the railway promoters, the new stores and new downtown buildings promised distinction and even perhaps renown. Everywhere houses were going up, streets being paved, and schools being built for children who hadn't even arrived yet.

The most immediate promise was at this stage mere rumour but nonetheless exciting in its massive implications. The Canadian Pacific, pioneer of the West, its biggest employer and its most

Glenbow Archives, NA-2479-2

During a two-year land boom Medicine Hat's population nearly tripled, reaching 15,000 by 1913. Young immigrants were pouring in, seeking land; in town, the housing shortage was acute. At top left is the Hollinger Real Estate Office in 1912. A 1912 Rimmer & Smith ad emphasizes the 'born lucky' theme with a swastika motif (left). E.C. Metzner (1913) provides an artist's aerial view of the city (above); the big square building near the lower right is labelled 'Proposed Depot Canadian Northern Railway.'

significant economic indicator, was said to be considering putting its western car shops not in Calgary but in Medicine Hat. This would do more than guarantee the city's future. It would set up Medicine Hat as a potential rival to the pompously presumptuous Calgary and the Ottawa-pandering Edmonton. Alberta would have three major centres, not two. The third would be "the town that was born lucky."

Ten years later when the decade ended, all these dreams would lie in ruin. Survival itself would seem in doubt. But the story of that decade, the soaring dream and the dismaying collapse, is integral to the history not only of Medicine Hat but of the whole province. Between 1910 and 1920, as the Hat went, so went Alberta.

There was more than optimistic hope behind the buoyant spirit of 1910. In the first seven months of the year, 4,138 homesteads, covering 822,000 acres, were gobbled up. Around the city, new towns sprang into being: Carlstadt "the star of the prairie," Redcliff "the smokeless Pittsburgh," Winnifred "another town born lucky"[1]. Then there was Suffield, the pride of the Southern Alberta Land Company, which was promoting an irrigation scheme in the area and also saw Suffield as a potential summer resort with a lake. Nearby, a British-financed stock company, Canadian Wheatlands Ltd., was selling wheat farms carved from a 23,000-thousand-acre tract.

[1] Carlstadt was 35 miles northwest of Medicine Hat. Originally named Langevin when the CPR rail line went through in 1883, it was renamed Carlstadt in 1900. In 1915 it was renamed yet again, and remained for the rest of the century as Alderson. Winnifred was on the CPR's Crow line, thirty miles southwest of the Hat. Named after a relative of an English shareholder of the Alberta Railway & Irrigation Company, Winnifred boomed from 1913 to 1916, then declined fairly steadily. By the 1960s just about all residents and businesses had moved out, and by the mid-'90s only grain elevators and a few residents remained.

The cover of a 1912 promotional brochure leaves no doubt about the town's industrial potential.

Suffield consequently boasted five grain elevators and three hotels.

Between February and June of 1911, Ontario land offices sold some 425,000 acres of land in Alberta and quite a chunk of this was in and around Medicine Hat. The CPR itself was selling some of the large tracts of farmland it held in reserve, with the somewhat strange belief that the "speculative element" could be eliminated and the land colonized.

The Medicine Hat Board of Trade mounted a massive advertising campaign, setting a new standard for the use of superlatives. In one year alone, it dispensed 40,000 pamphlets and folders, 16,000 copies of the *Medicine Hat Manufacturer*, 10,000 envelope slips and 200,000 gummed seals with a flaming gas well as their centrepiece.

One to three times a week the board sent special news stories, often illustrated, to all the major cities in Canada and to London. Frequently it quoted Rudyard Kipling's declaration that Medicine Hat was the "New Nineveh" (see sidebar). It provided major publicity pieces for the *Canadian Magazine*, the *Canadian Courier*, the *Traveller's Magazine* and to the *World Traveller de Luxe*, as well as regular news bulletins for financial journals.

Many British immigrants arrived, as did a large number of Americans — so large that between 1910 and 1914 the city celebrated July 4 as well as July 1. But the settlers came from other strange and exotic places as well. This diversity was made evident when Ira K. Jackson of the Alberta Bible Society distributed Bibles in fifteen different languages in the city.

The board even boasted, at one stage, that the health of the city was so good and business at the cemetery so bad that the Presbyterian Church had offered to hand over the land to the city to keep it as a public cemetery for all denominations. It pointed out repeatedly that Medicine Hat had one of the lowest crime rates in Canada. The city itself, with funding provided by industrial bureau subscribers, hired a second industrial commissioner in May 1912 to sell the advantages of Medicine Hat to the investment world.

By the end of 1913 Medicine Hat had thirty major industries, 25 miles of graded streets, 54 miles of waterworks and sewers, eight branches of chartered banks, eight public schools, four parks and twenty natural gas wells with a daily flow of fifty million cubic feet. At the beginning of that year, it also had 190 businesses listed. (Ominous portent of what was to come, many of them were mere names, registered by speculators.) In 1912 Medicine Hat led all Canadian cities in the rate of building-permit growth, increasing in the first nine months of that year by 340% over the same period in 1911.

Because of the effective propagandizing by the Board of Trade, the city and the railway, there

Determined settlers line up at the Second Street Post Office for what was called the 'Big Land Grab' in the winter of 1913. Police Sergeant Walter E. Grover is on hand to keep things calm.

To cope with the influx of pupils, ten schools had to be built in three years: six 'cottage' and four 'permanent.' In 1912 the Duke of Connaught laid the cornerstone for the one that would bear his name (left).

was an influx of comparatively young immigrants and the town grew rapidly. In 1906 the population stood at 3,000. By 1911 it was 5,606 and it all but tripled when it reached the boom's high point of 15,000 by the end of 1913. Mayor Nelson Spencer boldly predicted it would soon reach 25,000 or even 40,000[2]. Though houses were going up everywhere, a housing shortage was chronic and people still had to live in "Tent Town" beyond the South Saskatchewan River on the north side of the city.

Many British immigrants arrived, as did a large number of Americans — so large, writes Ed Gould in Medicine Hat's centenary book *All Hell for a Basement*, that between 1910 and 1914 the city celebrated July 4 as well as July 1. The latter predominated, however, and in 1912 the city imported "Professor" T.W. Hand of Hamilton, Ontario, to provide a $2,000 fireworks display for Dominion Day. A.F. Binning, chairman of the celebration committee that year, boasted that trains just hesitated at most western towns, but at Medicine Hat "all trains stay 25 minutes, so we must be doing things in a big way." But the settlers came from other strange and exotic places as well. This diversity was made evident when Ira K. Jackson of the Alberta Bible Society distributed Bibles in fifteen different languages in the city.

By the end of 1913 the city had fourteen churches, which also served as social centres for the city and surrounding countryside. Below is St. Barnabas Anglican, under construction in 1912. That was also the year when neo-gothic St. Patrick's Catholic Church (right), one of the first buildings in North America to be constructed entirely of reinforced concrete, rose on the riverside. For two decades the congregation would worship in its capacious basement, until the interior could be completed, but St. Patrick's would finally stand as one of southern Alberta's largest and most impressive churches.

[2] The *Medicine Hat News*, a persistent foe of Mayor Spencer, declared him a poor booster for the city. How could he tell the world of its prosperity, sneered the *News*, when his own phone had been cut off because he hadn't paid the bill?

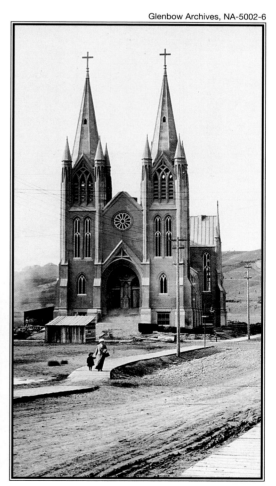

135

With verse and vitriol Medicine Hat takes out its wrath upon Calgary

NINE YEARS AFTER THE DECISION TO LOCATE THE CPR SHOPS THERE, FURY STILL RAGES IN THE HAT

The hard feelings Medicine Hat harboured for Calgary after losing the Canadian Pacific Railway shops kept breaking out for years after the decision, the first major industrial reversal the city suffered.

Particularly virulent was the *Medicine Hat Times*, which followed the announcement in tragic blank verse:

> *Farewell! Oh, thou fond dreams of affluence and sudden glory.*
> *Farewell, I weep.*
> *The car shops are no more.*
> *We loved this young child of our bright hope,*
> *We nurtured it.*
> *It became a thing of beauty — almost.*
> *But the CPR gave and the CPR have taken away!*
> *Blessed be the name of the CPR.*

"Where and what is Calgary?" asked the columnist, and he answers his question in purest vitriol:

Calgary, my dear innocent young friend, is nowhere. It is at present to be located several thousand feet up in the air. It is a name not mentioned in polite circles in this city. It is a creation superinduced by the application of an infinitesimal point of a powerful and continued draft of hot air. A similar result is often witnessed as a phenomenon on these plains in the so-called mirage. Calgary is a myth.

A week later, the paper returned to verse:

> *Oh tell me gentle stranger;*
> *Oh tell me, if you please;*
> *Is Calgary a city?*
> *Or is it a disease?*

For the whole decade the resentment persisted, and at one point even the clergy took it up. On Sept. 14, 1916, in a letter to the *Medicine Hat News*, a priest identified as Father O'Mara said: "To Calgary belongs the crowning glory of boasting of her slaughterhouse, and incidentally the number of hogs one finds running at large through the quarters of the city."

Father O'Mara was nothing if not fair, however. He went after all of Medicine Hat's rivals, not just Calgary: 'Let us not war against this pride of city nor expect to build ourselves up by pulling others down. Let Edmonton boast of her penitentiary, Ponoka her asylum, Red Deer of being the best place for mental defectives in the Dominion, Lethbridge in being a city of refuge for all the criminals of the province...

'Alas, the citizens of Medicine Hat can't compete in a list of honours similar to those which have crowned the labours of the citizens of sister cities in Alberta." — *S.K.*

The churches, too, were busy building. When the Roman Catholic diocese of Southern Alberta became a reality in 1912, Medicine Hat Catholics resolved to sell their frame church at the boom price of $65,000, and that September they turned the sod for St. Patrick's Church. It was already fairly clear Calgary would be chosen as the southern cathedral city, but inveterately optimistic Hatters cherished hopes that their city would one day become a diocesan centre as well. So they raised massive, neo-gothic St. Patrick's, one of the first buildings in North America to be built entirely of reinforced concrete. Money ran short by the time the main structure was up. It would take twenty years to complete the interior, while the congregation worshipped in the basement. Stained glass and imported rose windows would be added in the '50s, and the concrete roof (which had always leaked) was clad in copper in 1979-80. Although St. Patrick's never would actually become a cathedral, it undeniably looked like one. The imposing building with its magnificent marble altar and reredos stood as one of the finest and largest churches in southern Alberta.

The Anglicans, who had established a parish in the 1880s, built St. Barnabas Church and held their first service there Dec. 12, 1912. German-speaking immigrants, who had been flooding in since the turn of the century, raised St. Paul's German Evangelical Lutheran Church in 1911. Another was soon needed, and the chapel of St. Peter Evangelical Lutheran Church was dedicated in May 1912. Westminster Presbyterian Church ("west" for the area, "minster" for church, it was carefully explained — no connection to the famous London abbey) was dedicated June 21, 1914. These joined already existing Presbyterian, Methodist, Baptist and Congregationalist churches and,

Gas lamps illumine George Haystead's four-chair barber shop, established in 1914 at 238 South Railway Street and destined to provide Hatters with haircuts and shaves until 1928. For the camera, barbers and customers adopt expressions of unwonted gravity.

with them, served not only as religious but also as social centres for the city and surrounding area. By the end of 1913 the city had fourteen churches.

Schools were built in anticipation of the children who would arrive with the workers in the new industries. Plans were made for a technical school, one of the most up-to-date in the West, providing a full range of technical and vocational trade courses.

Residents regularly contracted railway fever and dreamed of the time when the Hat would be a focal point for transportation in Alberta. (Precisely the same dream was cherished by Lethbridge.) In 1912 businessmen decided that the local station could accommodate the seven railway companies operating in Alberta, Saskatchewan and Montana for the rest of the decade — and, indeed, for another thirty years. This optimism resulted in spasmodic buying and selling of land considered potentially useful for track development. Some of the speculators made money in

A few days later the announcement came. The CPR shops would be in Calgary. Having made so much of it, Medicine Hat boosters now had a new problem: how to prevent the blow from disheartening the whole city. Overnight, it was discovered that the shops really didn't matter that much.

1914 when the Canadian Northern Railway bought land and turned the sod for the start of its line to Hanna. The line was never completed.

Farms and ranches prospered all around the city. Particularly renowned was the Turkey Track Ranch, established by Texan Tony Day, who moved 22,000 head of cattle and 700 horses onto a 65,000-acre lease just outside Medicine Hat. When Guy Weadick, the promoter behind the Calgary Stampede of 1912, decided to hold a similar event at Winnipeg, Day provided all the livestock. He enlisted the aid of James Owen Gresham Sanderson, the grandson of a famous stockman

WHEREAS the insidious charms of California's allegedly balmy climate have lured from our fireside one for whom our regard is only equalled by the fear in which he was held by the wild and untamed Apaches in the warlike days of his youth, AND WHEREAS at the festive season, when not engaged in dodging our bankers and other creditors, we want to turn our thoughts to those who in the past year have departed from our midst and must seek fields and pastures new, AND WHEREAS those who have departed from us have, in departing, taken with them most of the available loose change which formerly grew in abundance in the vicinity of Medicine Hat and we are therefore unable to extend to you a more substantial token of our esteem than this little testimonial, NOW THEREFORE we, the undersigned members of the Cypress Club, send greetings and our best wishes for a happy, prosperous and more or less sober New Year, with the added hope that the easy chair which has been kept warm for you during the months in which you have been absent may before many moons be once more dented by your recumbent form, and the bar receipts be swelled in consequence thereof.

It was signed by 64 ranchers and businessmen.

in the area, who was using his horse-riding skills, including stunt riding, to earn enough money to go to medical school in 1917[3].

But reversals began long before the boom ended. In the spring of 1911, as word spread of the CPR's car shop plans, it set off a land-buying spree between Medicine Hat and Redcliff, supposedly the intended site. On June 1, the *News* described "a wild scramble for outside property." It continued: "Yesterday and today, every available automobile in the city is engaged in taking prospective buyers out. The sale of half a section across the river to Winnipeg people is taken as partial confirmation of the rumour. Mayor David Milne declares that he has not received any definite information, although promised the first word from [CPR] vice-president [William] Whyte. The mayor emphasized the word 'definite'." Medicine Hat was prepared to make major concessions to the CPR, including land deals and free natural gas — concessions which, because they were

Not everyone found life in Medicine Hat idyllic. Some loathed the weather. The swift temperature fluctuations brought by the kindly chinooks also brought on colds, and people digging water wells would hit pockets of natural gas which would burst out of the ground at 250 or 300 pounds of pressure.

offered to many other companies as well, ended up crippling the city financially for most of this decade.

But Calgary heard the rumour too, and launched a determined campaign to have the shops located in what Calgarians considered the only logical place, namely theirs. They recruited to their cause certain Winnipeg shippers, who threatened to divert traffic away from the CPR. This tactic infuriated people at the Hat, like business leader F.G. Forster, who wrote indignantly in the *News*:

> The attitude of Calgary has been one of smug security in the belief that every gift the CPR had for western Canada must go to Calgary... First divisional headquarters, then district headquarters, then the irrigation headquarters — everything thrown into the lap of Calgary — now a million-dollar hotel and other large improvements, yet Calgary is not satisfied, and threatening rebellion if anything is given to Medicine Hat or any other point. This is the most glaring sample of ungratefulness ever displayed in western Canada.
>
> Calgary has had enough; Calgary is big enough to stand alone; Calgary will have to recognize that there is room in Alberta for more than one big city and that Medicine Hat is going to give her a run for the stakes.

But it was all to no avail, and a few days later the announcement came. The CPR shops would be in Calgary after all. Having made so much of it, Medicine Hat boosters now had a new

The Alberta Clay Products brickyard sprawls from its factory across the landscape, circa 1914 (above). At left, an influential group, which includes former prime minister Sir Wilfrid Laurier and Premier A.L. Sifton, poses during a 1910 tour of the plant. Individuals were numbered and most of them identified when this historic picture was turned over to the Provincial Archives. At the rear are L.W. McBean (16) and company president John Dixon (15). The rest, from left to right, are: Warren Overpack (25); unidentified (24); A. Fish (23); W.H. Bridgman (22); L.H. Pruitt (21); future mayor M.A. Brown (20); former alderman Thomas Hutchinson (19); unidentified (18); CPR engineer James G. Millar (17); lawyer D.G. White (14); Senator Peter Talbot (13); Sir Wilfrid Laurier (12); realtor E.J. Fewings (11); unidentified (10); Saskatchewan Premier Walter Scott (9); Alderman Nelson Spencer, who would become mayor in 1913-14 and then MLA to 1921 (8); Alderman Peter Robertson (7); former interior minister Frank Oliver (6); merchant L.B. Cochran (5); G.P. Graham (4); Attorney-General and Medicine Hat MLA C.R. Mitchell (3); unidentified (2); Alberta Premier Arthur Sifton (1).

problem: how to prevent the blow from disheartening the whole city. Overnight it was discovered that the shops really didn't matter that much. "Businessmen Say That the Announcement Will Not Materially Affect the Progress of the City — Increased Population and More Industries Bound to Come — Can't Overlook the Natural Resources That the City Has to Offer, They Say." Mayor Milne concurred. "With fair treatment from any corporation, and without resorting to the tactics of our competitor, which doubtless had their desired effect, Medicine Hat need have no fear for the future," he said.

In fact, however, the loss stung deeply and the city even considered various ways in which it could retaliate. Raising city taxes on the CPR's subsidiary natural gas company at Medicine Hat — which would pump the fuel to the new Calgary shops — was considered and rejected. But never again, vowed the mayor, would Medicine Hat rely on "any abnormal impetus" from outside the city. And for years to come, the resentment of the "shops decision" would rankle (see sidebar).

The boom continued for another year and a half, however. In 1913 came the Medicine Hat Pottery Works (later Medalta Potteries). Alberta Clay Products was flourishing. John McNeely had built the first big flour mill, Medicine Hat Milling, in 1902, which was ultimately joined by three more flour mills. Again and again the city lured in small industries with tax concessions and cheap

Medicine Hat Museum & Art Gallery Archives, PC-9-1

Mayor Archie C. Hawthorne faced a critical financial and economic situation in 1915.

[4]Alberta children in those years were taught a rhyme to help them decide whether to trade or buy a horse:

One white foot, buy me.
  Two white feet, try me.
Three white feet, deny me.
  Four white feet and white on my nose,
Knock me on the head
  And feed me to the crows.

gas. But most of the growth was the consequence of homesteading activity; the city's rural links were everywhere evident. Many of the early industries had farm connections: bakeries, dairies and horticultural concerns, including massive undercover gardening — greenhouses — in which Medicine Hat's supremacy was said to be challenged only by that of St. Catharines, Ontario. These would fare much better when the crash came. In the town itself, the rural tie remained strong. Most residents kept at least a milk cow, several chickens, a pig and a horse or two in the back yard, and horse trading was brisk even within the city[4].

Not everyone found life in Medicine Hat idyllic, however. Some loathed the weather[5]. The swift temperature fluctuations brought by the kindly chinooks also brought on head colds and other ailments. Ironically, the natural gas that powered the city's growth could be a hindrance. When people digging water wells hit pockets of gas, it would burst out of the ground at 250 or 300 pounds of pressure.

Kipling's eloquence saved the city's cherished name

It's a liability, said the real estate men, and forced a vote, but the traditionalists appealed to the Hat's greatest booster

It was dreams of growth and grandeur that led Medicine Hat city council in 1910 to institute a plebiscite on whether the name of the city should be changed.

Medicine Hat, it was pointed out, had received much derisive comment about its name. Spurred by real estate and industrial interests, some decided no one could take seriously a city with such an outlandish name. The businessmen who advocated the name change even published their own newspaper, *The Call*, which also served as an extravagant booster of Medicine Hat.

Neither of the city's other two newspapers — the Liberal *Medicine Hat News*, which went daily on Jan. 1, 1911, and the Conservative *Medicine Hat Times*[a] — supported the change. The opposition of the *News*

Indignant postmaster Francis F. Fatt sent to the eminent author and poet a plea he couldn't resist.

Medicine Hat Museum & Art Gallery Archives, PC-525-190

to an idea from the business community was not, however, unexpected. All through the boom, businessmen deplored the *News* which, for example, vigorously opposed the proposal to build a street railway. When a plebiscite approved the project, the real estate agents who sponsored it celebrated their victory with a torchlight parade through the city and a ceremony in which an effigy of the editor was hurled into the river.

The proposal to change the city's name occasioned an equally bitter controversy. The issue became so heated that members of the city's Cypress Club wrote to the renowned British poet Rudyard Kipling, who three years earlier had penned an article on Medicine Hat for *Collier's* magazine entitled "The Town That Was Born Lucky." Referring to the city's natural gas deposits, Kipling said Medicine Hat had "all Hell for a basement."

Postmaster Francis F. Fatt asked Kipling to come to the defence of the city's curious name. In the letter, Fatt allowed his own anger to show. "Unfortunately," he wrote, "some newcomers have arisen and want to change the name of the city. It smacks too much of the Injin, smells fearfully of the teepee fire and kini-ki-nick and reminds outsiders of the whacking lies (may God forgive them) of the USA newspapermen in regard to our weather and so forth.

"In a moment of weakness, our city fathers have agreed to submit the question to the vote of the ratepayers, instead of ordering the proposers to be cast into a den of fiery rat-

Then there were the problems of ethnic groups. New arrivals, especially from central and eastern Europe, were often seen, in the words of one resident, as "outlandish nationalities and equivocal sects." Despite the prejudice, however, these settlers usually found life better than it had been at home. Andrew Klaiber, whose father had been among the first to arrive in the area from the Bessarabia region of Russia, recalled that his family chose to be as self-sufficient as possible: "It was a tough life, [but] we had lots of meat of our own, and lots of wild game. We made do with what was available, even making our own coffee from roasted wheat. It was a much better life than in Russia." People of Dutch and Nordic extraction, most notably the Icelanders, were better received and many were soon moving off the homesteads into town. Germans fared well too, at least until 1914.

However, the Chinese were not so fortunate. Lloyd Stepanic, writing many years later in the *Medicine Hat News*, noted:

Medicine Hat Museum & Art Gallery Archives, PC-55-139

Allegations of malfeasance defeated former mayor Nelson Spencer in 1915, but not for long.

[5]**Mrs. William A. Woolfrey Sr. moved to Medicine Hat from England in 1918. After her face was frozen in a ride by horse and sleigh into town from their homestead on the present site of the airport, she railed at her husband: 'You call this God's country? If this is God's country, well, give it back to Him — and a pound of tea for takin' it!' Like many other homesteaders, she found herself isolated and did not enjoy the three-hour drive into town.**

tlesnakes. Can you help us with a few words of encouragement in combating these heretics? Your influence here is great."

It was a challenge Kipling could not refuse. He wrote from Bateman's, his house near Burwash in the countryside of Sussex, England, on Dec. 9, 1910, "both as a citizen of the Empire and as a lover of Medicine Hat." The twin reasons for the change — that Medicine Hat had received some bad press in the U.S. about being the provider of all the bad

'Above all,' wrote Kipling, 'it is the lawful, original, sweat-and-dust-won name of the city, and to change it would be to risk the luck of the city, to disgust and dishearten oldtimers, not in the city alone, but the world over, and to advertise the city's lack of faith in itself.'

weather on the continent, and that another name would look better on a prospectus — Kipling dismissed as being inspired by the *Calgary Herald*: "I always knew Calgary called Medicine Hat names," he said, "but I did not realize that Medicine Hat wanted to be Calgary's little godchild."

He then warmed to his subject. Medicine Hat must be proud, not ashamed, of its reputation as the bad-weather capital of North America. It should declare itself "the only city officially recognized as capable of freezing out the United States and giving the continent cold feet." The name echoed the "old Cree and Blackfoot tradition of red mystery and romance that once filled the prairies. Also, it hints at the magic that underlies the city in the shape of your natural gas. Believe me, the very name is an asset, and as years go

Portrait by Sir Philip Burne-Jones

Kipling came vigorously to the defence 'both as a citizen of the Empire and a lover of Medicine Hat.'

on it will become more and more of an asset. It has no duplicate in the world: it makes men ask questions and, as I know, more than twenty years ago, draws the feet of the young towards it; it has the qualities of uniqueness, individuality, assertion and power.

No ethnic group suffered more in regard to discrimination, especially at the hands of the rougher elements of the land. Until the Manchu Dynasty fell in China in 1912, all Chinese males were compelled to wear a pigtail to acknowledge their allegiance to the emperor. Chinese immigrants continued to wear their pigtails and they brought much abuse from pranksters and drunks. Some people in Medicine Hat went so far as to snip off pigtails and this led to occasional bloodshed. Because they were unable to find anything but the most menial jobs, many of the early Chinese settlers opened their own businesses, including laundries, cafes and tailor shops.

By late 1913 the economic downturn became unmistakable. On October 11, a reported oil strike revived optimism, but only briefly. "Renewed Activity in Medicine Hat Real Estate Gives Promise of Return of Normal Conditions," prophesied the doggedly optimistic *Medicine Hat News* after reports of oil seepage at Small Creek, north of Redcliff, created forecasts that the field would be one of the biggest in Alberta.

But by August 1914 even the *News* was admitting that things were getting tough. The city, which had so lavishly handed out tax exemptions to lure in industry, now faced a crisis. Mayor M.A. Brown was forced to go to Winnipeg to meet officials of the Union Bank who agreed,

"Above all, it is the lawful, original, sweat-and-dust-won name of the city, and to change it would be to risk the luck of the city, to disgust and dishearten oldtimers, not in the city alone, but the world over, and to advertise the city's lack of faith in itself."

In passing he took another swipe at the *Calgary Herald*: "In the first case, the town would change its name for fear of being laughed at. In the second, it sells its name in the hope of making more money under an alias or, as the *Calgary Herald* writes, for the sake of a name that 'has a sound like the name of a man's best girl and looks like business at the head of a financial report.' But a man's city is a trifle more than a man's best girl. She is the living background of his life and love and toil and hope and sorrow. Her success is his success; her shame is his shame; her honour is his honour; and her good name is his good name."

Then he delivered the *coup de grâce*: "What then should a city be rechristened that has sold its name? Judasville?"

The plebiscite was soundly defeated by 351 votes to 28 and Kipling's letter was published in its entirety in newspapers around the world.

— *S.K.*

Medicine Hat Museum & Art Gallery Archives, PC-525-63

[a]The *Medicine Hat Times* became a daily paper in 1912, slipped back to a weekly in April 1916, and folded later that year.

Medicine Hat was extremely sensitive about its reputation as bad weather capital of North America, which stemmed from the fact that it was long the West's northernmost weather station. This January 1919 photograph of Mayor M.A. Brown ploughing a furrow was widely distributed, with an affidavit testifying that the thermometer stood at seventy degrees fahrenheit that day.

Like many another town, Medicine Hat regularly contracted 'railway fever' and dreamed of becoming a focal point for Alberta transportation. These dreams never became reality, and the worst blow was the CPR's 1911 decision to locate its western car shops in Calgary, not in Medicine Hat. Nevertheless, as one citizen observed, the station (above, photographed in 1910) was a busy place where trains customarily stopped a full 25 minutes. And who could fault a town that boasted such a fine city hall and post office as the ones shown here?

reluctantly, to increase the city's line of credit to $250,000, a move necessary because no buyers could be found for the municipal debentures. At that time council cut back on all capital spending except for projects that were absolutely necessary, and officially adopted a policy of retrenchment.

By October Medicine Hat was admitting that it was stuck with some $24,000 in bad cheques and 82 acres of land, as the result of uncompleted deals with industries. This led to charges of mass corruption in city hall, which were thoroughly covered by the *News* under headlines such as: "Whited Sepulchre Stripped."

At the centre of the "scandal" was that longtime nemesis of the *News*, ex-mayor Nelson Spencer, who was now the local Conservative MLA. Throughout Spencer's terms as mayor back in 1912 and 1913, the *News* had alleged unholy liaisons between council members and wildcat developers, the selling of civic franchises for personal gain, and preferential land purchases from members of council. All were largely overlooked in the optimism then captivating the city. In 1913 there were allegations that Spencer had misappropriated large amounts of government relief intended for city businesses. At the same time the city discovered, to its horror, that it had failed to secure land rights for six of its own gas wells.

Such allegations and denials continued through 1914, and in 1915 Spencer was back running for mayor against A.C. (Archie) Hawthorne. By now the *News* had another charge. When he was mayor, it said, Spencer had approved the purchase of land, at a hefty price, from Councillor S.E.

The magical gas supply fuelled burgeoning industries, and the occasional fireworks

Citizens gather (left) to watch a spectacular 1918 gas flare. Stinson tractors (above), manufactured in Medicine Hat by Martin and Phillips, parade downtown circa 1919-20. Below, workers pose at Alberta Foundry and Machine Co. Limited, which helped improve the city's sagging economy when it won a munitions contract, and later produced tractors — although not many.

The newspapers monitored the rise — and fall — of local hopes. Samuel Alexander Wallace sets type (above) at the Medicine Hat Times. *Below, Ford chassis are unloaded from CPR freight cars. In an older industry (below right) ice blocks are cut from the river for refrigeration.*

McClellan. Day after day, the *News* published accusations that Spencer had benefited from public service, and that he had actively driven away industries and businesses (although the *News* did not say how). Spencer was defeated, but his political life was not over. A distinguished career in the army followed, with more political adventures to come (see Vol. IV).

By 1915 the civic situation was critical. The city had 300 vacant buildings, 400 men unemployed and, at year-end, $400,000 in tax arrears and a whopping $3.7-million debt. On October 12, the *News* ran three pages, in its smallest type, of "Lands Liable for Sale for Arrears of Taxes in the City of Medicine Hat." By then the recession was compelling school trustees to cut back programs. The high school commercial program, and the manual arts and household economics courses were axed. All supervisory staff was released. Pupil loads in classes were increased drastically. Teachers, glad to have a job at all, accepted salary cuts of 20%. Many used their off-time to earn additional money as farm labourers. Plans for the projected technical school were abandoned and trustees found themselves tied up in litigation for years because the contractor had completed the foundation and had ordered lumber, boilers and other equipment.

The Great War did little to improve economic conditions. In the Suffield district, according to a July 1915 *News* story, Canadian Wheatlands had gone broke and could plant no crop[6]. Suffield was turning into a ghost village. By 1917 Medicine Hat itself, despite such things as a short-lived munitions contract awarded to the Alberta Foundry and Machine Company, and a surge in demand for automobiles and related services, was staggering under the financial burden of a mass of unpaid taxes. In a bid to raise revenue, the council raised natural gas prices, which in effect made things harder for the poor. (Nor did the councillors fulfil their promise to provide natural gas free to the dependents of soldiers serving away from Medicine Hat.)

In December 1918, at the city's annual meeting, citizens made it clear what they expected council to do: cut expenses to the bone, refuse to extend utilities to subdivisions, stop giving away land and industry tax breaks — and despite all this, somehow still encourage development. On Dec. 16, 1918, voters used recall to get rid of Alderman James J. Marshall, alleging he had rigged the election by having voters told one of the candidates had dropped off the ballot, and because he, like so many other Hatters, owed the city taxes. In 1915, when ratepayers' association president William Cousins donated 31 acres of hillside property to the city, it was discovered that he too had back taxes owing on the land, amounting to $1,425. The donation got him off the hook.

In January 1919 the new council raised water rates and caused a furore by charging for garbage collection. By the end of January returning servicemen were making the already high unemployment even worse. Some 200 men, and two women, registered at the government-run labour bureau. A crop failure in 1918 forced more than 40% of the area farmers to borrow money for seed to plant the 1919 crop. There were sporadic flurries of activity. Martin & Phillips (owned by A.P. Phillips and W.R. Martin, the well-drilling team that brought in Old Glory gas well at Bow Island in 1909) began manufacturing Stinson "Detroiter" tractors in the city, for example. But repeated crop failures soon crushed the fledgling tractor industry. The city population, which had risen to 15,000 in 1913, receded to 11,000 by the end of the decade. More than one out of every four people had left town. By May 1919 the unemployment situation was so bad that the

[6]As the real estate market dried up, according to the *News* story, local realtors F.M. Ginther and W.B. Finlay launched the Medicine Hat Grain Co., to plant a wheat crop on 6,000 acres leased from the bankrupt Canadian Wheatlands project. In July 1915 Ginther much impressed the *News* reporter by driving him out to the Suffield area in his six-cylinder Chalmers, at a speed of fully 35 or 40 miles an hour, to see the acres of waist-high wheat. Twenty-five binders were already lined up for the harvest, he said, and 96 horses. But this too was to be a temporary respite.

Medicine Hat Museum & Art Gallery Archives, PC-58-48

Harvesting with mule-drawn binders in the Canadian Wheatlands holding, Suffield district, in 1912.

'Photo taken the day I bought the Tony Day Ranch June 1917,' wrote future Alberta lieutenant-governor John J. Bowlen on the margin of this picture, noting that the spread then encompassed 100,000 acres and included 1,800 head of horses. From left to right, according to Bowlen's notation and information supplied to the Medicine Hat Museum & Art Gallery Archives, are Bowlen, Ford Day (nephew of Tony), A.J. Bryson, J.L. Peacock, Tony Day, Jack McLean, Bob Fleming, Jack Horne, and Tony Day's son Joe.

Medicine Hat Trade and Labour Council was threatening to call a general strike, similar to those staged in Toronto and Winnipeg. Repeated attempts to get rid of "Tent Town" proved futile, as more and more people lost houses and the number of wandering homeless increased.

Meanwhile, man-made disaster struck repeatedly and even nature herself seemed to have turned against the suffering city and its neighbours. In March 1913 a fire that resulted from a natural gas explosion at Malcolm Canneries killed five people, including two volunteer firefighters and a twelve-year-old boy. Ten others were seriously injured. In 1915, a tornado virtually wiped out the communities of Redcliff and Grassy Lake (see sidebar). In mid-decade, the plant of the Lake of the Woods Milling Company (Medicine Hat Milling under new management) was flattened by fire. So was the Dominion Harvester Company. Alberta Linseed Oil Mills was severely damaged.

A dryland farming crisis struck in 1917 and farmers, including large conglomerates, had massive crop failures because of drought. Bitterly cold winters caused huge cattle losses. This disaster occasioned the worst farm abandonment in Alberta history — four times greater than that in the same area during the Great Depression and the worst anywhere in Canada. Townships surrounding Medicine Hat would lose 83% of their population in the six years after 1918.

Floods repeatedly threatened, and repeatedly made the city's water supply undrinkable. In March 1918 the industrial section of the city was flooded by the South Saskatchewan River. People were rescued by boat and raft from the 300 houses that were under water, with rescuers having to contend with floating ice. Chickens and other livestock were drowned.

True enough, Medicine Hat still had its industrial base of ranching, farming, railroading, brick- and pottery-making, milling and greenhouse production, which should have put the city in a better position than many other Canadian centres. But the drought and the massive debt under which it staggered proved crippling. Fortune had turned her back, and a long, hard struggle lay ahead for "the town that was born lucky."

One of the many businesses wrecked by the 1915 tornado was the Redcliff Knitting Factory. The twister demolished most of the business section in both Redcliff and Grassy Lake, splintering frame structures, deroofing and splitting brick ones, wrecking a steel water tower. Redcliff Knitting never reopened.

With one terrible tornado Redcliff's future perished

UNTIL THAT STRANGE SULTRY DAY IN '15 ITS VISION WAS UNBOUNDED; THEN IN A GREAT ROAR, BUILDINGS AND DREAMS WERE TORN TO PIECES

It was Friday, June 25, 1915, in Redcliff and Grassy Lake, and for an early summer day the weather had been particularly hot, with temperatures climbing to over 100 degrees Fahrenheit. Residents welcomed that southwest wind.

But some noticed a range of ominously purple clouds forming along the southern horizon. They took children inside. Farmers and ranchers began moving livestock into secure areas. The wind rose. By dinner time, it was blowing dust and debris so violently that the sky darkened and Redcliff residents turned on their gas lamps.

Suddenly the wind stopped. Seconds ticked by. Then it struck, a killer tornado. Within the next few minutes much of both communities was destroyed.

In Grassy Lake, midway between Medicine Hat and Lethbridge on the CPR's Crowsnest line, a mother and her ten-year-old daughter died when their farmhouse was blown to pieces. Wood from the lumber yards was tossed all over the area. A freight train was blown right off the track. A hotel, a drugstore and much of the business section were flattened.

When it hit Redcliff, adjoining the South Saskatchewan River and six miles west of Medicine Hat on the CPR main line, only ten people were injured but property loss amounted to almost $1 million. Every large building and a steel water tower were damaged extensively. The roof was ripped off the Laurel Hotel and rolled up like a carpet. The Ornamental Iron Works lost its roof. A cigar factory blew over on its side. The post office collapsed. The Redcliff Knitting Factory was flattened and never rebuilt. The Dominion Glass Co. building lay in ruins. All over the area crops were obliterated; livestock just seemed to vanish.

Grassy Lake was rebuilt, and Redcliff would also survive, though the awesome visions some had for its future — boosters in 1910 had forecast a population of one million — never really returned. Some firms simply packed up what was packable and either sold it or took it with them when they left.

In many respects Redcliff had rivalled Medicine Hat. Like Medicine Hat, it was rich in natural gas. There was gold in the river and a large deposit of silica sand which for years sustained its glass industry. Volcanic ash found in the area was used in making hand-cleaner. Limestone, clay deposits in the riverside gullies, and high-grade shale created a local building materials trade, and there was a good supply of coal.

But by the end of the second decade of the 20th century, it was plain that Redcliff, Alberta, would survive only as a suburb of Medicine Hat. Its dreams of grandeur perished on that afternoon of June 25, 1915.

— *S.K.*

Tornados were rare — but fires and explosions were not

At left, the Medicine Hat fire department battles a 1911 blaze that destroyed three shops at Third Street and South Railway. The linseed oil mill (below left), gutted by fire in mid-decade, was rebuilt and carried on for another seven decades. Fire broke out at the Premier Brick plant, Redcliff, (below right) circa 1922. And in a city where someone digging for water was likely to strike gas instead, and where leaking pipes and fittings were not unknown, gas explosions were a constant danger. The 1913 explosion that levelled Malcolm Canneries (below left) was by far the worst, killing five people and injuring ten.

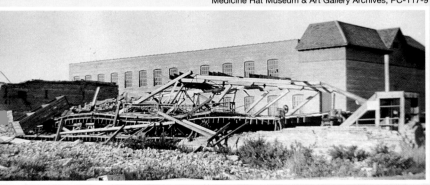

CHAPTER FOUR

Lethbridge was the world's capital of dryland farming, and then...

THE BIG CONGRESS OF 1912 SAW 5,000 VISITORS FROM AS FAR AWAY AS PERSIA DESCEND ON THE CITY, BUT THE BILL WAS HORRENDOUS

by STEPHANI KEER

There could be no doubt about it now. As Lethbridge residents watched the timbers going up to provide a special temporary arena for a world conference on dryland farming, this could only mean that the dreams of grandeur, so long cherished by the southern centre, were at last coming true. Just imagine: 5,000 visitors hosted by a city of only 8,400 people. The world at last was recognizing Lethbridge, Alberta.

Or so it seemed. The Seventh International Dry Farming Congress, held October 21 to 25, 1912, in conjunction with the Second International Congress of Farm Women and the International Conference of Agricultural Colleges was billed by the Alberta government as the largest gathering of agricultural experts and farmers ever assembled in North America. It drew representatives from fifteen foreign countries, including China and Persia. All Lethbridge hotel rooms, private billets, temporary dormitories and even tents were required to house the delegates. A temporary 2,500-seat convention centre was established around Galt Square for business meetings. It cost $2,500, though the city later recovered $1,600 from the salvage when it was dismantled[1].

The congress staff began arriving in Lethbridge the previous November (1911) and the 800 articles on dry farming they sent to newspapers and magazines all over the world generated enormous publicity for Lethbridge. More than 40,000 people passed through the gates during the six-day exposition and 13,000 were recorded as paid admissions.

[1]No detailed description of this structure was given at the time. Presumably it was housed in a tent like a circus bigtop, though this is mere conjecture.

This is Lethbridge in 1912, as presented on a real estate brochure. Notice the distant suburbs along the horizon and the plan for 'Dominion Square.' Lethbridge, in the thrall of boom-time development like the rest of the province, offered lavish tax incentives to attract industry, and later regretted it.

The dry farming congress was the high point of the Lethbridge boom. For three unbelievable years everything had spiralled upward. Lethbridge had become the undoubted Canadian leader in the relatively new science of irrigation. The entire city celebrated when area farmers won almost fifty prizes at the 1910 dry farming exposition in Spokane and earned Alberta the title of Sweepstake Province. In just one day that year, in a city of less than 9,000 people, more than 5,000 paid for admission to its annual Lethbridge fair.

Facts like those made Lethbridge the destination of choice for many of the land-hungry immigrants. There had been huge land rushes. In 1910 the Lethbridge Lands Office reported 4,952 applications for dryland homesteads and in the last major land rush, May 1, 1912, applicants lined up two abreast for four city blocks in the hope of getting homestead land in the Del Bonita area. Statistics on the city itself fanned the flames of boosterism. Between 1906 and 1911, the population had grown from 2,936 to 9,035, an increase of more than 200%.

This boundless optimism led to an orgy of overspending on schools and other facilities, and frantic subdivision of new housing areas. In 1911, more than $1 million worth of construction took place. In 1912, building permits to the value of about $500,000 had been issued by April and the city itself had set a budget of $2.35 million, with $1.1 million of that going to capital projects.

Euphoric Lethbridge expected it would soon become the province's railway hub, surpassing Calgary and Edmonton. Here elated residents ride flatcars as the first train crosses the CPR's viaduct bridge, highest of its type in the world, in 1909. In the next several years civic conjecture would run riot about an additional dozen lines — few of which would ever actually appear.

Some of these were undoubtedly inescapable. Services installed in the pioneer period had to be upgraded — like the water intake system, rebuilt in 1910 (and again in 1916 when a chlorinator was added to fight persistent outbreaks of typhoid, though even four years after that some residents still drew water and paid for it from horse-drawn tank carts or a standpipe). The sewage disposal system had to be rebuilt in 1911-12 because it did not conform to provincial standards. With the advent of three-storey buildings downtown, firefighting facilities had to be dramatically upgraded. A new power plant was required after fire destroyed the old one in 1910, causing a lengthy blackout. Generators from Galt Mines Nos. 3 and 6 provided emergency power. When garbage collection became a major concern in 1912, a coulee immediately south of Sick's brewery, later in the century the Third Avenue Extension, was designated as a public nuisance ground.

Finally, Lethbridge saw itself as the railway hub of Alberta, exceeding Calgary and Edmonton in the lines that were sure to intersect there. A map in the Jan. 23, 1912, edition of the *Lethbridge Herald* showed Lethbridge at the centre of a mass of railways, including four Canadian Pacific

The west side of Fifth Street, looking south from Third Avenue (above) and north (above right).

The city's northwest from the old water tower (above); looking east at Third Avenue and Fifth Street (right).

lines, three Canadian Northern Railway lines, four Grand Trunk Pacific lines, and several feeder lines from the Alberta Railway & Irrigation Company. The last mentioned grew out of the Galt mining company's decision to exploit the coal discoveries around Lethbridge, to build railways and to undertake irrigation projects. Late in 1912, the AR & I Co. was sold to the CPR.

Many of these lines were, of course, conjectural, yet one seemed utterly assured. The Canadian Pacific was definitely committed to bringing a line west to Lethbridge from Weyburn, Saskatchewan, a line that would make Lethbridge a main junction for grain coming out of southwestern Saskatchewan. Those words are "definitely committed," said Lethbridge boosters in their every communication with the CPR.

The dryland congress was certainly an impressive sight. For five days citizens of Lethbridge watched awestruck while prizes were awarded for all categories of sheafed grains and each evening seminar sessions were conducted on such topics as soils, tillage methods, and machinery used in dryland farming. But, like so many other things the city tried in those halcyon boom years, the results fell far short of the expectation. For one thing, there was a heavy financial loss. All the city's facilities had to be upgraded; people had to be fed and housed; other conference sites had to be constructed, apart from the main centre. What has been described as the ultimate

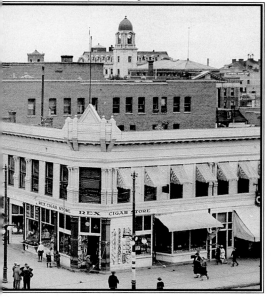

exercise in boosterism actually cost the city a great deal of money — money it simply did not have. However, it learned its lesson. A second international dryland irrigation conference, held in 1919, was not as elaborate and did not cost the city as much.

Lethbridge learned other lessons in those boom years, many of them much more painful. The city had joined the wild scramble for industries that epitomized urban Alberta, ignoring the fact that agriculture and coal were the real mainstays of its economy, and embracing the assumption that true affluence could come only from manufacturing. It competed with other prairie municipalities for the favour of investors, offering generous concessions — free sites, water and power at cost, and one or more decades of tax exemption. The development of the Bow Island-Lethbridge-Calgary natural gas pipeline, which brought natural gas to Lethbridge in 1912, also was an attraction, as was the rumoured billion-ton coal reserve discovered in 1885. Coal mining was still the main industry when the natural gas arrived.

Frequently Lethbridge found itself outbid by other Alberta centres, sometimes occasioning bitter recrimination. With lavish lures of free land and cheap utilities, for instance, the city competed

On an historic August day in 1912, Mayor George Hatch (far right) opened the city's first eleven miles of electric railway track, and also the annual fair on the new exhibition grounds. But on one of the very first trips a generator burned out and stranded fair-goers halfway there.

When racism ruled, Lethbridge enforced a Chinese ghetto
BEWILDERED PEOPLE ORDERED FROM THEIR HOMES INTO A RESTRICTED DISTRICT

Ratepayers of Lethbridge's North Ward and merchants on Round Street (later Fifth) persuaded city council in November 1910 to ban Chinese laundries and restaurants from their neighbourhoods. The bylaw applied to an area west of Smith (Fourth St.) and south of Ford (Second Ave.).

The bylaw, along with a similarly segregated school system, had the effect of moving virtually the entire Chinese population into that area, creating what amounted to a "Celestial" ghetto. (Contemporary slang referred to the Chinese as Celestials.)

Ostensibly, the move was to protect the area from the smells and noises associated with laundries, but the area was carefully drawn so as not to affect the white-owned Lethbridge Steam Laundry, which was, as the *Lethbridge Daily News*[a] pointed out, "a few yards outside the proposed limits." Neither of course did this explain the prohibition against Chinese restaurants.

Though the story was headlined "All Chinks Must Move," the *News* demonstrated a sympathy for the Chinese unusual for the times, particularly in Lethbridge. "The Chinese laundrymen feel as if they have been ordered off the earth," said the story, "for all of them that don't move from their present locations to the [segregated] part of the city sometime during the next eight days will be violating city bylaw No. 83. The Celestials are much wrought up over

the matter and have banded together to see if something cannot be done to amend the present bylaw."

Lethbridge's anti-Oriental disposition had two causes. Coal miners feared the Chinese who came to the city after the completion of the Canadian Pacific's Crowsnest Pass line would provide extra-cheap labour for the mine owners. Second, the Chinese community was viewed as a dangerous source of laudanum, an infusion of opium in alcohol, which was the drug of choice for white decadents in the first decades of the century. The Chinese were believed to be large and chronic users of opium.

The month after the bylaw was passed the *News* reported a shipment of opium had been seized by police. The story typifies the journalism of the day, utterly unconcerned that the press was in effect trying the case in print. "Detective Pat Egan Grabs Suspicious Celestial who Lands in Lethbridge with Seven Tins of Opium," said the headline.

The account continued:

Seven tins of opium were found in the possession of a Chinaman named Wong who arrived in the city on the 12:35 train last night from Vancouver. Wong got off the train carrying a small grip. Detective Pat Egan of the city force, who was standing close by, immediately became suspicious of the grip, and walking up to with Medicine Hat in 1911 as a western site for the Gordon Nail Works of Saint John, NB. Both lost to Calgary. Lethbridge and Medicine Hat had been "played for suckers," said the *Lethbridge Herald*, but Calgary was the biggest sucker of all. The only way it could have enticed the nail factory was to offer concessions far beyond those offered by the two southern cities.

Nevertheless many factories did accept the Lethbridge offer. Indeed, by 1920 Lethbridge was considered a logical visit for delegates attending the 1920 Canadian Manufacturers' Association meeting in Calgary, but by then the dubious fruition of all this enticement was plain. The city's financial stability had been gravely weakened. By 1913, when the boom ended, a third of the assessed city property was tax exempt and the city was still committed to heavy spending on facilities for the new industries. It was realized with great chagrin that many of the businesses wooed by Lethbridge would have settled there anyway because it centred a major agricultural area. Moreover, the gap between city revenues and city expenditures was widening alarmingly and small businessmen staggered under the tax burden caused in part by the earlier concessions.

Probably the greatest plunge into wild-eyed optimism was the street railway system. The idea had been kicking around since 1906 but it wasn't until 1910 that the project reached the committee stage, pushed by expectations for the dry farming congress. By the end of 1911, tenders worth almost $200,000 were being called. On Aug. 16, 1912, on what was to be a great and historic day for Lethbridge, Mayor George Hatch opened the first eleven miles of track.

It was a great day because it inaugurated more than streetcar service. The same ceremony launched the annual fair on the new exhibition grounds at Henderson Park. This 280 acres of land, surrounding what had hitherto been inelegantly known as Slaughterhouse Slough, was purchased by the city in 1910 and became the start of the parks system. It featured a grandstand and

the Chinaman, asked if he might see what was in it. The Chinaman refused and the detective, showing him his authority, demanded to see what it contained. Wong immediately thrust his hand into his pocket, found the key and threw it away, whereupon Detective Egan immediately arrested him... Wong is a big Celestial, nearly six feet tall, and a roughhouse was started outside the depot. He was very game, and put up a hard fight for freedom, but the detective overpowered him and started for the police station... The usual search being made, both of Wong and the bag, seven tins of opium each weighing about half a pound were found in the grip, while Wong had $95 on his person, besides the drug which is worth $15 a tin... The Celestial is an isolated smuggler. As far as the police can ascertain, he has no relatives in Lethbridge to whom he was bringing the opium but it is thought that he would not have had any difficulty in disposing of his goods if he had escaped the police.

The bylaw was rescinded in 1916 when the Great War had made the Germans the preferred target of hatred instead.

Ironically, Lethbridge would one day be given a chance to recant from its early anti-Oriental racism when Japanese evacuees from the B.C. coast were sent to southern Alberta sugar beet fields during the Second World War. Although initially forbidding the evacuees from entering the city, Lethbridge authorities finally relented. After the war many Japanese settled there and became some of the city's foremost citizens. Lethbridge's Nikka Yuko Japanese Gardens would become one of the tourist attractions of Alberta.

— *S.K.*

[a]The faltering *News*, initially a daily paper, was controlled by J.H. Woods with L.S. Gowe as publisher from November 1910 to March 1912 when it was sold to the Southam Company. It became a weekly in August 1913 and folded that December. The *Lethbridge Telegram*, another daily, began a year later. It folded in 1918.

Not all whites were hostile to the Chinese, as this photo evidences. It portrays the steps of a school for Chinese being conducted in Lethbridge early in the century. No further identification is available.

Glenbow Archives, NA-3092-3

THE NEW CITIES

How the charming Galt Gardens came to be

Townsfolk were accustomed to playing ball on the vacant property they called The Square. It became a park when Elliott Galt, manager of his family's extensive Lethbridge holdings, donated it to the city in 1910. Then landscaping began; growth is discernible even between 1914 (above) and 1919 (below). But amenities like this very much depended on the prosperity of the city, which in turn depended on settlers like the ones who lined up for the last major land offering, at the Dominion Lands Office on May 1, 1912 (below left).

Fritz Sick, founder of a brewing dynasty, poses beside the doorway of his original brewery in this undated photograph. His product (sample inset) would one day make Lethbridge famous. By 1913 this frame building had been replaced by a substantial brick structure.

racetrack. The slough was converted into a lake suitable for swimming and boating. The park also had a small zoo, with two bears in a pit and an eagle in a cage[2].

The double event stirred an unbounded exuberance, but here again the dream began dissolving almost immediately. On one of the first streetcar trips to the fairgrounds, a temporary generator burned out and left revellers stranded halfway to the park. CPR trains took over and transported fairgoers to and from the park every half-hour. This was a symptom of worse troubles to come.

It became apparent quickly that Lethbridge's small population could not support the expensive five-line system radiating out of the downtown core that the planners had conceived. One line was discontinued almost as soon as it was built. In 1914, the crew on each car was reduced from two men to one man. Later the same year, all workers were fired and then rehired at a lower wage. The firings coincided with other civic layoffs and led to labour unrest. Vandals cut several cables at the power plant and caused other damage.

In 1917 the city abandoned the longest of the five lines and continued to reduce service, adding workers to an unemployment line already lengthened by workers at Fritz Sick's brewery, shut down in 1916 when Prohibition became law. Operating only three of the five lines cost the city $45,000 annually. Eventually, in 1947, the city closed the street railway entirely.

Within a few months all the optimism seemed to vanish. In a 1914 report, civic officials said the city was in a great depression "which naturally made it a very difficult year to handle civic affairs from the monetary point of view and, in fact, from every point of view. The banks have all been remarkably conservative and, in our estimation, laid down conditions of borrowing that were very difficult to comply with and keep the city's affairs moving."

The report said that although taxes were coming in more freely than in any other city in Alberta, there were many delinquents, "which in combination with the banks' conservatism makes the navigation of the city's affairs at times a very difficult matter." However, the officials predicted confidently that the city "will come through 1915 with flying colours."

But by now the Great War was upon Alberta and it absorbed almost everyone's attention. Superficially, Lethbridge benefited from the war. A British company established a helium gas plant in the city. First gas, and then oil, was discovered by Ira Segur in the Sweetgrass-Coutts area. The coal mines, which had helped Lethbridge get established, increased their output in response to wartime demand and prices were good. There were bumper crops in 1915 and 1916 and, again, high wartime prices. In order to encourage food production, the Canadian government removed tariffs on small tractors entering Canada from the U.S. and in 1918 one local dealer sold more than 200 small gasoline tractors to area farmers.

However, these gains did not take into account the immeasurable loss of some of its finest young men. Almost a quarter of Lethbridge's population served in the armed forces. Ten percent of those did not return. There was a social price as well. Though the city enjoyed a period of relative prosperity from 1916 to 1919, the returning veterans did not share in it (see Vol. 4, Sect. 3, ch. 1).

Just at the end of the decade, however, came an event of unquestionable economic significance. After long negotiations, the government of Premier Charles Stewart agreed to bestow full provincial guarantees on all irrigation bonds. This led to massive irrigation projects in the Lethbridge agriculture area that would turn the 1920s into another boom.

But even that scarcely outweighed the increasingly bitter disappointment over the Weyburn railway line, linchpin (or so it was viewed) of the whole plan to make Lethbridge a major railway centre. The million-dollar project, to which the railway was "definitely committed," was "almost guaranteed" in January 1911. However, the bust intervened and the war intervened, and the on-again, off-again project generated more miles of newspaper than it did trackage. Each time the

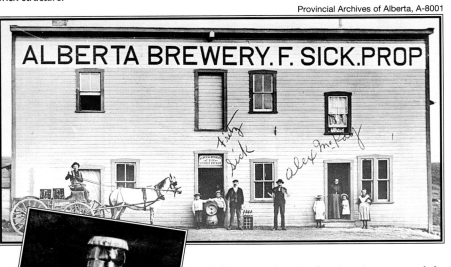

Provincial Archives of Alberta, A-8001

ALBERTA BREWERY. F. SICK. PROP

City of Lethbridge Archives, P19770145000-GP

A SMILE IN EVERY BOTTLE

THE NEW CITIES

CPR promised it, there were paeans on the editorial pages to the company's vision and integrity, and each time it didn't happen there were more columns of denunciation for its shortsightedness and lacklustre caution. Pleas to the federal government to take over the construction were rejected and other railways refused to attempt to buy the rights and the property from the CPR. In February 1920 CPR vice-president Grant Hall promised the line would be built that year "unless a cyclone strikes us." He was almost as good as his word and the line was finally completed in 1922, crossing from Saskatchewan through Manyberries and Foremost to Stirling, where a connecting line brought it into Lethbridge. But by then the dream of a great rail centre had vanished.

Even so, in 1920 those residents who had been there since 1900 realized that the city had changed unrecognizably. There were paved streets, streetcars, three-storey buildings and thousands more people. Staffordville had been annexed to become North Lethbridge and the city's population had topped 10,000. True the teen years had not fulfilled the promise the great dryland farming congress had portended, but neither had they been unproductive. Despite the bust, despite the awful war, much had been accomplished.

How Lethbridge finally got itself moved off the banks of the Belly

RESPECTABLE LADIES COULDN'T SAY WHERE THEIR CITY WAS LOCATED

by Alan Rayburn

In 1910, the Lethbridge Board of Trade declared itself "very much disgusted" with the name of the river upon which its city was situated. It was called "the Belly."

Lethbridge citizens were convinced their metropolis deserved a river whose name did not engender embarrassment. (In those days "belly" was a word avoided in polite company.) They had campaigned since 1886, but gaining a change took almost thirty years.

Alberta's Belly River rises some twelve miles (20 km) south of the 49th parallel in Montana and flows north to join the Oldman River eleven miles (18 km) upstream from Lethbridge. It was given its name during a survey in 1858 by Thomas Blakiston, a member of the Palliser Expedition, and the name first appeared on a map in 1865.

Blakiston derived the name from the Blackfoot *Mokowanis*, meaning "big bellies," referring to the local Atsina Indians. He applied it to the whole river from its source to its confluence with the Bow River, where the two rivers become the South Saskatchewan, 55 miles (90 km) northeast of Lethbridge. Thus when the city of Lethbridge was laid out near a series of rich coal deposits in 1885, it found itself on the east bank of the Belly.

Just one year later, Minister of the Interior Thomas White visited Lethbridge, and residents asked him to get the name changed. No action was taken, and in 1900 *Lethbridge News* publisher E.T. Saunders urged a change too. He wrote about the discomfort of strangers and the blushing embarrassment of ladies. He suggested that the St. Mary River, a tributary of the Belly upriver from Lethbridge, be designated the main watercourse, with the Belly as a branch of it. That way, Lethbridge would sit beside the St. Mary.

Six years later (and still no action), Saunders again appealed to the authorities. He claimed the name Belly made Lethbridge appear to be a crude settlement, and suggested extending the name South Saskatchewan River to some point upriver from Lethbridge.

In 1910, the Lethbridge Board of Trade wrote a letter to the Department of the Interior proposing the name Alberta River for the entire watercourse, including what would later become both the Oldman and South Saskatchewan rivers. The Geographic Board rejected the proposal, stating the new name had no authority based on usage, and noting in any case that the Bow was the principal tributary of the South Saskatchewan. The Board of Trade asked for other alternatives to Belly, but the Geographic Board responded by urging it to canvass local residents for their own alternatives.

The matter languished until 1913, when the Board of Trade again asked the Department of the Interior to replace Belly River with Alberta River, "a name citizens could call attention to with pride." The Geographic Board told the Board of Trade to obtain the views of local authorities and the endorsement of the province.

In 1915, the Board of Trade asked Premier Arthur Sifton to approve Alberta River, but Sifton said he preferred Lethbridge River. This new proposal was sent to the Geographic Board, which declined to accept it. Geologist and Geographic Board member Donaldson Dowling pointed out that the Oldman River carried considerably more water than the Belly at their confluence, and suggested carrying the name Oldman River to its juncture with the Bow. This would make the Belly the Oldman's tributary and put Lethbridge on the Oldman. It was the compromise the Geographic Board approved in August 1915, and thus Lethbridge finally got rid of its Belly River.

— *from* Canadian Geographic *magazine*

For 40 years Lethbridge was Alberta's sex capital
HISTORIANS CALL IT THE CITY'S 'GOLDEN AGE OF PROSTITUTION' AFTER REFORMERS LOST THE WAR AGAINST THE NOTORIOUS 'POINT'

The greatest single cause for Lethbridge's celebrity during the first half of the 20th century was not its skill in dryland farming, its significance as a source of coal, or the products of its famous brewery. The fact is, it was best known for sex. From the days of its inception until the late 1940s, it harboured the most renowned and most persistent prostitution business in the province.

The origins of this industry in Lethbridge are easily apprehended. The coal miners who came from central Europe were mostly single men. These, plus the cowboys from the ranches, plus the railway workers who built the Crowsnest line, plus transient farm labour, gave the industry its beginning. Consequently the most notable aspect of Lethbridge social and political endeavour during the second decade of the century was the effort of local church and women's groups to get rid of the bordellos. They failed.

The Temperance and Moral Reform League began the campaign against prostitution in 1909. The fact is, said the reformers, the city's brothels operate utterly undisturbed by any law enforcement whatever. The reaction of municipal

I have it from people living off the street leading to the district that the drunken rowdyism, obscene language and fighting there is almost more than they can bear. It is depreciating the value of their property, to say nothing of the abomination of the thing. With my own eyes in broad daylight I saw an automobile filled with half-drunken men go down Round Street [later Fifth] and turn down Redpath [Third Avenue S.]. Their loud brawling conversation was such that the men, women and children on the streets could not help but know where they were going.

The Galt Hospital was similarly annoyed. Its recently expanded building — later donated to the city by Elliott Galt, son of founder Sir Alexander — was also on the road leading to The Point.

The Knox Presbyterian Men's Club, after lengthy harangues from the clergy and women's groups, passed a resolution in the spring of 1910 urging city council to do away with the red-light district and the "evils of prostitution

---

It soon became evident to the clergymen that what opposed them was not merely indifference to prostitution, but a distinct if largely unspoken support for it. Some council members seemed quietly proud of this Lethbridge attraction.

---

officialdom to their demand was a mixture of scorn, futility and mirth. Most officials said closing the houses of ill repute was impossible. Some even saw them as "culturally positive." After all, they said, where but in the whorehouses could you hear such modern innovations as the phonograph, playing often into the small hours of the morning?

But by 1910 the league, now under the guidance of the Rev. Thomas Parker Perry of Wesley Methodist Church, had won some concessions. To much snickering, Perry disclosed that he had made a "personal investigation" into the notorious area known as The Point[a] and found at least five brothels operating there with thirty "inmates." Twenty-two were prostitutes, while eight were female servants. There were also several Chinese menservants. The Methodist minister shrewdly directed his attack on the sex business, carefully making no mention of the gambling houses that also ran unchecked on Round Street, which gave access to The Point. He would take on one evil at a time. The prostitutes, he said, were "of the most hardened types and, to top it all, most of them are aliens!" Their customers included married men of the town as well as single men. He continued:

as a menace and disgrace." Council should give "hearty support" to the police in this endeavour, they said. Finally, the city should offer all possible help to "the unfortunate women" in turning them towards "a pure and virtuous life." This resolution was presented to city council by Perry along with the Rev. Alex Gordon of the Presbyterian Church and the Rev. A.J. Prosser of the Baptist.

It soon became evident to these clergymen, however, that what opposed them was not merely indifference to prostitution but a distinct if largely unspoken support for it. Some council members seemed quietly proud of this Lethbridge attraction. Then, too, there was the factor of so many single men in the city. Police Chief Joseph Gillespie and Mayor Elias Adams believed in segregation and control of prostitution. Indeed, The Point was more formally known as the Segregated Area.

To appease the reformers certain moderate gestures were proposed. The street leading to The Point would become the most brilliantly lighted street in the city. A policeman stationed there would take the names of any men going to that quarter. Construction work in progress on a new bordello

Pauline Sylvia Fair, alias Irene Walker, aged 23 in 1919, Danish-born, keeper of a disorderly house.

Audrey Mauda, aged 28 in 1919, Norwegian-born, keeper of a disorderly house.

Pearl Newton, aged 22 in 1918, ordered to leave town on account of prostitution.

These ladies of the night were undoubtedly familiar to the patrons of The Point

Four of these women, filed in the Glenbow Archives, were well known to the Calgary Police Department as transient prostitutes or madams, and doubtless all of them at one time found work during the Great War period in Lethbridge's notorious red-light district, known as The Point. The picture of the fifth, Florence Phyllis Clark, turned up with the rest although she was charged not with prostitution but with bigamy, a much more serious offence.

Jenny Lebousky, alias Jennie Johnson, alias Babe Johnson, aged 23 in 1917, inmate of a disorderly house.

Florence Phyllis Clark, aged 23 in 1918, born in England, sentenced to one year for bigamy.

would be stopped forthwith, and the building of any additional houses of prostitution forbidden. The city called this "a policy of discouragement"[b]. In fact, however, most of these "improvements" never materialized, and the Segregated Area flourished for a further 35 years.

The city fathers, by now obviously irked, threw back a challenge at the churches. Mayor Adams suggested they restore these women "to respectable society" by building a home for them. "Where is your Christianity," he demanded, "when you come forward only with the request that we push the women farther down the path to ruin?" Perry replied defensively that he had the word of the resident captain of the Salvation Army that the women were "beyond redemption"[c].

Baptist pastor Prosser went much further, and came out

with rhetorical guns blazing: "How dare you try to foist the responsibility on to us! We are under no responsibility to do anything. It is up to you to enforce the law, for you have no right under the law to permit a segregated area of houses of ill fame to exist. You say things will be worse if the houses are closed. I say, close these houses and drive these evil women from our city and then, if you are correct, the law can be changed."

This 1910 confrontation, however, seemed to exhaust the reformers' zeal. Most were preoccupied with major church-building programs in more respectable parts of town. For two years there was a ceasefire in the war on prostitution. Then in 1912, it broke out again when Inspector Robert Nimmons of the Alberta Liquor Licence Board laid charges against the brothels for serving liquor, something

A westward view of The Point, source of delight for the unregenerate and bane of the reformers. Decade after decade The Point was the centre of acrimonious civic debate. In the background smoke rises from the municipal garbage dump.

they had been doing all along. This brought William A. Buchanan's *Lethbridge Herald* into action, Buchanan being a member of parliament, a former provincial cabinet minister and chief Liberal power-broker in southern Alberta. His paper was known as "Buck's Bible" and it demanded: "Where are the police when teenaged boys are permitted to buy liquor illegally and carouse around the streets?"

Answering so urgent a call, Chief Gillespie raided The Point and what the *Herald* called "five soiled doves from the Tenderloin" were charged with selling liquor to minors. Ultimately, only one was prosecuted and that case was dismissed for lack of evidence. Meanwhile, Frankie Berry, one of the "soiled doves," wrote to the *Herald*, which published her indignant letter. The boys, she said, were not getting booze in the brothels because they were not permitted inside. As a matter of fact, they were getting it from respectable Lethbridge citizens, she charged, then going to The Point and creating a disturbance.

Meanwhile all this community pressure had gradually eroded the position of Police Chief Gillespie. In 1912, he faced another crisis when two of his men, Detective Pat Egan and Inspector Leslie Silliker, appeared secretly before the police and licence committee and complained Gillespie was on the take.

Southminster United Church, Lethbridge

The council snickered as Rev. T.P. Perry told of the personal investigation he had made of 'The Point.'

Hearing this, Gillespie fired them. The council fired Gillespie and reinstated Egan and Silliker. Pummelled then by the pro-brothelists, they suspended the pair as well, sustained the firing of Gillespie, and asked for a judicial inquiry into the police department.

No sooner had the auditors begun a preliminary examination of the department's books than the court clerk suddenly resigned. Meanwhile Judge Roland Winters catalogued the assorted charges against Gillespie: taking money from madams, being drunk on duty, drinking in bars, and using obscene language in public.

Winters' investigation exonerated Gillespie on all but one of these charges. It seemed conclusive that he had not only taken money from the madams, but actively solicited it. However, said the judge, it seemed equally conclusive Gillespie had used this money to support local charities. On one occasion, when the Salvation Army was confronted with a financial crisis, the chief had actually escorted a Salvation Army representative, a woman, around The Point's brothels so she could solicit donations. His philanthropies notwithstanding, council fired Gillespie on Sept. 16, 1912, with a month's pay, and dumped Egan and Silliker with no severance whatever.

Gillespie's successor, William Davis, acted swiftly, raided The Point, closed the houses, and awaited the warm gratitude of the citizenry. Instead he found himself being pilloried. Business was on the decline, said the downtown merchants. People stopped coming into Lethbridge to shop. Meanwhile, the raids had scattered the prostitutes all over the city and simply reinforced the belief that the Segregated Area was preferable. The baffled Davis wearily let the girls return with some additional restrictions: they were permitted downtown only one day per week and delivery boys had to take them toiletries and medicinal supplies and mail their letters for them. A few months later Davis himself was gone.

For the next five years, while the Great War preoccupied Lethbridge and the world, business continued as usual at The Point with one distressing exception. Alberta voted itself dry in July 1915 — overruling Lethbridge which, predictably, was the only place in the province that voted to stay wet — but the houses continued to provide liquor anyway, their proprietors bitterly complaining that Prohibition made the supply uncertain, the quality dubious and the price outrageous. They were at the mercy of criminal types, like bootleggers and rumrunners, said the madams.

Then suddenly in 1917, with a new regime in office at city hall, the whole issue burst forth again. This time Mayor W.D.L. Hardie was said to be on the take, and the press printed charges that the madams operated under the protection of the city and paid $300 to $350 a month per house for protection. The provincial government hastened to investigate. An undercover police officer located forty active prostitutes where the city police had said there were none. However, insinuations of graft against Mayor Hardie were not proven.

Perhaps more from market forces than police forces, The Point nevertheless gradually lost its appeal. By the end of the decade it was virtually deserted and the houses and their residents had moved to a new Segregated Area bounded by First and Fifth Avenues and First and Fourth Streets.

In 1920, Pat Egan returned to the force, first as a detective under Chief James Harris, and then as chief himself. He quietly restored the prostitution trade to its Gillespie status; re-established and rigidly enforced a system of regularly scheduled medical inspections, ordered the women off the streets and laid down strict rules of decorum for the operation of the houses.

Police chief Joseph Gillespie (above) fired Inspector Leslie Silliker (inset) when Silliker secretly complained to the police committee that the chief was on the take. A judicial inquiry decided Gillespie was collecting graft from the madams — but also appeared to be handing it on to charities.

The new Segregated Area operated relatively unchecked until after the Second World War, providing for nearly three decades Lethbridge's main tourist attraction in what Lethbridge historians call "The Golden Age of Prostitution."

— *S.K.*

[a]The Point covered the triangular spit of land extending west between what would later be known as Lodge Coulee and Hospital Coulee, bounded on the east by Second Street South and on the north and south by the two coulees.

[b]As the city fathers well knew, the 'policy of discouragement' had wide gaps. Although prostitutes from other places officially were prohibited from entering Lethbridge, they did anyway, often taking up residence in another area called The Bottoms, whose houses seemingly served as farm teams for the gaudy and prestigious brothels on The Point.

[c]In the theology of nearly all Christian churches, it would be heretical to declare anyone 'beyond redemption,' Christ having admonished his followers to 'judge not.'

CHAPTER FIVE

In three wild and zany years Edmonton burst forth as a city

NEW BUILDINGS RISE, NEW BRIDGES APPEAR, STRATHCONA IS ENGULFED, WHILE 32 AVID BROKERS AND 336 AGENTS FAN A REAL ESTATE FRENZY

by VIRGINIA BYFIELD

Alberta from its inception was characterized by urban schizophrenia. Where every other province in the Canadian federation (with the single exception of neighbouring Saskatchewan) had one large city and numerous satellite ones, Alberta had two major cities competing for dominance. This duality shaped its history. Although Edmonton was the older, it was also the perpetual underdog obsessed with a constant challenge: keeping up with Calgary. By 1910 Edmonton had scored two grand coups: it had become the provincial capital; and Strathcona, on the opposite bank of the North Saskatchewan River, was the chosen site of the provincial university. Nevertheless, much was lacking. Calgary was still far ahead.

For one thing, Calgary was still ahead in population, recording 60,502 residents to Edmonton's 57,045 in the 1911 census[1]. For another, Calgary was a major divisional point on the Canadian Pacific Railway, still the only Canadian line to reach the west coast. True, Edmonton had both the Canadian Northern and the Grand Trunk Pacific and these were building westward, but they had a long way to go to the Pacific. Again, Calgary specialized in ranching and the allied meat-packing industry, and was therefore more focused economically. Edmonton, where occupations ranged from coal mining to flour milling, envisioned a fine future as a hub for the vast north country — but access to that region was still, to put it mildly, primitive.

Calgary, moreover, was more ethnically cohesive. With its complement of ranchers from affluent Ontario and British families, it had pretensions to social and cultural grandeur. Edmonton, already split between British and

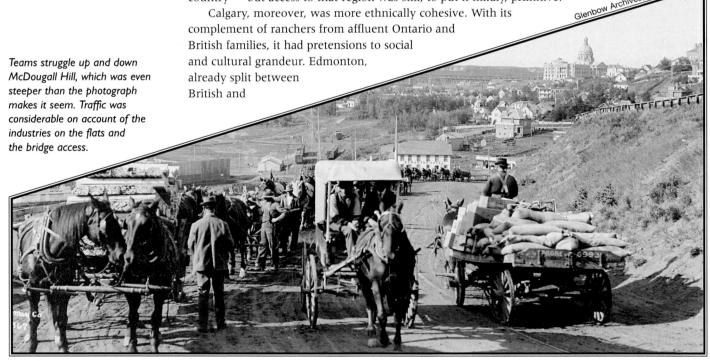

Glenbow Archives, NA-1328-64867

Teams struggle up and down McDougall Hill, which was even steeper than the photograph makes it seem. Traffic was considerable on account of the industries on the flats and the bridge access.

French, was rapidly adding a significant and vocal eastern European minority. The tea-and-tennis Ontarians who ran Strathcona across the river might make some claim to social and municipal dignity. But Edmonton had to endure such burdens as its city council which, as the new decade unfolded, proceeded from one scandal to the next, punctuated invariably with unseemly shouting matches and threats of personal violence.

Nonetheless, Edmontonians in 1910 were not inclined to brood much over these disabilities. They were too busy. As the prairie filled with homesteaders, and the railways finally came through, Edmonton's prospects, like those of every other city, town and village in the West, seemed boundless. The *Journal* reported in January that the city's 1909 debenture issues, worth more than a million dollars, had sold well over par in London and Toronto. The Grand Trunk Pacific was through the mountains and laying track westward towards Prince Rupert at a rate of two miles a day. The newspapers reprinted admiring articles from publications like *The Economist* and the *New York Commercial*. Edmonton's November air was "as stimulating as champagne," one such article reported, and its economic potential as a distributing point "impossible to compute." Another called the rapid development of western Canada "a 20th-century miracle" and Edmonton "one of the most progressive communities in the Dominion." It was "the prospective railway, commercial, educational and financial metropolis of this whole marvellous region."

Such encomiums in the outside world greatly enhanced the prospects of municipal debentures, immigration and, not least, real estate. Real estate fever, already epidemic both in Edmonton and Strathcona, would peak in the next three years. John G. Niddrie, in a reminiscence included in Hugh Dempsey's *The Best of Alberta History*, writes that in November 1911 real estate advertising filled columns of the three daily papers, real estate offices filled all available buildings,

Wagons, automobiles and a trolley mingle uneasily on Jasper Avenue in this 1912 photograph, looking east from 101 Street. The population of Alberta's capital had surpassed 57,000. The city's economic potential was 'impossible to compute,' declared one visiting newspaperman, while another called Edmonton 'one of the most progressive communities in the Dominion.'

The Hamly Press contrived to combine four photographs for a panoramic view of the city in 1909 (top). Then in 1913, at the peak of the boom, photographers Ole Voldeng and Eric Bolton almost precisely duplicated the 1909 pictures, providing a graphic record of growth.

[1]Neither Edmonton nor Calgary had anything to gain by slighting references to the other, the *Edmonton Journal* editorialized piously in March 1911, and Edmontonians fortunately weren't like that. Sad to say, however, a certain Calgary element, 'of which the *Albertan* is the journalistic spokesman, never loses a chance to disparage Edmonton.' The latest example was an *Albertan* claim that in 1910 Calgary's population had increased by 66 2/3%, to 50,000. Other western cities followed (e.g. Regina 26%, Saskatoon 25%). 'At the bottom,' fumed the *Journal*, 'appears Edmonton, which is generously allowed an increase of 10%. What our actual population is does not appear.'

and real estate blackboards outside the offices were filled with chalk-written "specials today." Young Niddrie, just married and working as an agriculture department clerk, got his brother-in-law to back a note for $250, bought a lot in Windsor Park near the site of the university for $650 on fairly tough terms for the times (one-third cash, balance in six and twelve months), and sold it a week later for $750[2].

A.F. Dreger, another young man who caught the fever, used to work a full day at his lumber yard, then hurry down to Whyte Avenue where "the real estate offices stayed open as long as there were any customers around." By the spring of 1912, he recalls in *A Most Diversified Character: A Pioneer's Memories of Early Strathcona and Edmonton*, "the city was buzzing no matter where you went. People were flocking in like bees to a honey pot... Hotels, rooming-houses and boarding-houses were filled to overflowing...people were forced to live in tents." Fortunately, he adds, the weather that spring and summer was "the best ever." The city council made the Granite Curling Club and some schools available as temporary housing, writes J.G. MacGregor in *Edmonton: A History*, and still some 2,600 people were camped about the river flats and the town's outskirts.

By 1912 *Henderson's Directory* listed 32 real estate brokers and 336 independent agents. A virtual war was in progress among established firms like McDougall & Secord, J.G. Tipton & Sons, York & McNamara and major new ones like Magrath & Holgate, and scores of transient operators known as "curbstone dealers." The latter, although not illegal, were seen as unfair competition. With no offices and no overhead, they hung about Jasper and Whyte avenues to waylay prospects before they reached the licensed realtors. Twenty-six established firms had formed the Edmonton Real Estate Exchange in early 1909, to curb the curbers and also to make sure all properties for sale, not just the high-priced ones, were openly listed. But a year later, the *Edmonton Bulletin* reported, "Wolves in sheep's clothing have been found within the fold." Four members of the exchange had resigned, accusing colleagues of offending on both counts (i.e. dealing with "curbstone men" and keeping choice prospects secret), and the exchange was disbanded.

The licensed agents all used runners, however, to steer buyers their way for lots in the new residential subdivisions that were being promoted in both Edmonton and Strathcona. Runners, who worked on commission, could be almost anybody and pop up almost anywhere. Anecdotalist Tony Cashman describes in *Best Edmonton Stories* how a trolley conductor and motorman did a thriving business from their streetcar, with a map of the subdivision they were pushing displayed in the motorman's compartment.

A realtor would survey a quarter-section farm into about thirty city blocks, thus producing about 300 lots, and give it an attractive name. If the farm was ten feet higher than the surrounding land, Cashman acidly observes, it was likely to be called "Something-View" (e.g. City View in Edmonton's then-remote northwest beyond the GTP tracks). If it was ten feet lower, "Something-Dale" was a favourite combination (e.g. Strathcona's Allendale). But the main thing was to convey a touch of elegance.

"STUDY THIS MAP," urged a York & McNamara full-page newspaper ad in early 1910. "Note also the key plan of the lots below and think quickly of BELVEDERE. It is the natural dwelling place for those who will be concerned in the development of this growing district." Belvedere, which seventy years later would give its name to an LRT station, was north of the GTP and Swift's packing plant. "Consider the prices," the ad implored, "either as a future resident or a present investor." Belvedere lots ranged from $60 to $180 — terms 10% cash and $5 a month, interest-free. That was standard.

"Park" was another favourite for development names. L.T. Murray (224 Jasper East Upstairs — Office Open Evenings) was promoting Garden Park, about seven miles southwest of the university. "The Proposed Saskatchewan Ave. Driveway Runs Past This Property," said his ads. Corner lots sold for $25, inside lots for $20, and buyers would also get to guess "the number of beans in a sealer on exhibition in this office." The promised first prize: a $1,200 house and five-acre lot.

The Seton-Smith Company offered property in Dominion Park, describing its location as "Cornering Edmonton City Limits on Alberta Avenue" (118th). It would not be subject to city taxes, and the St. Albert electric cars would soon pass nearby. Get in with the wise ones and expect a 300% return on investment, Seton-Smith urged, offering automobile transport to Dominion Park prospects.

Roads and streetcar service to the subdivisions were a vital point. That St. Albert line, for instance, did not survive[3]. To persuade the city council to make the steel bridge taking Athabasca Avenue (102nd) across Groat Ravine into Glenora forty feet wide, rather than twenty, developers Carruthers & Round offered the city twenty acres for parks. Glenora, on the city's western edge beyond the Groat Estate, acquired a single-track streetcar line after 1912. Even so, it long remained a sparsely populated upper-class rural enclave; title was restricted by a Carruthers caveat requiring all homes to be worth a minimum of $3,500.

William J. Magrath, whose Highlands subdivision opened in late 1910, spent $20,000 to

[2]Erstwhile realtor John George Niddrie (1887-1972), who had been raised on a ranch near Sundre, used the profit from his 1911-12 boom-time efforts to complete his teacher training. Meanwhile, he writes, a property deal he put through for Elmer Luck, modern language master at Strathcona Collegiate Institute, enabled Luck to go to Germany for doctoral studies at Leipzig University. There Luck was interned as an enemy alien in 1914, two weeks short of his degree, but he got home a year later and went to work for Victoria High School. Niddrie became one of the founding members of the Alberta Teachers' Association. He ended his career as principal of Westglen High School.

[3]In 1912-13 a private company, the Edmonton Interurban Railway, built a line from Alberta Avenue (118th) and 24th Street (124th) through Calder to Perron Street in St. Albert, following a devious route through a development called Summerland that was being promoted by an associated real estate firm. One car (with an electric motor powered by a gasoline engine) made four round trips daily until it exploded in the EIR car barn in April 1914. Efforts to restore passenger service and add freight hauling failed, Edmonton's transit system eventually took over the city trackage, and Summerland faded out by 1917.

Alberta's magnificent new Legislature

Below, the building under construction and as photographed complete from 104 Street and Jasper; top right, the elegant rotunda and (lower right) chamber. Opposite page (top), the imposing structure as seen from below; another view of the session room (lower left); and the marble central stairway (lower right).

There can be little doubt which of these gentlemen in the D.R. Bobeau Real Estate office (above left), circa 1912-13, are real estate salesmen and which are possible clients. Strathcona Land & Building Co. Ltd. (top right) features an appeal to German immigrants. At lower left, a Griffiths & Duffield agent makes his pitch right in the doorway.

extend the streetcar tracks to its east Edmonton riverbank location. This too was to be a fashionable district; Magrath and his partner, Bidwell A. Holgate, set the tone by erecting for themselves handsome brick mansions[4]. Other developers tried to figure out where the tracks were likely to go — or do what they could to influence the routing — and buy accordingly. By the end of 1913, sixty-three subdivisions were being marketed north of the river and 31 on the south side, some of them quite remarkably remote from the developed area.

In May 1912, however, there burst forth a real estate bonanza that was not at all remote. The Hudson's Bay Company, which still held a great block of empty land in Edmonton's northwest (the future 108 Avenue north to 118th, and 101 Street west to 121st), decided the time had come to sell[5]. The HBC promised to pave Portage Avenue (Kingsway), which ran diagonally across it; the city had agreed to provide a double streetcar line. A public lottery would be held at 2 p.m., Monday, May 12, at which 1,500 numbered tickets would be drawn. Each would entitle the holder to buy four lots, and the numbers would determine the order of choice.

The location of the draw was not to be announced until the last minute, but the secret leaked out. Rumour had it, the *Journal* explained the following day, that one Fenton T. Aitken had noticed HBC officials unloading a safe at a small unused church on Third Street (103rd) and Athabasca (102nd) on Saturday; on Sunday evening he planted himself at the door. By the time the HBC announcement duly appeared in the Monday morning newspapers, there were easily 1,500 men in a line-up stretching all the way to Sixth Street (106th), most of whom had been there all night.

It was an eclectic gathering — a local doctor complete with camp bed, realtors like D.J. McNamara, labourers, even a scattering of women. More women brought in lunches for their men. "At breakfast time the scene looked like the back yard of a restaurant," the *Journal* reporter wrote. Hopefuls who had journeyed in from Vegreville, Vermilion and other outlying communities were understandably indignant. Some of the earlybirds sold their places in line for anything from fifty dollars up. Arthur Davies, former mayor of Strathcona, reportedly got $1,000 for his spot, 87th in line.

HBC officials had the numbered tickets in a box suspended from rollers. At 2 p.m., when the box had been thoroughly whirled about, first-comer Aitken made his draw — and got No. 910. A brisk trade in tickets began as the crowd filed through. No. 28, the *Journal* said, was sold for $1,500. Cashman reports that No. 2, drawn by a man who happened to be visiting from Winnipeg, brought $5,000. Not a bad return for a night's vigil. The lot sales began next day and

[4]W.J. Magrath, who named the street along the riverbank Ada Boulevard after his wife, built a fourteen-room, portico-embellished mansion there in 1912. It featured a top-floor ballroom, basement swimming pool, hand-painted linen and silk wallpaper and frescoed ceilings. The similar Holgate mansion beside it had twenty rooms. Unlike the even more lavish downtown homes of early developers John A. McDougall and Richard Secord, which would both be demolished by 1975, these two would survive — still handsome — many decades later.

The HBC staged a land sale to end all land sales — and it nearly did

People lined up all night and most of the next day for a chance to buy a lot in the Hudson's Bay Reserve, the crowd reaching an estimated 1,500 and blocking surrounding streets. Some sold their place in the line-up, at $50 and far upward.

After years of negotiation, the High Level Bridge arises

The steel structure of the bridge progresses from the river's south bank towards the first of its massive 138-foot piers (above). The photo at left, when acquired by the Provincial Archives, bore the information: 'Roland, Sam and Sam's brothers taken on the High Level Bridge when it was under construction.'

went on for weeks. In the end 1,543 pieces of HBC property traded for a total of $4.3 million.

Meanwhile prices kept on escalating. The corner lot at Jasper and First Street, along with the one next to it, offered for sale in 1891 for $75, was sold by McDougall & Secord in 1913 for $500,000. Edmonton policeman Joseph Schreyer, who bought three lots at Isabella Street (104th Ave.) and Namayo Avenue (97th St.) for $15 in 1898, sold them in 1913 for $65,000 and decided to build himself an $8,000 house on Heiminck Street (107th Ave.).

Although flipping properties was the game of the day, actual building was booming too. In April 1912, the newspapers reported that the value of building permits had exceeded a million dollars in one month, surpassing every other Canadian city. Hundreds of modest structures, like W.F. Bresner's frame house on Houston Street (64th) and Gilbert Berg's barn on 25th Street (125th), were under construction. Meanwhile there was an orgy of downtown building such as Edmonton would not see again for six decades. By summer 1912 the Builders' Exchange was complaining of a cement shortage. The lavish sandstone courthouse stood resplendent on McDougall Avenue (100th St.). Stonemasons were putting the final touches to the dome of the Legislative Building, in time for its formal September opening by the governor-general, the Duke of Connaught. The Strathcona Post Office was under construction. So was Government House, the lieutenant-governor's residence[6]. Edmonton's utilitarian six-storey Civic Block would soon begin to rise on Queens Avenue and Elizabeth Street (99th St. and 102 Ave.[7]) overlooking the Market Square.

Among many other landmarks, the apartment building known grandly as LeMarchand Mansion on Victoria Avenue (100th) opened in 1910. In Strathcona, dominion government funding added the Connaught Armoury on Third Avenue (85th) in 1911 and a handsome stone downtown Edmonton Post Office in 1912. Edmonton's third permanent hospital, the 122-bed Royal Alexandra (which would be renamed the Glenrose when a new Royal Alex was built fifty years later), was also completed in 1912.

On Jasper Avenue the six-storey CPR office block (later renamed the Armstrong Block), with its massive two-storey Corinthian pillars, was completed in 1913. Banks proliferated on and near

---

One workman was crushed by a piledriver and three fell to their death, but the last girder of the High Level Bridge was riveted into place on the north side in early 1913.

Jasper, among them the three-storey Romanesque Union Bank and the pilaster-embellished new Dominion Bank (both in 1910). By 1911 work was begun on the GTP's magnificent Macdonald Hotel, which would open four years later (Sect. 3, ch. 1). The Tegler Building was rising, in successive stages, at First Street (101st) and Elizabeth (102 Ave.), to its full eight storeys — the tallest building in town. But already an Ontario Scot named Kenneth McLeod was aiming to top it.

McLeod was a carpenter who reached Edmonton in 1881. Local legend has it that he traded a sack of flour for some property and built himself a house. Thirty years later, having prospered in construction and real estate, he resolved to put up a truly magnificent edifice at McDougall Street (100th) and Rice Street (101A Ave.)[8]. So concerned was McLeod about strength, says Cashman, that he increased the architect's specifications for the steel framework by 50% and ordered concrete footings eleven feet square. The steel was up for the nine-storey McLeod Building, thirteen feet higher than the Tegler, in 1912. It had cost $400,000 and McLeod had run out of money. A year later, however, having persuaded the city to make him a loan, he finished it in style, with a marble lobby ceiling and terrazzo tile. Durable, too. Lightning hit it twice over the years, and only managed to knock off one cornice[9].

The East End Bridge, later known as the Dawson, was also completed, providing city access for Clover Bar farmers and the Dawson Coal Mine. With little fanfare a third bridge was opened in 1912 at the site of John Walter's old ferry and termed at first the "Central Low Level," later the 105th Street Bridge. And not least in importance to Edmonton, the Canadian Northern Railway line was opened to Athabasca Landing in August, replacing the old Athabasca Trail. Meanwhile the Canadian Pacific was finally bridging the North Saskatchewan from one steep bank to the other — a $2-million construction job, although they didn't know that when they began.

[5] As part of the deal whereby the HBC sold its vast territory of Rupert's Land to Canada in 1869, the company retained title to 1,000 acres around each of its forts. At Fort Edmonton this thousand acres, known as the Hudson's Bay Reserve, stretched from the river to what would become 118th Avenue, and twenty blocks west from the downtown core. In the 1880s the HBC began selling the southeastern part, future downtown Edmonton, for $35 a lot or thereabouts. There was no demand for the northern section until developers began planning subdivisions far beyond it.

[6] The imposing sandstone Government House, overlooking the valley of the North Saskatchewan at the Groat Ravine, cost $350,000 to build and only six lieutenant-governors would live there before Premier William Aberhart's Social Credit government ordered it closed in 1938. They cited maintenance costs, which had run as high as $24,845 in one year, but the fact that Lieutenant-Governor John C. Bowen had refused to sign three Aberhart bills is suspected as a factor. (Bowen had to move to the Macdonald Hotel.) In 1942 the furnishings, worth an estimated $300,000, were auctioned for $19,642. But after serving various utilitarian purposes, such as housing for Second World War veterans, the old residence was restored to its former grandeur in 1976. The renovation cost was $1.7 million.

[7] In the old street system, sometimes a street carried one name up to a certain intersection and another name beyond it. Thus, 102nd Avenue was Athabasca Avenue west of First Street (101st) and Elizabeth Street east of it.

[8] Rice Street (101A Ave.) appears on maps before the turn of the century. City historians have never determined where the name came from. More than sixty years later at 101A Avenue and 99th Street, the Citadel Theatre would appear, within which was the Rice Theatre. But this honours the city's founding broadcast radio entrepreneur and major philanthropist, Dr. G.R.A. Rice, a benefactor of the Citadel. The fact the theatre is on a street that once bore the same name is coincidence.

TEGLER BLOCK ON FIRST ST EDMONTON.

The McLeod and the Tegler each strive to top the other

The eight-storey Tegler Building on 101 Street and 102 Avenue (above) was the tallest in town in 1913, but in 1915 the determined Kenneth McLeod (below) topped it by thirteen feet with his nine-storey McLeod Building at 100 Street and 101A Avenue (at right). It would remain the city's tallest structure for almost forty years, and was still standing at the end of the century. Across from the McLeod Building is the new Edmonton Post Office with its 130-foot clock tower, completed in 1909 but not officially opened until 1910.

McDougall Ave

The remarkable High Level Bridge had been longer in the negotiation stage than in the building. The CPR, having bought the Calgary & Edmonton line, which terminated in Strathcona, proposed as early as 1903 to span the river and take the line into Edmonton. Immediate objections came from the Canadian Northern Railway, owners of the 2 1/2-mile Edmonton, Yukon & Pacific track that had been carrying trains into Edmonton since the previous year, across Edmonton's first bridge (later to be designated the Low Level). Both railways should use it, contended CNR promoter William Mackenzie, but the CPR was not so inclined. In May 1903 the company announced that it would build a quarter-million-dollar high-level railway bridge of its own.

This was the first mention of "high level," writes Eric J. Holmgren in a 1978 *Alberta Historical Review* article, and the federal railways minister promptly amended the enabling legislation accordingly, committing the CPR to a bridge at least 150 feet above water level. Much further negotiation was necessary, however. Strathcona was enthusiastic about the project, but wanted it to carry other traffic too, on a deck below the tracks, and was not so enthusiastic about helping with the cost. Most Edmontonians also approved, and wanted streetcars on it. But some residents along Ninth and Tenth Streets (109th and 110th) weren't pleased at the prospect of smoke and cinders. McDougall & Secord was holding out for $40,000 for some of the property needed by the line. East-end citizens wanted a more easterly bridge. And some Edmonton aldermen understandably wanted to know where else those tracks were going. What land would the CPR want for a station and yards? What about the streets that would be cut off?

However by 1910 both cities had accepted the CPR bridge proposal. Their citizens approved money bylaws to pay for the traffic deck and streetcar lines; the province contributed $175,000. The final price tag would be $1.6 million. Hundreds of men began work the following summer on the land piers over the flats and four massive 138-foot river piers, while the North Saskatchewan cooperated by remaining unusually low. Then the steel frame was erected, by means of a double-boom crane that straddled the upper deck, moving slowly forward from the south side on tracks laid on the deck's outside edges and lifting the prefabricated components into position. One workman was crushed by a piledriver and three fell to their death, but the last girder was riveted into place on the north side in early 1913[10].

On June 2, 1913, CPR Locomotive 2100, with seven coaches, left the station on Whyte Avenue at 11 a.m., and ten minutes later carried some 200 passengers across into Edmonton. Among them, the *Bulletin* noted, were "a number of prominent citizens." On August 8, Car No. 35

'Civic Block' was the right name for Edmonton City Council's strictly utilitarian new quarters, under construction (top right) in 1913 and (below) looking over the busy market square from its site on 99 Street and 102 Avenue.

[9]The McLeod Building was still in use when this volume was written (1993) and was expected to survive the century. The Tegler was demolished by implosion in 1982.

175

With a booming city to build, there was work and to spare

Excavating for a sewer (left); a two-storey house under construction in 1912 on 121 Street north of Athabasca Avenue (above); and a modest dwelling in North Belvedere subdivision (below). On the opposite page, top, men working on the Pantages Theatre and Brown Building in 1913 pause for a portrait. And enormous amounts of gravel (below right) were required for roads, watermains, sewers and other municipal projects.

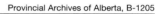

GROUP OF WORKMEN ON
PANTAGES THEATRE & BROWN BLDG

HAWLING GRAVEL IN EDMONTON

[10]Their 1909 agreement notwithstanding, the City of Edmonton and the CPR officials kept right on bickering about the cost of viaducts to take Jasper under the CPR tracks and a bridge to take Victoria Avenue (100th) over them. In 1910 Mayor Robert Lee had told the *Journal* that the CPR bridge engineer wanted to lower the tracks eight feet, which would make the idea of a Jasper subway 'an absurdity.' In 1911 Commissioner A.V. Bouillon, new on the scene, had reviewed the original plan and described the required gradients for the Victoria overpass and Jasper subway as 'little short of an engineering crime.' Crime or not, the CPR specifications were met. CP Rail removed the tracks in 1993 when they scrapped the long-pursued connection north from Strathcona into downtown Edmonton.

made the first trolley crossing. The streetcar tracks ran on the outer edges of the railway deck, nearly 200 feet above the river, and an awed *Journal* reporter described the sensation of looking "from a dizzy height down into the murky waters of the Saskatchewan without so much as a handrail to break the gaze into the abyssal depths below." Although the ride was perfectly safe, of course, he predicted that many passengers would suffer anxiety and dizziness.

He was right on both counts. The High Level trolley trip became a recognized "thrill," especially on windy days or when a large and noisy train was using the middle railway track. However, no streetcar came to grief in 38 years of operation. Just in case a trolley should stall on the bridge, however, the streetcars crossed it on the "wrong side" track, so that their doors faced the middle and in an emergency the disembarking passengers would be able to step down onto the ties, not into the void. By September 1913 the traffic deck below, with its attached sidewalks, was ready too, roofed with galvanized iron to prevent cinders from the locomotives dropping on the wagons, carriages and automobiles.

Edmonton and Strathcona, which for nearly two decades had each schemed and manoeuvred to eclipse the other and become the dominant metropolis of north-central Alberta, were now

---

Both councils ratified the deal in early September, the Strathcona one in a session the papers described as 'stormy,' and it went to the ratepayers on Sept. 26, 1911. Southside property owners approved it by 518 to 178, northsiders by 667 to 91.

---

being drawn inexorably together — and not solely by bridges. Alberta's new university town might remain secure in its sense of superior dignity, culture and financial responsibility, but it had begun to despair of outdoing those determined boosters across the river. Edmonton seemed to have blocked or surpassed the southsiders' every move. True, Strathcona had done well since its 1907 incorporation as a city, but it wasn't catching up. Edmonton still had four times the population, and had now attracted to itself not one railway, but four, since even the politically ill-starred Alberta & Great Waterways had been taken over by new management and was under construction. If we can't beat 'em, southsiders began to argue, why not join 'em?

Some Strathconans, characteristically cautious, still held back. They had water and sewer already paid for and in better condition than Edmonton's, they contended, and their municipal finances were in every respect sounder. To take on the debt of those wild men on the north side would be insane. Taxes were bound to go up, and there wouldn't be a thing they could do about it. But Strathcona mayor Arthur Davies favoured amalgamation, as did leading aldermen like J.G. Tipton and influential citizens like Henry Marshall Tory, president of the University of Alberta.

So far as Edmonton was concerned, the bigger the city the better for business. George S.

The Royal George (below left), built by clothier Abe Cristall where the Edmonton Centre would later stand, was a handsome hostelry; so was the King Edward (below right), at 101 Street and 102 Avenue. Much more modest but likely no less useful was the North Edmonton Hotel (centre).

Armstrong, a businessman and realtor, made amalgamation a prime plank in his successful mayoral campaign in December 1910. A joint committee appointed in early 1911 worked out a deal, which included a guarantee of at least three council seats (of ten) in the city-wide elections. Specified street railway extensions were also assured, as was the construction of the bridge at Walterdale's ferry.

Opposing Strathcona aldermen called the proposal so dangerously vague it was "no good at all." Only genuine south-side residents must be allowed to vote on this matter, they urged (i.e.

Commissioner Bouillon fired the power plant superintendent and street railway superintendent. He fought with the auditor. Police chief A.C. Lancey quit, complaining of interference. A committee of aldermen accused Bouillon of conducting a 'reign of terror.'

---

none of those Edmontonians who also owned south-side property), and amalgamation must pass by a two-thirds majority. At the very least, they declared, the vote should be postponed. They were defeated on all counts. If the ratepayers didn't know their minds by now, commented Alderman Tipton, they never would. Both councils ratified the deal in early September, the Strathcona one in a session the papers described as "stormy," and it went to the ratepayers on Sept. 26, 1911. South-side property owners approved it by 518 to 178, northsiders by 667 to 91[11].

Strathcona's mayor Davies did not run in Greater Edmonton's first municipal election, held in February 1912, and George Armstrong was strongly challenged by Lt.-Col. Bryce J. Saunders, a civil engineer who had run unsuccessfully in the 1910 mayoral campaign[12]. Provincial legislation had extended the franchise beyond property owners and tenants to anyone who paid rent. The *Journal* noted that the "labouring class" thronged to the polls between 5:30 and 7 p.m., and the "east end" vote was heavy. Ballot counting took until 3 a.m., chiefly on account of "considerable difficulty experienced" at the poll at Jasper and Fifth Street, which the chief returning officer had to "straighten out." Meanwhile crowds who had gathered at the *Journal* to watch the results flashed by stereopticon on a screen across the street were entertained with three motion pictures. When Armstrong was finally declared mayor (by 1,791 votes to 1,072) his supporters carried him through the streets on their shoulders, behind a brass band.

Mayor Armstrong was in for a lively year, which should not have surprised him. Having served on city council since 1908, he must have known how rambunctious it could become, good intentions notwithstanding. One manifestation of such good intentions, for instance, was its early adoption of the principle of commission government. Carefully chosen professionals, the aldermen reasoned, if given sufficient authority, would manage civic affairs more efficiently than they themselves could. After all, supervision of services in the expanding city was becoming a very big job.

[11]In a different kind of confidence vote, immediately before the amalgamation plebiscite, the Canadian Investment Company bought the Allendale development outside Strathcona for $175,000. Property values would rise as much as 100%, a company spokesman said. A week later a north-side realtor paid $112.50 per acre to J.G. Tipton & Sons for the William Fowler farm, two miles beyond the city limits. South-side building activity also increased, with the value of monthly permits reaching the much-to-be-desired million-dollar mark in 1913.

[12]Bryce Johnston Saunders, then 51, was a surveyor and civil engineer who had served in the Northwest Rebellion of 1885. He became deputy minister of Public Works for the Northwest Territories, based in Regina. He left that post to become a consulting engineer in Edmonton. In 1908 he became a major in the 19th Alberta Mounted Rifles.

Also aspiring to elegance was the Alberta Hotel (far right) with its corps of bellhops (centre). But curiously enough, of the five hotels shown here, the only one to survive the century was the plain, frame Transit Hotel (below), way out on the Fort Road.

Edmonton welcomes the dawn of a new age featuring electricity and the gasoline motor

Jasper Avenue (below) looking east from 108 Street, circa 1914. At right, crowds throng the corner of Jasper and 100A Street, with the McLeod Building under construction in the background. At far right, shooting northward from the Grand Trunk's Hotel Macdonald, the photographer achieved a fine view with the columned Imperial Bank in the foreground, backed by the McLeod Building steelwork and the post office clock tower.

Provincial Archives of Alberta, B-4796

The curiously designed Gibson Block (below), a so-called 'flatiron' building entirely typical of its period, not only survived to the century's end but in the mid-nineties was finally being restored after years of degradation. Below right, Jasper Avenue glitters after dark.

Provincial Archives of Alberta, B-4809

This cityscape, looking northeast from the Tegler Building evidences the new Edmonton much as it will remain until the 1960s.

The boulevard on Main Street (104 Street) in early Strathcona.

'Some types of Edmonton residences' in 1910, on 113 Street north of Victoria (100) Ave.

THE NEW CITIES

Another view of Victoria Avenue and 113 Street by photographer Ernest Brown.

Looking north on 125 Street, only just landscaped in 1910.

At the instigation of Mayor William Short the 1904 Edmonton charter had therefore specified that the city was to be run by the mayor, his council and two commissioners.

But the commission system had already proved far from foolproof. In 1910 the aldermen thought they had found just the man to relieve them of all their utility problems. The entire council, including then-alderman George Armstrong, eagerly endorsed the hiring (at the enormous salary of $10,000 a year) of A.V. Bouillon, Seattle's former utilities boss, seemingly unaware that his tenure there had ended in a gigantic fight with the Seattle city council. History soon repeated itself. Commissioner Bouillon fired the power plant and street railway superintendents. He fought

Arthur Davies (left), last mayor of Strathcona, favoured amalgamation with Edmonton. So did other Strathcona leaders like John G. Tipton, alderman, lawyer and sometime realtor (right).

with the auditor. Police chief A.C. Lancey quit, complaining of interference from Bouillon. A committee of aldermen accused him of conducting a "reign of terror" among civic employees.

The council split eight to two against the contentious commissioner, while the Board of Trade and many vocal citizens were staunchly pro-Bouillon. So were the newspapers. Looking elsewhere for the villains, they suggested that "the builders and contractors section of the council are unduly anxious to dismiss an unsympathetic commissioner whose business system contains no provision for accepting tenders 'by request.' " Cashman notes that before the aldermen could actually get rid of Bouillon it took months of private and public acrimony, and two obstructing court injunctions. Thereupon Bouillon went back to Seattle and became boss of a shipyard at $40,000.

So it was not unusual that Greater Edmonton's 1912 council began with accusations that the recent election had been "crooked." The charge was levelled at lawyer and amateur athlete Joseph

The following day Alderman Gus May appeared at the station and wanted to know why particular people were being persecuted when there were worse places in town. The chief challenged him to name one. The alderman helpfully named the St. Regis Hotel, a property coincidentally operated by the chief's sister.

Andrew Clarke, who had won a council seat as "the working man's friend." Clarke, widely known as "Fighting Joe," successfully defended himself and shortly declared that, if only he had enough money to prosecute the case, he could jail half the council in connection with certain December 1911 downtown property purchases. Where's the evidence, a chorus of indignant aldermen demanded. To their horror Clarke produced enough to bring on a judicial inquiry and force the immediate resignation of veteran alderman Dr. H.L. McInnis.

The inquiry lasted a full year. It seems the previous council had secretly passed a resolution to straighten the jog in Elizabeth Street (102nd Ave.) between Queens and Namayo (99th and 97th streets). Dr. McInnis had been informally assigned (just how and by whom never became entirely clear) to buy the necessary 26 pieces of property — including three lots of his own — with city money. Chief Justice Horace Harvey ultimately concluded that these procedures were highly irregular, but that none of the aldermen including McInnis was guilty of actual wrong-doing, and that taxpayers had not suffered in consequence.

The McInnis affair nevertheless cast a certain pall over the Armstrong administration. It suffered other setbacks, such as the recurring trouble with chief Lancey, who had quit in Bouillon's "reign of terror" the previous year. The city council had replaced Lancey with a former North-West Mounted Police staff sergeant named R.W. Ensor. But chief Ensor couldn't get along with anybody and seemed a violent man. When barely into office, he happened to attend (in plain clothes) a political rally, where a mild-mannered citizen dared speak up and ask a question. Ensor threw him out. When another citizen came to the chief's office the next day to complain about that, Ensor threw him out. "Fighting Joe" Clarke, not yet on council, took up the citizen's case and charged the police chief with assault. Decision: guilty. Fine: $1. But by now Ensor had had it, and the council sought another chief. They wound up rehiring Lancey at a higher salary.

But Lancey, instead of fighting with the citizenry like Ensor, took to fighting with the aldermen, in particular with Alderman Gustave May. There was, for instance, that alderman's unpleasant interference with the raid on the Afro-Canadian Progressive Association on Fraser Avenue (96th St.) The police had swept down on the place in the early hours of an August morning, and scooped up whiskey, cards, poker chips and 59 found-ins. The following day, who should appear at the station but Alderman Gus May. He was there, he said, at the behest of a "distressed citizen" who wanted to know why these particular people were being persecuted when there were 54 worse places in town. The chief, annoyed, challenged him to be specific. What 54 places? The alderman helpfully named one of them as the St. Regis Hotel, a property

George S. Armstrong, Edmonton's mayor in 1911, won a second term as mayor of Greater Edmonton. He was in for a lively time.

THE SCALES TELL THE TALE TRULY

Contentious city commissioner A.V. Bouillon (above) enraged the aldermen, but as this Edmonton Journal cartoon pointedly observed in February 1911, he had a lot of citizen support. Ousted at last, Bouillon reputedly became a Seattle shipyard boss at quadruple his Edmonton salary.

Picnics, dances, cruises made for a city that knew how to have fun

AND EVERY SPRING KIDS DAMMED UP MILL CREEK FOR A SWIMMING HOLE

Between 1910 and 1920 Edmonton completed its transformation from a muddy frontier town to a veritable small city, but it would long retain much of its small-town character. For one thing, although most of its citizens worked very long and hard for very modest wages, they clearly had a genuine talent for communal fun, and energetically pursued it.

Even allowing for the golden haze of nostalgia, for instance, their picnics seem to have been something pretty special. On weekends, for the price of a dollar, hundreds would board John Walter's big steamboat *City of Edmonton* for a picnic eighteen miles upriver at Big Island, with copious amounts of food and beer and (usually) speeches. Steaming slowly back in the dusk, they would dance on the hardwood floor of the big boat's upper deck to the strains of a local band.

Not that all Edmontonians approved of dancing. It was most severely condemned by many clergymen and also by certain residents of Kinistino Avenue (96th St.). The latter petitioned city council to close three dancehalls there because they were "a gathering place for all the riffraff of the city three or four times a week, to the annoyance of us all." On that occasion police chief A.C. Lancey, the *Journal*

reported, promised to take "rigid steps to have peace and quietness on the nights of Russian weddings and Scandinavian dances." It is not likely, however, given all the other preoccupations of the city police, that these festivities were much dampened.

Sports of the sort a later and less active era would call "participatory" drew no such condemnations, but often required from the participants a lot of work as well. Tony Cashman in *Best Edmonton Stories* describes how youngsters dammed Mill Creek with rocks and logs every year (since every spring the dam was flooded out) to make a swimming pool, just underneath the Edmonton, Yukon & Pacific Railway crossing. And young Norwegian enthusiasts had things called skiis made by local blacksmiths and harness shops, then challenged and beat local snowshoers in a race from the High Level Bridge to Whitemud Creek. They also formed the Edmonton Ski Club and built a jump on Connors Hill, where they put on spectacular exhibitions like nighttime flights through flaming hoops.

For summer picnics and winter skating there was McKernan Lake, near the Robert McKernan homestead on Strathcona's southwestern edgea. It could be reached for the price of a five-cent ticket on a streetcar (later affectionately known as the Toonerville Trolley) that for many years jolted

Glenbow Archives, NA-1328-66561

Glenbow Archives, NC-6-666

Glenbow Archives, NC-6-518

John Walter's steamboat (above) embarks on a gala Press Association picnic up-river, and motorists (right) watch the ski jumping on Connors Hill. Above right is the roller coaster at East End Park, a major attraction.

along its single track to the lake. The city also had a dozen parks, with bandshells for outdoor concerts, cricket pitches, baseball diamonds and even a couple of racetracks. East End Park (later Borden) was special, however. An entrepreneur from New York installed a rollercoaster there, and a feature called the Old Mill that floated people through a dark "tunnel of love" in little wooden boats, amidst ghostly noises and apparitions, and there was a merry-go-round.

Next door to Borden Park, on its new grounds, the great Edmonton Exhibition provided a midway that added a ferris wheel, acrobats, wild animal acts and midgets. It also brought exciting imported shows. It was there that Texas aviator Kathleen Stinson performed stunts in her Curtiss biplane in 1916; two years later people all along the CPR track watched her fly a bag of mail from Calgary, landing in front of the grandstand. In 1919, when John Philip Sousa's

famous band was the big grandstand show, attendance reached 111,710[b].

Horseracing, both regular and harness, was major at the six-day Ex, of course, and betting enthusiastic. When the management installed ten pari-mutuel machines the first-year profit was $6,781.15. Most of the exhibition was similarly home-grown, from its horse shows and livestock exhibits (after 1913 in the new brick Livestock Pavilion) to tug-of-wars, foot races, barrel races and greased-pig races in which any citizen could compete and many did.   — *V.B.*

[a]McKernan Lake, a depression in the prairie, lay south of the future 76th Avenue in the vicinity of 114th Street.

[b]At one point Sousa walked off in high dudgeon. It seems that wartime airmen Wop May and George Gorman, who were also performing that year in a Curtiss JN-4 donated to the city by realtor A.B. Carruthers, had decided to buzz Sousa's band as it played.

Provincial Archives of Alberta, B-8874

Glenbow Archives, NA-1328-64716

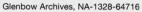

Glenbow Archives, NC-6-654

The ferris wheel (above left) was a big draw at the 1910 Edmonton Exhibition. Above right, sprinters get set for a 1912 Dominion Day race at the South Side Athletic Park. The ski association (below) pioneered their winter sport in Alberta.

When leading lawyer and former mayor William Short (at right) returned to contest the 1913 election on a reform ticket, he was heartily backed by both the Journal *and the* Bulletin. *The newspapers, agreeing for once, greatly feared that either realtor William Magrath or maverick populist Joe Clark might win. The* Bulletin *cartoon (below right) graphically expresses their sentiments.*

A VOTE FOR SHORT IS A VOTE
FOR THE SAFETY OF EDMONTON

[13]Financing for the new Robertson Presbyterian Church was substantially enhanced by the real estate boom. According to the *Journal*, the congregation sold its previous church on Sixteenth Street (116th) for $30,000, three times what it cost in 1910. Now it could afford Sunday School rooms for 600, a gymnasium, club rooms for young men, and ladies' parlours with fireplaces. Meanwhile First Presbyterian Church, which raised its own new red brick church (with a six-storey bell tower) in 1912, had also done nicely with real estate, says Jac MacDonald in *Historic Edmonton*. Downtown speculators paid $195,000 for its old building at Third Street (103rd) and Jasper. The congregation was able to replace it with a new one more than twice as big on Fifth Street (105th) for $186,000.

coincidentally operated by the chief's sister.

So the chief sued May for $30,000, for slander, and announced he was resigning, this for the second time. May made a public apology. In "the heat of the moment," he said, he had been unfair to the St. Regis. The chief dropped the lawsuit but not his resignation. Although some thought May should resign too, he vowed to continue doing his civic duty. He proposed a bylaw transferring control of the city clerk and the police, treasury, assessment, claims adjustment, health and industrial departments from the council to commissioners. This was adopted at once, but by now the Armstrong administration was finished.

What with one thing and another, at the end of 1912 William Short was resoundingly elected mayor on a reform ticket. "A Vote for Short is a Vote for the Safety of Edmonton" was the heading over a front page *Bulletin* cartoon on election day. It was a three-way race: Short, a member of the leading law firm Short, Cross & Biggar, who had been mayor a decade earlier, from 1902 to 1904; realtor William J. Magrath, who had announced his retirement from active business two months earlier; and the pugnacious populist Joe Clarke. Short won handily, polling more votes than his two opponents combined. "Edmonton Clambers Aboard the Safe and Sane Train of Progress for Twelve Months of Solid and Permanent Municipal Government," the *Journal* approvingly headlined.

And the Short regime did indeed prove a good deal quieter. It produced no scandal worth mentioning, and it set the municipal budget at $6 million, considered modest in view of the needs of the expanding city. According to the civic enumeration that year, the population had reached 67,243. Edmonton annexed a further fifteen square miles around its perimeter, bringing its total to nearly forty square miles. Ten more miles of telephone cable were completed, 27 miles of sewers, 23 miles of water mains and 335,475 square yards of new street paving. By 1914, writes J.G. MacGregor, the city had 35 miles of paved streets, 181 of graded ones, 140 miles of sidewalks and 128 miles of water mains.

Material progress continued on every side. Calgary meatpacker Pat Burns decided to open a plant in Edmonton, for example, as did the Cockshutt Plow Company and Northwest Biscuit. Property prices on Jasper Avenue hovered around $2,500 per frontage foot. The Windsor Hotel at First Street and Jasper sold for half a million dollars. Schoolteachers got a salary increase. The Edmonton Taxicab Company, based at the King Edward Hotel, provided the citizenry with "landaulet type" cabs that featured "cigar lighters, flower vases, taximeter system and uniformed drivers." There was a record grain crop. The country was "never so prosperous," the *Journal* declared in August, and interest had revived in Canadian investments.

The city's churches were prospering too — and building. The huge new McDougall Methodist, with seating for 1,800 including the gallery, was completed in 1910 on the First

· PROPOSED CIVIC CENTER LOOKING NORTH ·
CITY · OF · EDMONTON · ALBERTA · CANADA ·
· MORELL · AND · NICHOLS ·   · LANDSCAPE · ARCHITECTS ·

The three blocks of land for this magnificent civic centre (later site of Sir Winston Churchill Square) would have cost only $2.5 million in 1913 — a bargain, said the enthusiasts. But the voters turned it down, and a good thing too. It would have taken half a century to pay off the debt, and in any case the land soon reverted to the city for unpaid taxes.

Street (101st) site where the Rev. George McDougall built his first log cabin church in 1873. In 1913 the Anglicans built Holy Trinity (seating 650) in Strathcona. The Roman Catholics added the 1,000-seat Church of the Sacred Heart to their roster; St. Anthony's on the south side and St. Francis of Assisi in the northeast were packed to overflowing. The congregation of Robertson Presbyterian, having grown from fifty to 350 in three years, built a new brick 1,200-seat church at 23rd Street (123rd) and Athabasca Avenue (102nd)[13]. It was "a handsome addition to the already large list of magnificent city churches," commented the *Journal*.

In total, writes Carl Frederick Betke in his thesis *The Development of Urban Community in Prairie Canada: Edmonton 1898-1921*, Edmonton had about seventy churches by then of all sizes and descriptions. Thirteen were Methodist, twelve Anglican, and eleven Presbyterian. The Roman Catholics, Lutherans and Baptists had six each. The remainder belonged to a great diversity of

Burgeoning congregations raised bigger, higher, solider churches

A crowd of worshippers (below) leaves a downtown service, possibly at First Presbyterian on 105 Street. Below that is the new Robertson Presbyterian on 102 Avenue. Sacred Heart on 96 Street (at right) was the city's third big Catholic church. By mid-decade the total stood at about seventy churches of all sorts.

[14]Strathcona's New King Edward School helped bring the south side up to scholastic par with the north side of the river, where Oliver School at 102 Avenue and 117 Street opened March 1911 with twelve classrooms and, among other amenities, a rifle range. At the secondary level, Strathcona Collegiate Institute (later renamed Old Scona), which opened its doors in 1909 at 84 Avenue and 105 Street, had been matched and surpassed with the 1911 opening of the $150,000 Edmonton High School (later renamed Victoria) on Churchill Avenue near First (108th and 101st).

Protestant or nationally oriented denominations, and there was one synagogue, Beth Israel, built in 1911 on Syndicate Avenue (95th St.) on land donated by clothing merchant William Diamond.

The integrated seven-member public school board (it had two south-side trustees guaranteed) was also building as fast as it could. In 1913 there were 5,346 pupils enrolled, writes Michael Kostek in his history of the Edmonton public system, and the board's building commissioner reported over a million dollars spent on construction that year. Some of the buildings were temporary, like the two-room frame schools in Irvine Estates (near the future 73rd Ave. and 98th St.). Most were brick, ranging in size from four-room Garneau near the university site to seventeen-classroom New King Edward on Strathcona (on the future 101 St. between 85th and 86th Avenues). Its august namesake himself had not had the privilege of attending a school so grand, the *Bulletin* declared. Not only did the $180,000 building have special facilities for science, manual training and domestic arts, but "a turn of a set screw on the thermostat" in each room would regulate the temperature. The large indoor playrooms (one for boys, one for girls) even had lavatories with shower baths, "a novelty to many of the children, who never before saw hot water come down like rain"[14].

Thus as Edmonton began the year 1913, the sentiment was onward and upward forever. Within that year, however, this illusion would be shattering. The public school building program would grind to an abrupt halt, as would development all over the city. The wheat crop was good, but wheat prices were plummeting. Men laid off by Canadian Northern contractors were drifting into town. The value of building permits issued for the year had dropped by $5 million, news

Alderman H.L. McInnis was only trying to buy the city some property — but it took a year-long investigation to vindicate him.

reports said. In December 1913 city relief officer Thomas R. Turnbull told the *Bulletin* that there were between 500 and 800 unemployed men in the city.

All in all, however, Mayor Short had largely provided the "safe and sane train of progress" the *Journal* predicted. Curiously, he may be best remembered for something he did *not* do. Early in the year the council was offered the vacant three-block area between McDougall Street (100th) and Queens Avenue (99th St.) from Rice Street to Clara (101A Ave. to 103rd Ave.) at the allegedly bargain price of $2.5 million. Properly landscaped, said the enthusiasts, it would make a marvellous civic centre. A grandiose plan was being prepared. Many people, including most of the aldermen, saw it as too good a chance to miss[15]. The *Bulletin* quoted a Board of Trade spokesman as saying, "I don't think the city will be able to purchase the land at any time in the future for less money, or even for the same amount."

But $2.5 million was quite a bit for the city to borrow. When Edmontonians defeated the necessary bylaw — 3,079 to 2,636 — Mayor Short pronounced himself delighted. "There was quite an organization working in favour of the bylaw," he told the *Journal*, "and only the people against it. It will mean quite a difference to the city's finances, in the right direction I believe." Events would certainly vindicate him. It has been estimated that if Edmonton had bought that land it would still have been paying for it fifty years later. As things turned out, most of it reverted to the city within a few years anyhow, for unpaid taxes, and in 1957 and again in 1992 future city councils would construct two successive city halls and a park there, on property that was, in effect, free.

Perhaps Short was a bit too sane for Edmonton's taste at the time. He was defeated, if narrowly, in the December 1913 election. Realtor William James McNamara became mayor. Fighting Joe Clarke, apparently backed by a heavy ethnic/labour vote, topped the aldermanic polls. So one way and another, 1914 was going to be a rough ride (see Sect. 3, ch. 1).

Prophetic clouds mass over the city in this idyllic mid-decade view, with the old Edmonton Hotel annex in the left foreground. McKay School, where Alberta legislators held their first sessions, bulks large at the top of the hill.

[15] Concerning Edmonton's 1913 civic centre land controversy, J.G. MacGregor notes that the city owned only two lots in the three-block area, but several aldermen owned many and could buy more. They did too, he says, although prices headed upward as soon as the plan became known.

The birth traumas of Edmonton's streetcar system

DERAILMENTS, JAMMED CARS, UNCERTAIN ROUTES AND CHRONIC LOSSES FAIL TO DIM THE CITY'S PRIDE IN ITS BROWN AND YELLOW MONSTERS

A streetcar passenger disembarks at Jasper and 109 Street near the Canadian Pacific Railway station.

The first streetcar to run from Edmonton into Strathcona crossed the Low Level Bridge on Oct. 31, 1908, with Edmonton mayor John McDougall and street railway superintendent Charles E. Taylor aboard, and a crowd of excited Edmonton kids galloping behind. Strathcona mayor John Joseph Duggan and his council met them with congratulations. Then Taylor magnanimously offered all Edmonton children a ride back — and suddenly the trolley was jammed to the doors. Could all these youngsters have run the entire way over? The superintendent, nonplussed, began to question them. No, admitted one small girl with dignity, she was *not* an Edmonton child. But she was going to visit her aunt, she stated, and what's more she had her five-cent fare. Questioning ceased.

The trolleys would raise many harder questions in the years to come. By 1911, when the two cities amalgamated, the Edmonton Radial Railway had 31 streetcars serving six routes[a]. But successive city councils faced constant demands for more and better service, high capital costs for tracks, equipment and car barns, and recurring operating losses. "Heavy Rains and Steep 'Scona Hills Eat up a Lot of Good Money," the *Edmonton Journal* headlined in 1910, when the ERR lost $29,000.

The first profitable year was 1912, according to the system's 1983 official history *Edmonton's Electric Transit*[b], and in 1913-14 the passenger load rose to 40,000 daily. But this was not destined to last. By 1916 the effects of recession and the Great War would cut ridership and revenues almost in half.

Besides, as the ERR kept building tracks to new subdivisions, it chronically suffered from the same problem as

Building a system for 40,000 trolley riders

Workmen install an interchange at Jasper Avenue and 109 Street (top and centre left), and lay track on 124 Street (bottom left) and on Jasper Avenue (bottom right). At top right they show how the overhead trolley lines were installed in 1913.

Canada's railroads: too many long hauls over unpopulated areas that produced no revenue. One of these was the Packing Plant Route to north Edmonton, traversing two miles of countryside without one stop. Its daily operating cost in 1911 was $55, its revenue $40.

Another was the fabled McKernan Lake line, which travelled west along the largely uninhabited stretch of Sixth Avenue (76th) from Main Street (104th) to end abruptly in the bush at the future 116th Street. Beloved of lakebound skaters and picnickers, the line became the stuff of legend. Motorman Bob Chambers, it was said, used to recite the poems of Robert Burns as the car lurched and swayed along 76th Avenue, little more than a mud track. Other motormen would pick up groceries for the few residents. Bad boys

did not always work. On one memorable evening in 1913, for example, on the steep southern approach to the Low Level Bridge, only the action of an alert bystander prevented a collision between two northbound trolleys coasting downwards and another powering uphill around the curve. Then the crews all began arguing about who had the right-of-way and who must back off to a siding, which frequently occurred on these occasions. By the time it was all sorted out, they had five streetcars and a water sprinkler impatiently waiting behind them.

The ERR gradually worked out an elaborate routing system, but it was often hard for citizens to tell where a particular car was going until illuminated signs and coloured route markers were installed on them in 1912. More confusion followed during the year-long wrangle over changing the names and numbers of Edmonton streets. Nor do there ever seem to have been enough cars, at least until 1915. At rush hours, trolleys jammed to bursting routinely left crowds of fist-shaking passengers behind.

And there were accidents. The cars were driven too fast on account of their long routes and tight schedules, the *Bulletin* complained in March 1910 after two of them collided, a third hit a plank and damaged its flooring, and a fourth ran

Jolting along the largely uninhabited west end of Sixth Avenue (76th), one single-track trolley carried skaters to McKernan Lake, and picnic parties in summer. Much loved by citizens, the line remained a money-losing bane to the ERR.

occasionally shot out the lights at the terminus so that the motorman, groping through the darkness, ran the trolley off the end of the track into the bush. The line was never beloved by the transit system, which was obliged to provide the service under the terms of the Edmonton-Strathcona amalgamation agreement. One superintendent estimated that over its lifetime the line lost $350,000. It would be replaced by buses in 1947.

Maintenance costs were onerous over the whole system. Rain and frost buckled tracks that had been hastily laid along dirt roads. The city either had to pave the streets, which was expensive, or continually repair tracks and ballast them with gravel, which was not cheap either. It did some of both. And there was the expense of double-tracking.

Most early routes had only a single track, with sidings and a signal system to prevent head-on confrontations. This

down a horseman and killed the horse — all in one day. That year there were two fatal accidents, and unstable tracks derailed four trolleys in a week. In 1913 a Grand Trunk Pacific freight train collided with Car No. 23, tossing a boxcar and three flatcars into the air, splintering the trolley into fragments, and injuring the motorman (seriously) and five passengers.

Speeding complaints notwithstanding, the streetcars' normal speed was seven miles an hour, often much slower, which is why a baby was born on the Packing Plant Line in June 1914. The mother, who had been on her way home from work, had shyly confided to the conductor that she must get quickly to her doctor's office near Alberta Avenue (118 Ave.). Although the motorman tried, he didn't quite make it, but the *Bulletin* reported that mother and son were both fine.

Winter naturally posed particular hazards. There was a sweeper car for clearing snow, and the trolleys carried sand for icy tracks. If they ran short of sand it could take fully fifteen minutes to crawl up one block on a riverbank hill. And a bad winter day could cause a dozen derailments, of which the most spectacular occurred after a heavy snowfall in October 1919.

As Car No. 21, headed downtown on Athabasca Avenue (102nd) on its 7 a.m. run, braked for the trestle bridge near 30th Street (130th), ice and snow built up on its wheel flanges. Car No. 21 derailed and plunged thirty feet into the ravine, landing on its roof. It was demolished, and the motorman and four passengers were injured. The fifth passenger, A.J. Adams, crawled out from under the car and

The regiment, known formally as the 101st Regiment of the militia, headed by its band, was parading back from the CPR's southside depot after a week's encampment at Calgary, when it met up with an ERR trolley at McDougall Avenue (100th St.) and Jasper. Motorman Arthur Elliott, not about to compromise his schedule, spotted a gap between the band and the first company in line, and started through. The colonel, a veteran of the 1885 Rebellion, the NWMP, and service with the imperial forces in Nigeria in 1901-03, wheeled his horse and held up an admonitory hand. The streetcar "nudged" the horse and then, as the *Bulletin* recounted, the 101st began breaking the car's windows and smashing its headlights. Motorman and conductor both ended up in court, but were fined only a token $1 each. He didn't want

A snowstorm could cause a dozen derailments, and this was one of the most spectacular. Car No. 21 was travelling downtown on Athabasca Avenue (102nd) in October 1919 when ice built up on its flanges and sent it spinning off the bridge near 30th Street (130 St.).

helped rescue the others. Thereupon, according to the *Journal* report, he said, "Goodbye, I have to get to work," and set off on foot.

But the ERR kept working on improvements and extensions. So eagerly did they build, writes John C. Weaver in the *Urban Historical Review* (Vol. 2, 1977) that among western cities only Denver and Los Angeles had more miles of track per 10,000 citizens. And Edmontonians, despite their constant griping, seem to have been proud of their brown and yellow streetcars. Certainly the conductors and motormen took their responsibilities very seriously, as Lt.-Col. W.F.W. Carstairs, of the 101st Regiment discovered one Sunday morning in June 1912.

to get them in trouble, Col. Carstairs explained — he just wanted a little respect shown to His Majesty's service.

— *V.B.*

[a]The Edmonton Radial Railway, launched in 1908 by the McDougall administration, immediately bought the still inactive Strathcona Radial Tramway Company and assigned Charles Taylor to run the combined system (Vol. II, p. 97). Tony Cashman tells the free ride anecdote in *Best Edmonton Stories*.

[b]This delightful and bountifully illustrated history of Edmonton's transit system was written by Colin K. Hatcher and Tom Schwarzkopf and published by Railfare Enterprises in Toronto.

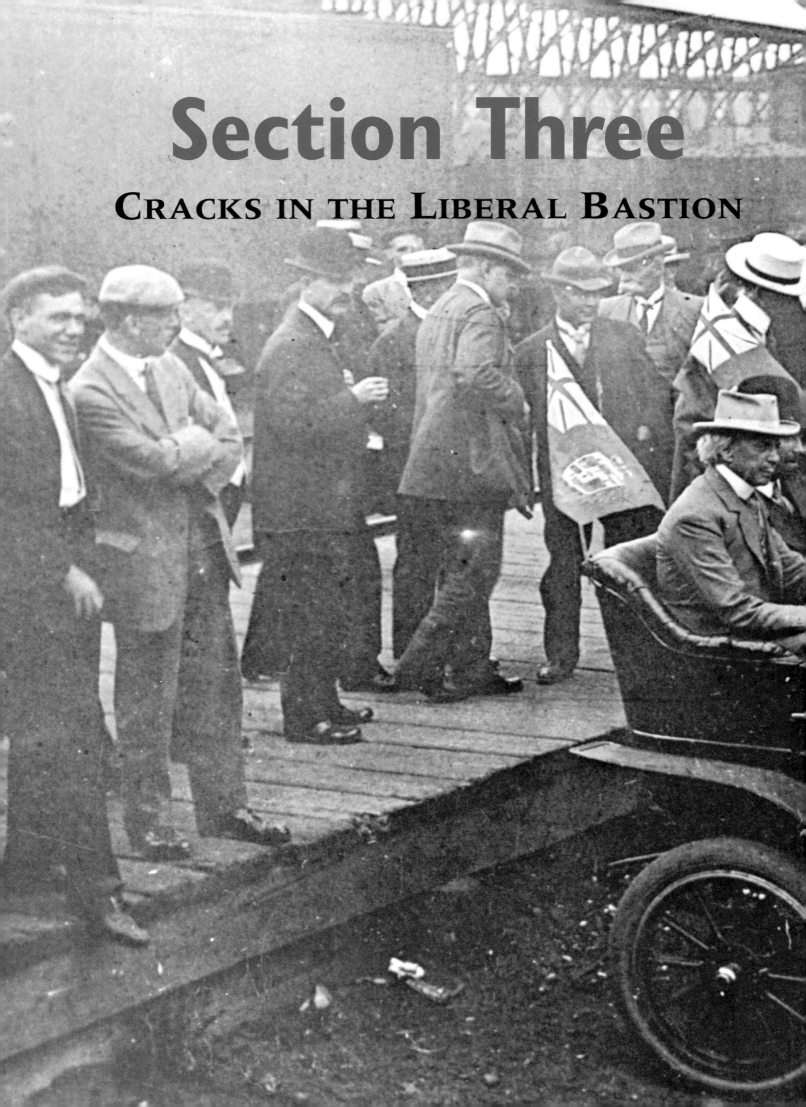

Section Three

CRACKS IN THE LIBERAL BASTION

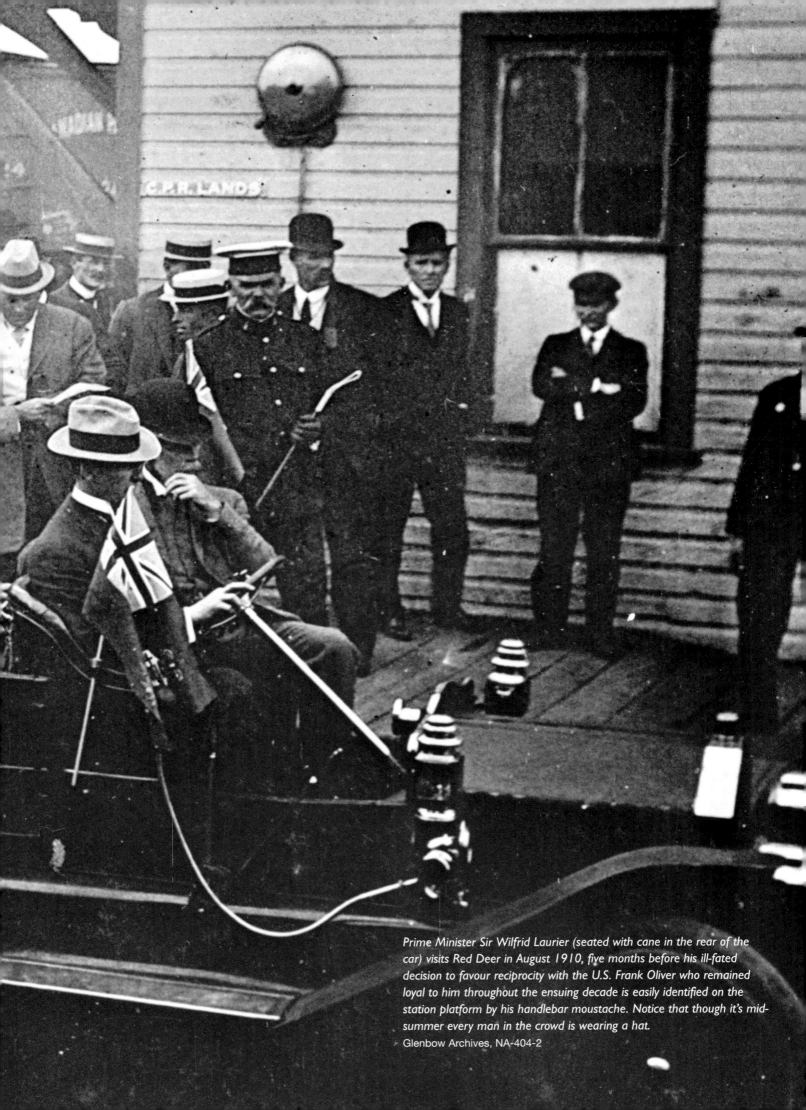

Prime Minister Sir Wilfrid Laurier (seated with cane in the rear of the car) visits Red Deer in August 1910, five months before his ill-fated decision to favour reciprocity with the U.S. Frank Oliver who remained loyal to him throughout the ensuing decade is easily identified on the station platform by his handlebar moustache. Notice that though it's mid-summer every man in the crowd is wearing a hat.

Glenbow Archives, NA-404-2

CRACKS IN THE LIBERAL BASTION

CHAPTER ONE

The 1911 election hands the West its first great political defeat

LAURIER'S TRADE TREATY WITH THE U.S. DESTROYS HIS GOVERNMENT, AS SUPPORT FOR HIM ON THE PRAIRIES IS OVERPOWERED BY ONTARIO

by GEORGE OAKE

Barely six years after Alberta had been carved out of the Northwest Territories its brash pioneers were struggling to change the face of a nation that many of them saw as still clinging too tightly to Britannia's apron strings. In 1911, Alberta's coal miners were on strike for better pay and safer working conditions. The province's women were agitating for voting rights and Prohibition. Most important of all, the province's farmers and businessmen wanted to scrap the tariff walls between Canada and the United States. Reciprocity with the U.S., meaning a mutual reduction of tariffs, had become the rallying cry across the Canadian plains. Albertans led the charge, perhaps because so many of the new province's citizens had American roots.

The silver-tongued Laurier at 68 could still rouse a crowd, as when the photo above was taken at 100 Street and Jasper Avenue in Edmonton in 1910. (Note the crowd on the roof of the Traders Bank Building.) Five out of six Alberta constituencies voted for him and for reciprocity in the next election. On the opposite page, he is speaking from Medicine Hat's Riverside Band Shell.

199

Apart from Calgary, Alberta did not represent hospitable ground for Conservative leader Robert Borden, and was not a place he much enjoyed visiting. Here, however, George Armstrong, first mayor of Greater Edmonton, reads a civic address to Prime Minister Borden, circa 1912, from a Jasper Avenue balcony.

In that year, 22% of Alberta's population was U.S.-born. Besides their skills and capital, the Americans had brought with them a fierce sense of essentially populist democracy that set the province apart from British-dominated Ontario or even neighbouring British Columbia, which had acted as a magnet for early English immigrants. But the great radicalizer was not the U.S. constitution with its emphasis on individual rights. Rather, it was two thick and well-illustrated annual anthologies of consumer necessities and delights. They began life being seized eagerly on their arrival in the prairie homestead and ended it well thumbed twelve months later in the prairie outhouse, the successor volume having arrived. These were the mail-order catalogues published by the T. Eaton Company of Toronto and Marshall Field & Company of Chicago. What caused much thought, agitation and eventually outright rage was the difference in the prices contained therein, especially those applying to agricultural equipment. The same piece of machinery was 25% cheaper in the U.S.

The West's grain farmers knew that being forced to buy from Ontario- and Quebec-based manufacturers, hiding behind their tariff wall, amounted in fact to a 25% toll on each bushel of wheat their sweat produced from the newly broken prairie. "The western farmer from the beginning was forcefully and vocally a free-trader," wrote Arthur M. Lower in his seminal history of Canada, *Colony to Nation.* "To him anything was welcome that would get his products over the American tariff wall, or American manufactured goods over to Canada."

Little real sympathy for the western farmer's plight had been evidenced in Ottawa. Sir John A. Macdonald's National Policy — protectionist tariffs for central Canadian industry and freight rates structured to prevent western manufactured goods from competing in the East — was, to the Tories, the doctrine that had founded the nation. The Liberals, some of them anyway, said they disagreed with the National Policy, but by 1910 they had been in office fourteen years and the catalogues still looked very different. The explanation for this apathy was not hard to discern. The

CRACKS IN THE LIBERAL BASTION

prairie provinces sent only 27 MPs to Ottawa in 1911, seven from Alberta and ten each from Manitoba and Saskatchewan, about an eighth of the 221-seat House of Commons. Indeed, Sir Wilfrid Laurier's Liberals had wrested power from the Conservatives in 1896 only after assuring eastern industrial barons that they wouldn't monkey with the tariff barriers that created and preserved Ontario's fragile industrial economy.

Even during a pre-election western tour in 1910 Laurier was careful not to endorse reciprocity, despite the clamour he heard at western whistle-stops. "Our American friends have been refusing the suggestion of reciprocity for fifty years," he declared. "So I have said, 'Good-bye, Washington.' We will make no more pilgrimages. We will be independent and try to build up trade for ourselves," This was his message to 250 unreceptive members of a grain growers' convention at

With the birth of the year 1911, a tidal change began occurring in Ottawa. After a series of cross-border meetings, a deal was reached that would require ratification by both the Canadian Parliament and the U.S. Congress. It certainly did not represent all-out free trade. It was termed modestly 'reciprocity.'

Brandon, Manitoba, the prairie province where the reciprocity pot boiled least ferociously.

But this Laurier apologia omitted certain relevant details. The Americans themselves, for example, had made a pilgrimage to Ottawa seeking free trade earlier in 1910, and it was Laurier, not the Americans, who had lacked the enthusiasm. In fact, it soon became clear to the Canadian negotiators that the Americans desperately wanted a reciprocity deal, on Canadian terms if need be. U.S. President Howard Taft could see his mandate crumbling in the U.S. The free-trading Democrats were knocking at the door and the progressive wing of Taft's Republican party railed against what it called "profiteers' tariffs." A strong Republican seat in Massachusetts had gone Democrat on a platform of reciprocity in 1910. The president could see the writing on the wall. He needed a win.

'Scrutineer Shot Man in Poll,' said the *Edmonton Journal* the day after the 1911 election. Frank Bancenyet, a scrutineer in the hamlet of MacKay, ninety miles west of Edmonton, had been 'scuffling good-naturedly' with another man in the poll during voting hours. Somehow Bancenyet had a revolver in his hand, and it accidentally went off, killing the other man. The victim was identified only as a 'Belgian,' and Bancenyet caught the train from Edson that night to surrender himself to the Mounties. A subsequent RNWMP report identified the dead man as Frank Van Cammeyet, said he was deputy returning officer, and explained that though Bancenyet was in custody, he could not be charged because many of the witnesses had been 'under the influence of liquor' and 'we are experiencing difficulty in getting the facts owing to the irregularities in the conduct of this poll.'

Glenbow Archives, NB-16-173

Prime Minister Robert Borden (in topper) speaks with Calgary's R.B. Bennett in this undated photo from the Glenbow collection. By creating an improbable coalition of Tories, Quebec nationalists and anti-reciprocity Liberals, Borden was able to defeat Laurier. Bennett was his only successful candidate in Alberta, and two decades later would himself become prime minister.

Glenbow Archives, NA-1328-61785

Sir Wilfrid gets a warm Alberta welcome in 1910

Clockwise from top left, Laurier campaigns in Lethbridge, addresses a throng of Edmontonians, has a carriage ride in Calgary (the only Alberta constituency to vote against him), attends a reception in Mundare, and greets friends in St. Albert.

Thus with the birth of the year 1911, a tidal change began occurring in Ottawa. Following a series of cross-border meetings, a deal was reached early in January. It would require ratification by both the Canadian Parliament and the U.S. Congress. It certainly did not represent all-out free trade, and therefore was termed modestly "Reciprocity." Seemingly, it offered something for everyone, and offended no one in the Canadian mix. Happily for the farmers and primary producers, it provided Canadian grain, meat, cattle, dairy products, lumber, minerals and fish free, or almost free, access to the huge U.S. market. American duties would be lowered on a sizable list of Canadian manufactured items as well. Unhappily for the farmers, the tariffs protecting Canadian industry would hardly be touched. All the U.S. received for its many concessions was a general lowering of Canadian tariffs on U.S. imports to levels enjoyed by European countries such as France. The catalogues, in other words, would still look very different. Little or nothing was asked in return by the Americans. British Empire Preference, the arrangement that gave Canadian grain

A man with an iron belly that was always upset

That was Robert Borden whose skilful coalition beat Laurier, who steered Canada through the war, and who always felt sick

Robert Laird Borden's leadership forged Canada's independence in the crucible of the Great War, yet he remains one of our least-known prime ministers. While Borden lacked the eloquence of Sir John A. Macdonald, the flair of Sir Wilfrid Laurier or even the Machiavellian will of Mackenzie King, his honesty and tolerance mark him as one of Canada's great prime ministers.

The man who was to become the nation's eighth prime minister was born in the small village of Grand Pré, Nova Scotia, in 1854, the same year that Joseph Howe's government began building a railway from Halifax to Truro. Even at the beginning of the age of steam, the Bordens had already been living in Nova Scotia for nearly a century.

Richard Borden had left Headcorn, Kent, England, in 1638 to settle in Portsmouth, Rhode Island. One of Canadian history's darkest chapters inadvertently brought the family north to Canada. Samuel Borden, Richard's great-grandson, was a surveyor, and he was commissioned by the Nova Scotia government to survey former Acadian lands — the Acadians had been deported from their ancestral lands by the British in 1755, some to Quebec, some to Louisiana — to make room for settlers from the British colonies.

Robert Borden's father, Andrew, married Catherine

provided with a classical education, much of it at home. He did so well at the local private school he became assistant headmaster at fourteen and by nineteen had the title of professor of classics and mathematics at the Glenwood Institute in Matawan, New Jersey.

Here, however, he was oppressed with homesickness. "I wish I could just step into Grand Pré tonight and surprise them all," he confided to his diary. "However, what cannot be cured must be endured." It was a maxim his political career would afford him every opportunity to observe.

Borden's biographer, Robert Craig Brown, said the future prime minister was a lifetime hypochondriac. The "dull daily routine of lesson preparations" and repetitious markings of a schoolmaster's life seemed to wear him down. "I feel very unwell tonight," he writes in his diary. "My brain almost refuses to act. I must have less brain work or I will not be able to bear up." He did.

Ambition led him into law. He articled at the firm of Weatherbe and Graham in Halifax. Haligonians of the period were rich and insular, thriving by supplying the British fleet anchored in Bedford Basin and on the West Indian and Yankee trade. Until Confederation (which the Nova Scotia Legislature rejected, but was over-ruled) Canada was largely

---

Borden himself was haunted by insecurity. 'I would be in a condition of such extreme nervous tension that I could hardly eat or sleep,' he wrote of his courtroom forays. 'It is tiresome work, but the longer I keep at it, the easier it is in some respects.'

Fuller, who bore him two children before her death in 1847. Andrew then married Eunice Jane Laird, daughter of a schoolmaster, in 1850 and the future prime minister was the first child of this union. Under the stern tutelage of his Presbyterian parents, particularly his mother, Robert was

an irrelevancy. A contemporary of Borden's, journalist William Stevens Fielding, led his provincial Liberals to power in 1886 on the pledge he would get Nova Scotia out of Confederation. (Unable to accomplish it, he later ran federally and became Laurier's minister of Finance.)

exporters access to a market in Britain, would remain unchanged.

Initially, the reciprocity deal appeared a pre-election bonanza for the Laurier Liberals. They could scarcely believe their good fortune. It seemed to guarantee them another term. "The government had achieved what every previous administration had tried in vain to win," wrote O.D. Skelton in his *Life and Letters of Sir Wilfrid Laurier.* "It had secured an agreement which opened a market in the United States for Canadian natural products without giving the Canadian manufacturer any legitimate and substantial ground for complaint. It had provided that in no case would there be discrimination against Britain. That Canada would not welcome this triumph of diplomacy seemed incredible."

The Tories were stunned. They listened glumly as Finance Minister William Fielding explained the deal to a hushed House of Commons on January 26: "There was the deepest dejection in our party," Conservative leader Robert Borden confided in his memoirs. "The western members were

Meanwhile, Borden excelled as a lawyer. Wallace Graham, senior partner in what had become the most prestigious law firm in Nova Scotia, praised him as "the fittest man for office I know of. His capacity for systematic work is unequalled. In fact, he has been doing two-thirds of the whole work of my firm..." But Borden himself was haunted by insecurity. "I would be in a condition of such extreme nervous tension that I could hardly eat or sleep," he wrote of his courtroom forays. "It is tiresome work, but the longer I keep at it, the easier it is in some respects." At 33, he married Laura Bond, daughter of a well-known Halifax hardware merchant. Though childless, the marriage never lost its lustre to its two partners in spite of long absences.

By 1896, Borden was making $18,000 a year and living in a house on the same street as Sir Charles Tupper, a father of Confederation and the last of the Tory prime ministers before the Laurier era. Borden was a Liberal, in fact president of the Young Men's Liberal Association of Halifax, but the Tories persuaded him to switch parties and run federally. He gained a seat for them in the Laurier sweep of '96. "The thought of a parliamentary career had never entered my mind," he later recalled.

Borden rose swiftly to prominence in the Tory caucus, all the while writing to Laura of his incessant "insomnia and stomach cramps." A New York physician eliminated spices, sauces and fatty foods from his diet, a regimen he followed for the rest of his life. He also told him to get out of politics. Borden agreed. "Unless I alter my mind greatly, nothing will ever induce me to again become a candidate," he wrote in July

Glenbow Archives, NA-1514-2

Borden soon after he became leader of the opposition. His leadership was never secure, but he had an unfailing formula for survival: Always offer to resign. Although he did this frequently, not until he had been party leader for nearly two decades was his resignation ever accepted. But by then he meant it.

1899. "I want to be rid of it and I am convinced that my health won't stand it."

He was then 45, putting in appalling hours, and much impressing the aging Tupper who, after losing the election of 1900, persuaded Borden to stay on and run for leader. Borden agreed to serve only as interim leader until a permanent one could be found. This device of shunning the office was, says his biographer Brown, a manipulation to which Borden repeatedly resorted. Every time his leadership was challenged, he would offer to quit. For nearly twenty years, the resignation was never accepted.

Along with his nervous stomach Borden possessed an iron will. He led the party in the 1904 election and lost even his own seat. They shoehorned him into an Ottawa riding in 1905. In 1908 he lost another general election. His victory in 1911 came about after he achieved one of the most extraordinary political alliances in Canadian history — a working partnership of Quebec nationalists, imperialist Tories and anti-free-trade Liberals (see main chapter).

Three years later he must see Canada through the whole horror of the Great War and an attendant rupture with Quebec that threatened the whole Canadian union, finally to emerge much less a British dependency and much more an independent nation. As events through the rest of the decade would testify, the man chiefly responsible for that pivotal achievement would be Prime Minister Sir Robert Borden (he was knighted in 1914), fretting the whole time over his health.

— *G.O.*

most emphatic in their statements that not one of them would be elected in opposition to reciprocity. One of them declared he dare not vote against the government proposals."

Meanwhile, the Liberal joy was boundless. The usually inscrutable Laurier boasted of a master stroke. He had found the formula that had eluded even the greatest Tory of them all. "It's almost word for word the tariff agreement which was offered to the U.S. by Sir John A. Macdonald," Laurier reminded the Commons. "John A. Macdonald was the Moses of reciprocity who had failed to reach the promised land. I am the Joshua who will lead the people to their goal."

It was plainly the moment to go to the country. But, as Laurier's biographer Joseph Schull notes, Joshua was so intent on blowing his own horn he could not hear the false notes, nor a certain dissonance in his own orchestra pit. Even after nearly fifteen years in power the Liberals had a majority of 47 in the Commons. Despite subsequent defections, they could easily have pushed through a reciprocity bill in 1911, before the Tories could catch their breath, and then gone to the country.

But certain qualms dissuaded Laurier, partly moral, partly the sagacious caution that had kept him in power so long. He was against using the parliamentary closure rule to cut short debate. Moreover, "Laurier always maintained the government should make important changes in legislation only on a mandate from the people," wrote Louis Aubrey Wood in *A History of Farmers' Movements in Canada.* Others have less flattering explanations. L. Ethan Ellis's *Reciprocity 1911*, for instance, blames Laurier's "natural unwillingness to act too precipitously, lest American rejection (by the Congress) make the government look ridiculous." But with the Tories apparently stunned and dejected — "Why not leave well enough alone?" seemed to be the only argument they could muster — the pressure on the 69-year-old prime minister to call a snap election was very heavy.

However, the Liberals stalled. "Let the Conservatives roast a little longer. We have seared them with the flame of reciprocity and there's no sense inserting the fork of an election until they're done to a turn." Such was the thinking. It was to prove disastrous.

"Geographically, the Ontario, Quebec and British Columbia papers were predominantly hostile, both in volume and in tenor of opinion expressed, to reciprocity," wrote Ellis. "In the Maritimes and the prairie provinces the burden of opinion was favourable, with a touch of regret in the latter areas at the slight reduction on agricultural implements." This was hardly the bound-

---

The Liberals stalled. 'Let the Conservatives roast a little longer. We have seared them with the flame of reciprocity and there's no sense inserting the fork of an election until they're done to a turn.' Such was the thinking. It was to prove disastrous.

---

less enthusiasm that the Liberals had expected. Nevertheless, they were undeterred. After all, had not Ontario itself voted for reciprocity in the 1891 election? Why could it not be brought around again? And Quebec was a Liberal fiefdom. Even Henri Bourassa's ultra-nationalists appeared to support reciprocity because it diminished the imperial connection they detested. And Laurier was "a man who had affinities with Macchiavelli as well as Sir Galahad," in the words of *Manitoba Free Press* editor John Dafoe. If anyone could sell such a deal it would be the prime minister, or so went the logic.

Who, then, were reciprocity's serious antagonists? Railway barons like the Canadian Pacific's Sir William Van Horne. "Bust the damn thing," he demanded. And Edward Gurney, president of the Canadian Manufacturers' Association, who declared: "I would make the tariff as high as Haman's gallows if it would keep the Yankee out." To his words, CMA conventioneers roared in approval. But it took two almost simultaneous events to turn what had looked like a cakewalk election into an eventual catastrophe.

The first reversal occurred in the United States, but made lethal headlines in every Canadian daily. Champ Clark, Democratic minority leader in the House of Representatives, praised the reciprocity deal with words that almost guaranteed its defeat in Canada. "I am for it," he told the U.S. House on February 15, "because I hope to see the day when the American flag will float over every square foot of the British North American possessions clear to the North Pole. They are people of our blood. They speak our language. Their institutions are much like ours." The Tories saw

CRACKS IN THE LIBERAL BASTION

the opening and jumped at it. Under a banner headline accented with illustrations of the Stars and Stripes, the *Calgary Herald* screamed, "Annexation is American Dream." The same cry crossed the country.

Then came the second blow, even more damaging. Clifford Sifton, Laurier's former minister of the Interior and owner of the *Manitoba Free Press*, was now out of the cabinet (see Vol. II, Sect. 1, ch. 3). But he had remained a powerful MP on the Liberal benches, indeed still the principal Liberal power broker in the West. On the first day of February 1911 Sifton led five other Liberals to Laurier's door, pleading with the old lion not to proceed with reciprocity until the U.S. Congress had approved it. Laurier refused. He had his reasons. He must have known, for instance, that Sifton's *Free Press*, the most powerful organ on the prairies, was editorially supporting reciprocity. Sifton in fact had summoned his editor, John W. Dafoe, to Ottawa for a renowned confrontation. Dafoe fully expected to be fired. They had argued for a week, and Dafoe returned to Winnipeg. The next day, the *Free Press* was still supporting reciprocity.

But Sifton was still opposing it, and he was thereupon summoned by the prime minister. Laurier's biographer, Joseph Schull, records their confrontation. Why, asked Laurier, did he oppose the deal.

Sifton replied: "Because I do not believe in it."

"You did once," shot back Laurier. [1]

"Yes, but conditions have changed," replied Sifton.

"No, it is you who have changed," said Laurier. "Your opposition is personal. What is it?"

The answer was a shake of the head and a retreat into depths "never probed through all the years of shouting down that ear trumpet," wrote Schull of Sifton, whose deafness gained him the reputation of "The Sphinx" in Parliament. (The same description came to be applied to his brother Arthur, premier of Alberta.)

Ethan Ellis advances the theory that Sifton had come to hate Laurier for not offering him a more powerful role in government. "Some contemporaries in a fair position to know the facts have intimated to the author that he desired revenge upon Laurier and the party for being ousted from his cabinet portfolio," writes Ellis. Whatever The Sphinx's

John W. Dafoe, editor of the Manitoba Free Press, *fully expected his newspaper's owner, Clifford Sifton, to fire him over the reciprocity issue. Sifton was militantly opposed to it, Dafoe just as determinedly in favour. They agreed to disagree, and Dafoe editorially supported reciprocity while Sifton fought it by other means. In the outcome, however, Manitoba did not join Alberta and Saskatchewan in voting for it.*

reasons, eighteen Toronto Liberal businessmen, including department store magnate John Eaton, published an "urgent protest against the reciprocity measure as injurious to Canadian interests" on February 20. That same day Sifton informed Laurier he would fight reciprocity, even on the floor of the House. Sifton's much-anticipated Commons speech even made *The Times* of London, something few Canadian events ever managed: "We are putting our heads in a noose. The best years of my life were given to the settlement of that country [i.e. the West], and I cannot tell you how I feel about that great country being made the backyard for the city of Chicago."

The Tory benches exploded into life, erupting in a bedlam of cheers and desk-thumping. By the time the fifty-year-old Sphinx from Manitoba sat down, they already smelled blood. Across the floor, on the Liberal benches, all was division and confusion. Day by day, matters grew worse, as the telegraph carried story after story back to Canada of American expectations and plans for the annexation of the British dominion.

This shaped the Conservatives' strategy. They would cool their attack on the economic aspects of the agreement and focus on fears of Americanization. Commercial union will follow reciprocity, they would say, and political union will follow commercial. Meanwhile, imperial preference, and with it access to the markets of Britain, would be long gone. No sooner was this cry uttered than it was taken up across the country.

[1] **While a member of the Manitoba Legislature in the 1890s, Sifton had spoken in favour of reciprocity. Notes kept by Alexander Smith, better known as 'Silent Smith,' an Ottawa lawyer and Liberal wheelhorse at the turn of the century, show Sifton speaking in favour of reciprocity as late as 1905. Sifton's biographer, David Hall, attributes Sifton's turn against reciprocity to his 'instinctive distrust' of Americans. However, L. Ethan Ellis, in his *Reciprocity 1911*, has another theory, notably that Sifton's increasing wealth would have been threatened by American competition. When he died in 1929, he left an estate of $3 million.**

By then, Laurier's party was feeling the effect of another reversal, not related to reciprocity. To sustain his reputation in Ontario as a true son of the Empire, Laurier was proposing to create a Canadian navy that would assist the Royal Navy. This was also backfiring. While reciprocity was increasingly viewed as the first step towards republicanism by Ontario's Orangemen and other anglophiles, the navy plan was viewed by Quebec nationalists as an imperialist plot.

A Canadian navy was not exactly a new idea. Since the British Colonial Conference of 1902, the Laurier government had been on record as promising to aid the mother country in times of war. Though imperialistic sentiments had waned somewhat since the Boer conflict, Britain itself was now appealing for naval help. The German government had begun building a fleet of new super-battleships known as "dreadnoughts" to challenge the British fleet and Britain appealed to her dominions to help her meet the German threat. Canada should "fling the smug maxims of commercial prudence to the winds and place dreadnoughts, or the money for dreadnoughts, at the disposal of the British government," intoned the Toronto's Liberal *Globe*. Laurier concurred. So did Borden. A "naval bill" had received first reading in the Commons in January 1910, not to finance dreadnoughts but to provide five cruisers and six destroyers at a cost of $11 million to be staffed by a volunteer force of Canadians and assist the British fleet in an emergency. The bill provided that Canada, not Britain, would decide what constituted an emergency, and the measure had passed through the Commons in April with hardly a murmur of dissent.

Quebec Nationalist leader Henri Bourassa found himself in strange company, teaming up with British imperialists and Ontario anti-reciprocity Liberals to defeat Quebec's own Sir Wilfrid Laurier.

However, it soon became obvious that while Borden had put his imprimatur on the government bill, much of his party was out to torpedo it. Imperialists, like Manitoba Premier Rodmond Roblin, sneered at the idea of a "tin-pot" Canadian navy and demanded that Laurier write a cheque so that the Royal Navy could buy dreadnoughts instead. More serious trouble was brewing in Quebec. The Quebec federal Conservatives, led by Frederick Debartzch Monk, knew Tory fortunes were doomed in the province at the merest hint of Canadian involvement in the British Empire's colonial wars or gunboat diplomacy.

It is the province of Ontario which has defeated us. Our losses elsewhere were not very serious and would simply have reduced our majority, but Ontario went solid against us. It is becoming more and more manifest to me that it was not reciprocity that was turned down, but a Catholic premier. All the information which comes to me from that province makes this quite evident.

— from a letter by Sir Wilfrid Laurier to a Prince Edward Islander, Oct. 5, 1911.

Then, in a curious contortion that only Canadian politics could produce, there appeared an amazing coalition. French-Canadian nationalists led by Henri Bourassa, a grandson of rebel Joseph Papineau, joined with Quebec's Tory imperialists in opposing the naval bill. Bourassa, who had once been a Quebec Liberal MP, had resigned in 1899 to sit as an independent. He was now the leader of the Nationalist movement, which emphasized the central place of Roman Catholicism in the French-Canadian life. A fiery orator, he attracted much support in Quebec from conservatives of all stripes, including students, teachers and priests in the classical colleges that dominated Quebec's intelligentsia. In January 1910 Bourassa founded *Le Devoir*, which became the bible of the nationalist movement and provided him with a far-reaching pulpit from which he could proclaim that the naval bill was a "national capitulation."

By the middle of 1910, Monk was appearing on the same platform with Bourassa — the British imperialist and French-Canadian Nationalist united by a common determination to oust Laurier's Grits. Borden promised to hold a national plebiscite on the naval issue should he form a government. In return, Bourassa's Nationalists agreed not to oppose Tory candidates in many Quebec constituencies and urged Nationalists to vote Tory. Laurier labelled it "the Unholy Alliance." But had such a Tory-Nationalist deal been spelled out in specific terms? Borden's biographer, Robert Craig Brown, seemed to think so. "Borden may indeed have seen Bourassa on

power," wrote Howard and Tamara Palmer in *Alberta, a New History*. "Thousands of Alberta farmers began to feel a common sense of exploitation and grievance, and a common determination to change their status."

While Laurier wept, Borden's troubles had only begun. Jubilant Tories soon were converging on Ottawa in the hope that they would be in line for patronage from the new regime. "There was hardly a member of the party who did not rush to him and say he had to make him a cabinet minister. It was a most humiliating spectacle, this rush for the spoils of office, this playing pussy in the "Repatriation of French Canadians."

Despite crude communication technology, it was a surprisingly sophisticated operation for the time. The tracts and stories — often called boilerplate in the newspaper trade — were given to printing companies, which then supplied "ready press service" to hundreds of weeklies across the nation. In addition, some 9,500,000 pieces were sent by direct mail on a list compiled from party membership rolls and the customer register of the Massey-Harris farm machinery company. However, the biggest bonanza of all — the T. Eaton Company mail-order catalogue list — was turned down by Eaton's.

Despite his onerous editing duties in the backrooms of the CMA, Leacock also managed to crank out a series of articles under his own name during the campaign and anti-reciprocity papers displayed them prominently. "Rip and Tear the Soul of Alberta," said the large black type on the front page of the *Calgary Herald*. A subheadline proclaimed: "Written for the *Herald* by Professor Stephen Leacock." There was little sunshine in these sketches:

National Archives of Canada, PA-110154

Radio Times Hulton Picture Library

Kipling (above) and Leacock (left). Stephen Leacock was at least a Canadian and his fear of annexation by the U.S. overrode even his disgust with the Canadian Manufacturers' Association. Kipling on the other hand wouldn't have known there was an election if the Montreal Star hadn't told him.

> The ravenous maw of American industry opens wide, the restless eye of the trust looks abroad for new fields... And meantime smile, if you can, with the simper of the fool's content at the sale of your little peck of potatoes in the Boston market. Clutch tight the Yankee nickel of your profit. You may well treasure it. You have sold it for your birthright and your future.

Leacock plainly cared deeply about the fight against reciprocity, which he viewed as the first step towards a political union with the United States, a prospect that horrified him. What he regarded as distasteful was those in whose company he found himself, the members of the CMA, or "the moguls of the Mausoleum Club," as he called them. He made no secret of his antipathy to Canadian banks and business.

"The rise of the great trusts, the obvious and glaring fact of the money power, the shameless luxury of the rich, the crude, uncultivated and boorish mob of vulgar men and overdressed women that masqueraded as high society — the substitution, shall we say, of the saloon for the salon — all this seemed to many an honest observer of humble place as but the handwriting on the wall that foretold the coming doom." Such was his prophecy in *Democracy in Progress*, an essay in *The New Era in Canada*, edited by J.O. Miller.

Thus the ambiguity of a strange and contradictory man who denounced the captains of the side he fought for. Undoubtedly, Leacock played a key role in fuelling the Tory anti-reciprocity propaganda machine, and while history does not give him credit for Laurier's defeat, his tireless writing and editing may have been instrumental in changing the course of Canadian history.

— G.O.

[a]Kipling had already been primed to dislike Prime Minister Sir Wilfrid Laurier by his friend, Sir Leander Starr Jameson, whose raid on Johannesburg had set off the Boer War (Prologue chapter, Vol. II) and who became premier of Cape Colony. Jameson, an avid imperialist, took an instant dislike to Laurier at the 1907 Imperial Conference in London and described the Canadian prime minister to Kipling as 'that damned dancing-master' who 'bitched the whole show.'

1910
Out of Office.

1913
In Office.

Dr. W.J. Roche, Borden's minister of the Interior, is razzed for his failure to carry out a Tory promise and give the prairie provinces control of their resources, a right conferred on other provinces when they entered Confederation. Since Roche sat for a Manitoba seat, it was a particularly difficult issue for him. The Eye Opener, *Sept. 27, 1913.*

the corner," wrote an unknown Tory quoted in Skelton's biography of Laurier.

"One should never select a colleague by the standards of one's personal likes and dislikes," Borden later reflected. He adhered to that principle in appointing a cabinet. His troublesome Quebec lieutenant, Frederick Monk, was named to Public Works, despite a warning from the meddlesome British governor-general, Lord Grey, that "the presence of Mr. Monk as one of your colleagues on the Treasury Bench" might "mean a weak or retrogressive naval policy." The other half of the "unholy alliance," Henri Bourassa, refused a cabinet position and chose to stay at the helm of *Le Devoir* where he hectored the government and, when the Great War came, fought tenaciously against Borden's conscription policy.

Clifford Sifton, the enigmatic Liberal who had joined forces with Borden's strange coalition to defeat reciprocity, might have had his pick of cabinet positions. But while he advised Borden on his ministers, he remained out of office. "He knew that politics at Ottawa would not attain the same glamour under Borden," wrote his biographer, David John Hall, the University of Alberta historian. "He was abandoning politics at age fifty, a time when many men were just beginning a public career."

Sifton did retain his position as chairman of the conservation commission, a body created by the Laurier administration to consider water resources, forestry, agriculture, irrigation and their inter-relations, but he was clearly tired, and unsure of his health after 23 years in politics. "I have been troubled with my head and nerves the last couple of years and...I shall have to refrain from public speaking for some time," Sifton wrote in 1912, just before he fell ill with serious pneumonia. He was also plagued by insomnia, severe headaches, high blood pressure, and "a serious worsening of his deafness," writes Hall.

And while the restless Monk held an important if mundane portfolio, he was never a team-player and couldn't abide Borden's naval policies. He resigned from cabinet a month later when it became clear the prime minister would not honour his promise to hold a plebiscite on the naval issue. Instead, Borden introduced a Tory naval bill, proposing to shell-out $35 million to buy three battleships for the Royal Navy to use as they wished.

This brought Laurier to his feet in the Commons with something of his old vigour. "O ye Tory jingoes," he jibed. "You give England two or three dreadnoughts to be paid for by Canada, but to be equipped, maintained and manned by England... You leave it to England to supply the bone and sinews. You say that these ships shall bear Canadian names. That will be the only thing Canadian about them. You hire somebody to do your work; in other words you are ready to do anything except the fighting."

But Laurier and the Liberal Party were devastated by the defeat. Powerful ministers such as Alberta's Frank Oliver had to fight to get nominated in the first place when former Alberta premier Alexander Rutherford initially challenged the minister of the Interior for his seat. Rutherford withdrew from the race, Oliver won the nomination and went on to a handsome victory, only to find himself forlorn in opposition, an outsider who would remain loyal to Laurier in the conscription crisis of 1917.

The aging Liberal leader himself, who had spent 38 years in the House of Commons, offered to resign at the start of the first parliamentary session after the election, a pro-forma gesture that was rejected by the diminished party. His dreams of retiring to his home in Arthabaskaville, Quebec, and writing a history of Canada were just idle ruminations because "he was frankly fond of power and fond of the game of politics," as Skelton put it.

The Great War, the conscription crisis, and the Union government were ahead. Laurier would live to see it all, including the division of his own party over conscription, before he died on a cold February day in 1919.

Homeless

Joy (dubious) over one sinner that repenteth

The Down-and-Outers.

In 1910-11 the Eye Opener divided its cartoon venom between editor Bob Edwards' loathing for Clifford Sifton, somewhat unfairly pilloried above and below, and his gloating over the Liberal defeat. Above right, a besotted Laurier leans on an equally inebriated U.S. President William Howard Taft. Below right, horror-stricken Grit patronage appointees face the political guillotine.

He's A Bird Alright

THE REIGN OF TERROR

CHAPTER TWO

The unbeloved 'Little Arthur' salvages the shattered Grits

COLD, CIGAR-PUFFING SIFTON SOLVES THE A & GW CRISIS BY UNITING
THE FEUDING FACTIONS IN HIS CABINET AND PRESERVING LIBERALDOM

by GEORGE OAKE

The enigmatic Arthur L. Sifton after taking office as premier of Alberta in 1910. Stay clear of that appointment, his brother Clifford had advised. 'I shall accept it if it is offered,' Arthur replied, and offered it was.

When Arthur Sifton lit up one of his trademark black cigars and surveyed his new realm in the summer of 1910, he must have been a touch nervous. "Little Arthur," as he was known behind his back, had stepped down from his comfortable perch as the chief justice of Alberta to take over the reins of the ruling Liberal party, still mired in and divided over the northern railway scandal (Vol. II, Sect. 6, ch. 2). He was now premier of Alberta, but few would envy him the job.

Sifton had not been an overwhelming favourite to replace Alberta's first premier, Alexander Cameron Rutherford, who had been fingered to take the fall for the Waterways scandal. Even Sifton's brother, Clifford, for nine years Prime Minister Wilfrid Laurier's interior minister and still the top federal Liberal power-broker in the West, had warned Arthur to stay clear of Alberta's rancorous Grits.

"Would on no account accept it if offered," Clifford had wired his brother from Ottawa early in 1910 when the premiership was being mooted. "I shall accept it if it is offered," shot back Arthur, providing a glimpse of his stubborn nature that would rule Alberta for another seven years .

The Ottawa Liberals, who had carved Alberta and Saskatchewan out of the Northwest Territories in 1905, had lost little of their brash confidence. Rutherford had been given an overwhelming new

Provincial Archives of Alberta, A-10615

Alberta's legislators, ensconced in their handsome new chamber, take time out from political infighting and backbiting to solemnly pause for an official photograph.

mandate in 1909, but had fallen swiftly when a group within his caucus had teamed up with Tories over the ruinous contract to build the Alberta & Great Waterways Railway from Edmonton to Fort McMurray. Their chief target was Rutherford's attorney-general, Charles Wilson Cross. Rutherford had appointed a royal commission, but it had been too late. Political gangrene had set in, and the Ottawa Liberals were still powerful enough in the provincial party to force his resignation.

But before he went, it must be decided who would succeed him. There had been no lack of aspirants. Former Public Works Minister William Cushing thought he was a shoe-in because he had quit the Rutherford cabinet in a huff, ostensibly over the government's railroad policies. Cross had quit, too, over his murky role in the affair, but then rejoined the government. He too wanted the first minister's job and had a sizable rump of supporters [2] Even Frank Oliver was suggested. He had replaced Clifford Sifton as Laurier's Interior minister and was, in title anyway, still publisher of the *Edmonton Bulletin*. Another nominee was Senator Peter Talbot, president of the Alberta Liberal Association and a trusted servant of Laurier.

But all had fatal disabilities. The rebels in the caucus favoured Cushing, but this would alienate the Rutherford loyalists, and besides, Cushing had contradicted himself in testifying before the royal commission. Oliver and Talbot had been so long in Ottawa they had lost much of their local support. Cross was a marked man due to the railway scandal. This left Sifton, whose judicial responsibilities had necessarily distanced him from provincial politics.

But how would he be chosen? By a provincial convention? By a vote of the caucus? Not at all. Lieutenant-Governor George Hedley Vicars Bulyea, Ottawa's appointee and Ottawa's point man, met privately for two days and two nights with the recalcitrant provincial Grit leaders in both camps and coerced them into accepting Sifton. Then on May 26, 1910, he called the provincial House into session at what was known as the Legislature Hall behind the Terrace Building. (The future Legislature Building was then under construction.) Bulyea flatly announced Rutherford's

[1] The usually reticent Premier Sifton uncharacteristically told this anecdote to reporters from the *Medicine Hat News* and the *Toronto Star*. It is virtually the only evidence on record of the personal relationship between the two brothers who played such dominant roles in western Canada in the first two decades of the century. The term 'sphinx' came to be applied to them both, particularly to Arthur who was frequently portrayed in stone by political cartoonists.

[2] Cross waged a fifteen-year backroom battle with Frank Oliver for the control of the Alberta Liberals. The province's first attorney-general had such an indisputable following that both Premiers Sifton and Stewart reluctantly put Cross in their cabinets to ensure unity in the fractious party.

resignation and Sifton's appointment, tipped his hat, wished the gaping legislators a pleasant summer, and rode off in his viceregal carriage. Through it
all, Little Arthur had peered on implacably from the gallery.

The predictable explosion followed. The Conservative opposition
howled that Bulyea's moves were unconstitutional. This was never tested.
That they were undemocratic didn't need to be. "Had a vote of want of confidence in the Sifton government been carried, a dissolution could scarcely
have been avoided and in the ensuing general election the Conservatives
might have made substantial gains," wrote Lewis G. Thomas in his definitive work on early provincial politics, *The Liberal Party of Alberta*. "By defer-
ring the general election, the Liberal party would have a further
opportunity to close the breaches in its ranks."

All this flagrant fiddling by the federal Liberals had, of course, bought
the new premier some desperately needed time. Sifton gave himself six
months to pull the party, the caucus and the government together again,
and decided to call the House in November. By then, the Royal Commission
on the Alberta & Great Waterways Railway contract would have tabled its
report in the Legislature.

On June 1 the former chief justice announced his cabinet. Cross supporters had staged an extraordinary parade through Edmonton, demanding
their champion be restored to his post of attorney-general in the new government (Vol. II, p. 436). Parade or no parade, Sifton kept him out. In fact,
he wisely excluded all of the former cabinet ministers or MLAs who had
supported the Alberta & Great Waterways deal. This would alienate the
Rutherford-Cross contingent, but seemed to have the desired effect on most
Alberta voters. When three by-elections were called for June 29, the
Liberals won all three.[3]

But the by-elections saw the appearance in Alberta politics of the farm
associations whose members supported the Liberal candidates, but the very
existence of the farm movement gave evidence that Alberta voters might be
losing faith in the traditional parties. This made the Liberals nervous. In
fact, the farm revolt was one of the three radical movements within Alberta
with which the new premier had to contend, the others being the women's
movement and the labour movement. Sifton deftly overcame them all,
yielding to and co-opting the women's movement, making his Liberals the instrument of the farm
movement, and simply defeating the labour movement.

With seeming ease, Little Arthur coasted through the summer of 1910, sucking on his long
black cigars plucked from a Morocco leather humidor, and contemplating his next move in consol-
idating his grip on government and the still simmering caucus. A provincial election could be postponed until 1914, but the Royal Commission on the A & GW had rekindled public interest in that
mess and the government would have to somehow bury it once and for all.

The Royal Commission, made up of Chief Justice Horace Harvey and two of his colleagues on

**The by-elections saw the strong appearance in Alberta politics of the
farm associations whose members supported the Liberal candidates,
but the very existence of such a movement gave evidence that
Alberta voters might be losing faith in the traditional parties. This
made the Liberals nervous.**

---

the provincial Supreme Court, D.L. Scott and N.D. Beck, finished its reports on July 6 of 1910, but
did not present them to the government until November when the Legislature met. Did Sifton's
Liberals get a peek at the report before it was presented to the Legislature? There was certainly a
noticeable lack of anxiety about it when it was made public.

After taking 3,225 pages of evidence, the commissioners could find nothing conclusive against

[3] Sifton himself won Vermilion
by 1,018 to 710 against a Tory. He
represented Vermilion until he
moved to the federal cabinet in
1917. Charles Mitchell, a former
district court judge and Sifton's
new attorney-general, won
Medicine Hat 1,134 to 670.
Archibald J. McLean, a rancher and
one of the 'Big Four' guarantors of
the first Stampede, was acclaimed
in Lethbridge. McLean became
provincial secretary and later minister of Municipal Affairs. All three
by-elections were made possible
when sitting Liberal members
resigned.

Arthur Sifton, fresh from the calm of judicial office, returned to the rough-and-tumble of politics when he became premier in 1910. He addressed this audience in Wetaskiwin that summer, during a light shower.

the government or any member of it.[4] Indeed the main question was scarcely addressed: Did any member of the Alberta Legislature profit from the A & GW contract? Scott and Harvey submitted a majority report that was little more than a chronology of what occurred. True, it did question the sagacity of Premier Rutherford and Attorney-General Cross in negotiating the Alberta & Great Waterways contract without investigating the background of the "bankers" with whom they made the deal, but they found no one guilty of misconduct. Beck's minority report was even more innocuous in its conclusions. It found nothing unusual in special exemptions to the provincial railway act granted the A & GW consortium, and no "suspicion of intention" on the part of Cross to favour the company unduly (see sidebar).

There appeared to be a reluctance on the part of the judges to examine the attorney-general's relationship to the railway company. Why, for example, had Cross removed between fifteen and twenty boxes of files from his office at midnight on March 8, the day before his brief resignation? Why, in particular, since members of the Legislature were complaining at the time that the government was not providing the commission with the files the commission was asking for? Yet the commissioners had not asked Cross about this.

Public Works Minister Cushing's testimony contradicted that of Rutherford and Cross about certain dates of meetings, but the inconsistencies were not queried. "The result is that one is left questioning either

Sifton refused to name popular Edmontonian Charlie Cross as attorney-general because of Cross's involvement in the scandal-ridden A & GW contract (see sidebar). He chose Charles R. Mitchell (left), who got a seat in a Medicine Hat by-election.

[4]Jay Stewart Heard in a 1990 University of Alberta master's thesis entitled 'The Alberta & Great Waterways Railway Dispute' provides a wealth of detail from more than 3,200 pages of testimony resulting from the royal commission struck in March 1910. The scandal and resulting inquiry are described in the last chapter of Volume II in this series.

Cushing's memory or his honesty," concluded J.S. Heard in his thesis on the Alberta & Great Waterways Railway scandal.

Even more incredible, R.B. Bennett, the Calgary lawyer and Conservative leader who would later become prime minister and as counsel for the Canadian Pacific knew more about the technological inadequacies of the contract than most people in the province, was never called upon to testify. He appeared before the commission only in the role of counsel for the dissident Liberal members, known as "the insurgents." Indeed it was Bennett who had set off the inquiry by charging government with "culpable negligence." He had told the House of being "approached by great financial interests in an attempt to keep him from protesting against this thing." Heard describes

Alberta's first Liberal premier turns to the Tories

THOUGH OUSTED PREMIER RUTHERFORD INSISTED HE WAS STILL LIBERAL HE FOUGHT FOR THE CONSERVATIVES AND WAS NEVER ELECTED AGAIN

by Virginia Byfield

When Alexander Cameron Rutherford was relegated to the back benches of Alberta's Liberal government in 1910, after his ignominious resignation as premier (Vol.1, Sect. 6, ch. 2), the political enemies who brought him down may have thought they were rid of him. They were not. True, Rutherford would never win another election. But in the next eleven years he would throw assorted monkey wrenches into the Liberal works, thereby very likely helping to consign that party to political oblivion in Alberta for most of the remaining century — and always apparently with the noblest intentions.

That a man would so readily turn on his own party was a puzzle, however, in those times of strict political loyalties. Was Rutherford unusually honest and brave, his contemporaries wondered, or just politically naive? Probably something of all three. He was still Liberal MLA for South Edmonton when he let off his first bomb just before the 1913 provincial election. Rutherford was planning to stand again, and he wrote a most unusual letter to the president of the South Edmonton nominating convention.

In *Alexander Cameron Rutherford: A Gentleman of Strathcona*, D.R. Babcock describes this curious episode. So opposed was he to the policies of Liberal leader Arthur Sifton on the A & G W Railway issue, Rutherford confided in his

Glenbow Archives, NA-1514-5

Alexander Cameron Rutherford, deposed as premier in 1910, became a thorn in Sifton's side by campaigning for the Tories while avowing that he was still a Liberal. This photo was taken on a visit to Britain.

letter, that if the Conservatives would refrain from running a candidate in South Edmonton, he would personally campaign for the Conservative cause anywhere else in the province. This was, to say the least, a strange offer to come from the previous Liberal premier. When it was read to the Conservative convention March 29, some of them wanted to take him up on it. The majority, however, voted it down.

Two days later, Rutherford's name was duly presented for renomination at his own South Edmonton Liberal convention, and some puzzled constituents not unnaturally called for an explanation. But the candidate was in no sense abashed. "I am glad to meet such an enthusiastic audience of Liberals," he blandly told them. "I am a Liberal of the Liberals myself..." Then he read his letter to them, and emphasized that he had all along opposed the Sifton "solution" to the A & G W problem, because it was no solution. It was unbusinesslike, had been declared illegal by the Privy Council, and was not going to produce the railway which northern Alberta needed.

Surely his constituents would not expect him to support "measures that are not in harmony with good Liberal principles," wherever they came from. Anyhow, he was not offering himself as "a Sifton candidate." He would run as a good independent Liberal candidate. So his constituency association happily nominated him, although the *Edmonton Journal* described his actions as unparal-

Bennett's charge as "a provocative statement that begged queries," but he says none was ever made.

The reaction to this inconclusive commission report was as curious as the report itself. The *Edmonton Capital*, which strongly supported Cross, was understandably relieved. [5]The report had cleared everybody of wrongdoing, it noted. The Conservative-leaning *Edmonton Journal* was careful to observe that the commission's verdict was in fact more a case of "not proven" than "not guilty," and let it go at that. It was as though the commission had been an embarrassment to all concerned, an impediment to the province's boosterism. On November 11, the day after the report was made public, it was widely published. Thereafter, there is no mention of it in newspapers [6]

[5]It was assumed by many at the time that Cross in fact owned the *Edmonton Capital*, though no record survives of his having done so. The *Capital* was published from December 1909 to November 1914. For the first year its publisher is listed as Arthur Balmer Watt. From then until it folded its publisher was William MacAdams.

SIC VOS VON VOBIS.
"Well, what do you know about that?"
Hamlet, Act V, Scene II

The Calgary Eye Opener *depicts Liberal dissidents Cushing and Boyle, who had led the attack on the now down-and-out Rutherford, looking on furiously while 'Little Arthur' collects the fruits of their victory.*

leled in Canadian history. Nor did the Liberal party nominate against him. But a majority of his constituents, who may have been thoroughly confused by election day, voted for his Tory opponent. Hence the Tories took their first Edmonton seat when Herbert Howard Crawford, a Strathcona merchant, auctioneer and council member, defeated Rutherford 1,523 to 1,275.

For the next eight years Rutherford kept busy with his law practice, overseas travel, war work, myriad community activities and, above all, the University of Alberta of which he was in effect the founder. He served as chancellor from 1927 until his death in 1941. But in the 1921 provincial election he felt once more the old stirring to political battle, and it moved him to attack his own party again — but still, of course, as "a lifelong Liberal."

As the campaign got going, Rutherford appeared as the star attraction at a Conservative rally, speaking on behalf of five Tory candidates. The present "rotten" Liberal administration had put the province disastrously into debt, he proclaimed, and the party itself was sadly disorganized. He even suggested a new Liberal slogan: "Get Rid of the Barnacles and the Boyles!" (In 1910 J.R. Boyle, Liberal member for Sturgeon, had led the party rebellion that destroyed Rutherford as premier.)

A week later the reigning Liberals were decisively defeated by the United Farmers, and the Tories almost wiped out. Although it cannot be argued that Rutherford was central to the Liberal demise, he certainly helped discredit the party.

But then, he never had been a satisfactory party man. As Babcock observes, when campaigning for his big electoral victory in 1909 he had proclaimed that "the province must stand before the party." That, along with "good Liberal principles" and a certain naive and stubborn honesty, was his political credo.

The forces of Frank Oliver vie with those of ex-premier Rutherford to tear asunder the provincial Liberal party, in this 1911 Edmonton Journal *cartoon.*

One thing that eased life for Premier Sifton was the departure to federal politics of Tory provincial leader R.B. Bennett, the opposition's most effective man. Here Bennett unveils a South African war memorial in Calgary's Central Park in June 1914, while RNWMP veterans look on.

Thus Sifton's administration had survived its first test with no hits, no runs, and no errors. But the question remained: What about the railway? Some $7,400,000 had been raised to build it by the sale of bonds; the province had guaranteed the issue; the money was in the bank. But where was the railway to Fort McMurray?

That July, two months after Sifton took office, the A & GW defaulted on the interest payment. The government met the payment, and in November Sifton introduced a bill that would transfer the $7,400,000 to the credit of the province. This would shut out the old A & GW management, and provide the province with a cash transfusion.

It would not, however, placate the Rutherford-Cross faction, excluded from the new cabinet and festering on the backbenches. They attacked the bill as dooming all further northern development. Bennett called it a money-grab, un-British, and "an act of confiscation." After all, what of the bondholders? Their cash would be in the hands of the government and there was no railway to secure them. Sifton argued that the bill was simply foreclosure on an agreement that had not

---

Sifton's administration had survived its first test with no hits, no runs, and no errors. But the question remained: What about the railway? Some $7,400,000 had been raised to build it by the sale of bonds; the province had guaranteed the issue. Then the A & GW defaulted on the interest payment.

---

been fulfilled. There was little danger of legal action from either the banks or the A & GW if the legislation were passed, he said.

But if the Rutherford forces were displeased, those Liberals who had opposed the Rutherford government on the A & GW contract were equally disagreeable. One of them, E.H. Riley, Liberal member for Gleichen, had resigned his seat and ran for it again as an Independent. In this, another by-election, his Liberal opponent A.J. McArthur had defeated him 1,119 to 919. That vote was held October 3, and the result seemed to sober Sifton's critics.

Thus the outcome was something of an anomaly. Only Sifton himself spoke in support of the

[6]Railway development was an article of faith for both Alberta's Liberal and Conservative parties. While the A & GW was an admitted scandal, neither party exploited the issue. Meanwhile, four other rail lines were under construction in Alberta.

CRACKS IN THE LIBERAL BASTION

Alberta's first A-G — they couldn't live without him, or with him either

ATTORNEY-GENERAL CHARLIE CROSS WAS THE POWDER KEG OF THE LIBERAL ERA; TWO PREMIERS LOATHED HIM, BUT HOW COULD THEY GET RID OF HIM?

Alberta Attorney-General Charles Wilson Cross at the peak of his career. The mud flew constantly but none ever stuck.

Through the entire sixteen years of Alberta's Liberal era, the lightning rod of all three of its administrations was Charles Wilson Cross, Alberta's first attorney-general. He was the central target in the Waterways railway scandal, the man chiefly blamed by the Tories in the so-called "crooked election of 1913," and under constant criticism and suspicion in the Prohibition wars that followed.

At the same time, he was one of the most popular politicians that the 20th century was to see elected in Edmonton, and although his foes endlessly accused him of graft, corruption and sleaze politics, never once was any of these accusations made to stick.

And when the Liberal era came crashing down in the election of 1921, there standing tall among the few survivors, re-elected as usual, was Charles Wilson Cross.

Even the then-rabidly Tory *Edmonton Journal*, which called Cross "the weakness" of Premier Arthur Sifton's regime and hinted that he plugged ballot boxes to win elections, buried him with praises when he died in 1928.

"To few men in the public life of the province has it been given to have made so many friends as did Charles Cross, for

At Edmonton he soon enmeshed himself in politics and gained a reputation as a popular politician and Liberal vote-getter. Premier A.C. Rutherford made him attorney-general and No. 1 provincial party wheel in the capital. This soon brought him into conflict with Frank Oliver, publisher of the *Bulletin*, member of parliament, and minister of the Interior. It also alienated another Edmonton Liberal lawyer, John R. Boyle.

These internal conflicts within the Rutherford party exploded in the Alberta & Great Waterways Railway scandal (Vol. II, Sect. 6, ch. 2), which saw Boyle, doubtless with

After Prohibition came to Alberta in 1916, there were so many accusations of corruption levelled at politicians that some were probably true. As usual, charges against Cross commanded the biggest headlines.

it is as Charlie Cross that he was known from one end of the province to another," said the *Journal*.

Cross was born in Madoc, Ontario, in 1872. He had an impeccable education at Upper Canada College and the University of Toronto, then studied law at Osgoode Hall. At 25 he packed up and moved to Edmonton, then a small town in the vast Northwest Territories, opened his own office, and later became a partner in the firm of Short, Cross, Biggar and Ewing. In 1900 he married Annie Louisa Lynde, who bore a son and two daughters.

Oliver's backing, pitted against Cross, who had Rutherford's unflagging support. The inquiry did not exactly exculpate Cross. Rather, as the Tory *Edmonton Journal* pointed out, it merely declared the charges against him "not proved."

Cross resigned as attorney-general on March 9, 1910, resumed his portfolio a few days later, and was sitting beside Premier Rutherford on the front bench when Lieutenant-Governor Bulyea announced the demise of the Rutherford government. But Cross retained his seat in the Legislature, and even arranged a mass rally of Edmontonians to demand

The Tory Edmonton Journal *makes sure a disgusted 'Alberta' knows all about the behind-the-scenes feud in the Sifton cabinet.*

a seat for him in the new Sifton cabinet. This unusual performance, complete with two brass bands, a parade down Jasper Avenue and a speech of appeal on Cross's behalf by the deposed Premier Rutherford (Vol. II, p. 436), evidenced Cross's powerful popularity in the capital.

But Sifton wanted no part of Cross when he formed his first cabinet, doubtless because he realized Cross had ambitions to replace Frank Oliver as Alberta's top Liberal power broker. Despite the scandal, Cross and Rutherford still had many friends in the Alberta party who resented Sifton as an Ottawa cat's paw.

The popular Cross could not be long kept from power, and Sifton brought him back into the cabinet as attorney-general in 1913. A by-election was then required whenever an MLA was appointed to a ministry, and an incident in that by-election campaign eloquently illustrated how determined the Tories were to defeat him and how innovative Cross was in an election fight.

Dr. George D. Stanley, Tory member for High River, charged that Cross received big payoffs from hoteliers seeking liquor licences. It was never proved.

On the eve of the vote, a Sunday night, Cross had arranged a session with Edmonton's small Jewish community in an Edmonton synagogue, to rout out a few last-minute votes. "The meeting was a clandestine affair," reported the *Edmonton Journal.* "The outside world was not supposed to know anything about it, but every Jew in Edmonton was welcome, according to the word passed around."

However, when a man identified as S. Kaplan tried to enter the synagogue to attend the meeting his way was blocked by one I. Goodman, who refused him entrance. Though Goodman was a large man, Kaplan apparently knocked him down, and was intent on administering more punishment still when bystanders intervened.

"The trouble caused such a disturbance that the entire neighbourhood was aroused and a riot call was sent to the police station," reported the *Journal.* Two constables arrived on the scene and demanded admission to the synagogue, wherein the attorney-general was working the crowd. Admission was barred to them as well. The police "pounded on the front door," reported the *Journal.* When they were finally admitted, they demanded an explanation of why a political meeting was being held on Sunday. A "wheezy orchestra" drowned them out.

Four men, D.R. Fraser, A.L. Gilpin, A.C. McDonald and Alexander Rankin, "who happened on the scene," said the *Journal,* were so incensed they demanded that the police eject Cross from the synagogue for violating the Lord's Day Act. Meanwhile, Kaplan swore out a warrant for the arrest of Goodman on charges of assault, and said he was trying to enter the meeting to unmask some of Cross's supporters, who were corrupt and willing to sell their votes for a dollar. The next day, in what the *Journal* described as a "heartless downpour," Cross won by a comfortable margin. The charges are not mentioned again and presumably were dropped.

A year later the attorney-general was in hot water again, this time in the "crooked election of 1913." Cross's role did not surface until a 1915 trial that led to the ouster of independent Liberal MLA Andrew Shandro from office, for vote-buying in the riding of Whitford. Evidence presented at the trial included a letter from the attorney-general to Liberal candidate Paul Rudyk, written during the 1913 election campaign:

"Dear Sir: If you are desirous of having any appointments made of justices of the peace, notaries or commissioners in connection with my department during the election, kindly write to me at government offices, Edmonton, and the appointments will be attended to at once by Mr. Thom. [Signed] C.W. Cross." Though appointments by patronage were very much a part of Alberta politics, the practice was rarely proclaimed quite so blatantly. Even so, the disclosure brought no censure whatever on the attorney-general.

After Prohibition came to Alberta in 1916, there were so many accusations of corruption levelled at most politicians that some were probably true. As usual, charges against Cross commanded the biggest headlines. These occurred when Dr. George Stanley, Conservative member for High River, charged that Cross and other government members had received large payoffs from hoteliers, either for liquor licences, to stifle prosecution, or for future immunity. None of this was ever proved.

When in 1917 Sifton decamped to Ottawa to join Borden's Union government (a coalition of Tories combined with those Liberals who favoured conscription for military service) this presented Cross with a new problem. Sifton's successor was Charles Stewart who was appointed Alberta's third premier by the Liberal caucus. Stewart didn't like Cross much. The new premier was a Unionist, in favour of conscription. Cross refused to support the coalition, remaining loyal to Sir Wilfrid Laurier, who was still the national leader. Stewart, like Sifton before him, nevertheless had to bow to Edmonton pressure and reluctantly reappoint Cross as attor-

ney-general. There is little doubt, however, that Stewart felt uncomfortable with a colleague who carried so much bad baggage from two previous administrations. Within a year, therefore, Stewart was resolved to rid his government of Charles Wilson Cross, which precipitated yet another crisis because Cross refused to quit.

"A story was current to the effect that just before the [1918] session opened Cross had been given a stated period to resign, that at first he had agreed, but that later he defied the premier to remove him," wrote L.G. Thomas in his 1959 book *The Liberal Party in Alberta*.

Stewart offered Cross the province's agency-general in London, an offer that caused Oliver's *Edmonton Bulletin* to sniff that "it was one time when the generosity of the premier outran his good judgement."

The Cross home on Hardisty Avenue, later 98th, stood across the street from the future site of the Legislature and was certainly unpretentious compared with others that would arise during the boom. When work on the Legislature began the Crosses moved to Stony Plain Road near 127 Street.

But Cross wouldn't budge. Stewart next took the unusual step of announcing that the attorney-general had been asked to resign and wouldn't. Even this didn't pry Cross out of his job. Finally, Stewart resorted to an extreme measure. He simply rescinded the order-in-council appointing Cross to begin with. At that, Cross gave up.

He remained a member of the Legislature, however, and was one of the few survivors of the 1921 disaster. By then his interest had shifted to the federal scene and he only occasionally attended legislative sessions. He moved into federal politics and won the riding of Athabaska for the Liberals in 1925, but was defeated by a United Farmers of Alberta candidate in the 1926 general election.

Two years later, in Calgary, he died. Undoubtedly Cross was one of the shrewdest politicians in the province's history, even if many people regarded him as not entirely honest. He served under two premiers who actively disliked him, but could not do without him.

At Osgoode Hall where he studied law before migrating west, he earned the nickname "Slugger" Cross for his prowess at the rough game of lacrosse. In politics he was also a slugger — and no one ever put a glove on him.

— *G.O.*

bill. Not one Liberal or Tory MLA spoke in favour of it and many attacked it. Yet it passed 25-14 on December 14 with little comment from the partisan press. How Sifton managed this result, or why it happened if he didn't manage it, has never been explained. The legislation did not heal the fundamental schism between the Cross-Rutherford group and those who opposed them. As for

the acquiescence of the banks, on this Sifton proved sadly mistaken. They refused to turn the $7,400,000 over to the provincial treasury and their ensuing legal battle with the Alberta government lasted two years, financially hamstringing the province.

But those voting for the bill included not only the Liberal "insurgents" in Rutherford's caucus — men like John R. Boyle, who had bitterly opposed the Cross-Rutherford group on the A & GW contract deal — but strangest of all, Cross himself, who voted for it. He spoke one way and voted another, but the explanation was not long in coming: In 1912, Sifton increased the number of Alberta government departments from four to eight, a move that would require the appointment of more cabinet ministers.

"The long-lived antagonism between Cross and the government had been a serious political problem for the Liberals, and the return of the popular Edmonton lawyer [Cross] as attorney-general brought an official return to party unity," wrote G.K. Wright in his 1952 University of Alberta thesis, *The Administrative Growth of the Government of Alberta 1905-1921*.

Cross's mortal foe, John Boyle, another Edmonton lawyer who sat for Sturgeon, entered the cabinet as minister of Education. This, adds Wright, "served to soothe still more of the electorate in view of his strong attitude about the A & GW affair." Thus was peace made among Sifton's Liberals.

The cabinet expansion also brought in a new minister of Municipal Affairs, Charles Stewart, a 45-year-old Ontario-born farmer from Killam who sat for the riding of Sedgewick. He would become the third Liberal premier of Alberta in 1917.

Why is Sifton ?

THE SPHINX SMILES

Meanwhile, the battle between the banks and the Alberta government had worked its way to the top, that is to the judicial committee of the Privy Council in Britain that served as a final court of appeal for the British Empire. The Privy Council ruled that Alberta's attempt to expropriate the proceeds of the A & GW bond sale from the banks was *ultra vires* because it infringed on the civil rights of bondholders outside the province. However, it affirmed the province's right to repudiate its contract with the A & GW.

If another company could be found to take over the A & GW contract it would free up the

---

Sifton proved sadly mistaken as to the acquiescence of the banks. They refused to turn the $7,400,000 over to the provincial treasury and their ensuing legal battle with the Alberta government lasted two years, financially hamstringing the province.

$7,400,000 held in escrow by the banks and ensure northern rail development, which would cheer everyone on the Liberal benches. Thus one of Alberta's most enterprising though ill-starred railway-builders enters the province's history. Right on cue, J.D. McArthur of Winnipeg, who was already planning a railway into the Peace country, to be known as the Edmonton, Dunvegan & British Columbia, surfaced with an offer to build the A & GW as well. Sifton quickly introduced legislation that allowed McArthur to take over the contract and, while the Tory opposition complained, the Liberals nodded assent. For the first time since February 1910 the Liberal government was united over the construction of a railway from Edmonton to Fort McMurray. All 36 Liberals voted for the measure, thereby ending a divisive issue that had almost torn the party apart. The government, so bitterly divided, would live to triumph in two more provincial elections.

The Calgary *Eye Opener* snipes away at Sifton

Bob Edwards had a running feud with the Siftons, and when Little Arthur became premier he didn't spare him. In these Eye Opener cartoons, Sifton picks the pocket of the farmer while smiling upon him, remains sphinx-like until he pays off with appointments, hatches anti-Calgary plots with Oliver, and confidently counts on farmers who would push him off a cliff. In fact, however, the farmers strongly supported Sifton.

Their Little Joke

On the Brink

Yet relatively little is known of the enigmatic figure who accomplished this. There are no biographies of Arthur Lewis Sifton, a man who had always lived very much in the shadow of his flamboyantly successful younger brother. There is at least one panegyric. "Imagine a man of rather middle stature, with fine features, delicately coloured skin and very little natural adornment on the top of his head," wrote R.B. Cooke in a cloying portrait carried by the *Medicine Hat News* on Aug. 30, 1913. "Imagine a man so reserved that his very silence is attractive. Imagine a man who walks delicately, talks softly, acts gracefully and yet is almost grim in his determination, inexorable in the execution..."

Others describe the same traits less fondly. They picture a bald, coldly calculating and arrogant man who enjoyed the exercise of power. In fact, in yet another "pen picture" of Sifton, carried by the Liberal *Toronto Star*, the anonymous author almost apologizes for Sifton's remoteness: "His coldness, his dryness, is said to be his greatest handicap," he wrote soon after Sifton was appointed premier. "Short-sighted electors do not always understand it. He convinces the intelligent, and appeals to the lover of fair dealing and honesty." It was as though the *Star* man was desperately seeking something nice to say.

Two qualities seem to come through. Sifton had an astonishing memory and an astonishing inattentiveness, the latter perhaps feigned. Both the *Medicine Hat News* and the *Toronto Star* quoted versions of a story in which the chief justice of Alberta endlessly wrote his signature, "Arthur L. Sifton," on pieces of paper as defence and prosecution argued.

When they had finished their long petitions both lawyers expected that His Lordship would reserve judgement while he considered the fine points of law. Instead, Sifton proceeded immediately to give his judgement. Observing the consternation of the two lawyers in front of him, he paused and explained. "Don't worry now, gentlemen. I had made my decision before you began your very able addresses."

Sifton was born near London, Canada West (later Ontario), in 1858, two years before his brother Clifford. The Sifton family moved in 1875 to Winnipeg, where both the Sifton boys were educated. Both became lawyers after attending university in Ontario. Soon after completing his law training Arthur married Mary Deering in 1882 and little is heard of her again. Arthur practised at first with his brother in Brandon and joined in the family's crusade in favour of temperance (though not, presumably, against tobacco).

He and his wife moved to Prince Albert and later, in 1889, to Calgary, where they produced a son, Lewis Raymond, and a daughter, Nellie Louise. Within six years he was appointed commissioner for public works in Frederick Haultain's territorial government. He ran twice for the territorial Legislature — in 1898 and 1902 — and was member for Banff. An anecdote survives of his days as a territorial politician, recounted in the Banff newspaper *Crag and Canyon* after Sifton became premier:

Sifton was running against the popular Banff physician, Dr. R.G. Brett. Though political rivals, they were close friends and slated a number of joint evening meetings throughout the constituency. They took turns speaking first, the other making a reply. Detained by a medical call, Dr. Brett was late for their meeting in the community of Anthracite. Sifton spoke, and still the doctor had not appeared. Rather than

HON. J. R. BOYLE.

Sifton's method of reuniting the party was to keep the leaders of the rival factions out of the cabinet until they could get along. This eventually brought John R. Boyle (above) back in, along with his arch-foe Charles W. Cross.

Provincial Archives of Alberta, A-2688

A cabinet newcomer was Charles Stewart (at right), a farmer from Killam, who would succeed Sifton and be Alberta's third premier.

Provincial Archives of Alberta, A-2698

HON. CHAS. STEWART.

The Silence May Be Broken Soon

PREMIER SIFTON'S POLICY

The Prime Minister has announced that he is in favor of turning the Great Waterways capital to the public works department to be used in the erection of public buildings instead of coming a railway to Fort McMurray.

The Tory *Journal* lambastes Sifton

The Edmonton Journal's *cartoonists sniped constantly at the 'Sphinx,' Little Arthur, seeing him conked on the head by northern development problems, or ignoring the North while feeding the party's lapdogs, or beset by problems as though by mosquitoes, and finally being ignominiously demoted from the 'head of the class' in the 1917 election. (He wasn't).*

Welcome Home !

By 1913 there were major changes on the Sifton front bench. Boyle and Charlie Cross are discernible, back in power and in the favour of the premier, and the government is preparing for an early election — one destined to win a reputation as the most crooked in Alberta history (see sidebar). Sifton himself is seated at the extreme right, his hand to his head.

see the meeting break up, Sifton offered to deliver Brett's speech for him. He had heard it so often, he said, he knew it by heart. The crowd cheered its approval, and Sifton proceeded to give Brett's speech, complete with anecdotes and gestures. In the middle of this, Brett appeared. Sifton instantly sat down, and Brett then delivered the same speech. People began snickering. Brett couldn't understand it — didn't understand it, in fact, until many years later when someone finally told him what had happened.

Sifton was named chief justice of the Northwest Territories and then, in 1905, of Alberta. His rise to power is "scarcely coincidental," says Clifford Sifton's biographer, David John Hall, his Ottawa connections being what they were. Yet when Arthur Sifton accompanied Frederick Haultain to Ottawa during the negotiations for Alberta's provincehood, they found themselves up against the younger Sifton and in the end they gained almost nothing of what they went there to get (Vol. II, p. 35).

Arthur's kinship to Clifford doubtless helped his career, but he had other things going for him. He was a quick study with a remarkable memory for details. The *Lethbridge Herald* recalled how

The crowd cheered its approval, and Sifton proceeded to deliver his opponent Brett's speech, complete with anecdotes and gestures. In the middle of this, Brett appeared. Sifton instantly sat down, and Brett then delivered the same speech. People began snickering. Brett couldn't understand it.

Haultain had once asked his public works commissioner to reply to a strong opposition attack on the territorial government in Regina. Sifton appeared to be asleep as the opposition ranted, much to the chagrin of Haultain, who thought his lieutenant had forgotten. When the opposition speaker ran out of breath, Sifton rose to his feet and refuted every argument in the order of presentation without a note. "He had the faculty of pointing out defects in proposed legislation and disentangling the threads of a subject with unerring accuracy," said an anonymous friend quoted in a legal magazine of the time.

Even his enemies respected his shrewdness and intelligence, but the image of a cold, dispas-

The Liberal press fights for 'Little Arthur'

The province's Liberal newspapers did what they could to defend Little Arthur. The Lethbridge Herald *has the opposition 'buried' by Sifton's legislative agenda. The* Edmonton Bulletin *sees him converting Tories, and the Southam newspapers encouraging a 'jackass' opposition to batter Alberta's credit rating. The* Medicine Hat News *sees the Tories dreading an election as farmers dread a tornado.*

This curious picture of Sifton, his wife Mary, his daughter Nell and his son Lewis, mounted on camels in Egypt with a pyramid and the Sphinx in the background, is on file at the National Archives. That the man so long panned by the media as 'The Sphinx' should have himself photographed in front of the real Sphinx may be a sample of his much-concealed sense of humour, which emerged on such occasions as the time when he delivered an absent opponent's speech for him.

sionate man floats down through the years, an image that lacks human warmth and compassion for the people he governed.

Neither was he sparing of political sensitivities. Alberta MLA Robert E. Campbell in his book *I Would Do It Again* recounted how Sifton seemed incapable of understanding the suffragette movement. Two hundred women had gathered in the rotunda of the Legislature to argue for female votes in February of 1914 and Sifton refused to let them inside the legislative chamber to present their arguments. "He stood on the second step leading to the chamber and heard their case. Then he asked them if they had washed their dishes before coming to ask him to give them their votes. He couldn't have been more impolitic," Campbell wrote. Yet these same women supported Sifton in the 1917 election.

Despite what historians Howard and Tamara Palmer have described as Sifton's "autocratic and aloof style," he had put the Alberta Liberal party and government back together again and in 1913 was ready to test it at the polls. Nothing was left to chance. Skilful redistribution in 1912 — which the Conservatives called "a bare-faced gerrymander" — ensured a strong Liberal vote.

Neither Liberals nor Conservatives wanted by now to revive the A & GW problem and the Tories had lost their most eloquent voice when R.B. Bennett decamped to Ottawa. In addition, the increasing clout of the United Farmers of Alberta backed Sifton's agricultural policies. What followed is known as the most crooked election in Alberta history (see sidebar). But when it was over, the Liberals had a comfortable majority, 37 seats to the Conservatives' seventeen. And the abstemious Sifton must have celebrated by lighting one of his long black cigars and contemplating the good life in a province where Liberals reigned supreme.

Now I know what a statesman is; he's a dead politician. We need more statesmen.
– Bob Edwards, no date

Politics has not ceased to make strange bedfellows; at least, the politicians of both parties continue to share the same bunk. You know the kind of bunk we mean.
– Bob Edwards, Oct. 2, 1912

Beatings, bribery, theft, thuggery and fraud

THAT WAS ALBERTA'S 'CROOKED ELECTION OF 1913' WHICH EVEN SAW ONE ELECTION WRIT STOLEN SO THE TORIES COULD WIN THE NORTH

It was billed as the crookedest election in Alberta history and the 1913 campaign lived up to its name in every corner of the province. Ballots were fiddled, an election writ was tossed in a lake, and voter bribery was rampant as the Liberals and Tories went for the jugular.

Premier Arthur Sifton had ruled by viceregal decree since he was anointed by the Liberal establishment in 1910 after Premier Alexander Cameron Rutherford took the fall for the Alberta & Great Waterways Railway scandal.

Sifton could have put off the election until 1914, but why press the Liberals' luck? There was a corporal's guard of only seven opposition members and their best man, R.B. Bennett, had deserted to Ottawa in 1911. The premier had defused the A & GW scandal by adroit legislation and deft cabinet appointments that mollified fractious elements in his own caucus. Redistribution had ensured a strong Liberal vote. The real estate bust was looming and expected, but had not yet occurred. All this suggested it was a fine time for a provincial vote.

The Legislature was dissolved March 26, 1913, the vote called for April 17, and the fight was on. The Liberal *Edmonton Bulletin* charged the Conservatives with importing an army of election workers from Saskatchewan and Manitoba, the so-called Rogers Gang, controlled by Manitoba Tory Robert Rogers[a].

According to the *Bulletin*, this "army of thugs" was sneaking about the province posing as farm machinery salesmen and demanding payment for implements. Sometimes they would be in the guise of land and immigration officials bent on intimidating or coercing homesteaders or immigrants. The object, of course, was to portray the government as tyrannical oppressors.

Attorney-General Charles Cross retaliated by swearing in 250 special constables to arrest any of these infiltrators on

sight. The Liberal papers were beside themselves with indignation, reporting arrests in small towns throughout Alberta and urging vigilante justice for Rogers' army. Under the headline, "Manitoba Thugs Over-Running Province of Alberta," the *Lethbridge Herald* advised its readers to take the law into their own hands. "When you meet one of these chaps swat him good and hard," said the *Herald*.

The Tories hit back, accusing the Liberals of offering immigrants citizenship papers if they promised to vote for the local Liberal candidate. "Foreigners are Deluded in Every Constituency by Cross-Sifton Forces," warned the *Edmonton Journal* in a front-page headline. Apparently, the Liberals had promised bewildered immigrants, "many of them unable to speak or comprehend the English language," naturalization papers in return for their votes in Edmonton.

Cross's special constables arrested Calgary teamster Joseph Crutcher in the southern Alberta town of Carmangay and charged him with buying votes with liquor. The *Calgary Herald* rushed to his aid when he was jailed without bail. In a front-page story the *Herald* said the teamster had been arrested on a "trumped-up charge" and was being held illegally by a "Sifton judge."

"The arrest of Crutcher is the climax to the campaign of thuggery and despotism which has been waged by the heelers of the Liberal government in southern Alberta," said the *Herald* on the eve of the election. "There are apparently no depths of political thuggery too low for the Sifton forces to descend to in an effort to carry ridings in which they deem they have a chance at all of winning."

A $250,000 fund contributed to by the province's liquor interests was being distributed to Liberal candidates, claimed the *Edmonton Journal*. Edmonton hotel men contributed $30,000 to the "graft and election fund," which supposedly was collected by a deputy minister in the Sifton government

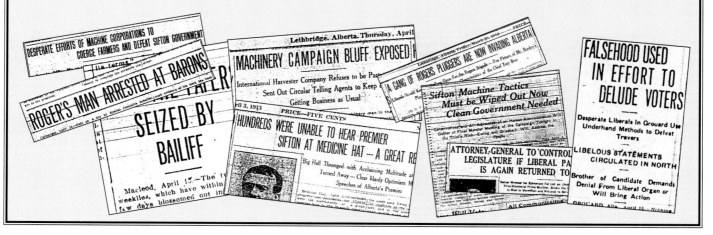

for a non-existent organization piously called the Alberta Moral Reform League.

The chicanery on both sides reached a crescendo on election day and the reverberations would be heard for years in recounts and judicial inquiries. In the northern riding of Peace River the election had to be deferred from April 17 to September 2 because the writ was seemingly never delivered there.

The bizarre explanation for that occurrence was recounted by Alexander Hugh McQuarrie[b], a former district engineer for Peace River, in the *Alberta Historical Review*. One cold morning in April 1913, Frank Christie, dominion government land agent at Grande Prairie and a provincial Tory organizer, was standing on the Canadian Northern Railway station platform in Edmonton, waiting for the Athabasca train. He fell into casual conversation with a well-known Peace River pioneer, and the two men naturally discussed the imminent provincial election.

Christie told the other man (McQuarrie identifies him only as "Bob") that the Tories would have a better chance in Peace River if the election was somehow delayed so they had more time to organize. Bob then asked how the election could be delayed. Christie pointed to another man on the station platform who, he said, was on his way to Peace River with the election writ in his pocket. "If you can get the writ from him the election will be delayed," Christie replied.

In those days the journey into the Peace River country

Provincial Archives of Alberta, A-2750

The election of Andrew S. Shandro as Whitford MLA was voided after the courts concluded he had bribed the voters.

included a steamboat trip from Athabasca to Mirror Landing on the Athabasca River, then up the Lesser Slave River and across Lesser Slave Lake. Somehow Bob got assigned to the same stateroom as the Liberal electoral official. When the steamboat was in the middle of the lake the official complained that his bag, which contained the writ, had suddenly disappeared.

The Peace River election was deferred in consequence, and when Christie chanced upon Bob some time later, he asked him about the strange disappearance. "I looked in the grip and there was not much in it besides a nightshirt and the writ, so I put a marlin spike in it and shoved it out through the porthole, and it is on the bottom of Lesser Slave Lake," Bob told Christie. When the deferred election was eventually held on September 2, the Conservatives, having been given more than four extra months to organize, won by a small margin.

But in the election of 1913 such an incident was typical. There were gross irregularities everywhere. A ballot box simply vanished in the Peace River riding before the votes could be counted. The chief election clerk went missing with it, having failed to fill out any of the requisite forms. The clerk turned up a few months later and the missing ballot box was found several years after that at the bottom of an abandoned well.

In Pembina, west of Edmonton, one poll was not opened on election day. In Edmonton 27 votes were assigned to a vacant lot. At another Edmonton poll a Tory scrutineer, try-

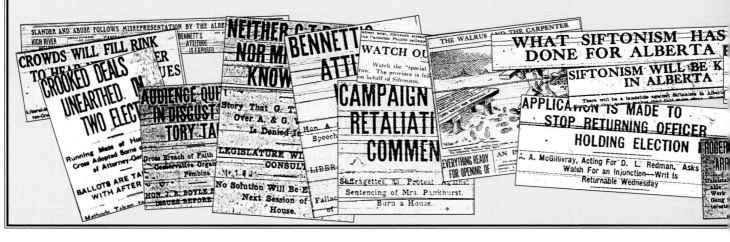

ing to take up his post, was beaten up. The Conservative *Journal* tells the story with appropriate indignation. "The first excitement of election day was caused this morning when a Liberal scrutineer refused to allow the Conservative scrutineer to enter the poll at the Senate Hotel. The Conservative worker got in, however, but when he did so, one of the Cross special constables attacked him with such violence that the man is hardly able to walk. His right leg was thought to be broken and one of his arms has to be carried in a sling."

Tampering with ballots was commonplace. Nelson Spencer, the mayor of Medicine Hat and Tory provincial candidate, said he had been told by six or eight of his supporters that their votes had been changed. He had affidavits from them, he said, that "their votes were disputed and placed in envelopes, and every one of these legal declarations goes to prove that these six men cast their ballots for me. [But] when the eight ballots were opened by the returning officer, not one among them was marked for me. There is no such thing as election by the people. The whole thing is in the hands of governmental machinery."

Sifton's Liberals were clearly the villains of the piece. In almost every case it was a Liberal who beat up some election officer, or tried to skew the vote by any available means in favour of the governing Grits. In the riding of Clearwater north of Edmonton a two-vote margin favoured the Liberal candidate. Five Tory votes had been disputed by the Liberals, and while they appeared legitimate, the law required the five voters to attend a court of inquiry to validate their ballots.

If three of the Tory votes were validated the Liberals would lose a seat. Enter Liberal worker William Lawrence Lawlor who visited the voters and tried to persuade them to leave town before the court of inquiry started. "He suggested long trips, short trips, any kind of a trip that would take each of the young men out of Clearwater over the day of the court of inquiry," reported the *Edmonton Journal*, which covered Lawlor's trial in Clyde.

"Offers were made of fares to Edmonton with passes for the moving picture shows every night and sometimes daily," the *Journal* reported from testimony. "A free immersion in the hot springs of Banff was suggested in lieu of a trip to the United States, asked for by one of the young Englishmen..."

When the dust finally settled the Liberals had 38 seats to the Conservatives' eighteen in the 56-seat Legislature. But it was not until early in 1915 that the last fish was caught in this particular shoal of scandal.

Liberal Andrew S. Shandro's election in the riding of Whitford was declared null and void after a lengthy court case before Mr. Justice James D. Hyndman. Shandro, who was found guilty of bribing voters, was ousted from office and ordered by the court not to hold any public office for eight years. Thus the crookedest election in Alberta's history was finally laid to rest in a bitter trial that brought public shame to an honourable member.

Back in Clearwater, where Lawlor had bribed the young English immigrants with the promise of trips, former Edmonton alderman and future mayor Joseph Clarke, an unsuccessful independent candidate in the provincial election, summed it all up. "It's been the most crooked election I've ever been in," Clarke told a court of inquiry. "The agents of both candidates [Liberal and Conservative] were the crudest I ever met. Their tracks were so wide you can walk in them... I've been twenty years engaged in elections, all crooked ones, and yet I've never seen anything quite so crooked as this Clearwater election."

— *G.O.*

[a]Repeated accounts of the 'notorious Rogers Gang' appeared in the rabidly Liberal *Edmonton Bulletin* and *Lethbridge Herald*. Whether there ever was such a gang and whether it ever came to Alberta remains a mystery. No member of a 'Rogers Gang' was convicted in an Alberta court and the published reports may have been totally contrived for an election campaign in which such skulduggery is altogether plausible. A check of the newspapers in Manitoba at the time turned up no references to a gang-leading Robert Rogers.

[b]Alexander Hugh McQuarrie was first employed by the Northwest Territorial government in what is now Saskatchewan and came to Alberta in 1907. He was inspector, bridge and road builder for the Department of Public Works, a position that often took him north. He was eventually appointed district engineer for Peace River. He retired in 1939 and moved to Ontario.

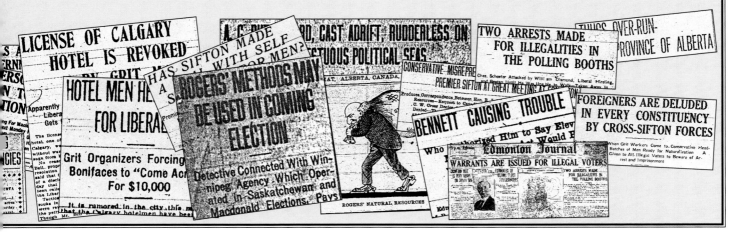

Section Four
THE SOCIAL UPHEAVALS

Women voters line up before F.E. Hawey's Jasper Confectionery on Edmonton's Jasper Avenue west of 121 Street, after casting ballots for the first time.
Glenbow Archives, ND-3-626

Members of the Woman's Christian Temperance Union parade south on 96th Street to Jasper Avenue on July 20, 1915, the day before Alberta voted itself dry. Twelve thousand were in the parade.

CHAPTER ONE

The women's war against the bar became a fight to get the vote

MANY WOMEN DIDN'T WANT IT, BUT NELLIE MCCLUNG DECLARED THAT JUSTICE MUST PREVAIL, AND A QUAILING LEGISLATURE AGREED

by MARY FRANCES DOUCEDAME

At the beginning of the province's second decade, the Alberta woman might be one of three things — housewife-mother, teacher or nurse. Few other fields were open to her, and few Alberta women would have aspired to them if they had been. Politics, the law, the other professions, industry, all these were male affairs. She was usually an equal participant in the development of a homestead but had no legal claim to it unless her husband left it to her. By the decade's end, or shortly after, all this had radically changed. She could vote or run for any public office. She could practise law and serve on the bench. She could and did work in scores of city occupations and she had a legal claim to the family farm.

These changes had been wrought all over Canada, but it was Alberta and the prairie provinces that led the way. Three things brought them about. One was the Great War, which thrust women into men's jobs. Another was the female suffrage movement. But far more than these, what goaded women to demand change was the third: the bar and its inevitable companions, gambling and the brothel. These hoary if not hallowed institutions drove women to quiet and often desperate fury and that fury was soon translated into decisive political action.

Men outnumbered women by as many as three to two in the booming cities and, for many men, drinking, gambling and prostitution were about the only recreation available. Since men

What goaded women to demand change was the bar and its inevitable companions, gambling and the brothel.

usually liquored up before gambling or visiting the countless brothels, it was assumed the three vices were linked. A visitor commented that revelry and debauchery were far greater in Alberta than in the New York slums. Reeling drunks and prostitutes adorned many a downtown corner. Even a teetotaller's wife could dread a shopping trip downtown, negotiating a course around hookers and drunks, some of the latter out cold on the sidewalk. Through the lace curtains of street-level rooms, one could see hookers performing their services. (One council resolved this by requiring whorehouses to put up blinds.) Yet when indignant citizens petitioned their city councils to clear up the disorder they were usually ignored, and the suspicion arose that some officials were in the pockets of those permeating the vice.

Drinking to excess — the word "alcoholism" had not yet been invented — created other miseries: families left in poverty, women and children beaten senseless, street fights, lives lost to carriage and now motor accidents. The Protestant churches, acting through a growing international movement known as the Woman's Christian Temperance Union (WCTU)[1], had railed against it for years (Vol. II, Sect. 5, ch. 10). The goal of the WCTU was temperance (i.e. moderation). They tried to talk drinkers into signing pledges for total abstinence, or, failing that, anti-treating cards. (Treating, the custom of buying a round, was seen as especially odious.) All to no avail. Drinking grew worse. Temperance didn't work. So women decided the law must be changed and the sale of booze prohibited. However, compelling politicians to act meant women must have the vote. Hence

[1] The WCTU, founded in Cleveland, Ohio, in 1874, led in establishing the Anti-Saloon League in 1895. Its leader from 1879 to 1898 was Frances Willard, for whom WCTU residences for women in cities are named (Willard Hall). The movement spread quickly to Canada, with the first meeting of a Canadian branch at Owen Sound, Ontario, in 1874. By 1885 a national WCTU was organized in Canada under Letitia Youmans, who had been active in temperance work in Ontario for many years.

the crusade to close the bars became inextricably joined to the campaign for women's suffrage.

The transition from temperance to a drive for outright Prohibition can be dated to the year 1907 in Alberta with the formation of the Alberta Temperance and Moral Reform League. While the WCTU continued to pass its resolutions, the league became far more activist. Its secretary and chief incendiary, the Rev. W.G.W. Fortune, began hounding drinkers from every available Protestant pulpit demanding: "Ban the Bar." At the same time the league zealously pressured town and village councils to prohibit liquor sales under the Canada Temperance Act of 1878,

This float, produced and manned by Calgary's Hillhurst Presbyterian Church Sunday School, furthers the anti-liquor campaign.

The four gents at Chevigny's store in Plamondon do not exactly look penitent, probably because in the French-Canadian tradition alcohol did not suffer the disapprobation it had to endure in Anglo-Saxon Protestant towns.

which gave municipalities the local option to do this. By 1910, Fortune could declare in a sermon at Strathcona that eight towns south of Lethbridge had gone dry where "a drunk is not seen from one end of the week to another."[2] True, one man had been arrested with two bottles of lemon extract. "But do you think that a man would get drunk on lemon extract if he could obtain liquor?"

By 1912, the league had acquired another ally, the United Farmers of Alberta, the most powerful lobby in the province which, an uneasy Liberal government noted, was threatening to

[2] The eight 'dry' towns that Dry crusaders referred to were probably Mormon communities where drinking had been suppressed by municipal bylaw.

Fred Stubbs at work in the Seven Persons Hotel bar (above) with the bartender 'Curly' beside him. On display, among other brands, are 'Hogans Whiskey' and 'Mountain Dew.'

The precise date and locale at which these three clowned for the camera (at right) are not known, though the photo was obviously intended to taunt the Drys.

Purity versus iniquity: that was the whole issue as far as the Drys were concerned

The case before the Alberta electorate was not one of Drys versus Wets, in the view of the Drys, but one of virtue versus sin, or purity versus iniquity. On every possible occasion the Drys presented the issue in these terms, opposing the bright innocence of children's faces against what they considered the dissolute faces at the bar. And just about every town in Alberta had one of the latter.

become a political party, and its associate organization, the United Farm Women of Alberta. That year, the league, aided by the UFA and the WCTU, sent no fewer than six deputations to the Legislature. Their demand: Prohibition. The government remained impassive. For one thing, booze meant revenue. For another, only men voted.

However, the following year the Legislature, bowing to the populist ideas of the UFA, passed the Direct Legislation Act, a bonanza opportunity for what was now everywhere known as the "Dry" movement. Under the act, a petition signed by at least 20% of the electorate with 85% of

the constituencies canvassed could force the Legislature to submit a law to a binding referendum. No sooner was the Direct Legislation bill become law than 500 canvassers were at work. They needed 20,000 signers. They hired billboards, took out newspaper ads. The Alberta Medical Association endorsed their cause. On Oct. 12, 1914, they presented Premier Arthur Sifton with a 23,656-name petition. He had no choice but to act. A week later he moved to submit to referendum the following July the Prohibitory Liquor Act, cutting off sales of liquor in shops, bars, clubs and trains. Aha, Bob Edwards in his *Eye Opener* chided the bar owners, for all their fat contribu-

As the doom of the bar nears, the faces seem to grow solemn

(Upper left) The bar in Edmonton's Empire Hotel. (Above) The bar in the Alberta Hotel at Crossfield. (Right) The bar in the Arlington Hotel, Lethbridge. (Left) The bar in the Wainwright Hotel.

tions that kept the "Sifton bunch" in power for so long, they were now "being bitten by the dog they fed."

The Drys must now persuade the whole electorate. They vowed to raise $30,000 in funds. They set up volunteer groups in the 52 constituencies. From New York, they brought in Clinton N. Howard, leader of what was known as the "Flying Squadron," who boldly took the podium in Lethbridge where the Dry cause was weakest because a brewery was one of the biggest industries in town. "Open Fight!" headlined the *Lethbridge Herald*, "Drys Turn 42-Centimetre Guns on Enemy in Big Campaign Against Alberta Bars." Howard's appeal was essentially religious. The Drys would triumph because of "the woman, on her knees praying the Son of God to bring vengeance on the saloon which has robbed her of her husband and her beloved son." Christ had said if your hand or

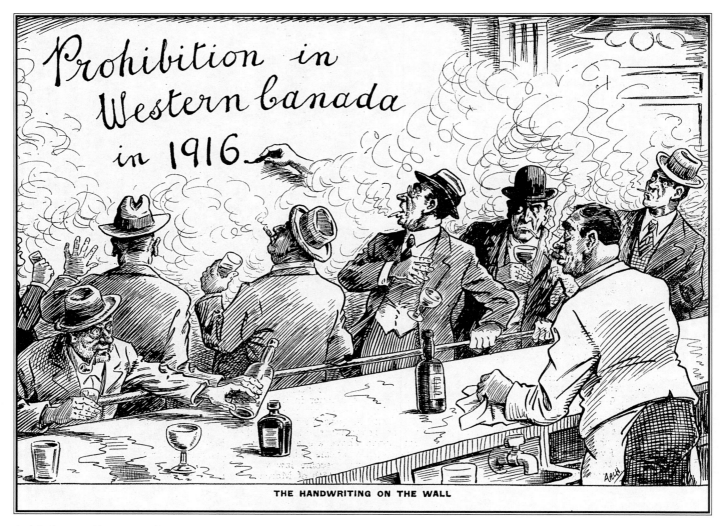

THE HANDWRITING ON THE WALL

Arch Dale, viewed by many as the poisoned-pen cartoonist of the Grain Growers' Guide, *captures the 'spirits' of the much-deplored booze trade in this 1916 observation.*

foot offends, cut it off. Therefore "we are done with toleration, segregation, taxation, local option, regulation and nullification... Now must the axe be laid at the root of the tree... Prohibition is the only cure. To let the bar live on any condition is the remedy of perdition. To kill it is the divine remedy for the sin... In the high court of heaven I indict the liquor traffic as the curse of the cradle, the nightmare of the family altar, the vulture of human society and the populator of the cemetery."

Who could resist such talk? The *Calgary Herald* and *Edmonton Journal* for starters, now both owned by the Ontario-based Southam Company. They boycotted many of the Drys' mass meetings. They attacked them editorially. The *Journal* closed its letters columns to both sides. Paradoxically, however, the reprobate Bob Edwards came in on the Dry side (see sidebar).

The Licensed Victuallers' Association and the Bartenders' Union likewise rallied to the Wet cause. So did the Alberta Federation of Labour, with a plea for the jobs of the brewery workers and the working man's right to a glass of beer. The Wets took out huge newspaper ads pointing out the proposed law's undoubted loopholes, the huge benefits to bootleggers and the possibility of corruption. They too imported an American orator, Chicago magazine editor Dr. A.C. Windle. The Drys attended his meetings to heckle him, noting especially his magazine was pro-German. "Herr Windle of Chicago," sneered the pro-Dry *Edmonton Bulletin*, "has suspended his efforts to help Germany beat the Allies long enough to come to Alberta and try to beat Prohibition."

The Drys took out ads refuting the Wets' arguments point by point. But they didn't stop at speeches and advertisements. In April 1915, a committee of the Central Methodist Church bent on proving the intemperance and immorality of soldiers in a battalion based just outside Calgary, went spying at the bars, counted heads and took down names. Women of ill fame were carrying on a regular business with the soldiers, they reported. Two women "took quarters in a livery near a hotel, and were visited during the evening by a large number of men." Some of the spotters were chased through the streets by soldiers and civilians. Their scandalized report, published in the *Calgary Herald,* almost provoked a mutiny back at the barracks.

The soldiers stationed at Calgary's Sarcee reserve would be denied a vote on the Liquor Act. Although they petitioned for it, the government decided they couldn't vote out of their own constituencies and it would be impractical to let them go home just to vote.

On Tuesday, July 20, the eve of the plebiscite, a parade three miles long with banners flying marched through Edmonton in support of Prohibition. The *Bulletin* estimated the crowd at up to 12,000, from "tiny tots to grey-haired veterans." A similar parade was staged in Calgary. In seeming desperation, Lethbridge Brewing & Malting Company bought a three-quarter-page ad in the

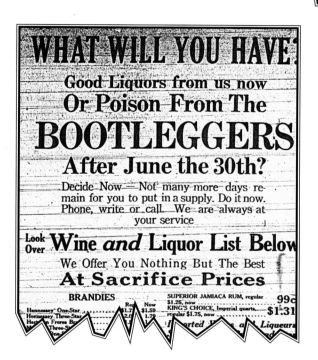

(Top) A handbill distributed by the WCTU in the 'Ban the Bar' campaign. (Below) A poster advertising a Calgary meeting of the WCTU as the crusade for Prohibition mounted. (At left) With the approach of 'Dry Day,' liquor stores dumped their stocks at bargain prices, and warned of the evils of bootlegging. This appeared in the Edmonton Journal *June 8, 1916.*

Edmonton Daily Bulletin.
MORNING EDITION

First News of Women's Fall Suits—SEE PAGE FIVE

VOL. VI. NO. 71   EDMONTON, ALBERTA, THURSDAY, JULY 22, 1915.   TEN PAGES TODAY   PRICE FIVE CENTS

ALBERTA GIVES 20,000 MAJORITY FOR PROHIBITION

Many Rural Districts Have 3 to 1 Majority For Act---Only 13 Out of 55 Ridings Go Wet

EDMONTON CONTRIBUTES 3,200; CALGARY ADDS 3,000

Returns Show That Liquor Interests Snowed Under by Majority of 2 to 1

Total Figures Early This Morning Were: Dry 46,987; Wet 27,752—Almost Every Part of Province Declares in Unmistakeable Terms That Bar Must Go—Liquor Act Comes Into Force on July 1st of Next Year—Big Majority Exceeded Expectations of Even Sanguine Prohibitionists.

The electors of Alberta yesterday sounded the death knell of John Barleycorn. The returns still are far from complete, but those received up to an early hour this morning from all parts of the province show that the liquor interests have been snowed under by a majority of two to one, and this may be increased by the time the final figures are received. Never was a victory more complete. The ...

THREE OF THE PROHIBITION LEADERS

GREAT BATTLES ARE IN PROGRESS NOW FOR WARSAW

Biggest Fight For Possession of Lublin Chalm Railway

RUSSIANS IN WELL FORTIFIED POSITION

Bombshell in Calgary: Edwards supports the Drys

BUT HE GOT SO DRUNK THE NIGHT BEFORE THE PAPER WAS PRINTED THE WETS WERE NEARLY ABLE TO DESTROY THE WHOLE EDITION

Though apt to extol the pleasures of drink in his influential *Eye Opener*, editor Bob Edwards was, like many drunks, ambivalent about booze. It had claimed the life of his own brother (Vol. II, p. 346), and he resented the hotelmen for serving "rotgut" whiskey and overcharging for beer. Therefore when the booze industry heard he might come out in favour of Prohibition, they feared he might sway the votes of many drinkers.

As Robert Gard tells it in his book, *Johnny Chinook*, a delegation of hotelmen went to see Edwards in March 1915,

the next edition of the *Eye Opener*, due out the following Saturday. That Tuesday he sent his article over to the *Albertan*, where editor W.H. Davidson had taken on the job of printing the *Eye Opener*.

On Thursday a couple of bar-boys brought over a few bottles of "first class Grade A, bottled-in-bond." That afternoon when Charley Taylor brought the *Eye Opener* over from the *Albertan* to be proofread, Edwards, barely able to see straight, took a pencil and marked a big X right across the whole front page, then said and did nothing more. Some of

'I've never sold the old rag yet and I never will,' said Edwards when the hotelmen offered him $15,000 to back off.

three months before the plebiscite, and offered him $15,000 for his support. Edwards had to think a moment. Then he held open the door: "Gentlemen," he said, "you can leave my office. I've never sold the old rag yet and I never will."

That same day a Drys' delegation came to ask for his support. Edwards told them the hotelmen had offered him fifteen grand. How much would they offer?

"We haven't got a dollar, Bob," said one delegate.

"It's a good thing," he replied. "I won't be bought or sold." He then agreed to come out in favour of Prohibition in

his friends carried him over to the hospital, to his usual room there. The Prohibitionists heard about it and rushed to Davidson. "Well boys," he conceded, "Bob told me to print the *Eye Opener*. So far I haven't seen or heard an order countermanding that." So Davidson proofread the paper himself and printed it.

Friday morning two hotelmen visited Edwards' office, where a girl-Friday was holding the fort while he was recovering, and demanded to buy up all copies of the *Eye Opener* as soon as they arrived. But Davidson heard of it, locked the

---

Herald, detailing its mammoth annual contribution to the city in wages, taxes, and expenses. "Businessmen," it half pleaded, half threatened, "Don't Vote Yourself Out of Business."

Prohibition won with a huge margin — 58,295 to 37,509 — sweeping every centre except, notably, Lethbridge where the vote was 1,371 against, 989 for. Unable to refute such a clear mandate, the Liberals passed the Prohibitory Liquor Act the following spring, and on June 30, 1916, the hotels sounded the last call. Drinkers took it good-naturedly, gathering in bars to steel themselves for the long "drought," and at 10 p.m. they toddled quietly off to bed. The next day, July 1,

The government remained impassive. For one thing, booze meant revenue. For another, only men voted.

1916, Alberta was officially dry, one month after Manitoba. Saskatchewan would move to complete Prohibition less than a year later. Historian James Gray would call Alberta's Prohibition campaign the shortest and sharpest in history.

The new law, as foreseen, was riddled with loopholes. Breweries, under federal jurisdiction, went right on brewing, knowing they could market their product by exporting it to other provinces. Albertans could mail-order in liquor for personal consumption from outside, often Alberta-made, exported to be re-imported. There was also the inevitable bootlegging, moonshine and illegal sales. The RNWMP would shrug their shoulders, busy with more serious crimes. So the

> **A vendor may sell** alcohol for mechanical or scientific purposes, but no sale shall be made except upon the affidavit of the applicant, duly signed and sworn before the vendor, which affidavit shall be in a form prescribed by the Lieutenant-Governor-in-Council, and which shall set forth that the alcohol is required for mechanical or scientific purposes only, stating how and where the same is to be used, and that the same is not intended to be used as a beverage or to be mixed with any other liquid for use as a beverage...
> – *The Liquor Act,*
> *April 19, 1916*

Glenbow Archives, NA-937-12

Eye Opener in the vault and then shipped it out directly on Saturday, bypassing Edwards' office. In a front-page article that Monday the *Albertan* announced Edwards' change of heart as a "fatal blow to the opponents of Prohibition...The *Eye Opener* has a large circulation — the largest of any paper circulated in Alberta...Its editorial advice is always read and very generally heeded, as its attitude in previous elections proves."

However, Edwards' lengthy declaration was hardly a full endorsement of the Drys. "The Temperance cranks do not understand the game," he complained in that historic April 3 issue. "Nor will they take advice from old stagers like ourself. We maintain, speaking as one singularly well posted on the topic, that the only solution of the problem is cheap beer." (Edwards had always condemned the hotelmens' "greed" for charging fifteen cents for both a glass of "weak slop" [beer] and for whiskey. This only encouraged drunks to choose the latter, he said. Had five-cent beer been available there wouldn't have been such a problem with drunkenness.)

"Had this bill permitted the sale of beer and California or French light wines, we should have supported it with a better grace...In any case, the bunch at Edmonton who constitute our government are a fine set of ducks to be entrusted with the task of regulating the morals of this or any other community. It will be interesting to note the class of men who get jobs as government vendors."

— *M.F.D.*

Bob Edwards during the Prohibition war: Unhappily, he said, 'the Temperance cranks do not understand the game.'

WOMEN'S INDUSTRIAL AUXILIARY RECEPTION COMMITTEE AND DELEGATES OF WOMEN'S SECTION, UNITED FARMERS OF ALBERTA CONVENTION. JAN. 19. 20. 21- 1915 EDMONTON, ALBERTA

CIRKUT PH

Glenbow Archives, NA-4176-4

Provincial Archives of Alberta, A-1796

Terrible as an army with banners, their numbers and grim determination terrified the politicians

(Clockwise from top left, opposite page) The Women's Industrial Auxiliary reception and delegates to the United Farmers of Alberta meeting in Edmonton, 1915; the WCTU convention in Olds, 1911; the Stony Plain Women's Institute, 1916; the Edmonton Diocesan Women's Auxiliary of the Anglican Church about 1910; the Women's Institute at Entwistle, 1917; and (centre) the Hillhurst Sunday School Crusaders in Calgary.

Nellie McClung's wit was a terror on the platform

SHE'D MIMIC AND ATTACK OPPONENTS, AND HID HER KIDS FROM THE MEDIA

The early Alberta suffragist who foresaw the day when women would be "economically free and mentally and spiritually independent" began life on a stony Ontario farm in 1874 as Nellie Letitia Mooney. When she was six, her strong-willed mother prodded her father into moving to Manitoba, where she believed prospects for their sons would be better.

The family of eight spent the first lonely winter of 1880 in a one-room log cabin, 180 miles west of Winnipeg. At sixteen, with just six years of schooling behind her, Nellie became a teacher in Manitou, and was taken under the wing of Woman's Christian Temperance Union activist Mrs. J.A. McClung, her future mother-in-law, who pushed her into writing and public speaking. Nellie would write fifteen novels, of which a few were bestsellers, some short stories and a two-volume autobiography.

At nineteen she married Wesley McClung, a pharmacist who later switched to selling insurance. While gossips often implied the marriage was breaking down because of her campaigns, it proved cohesive. But Nellie was often away giving speeches, for which she was well paid, leaving her five children in the care of two Irish girls. Their youngest son, Mark, recalls that his father advised him to shaft people good-naturedly about being a suffragette's son, by claiming that he'd never known a mother's love. If the older children found little Mark looking ragged after a day of frolic, they'd hustle him home before some news photographer got a picture of Nellie McClung's neglected child.

Mrs. McClung's first big coup came in Manitoba in January 1914, at Premier Rodmond Roblin's expense. Roblin contended that politics would take the woman "off the pedestal where she'd sat for centuries" and that franchise was only supported by "short-haired women and long-haired men." When the first major suffragists' delegation marched to the Manitoba Legislature, he shooed them away, saying nice women didn't want to vote and it would break up the home.

The next day the Political Equality League staged a mock

Glenbow Archives, NA-1514-3

Nellie McClung about 1910: The eyes always shone, with laughter, or sometimes anger.

parliament with women acting as legislators receiving a delegation of men. Acting the part of Roblin, Nellie congratulated the men on their manly appearance but denied their request lest they "vote too much" or become "unsettled by politics." She had studied Roblin's mannerisms and pet phrases at the Legislature the day before and practised in front of the mirror that night. Now she mimicked him so well her performance won rave reviews.

Nellie McClung's brown Irish eyes, it was said, always shone, sometimes with laughter, sometimes anger. Her rhetoric would have done latter-day feminists proud:

On women in marriage: "Her husband wanders free while she stays home...the tied-up woman and the footloose man..."

On women in the church: "The women may lift the mortgages, or build churches or any other light work, but the really heavy work of the church, such as moving resolutions in the general conferences, must be done by strong, hardy men."

In her entertaining autobiography, *The Stream Runs Fast*, she claims she loved the opportunity hecklers gave her to show her stuff. Assessing their personalities and weaknesses by their appearance, she'd invite them into debate and instinctively hit below the belt.

Although she once said women would accomplish more if they didn't care who got the credit for it, her other speeches belied this. She did want more credit for women: "The great army of women workers are ill-paid, badly housed and their work is not honoured or respected... What share have they in man's chivalry?" It wasn't chivalry that made men want to keep women out of politics, but "the thought of [women] getting comfortable and well-paid positions which wrings their manly hearts."

Nellie McClung was elected to the Legislature in 1921. She lost the next election when her Liberal party and her strong Prohibition stance were both out of favour. She died in 1951, disillusioned, it was said, by two wars and the erosion of causes she'd held dear.   — M.F.D.

government created the Alberta Provincial Police to enforce the liquor law (see Vol. IV).

Ironically the women of Alberta had not been allowed to vote on the Liquor Act, even though they'd gained the provincial franchise just a few months before the referendum. A referendum had to be held under the same franchise as the petition that incurred it. As it turned out, therefore, their participation hadn't been critical after all. Prohibition had passed without them.

While women's view on Prohibition was unanimous enough, their attitude towards the franchise was not. True, women in New Zealand, Australia, Finland, Norway and eleven American states had won the vote over the previous two decades. British suffragettes were resorting to such military tactics as trashing art galleries and hurling stones. Their leader, Emmeline Pankhurst, once wrapped herself in barbed wire to prevent the police from toting her off as she spoke publicly. But

Her career began the day the judge ordered her out

A SELF-TAUGHT LEGAL EXPERTISE PUT EMILY MURPHY ON THE BENCH

Judge and best-selling author Emily Gowan Murphy (nee Ferguson) was raised in Toronto. Her three brothers became lawyers and she was always interested in the law. At 19 she married an Anglican minister, Arthur Murphy, whom she would affectionately come to refer to as "the padre." They'd have two daughters. After a brief sojourn in England and Toronto they came west, for eight years farming 320 acres near Swan River, Manitoba, where Emily wrote literary reviews for the *Winnipeg Telegram*.

In 1907 they moved to Edmonton, Emily travelling the countryside for stories. Her best-selling novels starring "Janey Canuck" (also Emily's penname), with their vivid descriptions of prairie life, are thought to have inspired many to immigrate. Meanwhile, she became a self-made expert on women's law. She worked, it was said, with such quiet efficiency people could scarcely believe her awesome accomplishments. She was a director of the Canadian Council of Child Welfare, president of the Canadian Women's Press Club and president of the Federated Women's Institutes which sought to establish community halls and social activities in isolated areas.

Her connection to the Council of Women led to a legal career. In 1916, the council sent two women to study the treatment of girls charged with vagrancy or prostitution. The crown prosecutor wanted the two observers removed from the court. "Ladies," he said, "should not hear such sordid evi-

Judge Emily Murphy: Her complaint to Alberta's A-G produced an astonishing reaction.

City of Edmonton Archives, EA-10-1996

dence." The women left the court in confusion and appealed to Mrs. Murphy.

If such evidence was unfit for mixed company, she reasoned, then the accused were entitled to a hearing with only women present. She saw Attorney-General Charles Wilson Cross who knew of her legal expertise. He not only agreed, but asked her when she'd be ready to be sworn in as police magistrate and judge of the Juvenile Court. A year later she was promoted to a full magistrate.

On her first day in court a lawyer objected that she was not a "person" within the meaning of the statutes, therefore unqualified to be a judge. Under the British North America Act, only "persons" could qualify for judgeships or the Senate, and "persons" had always been interpreted to mean men. Judge Murphy ignored the objection and proceeded with the trial.

But the question of female non-personhood persisted and in the coming two decades would become a celebrated constitutional case. Emily Murphy and four other Alberta women[a] assisted by her lawyer brothers, would take it beyond the Supreme Court of Canada to the Privy Council in Great Britain. — *M.F.D.*

[a] With Judge Murphy, these would become known as the "Famous Five" of Alberta: Nellie McClung, the MLAs Louise McKinney and Irene Parlby, and another self-made expert on women's law, Henrietta Edwards, all of whom emerged in the women's movement of 1910-20.

it was never clear that most Alberta women even wanted the vote, Nellie McClung, Alberta's leading suffragist, later acknowledged. But after all, she added, women had been given many things they didn't want. Justice must prevail. She had only contempt for "gentle ladies who relied on sexuality, tears and fainting to get their way, whose ears could not stand to hear an unpleasantness and who worried more over a stain in the carpet than on the soul."

Whatever the silent majority of women thought, a loud minority made their opinions known from 1910 onward. Certainly many women joined the scores of groups such as their local units of the National Council of Women, the Equal Franchise League, and the Womens Institute, the latter providing education courses for women in isolated areas. All these groups advocated the franchise.

Women first began acquiring the franchise in civic elections. In July 1914 the Equal Franchise League presented a petition bearing 3,767 signatures to Edmonton city council, which then had its charter amended by the Legislature to grant suffrage to all women. Calgary similarly adopted an almost universal suffrage, stipulating only that voters (of either sex) had to be able to read the Grade 2 reader. Lethbridge limited its female suffrage to property owners or wives of such. While the government was modifying Wetaskiwin's charter in 1918, it announced it would put provisions in every city charter giving women whatever local rights to vote and be candidates that their husbands had.

Getting the provincial vote, however, was a much more formidable task. A women's delegation approached the government in 1914 with a petition. They were rejected on the grounds "more widespread demand for the reform had to be shown among women themselves." It was

Women saw themselves bringing purity to politics
THE EARLY FEMINISTS WERE FORERUNNERS OF THE LATER MOVEMENT BUT THEIR EMPHASIS ON FAMILY AND MOTHERHOOD DEFINED THEM

Was the feminist movement that burst into activity during the century's second decade the forerunner of the feminist revolution that shook society a half-century later, or were the early-century crusaders pursuing very different ends? The answer is not at all self-evident. In some respects their principles were in direct opposition. For example, while they endorsed a woman's right to work if necessary and to be paid equally for it, they embraced, indeed enshrined, the homemaking role. As Eliane Silverman, professor of women's studies at the University of Calgary, points out in *The Last Best West*, their main concerns — temperance, child welfare, allowances for mothers, labour reform and the teaching of domestic science in schools —"were all aimed at making the world more homelike."

They sought to achieve in society what they'd presum-

There were other serious differences. While their successors would see childbirth as a trap and abortion as a right, Alberta's early feminists glorified motherhood. In her book *Emily Murphy*, latter-day feminist writer Donna James contends this was just to foil men's objection that women's liberation would result in neglected families. In other words, she didn't really mean it. But that thesis must contend against great evidence to the contrary. A reverence for motherhood threads through so much of their writings. Mrs. McClung, mother of five, wrote that "every normal woman desires children...Deeply rooted in every woman's heart is the love and care of children...The woman's outlook is to serve, to care for, to help."

Something else distinguishes the two generations. "There was an overriding sentiment that women were possessed of

They sought to achieve in society what they'd presumably already achieved in their own households: to make and enforce rules of good conduct and to clean it up.

ably already achieved in their own households: to make and enforce rules of good conduct and to clean it up. "Women have cleaned up things since time began," their most noteworthy leader, Nellie McClung, once said, "and if women get into politics there will be a cleaning up of pigeonholes and forgotten corners in which the dust of years has fallen."

a higher morality than men," writes Michael Palamarek in *A History of Women and Politics in Alberta*. "This untapped force would rid the world of all its problems, if only women were allowed to express it through the vote." That's why female suffrage was advocated by moral reformers as well as the United Farmers of Alberta, whose leaders were often lay then that Nellie Letitia McClung came west. Witty, sharp, outspoken, she had been a leader in Manitoba's suffrage movement, and a thorn in Premier Rodmond Roblin's side (see sidebar). Once in Edmonton she swiftly became vice-president of the Equal Franchise League. In February 1915, a year after her run-in with Premier Roblin, she was face to face with Premier Sifton. If the politicians wanted to see "widespread demand," she said, then they'd demonstrate it. With Alice Jamieson, president of the National Council of Women of Calgary, she led the largest deputation ever to address the Legislature up to that time. "When the premier and his colleagues arrived they were at a loss to know where to place themselves," the *Journal* reported. The women brought with them a 12,000-name petition. After a resounding address from Mrs. McClung, the premier rose to speak — surrounded by his ministers, one report noted, "in an almost protective gesture."

But Sifton, a master of the non-answering answer, was also in top form. "I've learned never to argue back with a lady," he said, thereby dismissing all her points. A stream of noncommittal observations followed, said the *Journal,* abounding in terms like "liable to" and "probably," so that his response amounted to: "Anything is liable to happen, probably nothing will." Sifton concluded: "My own personal opinion is that there are only two logical reasons against equal franchise — that of doubling the expense, and uncertainty as to the desire for the franchise by the women themselves." Mrs. Jamieson of Calgary curiously confirmed his doubts. She felt she must explain, she said, why so few of the 3,000 members of her local council had been active in the suffrage cause. They'd been "too busy with the war effort to give attention to suffrage."

Mrs. McClung and Emily Murphy (see sidebar), however, were not too busy. A week later

---

ministers pushing the social gospel. The United Farmers of Alberta local at Lake Thelma[a], for example, stated it believed women "would cast their votes on the right side of all questions affecting the home, the community and the nation," while the *Grain Growers' Guide* published an article claiming women had cleaned up the state of California as a result of the franchise.

However, the later feminists did in one respect share some such assumption. Changes they advocated for sexual assault laws, for instance, often assumed that no woman would lie about this and accuse an innocent man, so that the usual innocent-until-proven-guilty safeguards in the law were removed. Similarly, a woman accusing a man of rape could not be publicly identified, though the accused's name could be published as soon as the accusation was made in court.

In other respects, however, the later feminists held out for "equality," contending men and women should be treated the same because the differences between them were largely the result of "learned behaviour." Pioneer feminists believed women not only different but better. Indeed, their opponents used this contention to argue against suffrage. Politics, they cautioned, was much too dirty for such innocent beings. — *M.F.D.*

Glenbow Archives, NA-6-1746

Emmeline Pankhurst with Nellie McClung, 1916: Was the family emphasis conviction or ruse?

[a]Lake Thelma was originally a post office. Situated just east of Sullivan Lake, near Coronation, it opened in 1912.

Ruthenian (Ukrainian) women like these, who posed in their native costumes for this postcard photograph, played little part in the women's movement. Most were preoccupied with the struggle to earn a livelihood on the province's northern parkland farms.

they were back to see Sifton in what they called a "neighbourly visit...a private chat." Sifton reportedly told them acidly that he believed it impossible for them to do anything privately. They asked whether he would consent to an equal-franchise question being brought before the House that session. He gave them the usual non-answer and later noted that they were "very determined women."

However that September of 1915 Sifton suddenly acquiesced. He announced a bill would be introduced at the next session. "Thus," said the *Journal*, "in a little over two years has the chief executive of the province flopped from a scoffing antagonist to a proponent of equal suffrage." Possibly Sifton was shaken by the resounding support for the summer's Prohibition plebiscite (thought to have the same supporters as Women's Suffrage) and was wondering how he'd weather the next election. The statute would also allow women to hold office in the Legislature but not to be jurors. Juries fell under federal jurisdiction.

On Feb. 26, 1916, Sifton introduced bills to enact Prohibition and to confer the franchise on women. The franchise bill's second reading a week later drew another large, mostly female crowd — the Women's Institutes of the province, Edmonton women's societies and a delegation of "the women of Calgary" — all peering belligerently down from the galleries as the legislators passed the suffrage bill 55 - 1.

Oddly, the lone holdout was little Lucien Boudreau, member for St. Albert. Though himself French Canadian, he reminded his fellow legislators that female suffrage was not in the British tradition. Indeed the British parliament had so far rejected it. He felt it would degrade rather than elevate women. Looking at the galleries, he declared: "The woman who is against this measure is not here. She is at home. The duty of her home is more important than public life." His observation was met with "a perfect tornado of hisses," the *Lethbridge Herald* reported. His legislative colleagues looked on sheepishly. Several later took him aside to whisper their congratulations. He'd expressed their sentiments exactly, they said. They wished they'd had his courage. Boudreau was returned to the Legislature in the 1917 election in which women voted.

Women now had the right to take public office, though many of their leaders discouraged it. Even Mrs. McClung felt they should first only study the issues and act as a moral influence. However, they had already infiltrated civic affairs. In 1912 Bessie Nicholls of Edmonton was elected school trustee. During her candidacy it was found Miss Nicholls was ineligible under the act and an amendment to the city charter was rushed through the Legislature.

Their venture into office was not

Alice Jamieson of Calgary, probably the first female police magistrate in the British Empire.

always welcome. Teacher Jennie Stork Hill was running for Edmonton school trustee in December 1913, endorsed by the 35 women's societies comprising the local branch of the National Council of Women. Her speeches were reported in the *Bulletin*. Mrs. Hill was appalled at the "snake in the grass" tactics of her opponents, one in particular. She accused Dr. F.W. Crang of getting an "Alice Hill" put on the ballot to confuse the electorate. Her name was "Jennie" and "Stork," she stressed, "the bird that is supposed to have the especial care of little children." She added that Crang might know how to diagnose disease, "but he has shown he doesn't know how to diagnose a woman's mind." Although 867 votes were diverted to the bogus opponent, Jennie Stork Hill was elected.

Calgary elected Mrs. W.J. Gale to be Canada's first female alderman in 1917. When she sat as acting mayor in 1919, it was thought to be a first for the British Empire.

The results of the 1917 provincial elections, the first in which women could vote and run, were disappointing. Of two original female contestants, only Louise Crummy McKinney won, running in Claresholm for the Non-Partisan League. She thus became the first woman legislator in the British Empire. Ontario-born, a former school teacher, she predicted that women's role in the future would be for the "purification of politics." As provincial head of the WCTU, she had tried to prevent cigarettes and tobacco being sent to the men in the trenches.

Two months later 36-year-old war nurse-dietician Roberta MacAdams was chosen by the 13,286 eligible Alberta soldiers and nurses stationed overseas as one of their two MLAs under the Alberta Military Representation Act. Her campaign was orchestrated by Beatrice Nasmyth, publicity secretary for the Alberta government in England. The only woman in a field of about twenty, she came second behind the "fighting parson," Capt. Robert Pearson. Miss MacAdams said her main concern would be seeing to the welfare of returning soldiers. A week after she was sworn in at the opening session of the Legislature in February 1918, she brought in a bill to incorporate the

Only St. Albert's Lucien Boudreau voted against the suffrage bill, while women hissed their objections from the gallery.

Women voters outside the poll at Westcott in the 1917 provincial election.

Bessie Nicholls, who was elected an Edmonton school trustee in 1912, four years before women got the vote provincially.

War Veterans' Next-of-Kin Association, thereby becoming the first woman to introduce legislation in the Commonwealth.

She did not run for re-election in 1921, although she stayed active in various charitable societies. By then she had married lawyer Harvey Stinson Price and was starting a family. A gentle woman, not prone to seek recognition, she'd later sum up her political stint to her son, Bob, in a letter: "It was something that just happened to me."

In the 1921 elections, Nellie McClung would win on the Liberal ticket and Irene Parlby[3] become minister without portfolio in the new UFA government. If Alberta's women had been scrambling for firsts, they could hardly have done better. When Alice Jamieson, wife of the superintendent of the Canadian Pacific Railway, was appointed judge to the juvenile court of Calgary in 1913 and then three years later commissioned as a regular police magistrate to deal with female offenders, it was touted a world-wide first[4]. In Edmonton in 1916 Emily Murphy was appointed a police magistrate for women and juveniles in Edmonton and promoted to provincial magistrate the following year.

There were lesser though equally significant triumphs. Toward the end of the decade newspapers reported two "Portias" or "lady lawyers" being called to the bar. But most women were entering the working world in far humbler professions — as waitresses, bookkeepers, hospital aides,

Women had to fight for the right to inherit the farm

Dower rights seemed self-evident but powerful opposition arose when the move began to implement them in the West

Hear tell, said the *Grain Growers' Guide* in 1914, "the story of Jennie and John Tightwad."

The Tightwads settled on a homestead and after 15 years Tightwad owned two sections of land, clear, many head of stock, a splendid barn, a fair-sized house and six children. All that Jennie owned of his was her rather dowdy wardrobe. She hadn't even a legal share in the children. John made it very clear to her that the money and the house and the family were all his, though she had grown horny-handed in working for them. Her husband was quite within the law. She had no legal claim on anything. She discovered, to her chagrin, that her position in the home of her husband all these years had been that of an unpaid domestic.

Fictitious though the story was, it had countless parallels in reality, due to an 1886 statute that abolished dower, a widow's right to a share in her husband's estate[a]. Re-estab-

cause undue delays while getting the wife to sign.

Women could not even acquire a new homestead unless they were heads of household. Homesteads were granted to make the land productive, Interior Minister Frank Oliver argued, "and this would not be the case if held by women," although a 1916 farm journal survey showed that in Alberta alone at least 21 women were operating farms.

But as newspapers published stories of men selling out to the highest bidder, leaving the wife and children homeless and requiring community relief, the Woman's Christian Temperance Union under Louise Crummy McKinney and the Alberta Council of Women under Henrietta Muir Edwards[b] petitioned in 1909 for legislation that would limit a married person's right to will away his property.

The reception was chilly and when Alberta Opposition Leader R.B. Bennett introduced a bill in the Legislature in 1910 that would adequately protect the interests of women

When R.B. Bennett moved to implement them, he was called 'a susceptible young man affected by the pleadings of the ladies.'

lishing dower, therefore, became a primary objective of the Alberta women's movement.

The unfairness of the existing law seemed self-evident, but arguments were nevertheless advanced to preserve it. Dower would create dissensions within the home, some said. During the hot property dealings of the land boom, it could

and children, it was defeated in favour of a much weaker one and Bennett was dismissed as "a susceptible young man affected by the pleadings of the ladies."

Five years later, however, Arthur Sifton's Liberal government passed an act that entitled a woman to file a caveat against the homestead. As this required her to know both hairdressers, tailors, post office clerks, saleswomen of ladies' clothing, telegraph and telephone operators. They considered themselves lucky to have a job, despite labour shortages, and didn't complain about lower wages. University of Calgary women's studies professor Eliane Silverman in her book *The Last Best West: Women on the Alberta Frontier 1880-1930* writes that it was generally assumed they worked just to pay for luxuries, "for pin money, and one didn't reward people for that." However, with the war their role became more significant. Lt.-Col. Craig, commander of the 194th Highlanders Battalion, known as the Kilties, urged women to take over every possible job and free men for the front — driving taxis, delivery trucks and streetcars and delivering mail, as women already did in England.

Not all professions or trades welcomed women. Police forces, for instance, resisted them. As early as 1912, there were proposals for a woman officer on the Edmonton force to handle delinquent girls. It was rejected. The following year 53 Calgary women's clubs proposed female officers be hired to deal with women and children, and to operate undercover in centres of vice such as movie theatres and fairs. Chief Alfred Cuddy staunchly opposed this. And Cuddy, noted the *Albertan*, had moulded a disorganized force into one of the most efficient in Canada. So he should be left to do his job as he saw fit. He was. But finally, in 1919, two females made it into the Edmonton constabulary.

Louise McKinney, elected for the Non-Partisan League in 1917, who became the first woman legislator in the British Empire.

EVERYBODY VOTES BUT MOTHER

The Grain Growers' Guide, *always a strong voice for the women's movement, throws itself into the suffrage campaign. It ran this cartoon in 1914.*

the law and her husband's intention to sell, and as it applied only to the house and buildings, women dismissed it as a "delusion and a hoax."

However, a year later the United Farm Women of Alberta was founded as an auxiliary to the powerful United Farmers of Alberta. Led by Irene Parlby, the UFWA submitted a resolution calling for a dower law guaranteeing a wife's interest in her husband's property. The male-run UFA amended it to read "one-third interest."

In 1917, the Liberal government, by now fearing the growing might of the UFA, put a Dower Act through the Legislature. At first it seemed sufficient. It required the written consent of a non-owning spouse for selling or encumbering property and guaranteed the use of the property to a surviving spouse. But the courts interpreted the act so narrowly it didn't allow a widow to sell, mortgage or convert the homestead, leaving her, as Mrs. Edwards pointed out,

with the "bare home or homestead without the wherewithal of making a living."

Disillusionment with the 1917 legislation brought about renewed attempts to pass a community property act. It was defeated in 1928, in part because of disagreement among women as to what a woman's rights to property should be.

— *M.F.D.*

[a]The territorial Real Property Act of 1886 was passed because dower rights were seen as conflicting with the land registration scheme for the prairies, writes Catherine Cavanaugh in her 1986 MA thesis *The Women's Movement in Alberta Seen Through the Campaign for Dower Rights.*

[b]Henrietta Muir Edwards, a doctor's wife, was born in Montreal and moved to Macleod, Alberta, in 1903 at the age of 54. In the East she had published a journal for working women and written articles on women's legal and political status.

An Englishwoman, Mrs. Parlby immigrated with her husband in the 1890s and ranched in the Lacombe area. She was president of the United Farm Women of Alberta from 1916 to 1920. The reason Alberta was so advanced in suffrage, she believed, was because men were grateful for the role women had played in opening up the West, sharing the hardships, loneliness and privations.

Teachers led the fight for equal wages. In Edmonton they were making about $200 less than their male colleagues. (Annual salaries for men started at $1,600.) In 1919, eleven of them politely petitioned for equal pay. It was granted that year to high school teachers only, but wouldn't become an across-the-board policy until 1946. The women used the argument that they were equally qualified and had equal expenses. In fact, their government annuities cost more than a man's.

Such inequities naturally ruffled the feathers of any thinking woman. Nellie McClung, who generally took out insurance policies when she travelled by train, one day read the fine print to

---

Sifton, a master of the non-answering answer, was in top form. 'I've learned never to argue back with a lady,' he said, thereby dismissing all her points.

---

discover that as a female she was insured only against death, whereas men were compensated for all disabilities. Women, an insurance agent explained, were more frail and highly strung, therefore more likely to imagine they were hurt.

Such "unwritten laws," Mrs. McClung contended, endlessly worked against women. She cited

Glenbow Archives, NA-1328-2692

With the second decade, women's fashions began the startling changes the 20th century would see

This catalogue, issued by the Edmonton retail store James Ramsey Ltd., gives the first clues to the astonishing changes that will occur to women's fashions in the 20th century. For the first time, dresses become form-fitting. The bustle and the wide skirts have gone. Skirts begin to follow the hip and leg line. In the forthcoming war women will be called upon to perform jobs hitherto entirely male, and when the war ends, skirts will rise from the floor to the knees and higher, and the process of emancipation will confer freedoms unimaginable to this generation.

the case of Jennie Hawkes, tried for murder in 1915. When her husband brought his mistress into their home and "paraded his affection before her eyes," she flew into a rage and killed the woman. Men had been acquitted under similar circumstances, Jennie Hawkes was sentenced to death. About 300 people, mostly women, rallied to a meeting appealing for clemency. A petition was circulated pleading for a commutation of her sentence, which was later reduced to ten years imprisonment in the Alberta Penitentiary.

There was another unwritten law in cases of rape, as Terry L. Chapman documents in her thesis *Sex Crimes in the West 1890-1920*. Consent was supposedly the issue, but a woman had to be gravely injured in the struggle to prove she hadn't consented. In theory, consent was not even a factor in cases involving minors: anyone who "carnally" knew any girl under fourteen who was not his wife was guilty of an indictable offence and liable for imprisonment for life and/or the lash. But in practice, the consent argument was used in case after case, and the men frequently got off.

Max Rudneff, for example, appeared before the Supreme Court in Calgary in 1914 on charges of carnally knowing an eleven-year-old. Although the girl told the court he'd had intercourse with her despite her pleading, crying and protests, he claimed she had asked him

Irene Parlby of Lacombe, president of the United Farm Women of Alberta, who was elected MLA in 1921 and served in the UFA cabinet.

4Although a little woman, Judge Jamieson was tough. The book *Pioneer Women of Western Canada* tells how an angry woman came one night to "bust her," and grabbed her by the lapels. By ordering a foster child removed from her daughter, said the woman, the judge had deprived her household of government support. She wanted the child back. Judge Jamieson managed to walk her to the door and thrust her gently through it. On another occasion she received a marriage proposal in court from a gallant but drunk French Canadian whose wife she had just tried under the Children's Protection Act.

for sex and to "the best of his recollection, not complained. In other words, she had consented." The jury found him not guilty.

The final right of suffrage, the federal vote, seemed inevitable after provincial franchise was granted, but proved far from automatic. All the old arguments reappeared, along with new legal technicalities that baffled even amenable MPs when they discussed it in May 1917. A debate in

---

Central Methodist Church in Calgary went spying in the bars. Some of the spotters were chased through the streets by soldiers and civilians.

---

the Senate the following April almost came to blows. In the previous election, the relatives of departed soldiers had been allowed to vote. Senator Henry Joseph Cloran, a lawyer and Quebec Liberal, complained that women with "no more capacity than children to vote intelligently" had been duped into voting for Union government by promises of furlough for the soldiers and increased separation allowances. Senator Lindrum McMeans, a lawyer and Manitoba Conservative, jumped to the defence of the "noble women who had given their all to the Empire in this mighty struggle." Soon the two were shouting at each other over cries of "Sit down!" and "Order!" After mutual threats of physical violence the two eventually took their seats. The federal franchise wasn't granted until 1918, and it first applied to the federal election in 1921. Few women would run in that year's election, only one, Agnes Macphail from Ontario, would win, and no women from Alberta would run federally until 1935.

The suffrage movement ended, that is, in something of an anticlimax. Women gained the right to hold legislative office and then for decades exercised it only sporadically. Apart from school boards, few elected bodies and no legislatures came even close to equality of membership. Even in the 1990s, parties would have to impose quotas to bring up the numbers of female candidates. But this indifference was evident in the movement from the start. During the Great War most women were far more worried about "the fatal telegram," announcing the loss of a husband or a son, than they were about the visions of their political sisters. Many rural women were running farms singlehandedly, while the urban middle class were busy with Red Cross efforts, knitting socks for soldiers and sending them Christmas presents, as well as such ongoing charitable causes as children's aid.

In his essay, *The Votes for Women Movement*, University of Alberta history professor Paul Voisey concludes that "suffrage didn't radically alter the political and social life of the West as its supporters had claimed it would." While women may have contributed to reforms on child welfare, they didn't eliminate prostitution or noticeably clean up politics. Prohibition reduced but did not eradicate drinking, and was soon repealed as unenforceable.

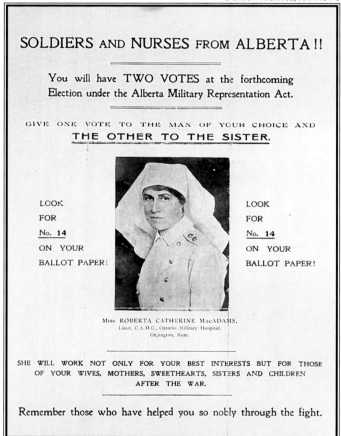

SOLDIERS AND NURSES FROM ALBERTA !!

You will have TWO VOTES at the forthcoming Election under the Alberta Military Representation Act.

GIVE ONE VOTE TO THE MAN OF YOUR CHOICE AND **THE OTHER TO THE SISTER.**

LOOK FOR No. 14 ON YOUR BALLOT PAPER!

LOOK FOR No. 14 ON YOUR BALLOT PAPER!

Miss ROBERTA CATHERINE MacADAMS, Lieut, C.A.M.C., Ontario Military Hospital, Orpington, Kent.

SHE WILL WORK NOT ONLY FOR YOUR BEST INTERESTS BUT FOR THOSE OF YOUR WIVES, MOTHERS, SWEETHEARTS, SISTERS AND CHILDREN AFTER THE WAR.

Remember those who have helped you so nobly through the fight.

An election handbill distributed to the troops on behalf of the candidacy of Lt. Roberta Catherine MacAdams, a nursing sister, who was one of the first two women to serve in the Legislature. She retired from politics in 1921.

Nor would women prove themselves morally superior. As Voisey tells it, Nellie McClung would write in 1945 that the sight of women lined up at liquor stores filled her "with a sense of withering disappointment." Although she knew women had as much right to drink as men, she wished they wouldn't. "It is not in keeping with their character."

Yet there's little doubt that women's acquisition of the right to a political voice did have a profound effect on society, not all of it universally viewed as positive. For example, the influence of women lay behind the softening of academic standards that began in the 1950s and the dismantling of classical education. The early feminists loudly deplored history courses as "dry as dust"

The 'temperance hotel' at Priddis represented what the Drys foresaw as the new regime in Alberta accommodation. Hoteliers later complained they were going broke.

(McClung), the amount of homework (Murphy), and the glorification of war heroes (McKinney). They advocated practical courses for girls preparing them for the "profession of motherhood." Thus "domestic science" was born as an academic course, leading the way for a host of other more "practical" options that over the decades would tellingly erode the time spent on basic academics.

When the opponents of female suffrage like the redoubtable Lucien Boudreau warned that the liberated woman would neglect her husband and children, were they simply speaking from tradi-

During the Great War most women were far more worried about the 'fatal telegram,' announcing the loss of a husband or son, than they were about the visions of their political sisters.

tionalist prejudice? Or did they prophetically foresee the full implications of enfranchising women? By the end of the century, when women had gained their place in society, pursuing careers while someone else brought up their children, the argument would persist that the real price of "liberation" would be paid not by the man but by the child.

Could those "maternal feminists" of the second decade have imagined a society where fully half the children would come from "broken homes" and where (statistics would show) such children would turn more readily to drugs and crime; a society where frightened and lonely latchkey youngsters would call hotlines for reassurance from a stranger's voice? Undoubtedly they did not.

And just as the early feminists had blamed men's immorality and political mismanagement for the social ills of their day, the blame for many of these new "social ills" would increasingly be laid at the door of the emancipated woman, putting her career or personal needs before her marriage, absent from her home.

The die, however, was cast. For better or worse, Alberta women of the province's second decade led their Canadian sisters into the 20th century.

The water wagon is certainly a more dangerous vehicle than the automobile. At least more people fall off it.

Booze acts on the human character as developer on a photographic negative. It brings out the lights and shadows. It shows up the black spots...

When a man is driven to drink he usually has to walk back.

It is our firm conviction that blending of women's ideas with those of reasonably thoughtful men will some day bring about an era of common sense.
– Bob Edwards, quoted in the Eye Opener

CHAPTER TWO

Blood flows, fists and rocks fly, as the miners strike Drumheller

ALBERTA WAS A LABOUR-DOMINATED PROVINCE BEFORE THE GREAT WAR BUT WHEN THE BIG WALKOUT OF '19 FAILED, SO DID THE REVOLUTION

by ROBERT COLLINS

Although Bolshevism was doomed to extinction, warned an organization called the 'Canada First Publicity Association' in full-page ads like this one from a 1919 Lethbridge Herald, *it might not die 'before several nations of the earth have had a big dose of it.'*

By 1910 the workers of Alberta had grasped one of life's little verities: class warfare between them and their natural enemies (governments, police and corporate princes) was as fierce and enduring in this brave new land as in old Ontario or older Europe.

Wages were as low, working conditions as bad or worse, and bosses as insensitive. It led to a decade of fervent unionism and unprecedented conflict. New factions, with charismatic leaders, flared up like shooting stars and vanished as quickly. At the end labour was a little wiser, a little better off, but a long way from Utopia.

By 1913 Alberta had 171 union locals with a total membership of around 11,500[1]. During 1912-1920 inclusive the province recorded 137 strikes, some trifling, some long and vicious. Dissension built to a thundering crescendo in 1919. "In the 2 1/2 years from 1917 to June 30, 1919, more than 600,000 working days were lost because of strikes in Alberta," wrote labour specialist Warren Caragata in *Alberta Labour: A Heritage Untold*, "almost two-thirds of all the man-days lost in the first twenty years of the century."

There were reasons aplenty. In 1910 a union man sent the

CANADIANIZE OUR ALIEN WORKERS

The Grasping Hand of the I.W.W.

It is antagonistic to the ideals of honest labor

An underground crew (right) working at the Alberta Coal Company mine in Edmonton typified the labour force of the Alberta mines. They helped form District 18 of the United Mine Workers, which combined with management in 1918 to defeat the One Big Union movement that was regarded as seeking a Soviet-style Bolshevist revolution.

Miners' living conditions were a subject of endless scandal, but few photographs survive to illustrate them. This is a Canadian worker bunkhouse, preserved by the National Archives without identification.

[1]Thirteen representatives of the United Farmers of Alberta (UFA) attended the founding convention of the Alberta Federation of Labour (AFL) in 1912, but soon drifted away. A speaker at a United Mine Workers convention said farmers were miners' worst enemies: 'They are cheap guys and do not recognize any unions.' By 1918 the UFA was out of the federation.

[2]Those were conservative figures. At the time a four-room house in Edmonton rented for $40 a month and up.

[3]In June 1911, eighty road graders quit a CPR project because of bad work conditions. The railway brought in 100 replacements. A pitched battle ensued with clubs, frying pans, stones and buckets of scalding water. The Mounties finally quelled it.

Lethbridge Herald a typical monthly budget for an average family of five:

Groceries:	$20
Butcher:	$10
Baker:	$ 4
Coal:	$ 5
Light:	$ 1.50
Water:	$ 1.50
Rent :	$15 (five-room cottage)
Clothing:	$20
Druggist:	$ 2
Doctor:	$ 2 (average over five years)
Incidental:	$ 5
Total:	$86 ($1,032 a year)[2]

Suppose, the writer continued, the breadwinner were a carpenter earning 45 cents an hour in a nine-hour day, 26 days a month (no Saturdays off) and a typical eight months a year. He'd earn $842.40 (there was no income tax), but end up $189.60 in the hole.

Not every working man earned 45 cents an hour (men who mixed concrete or dug holes got 35 cents). Nor did all have a house or even a room, however humble. In 1912 Edmonton transient workers lived in a shack-and-tent town surrounded by open pools of stagnant water. Labourers building the Calgary waterworks in 1909 slept 44 to a tent and ate their meals sitting on boxes of dynamite.

Conditions were even worse in railway building camps[3]. Twenty to 35 railway labourers might be housed in one stinking boxcar crawling with vermin. Death and injuries were common. Sick leave, in any labouring job, was unheard of[4]. Immigrants laying steel for the Alberta & Great Waterways Railway in 1916 worked a ten-hour day at 15 cents an hour. From that $1.50 they paid $1 daily for food and lodging and $1 a month for a doctor's fee (although they never saw a doctor).

A Humane Society inspector wrote to the *Edmonton Bulletin* that railway camp "conditions for

labourers and teams are unspeakably abominable and cruel beyond conception... Men have been discharged for refusing to drive teams whose necks and shoulders were a mass of festering sores... Dead horses and mules have been left unburied in the vicinity of camps, infested by clouds of flies... Some of these camps appear to have been nothing less that pestilential centres from which disease and death have radiated in every direction."

Mining life was no better. "Some of Alberta's coal towns were as bad as any in the world," wrote Alberta historian David Jay Bercuson in his introduction to a transcript of the Alberta Coal Mining Industry Commission of 1919. "Housing was generally poor with families living in small frame shacks. Single men were often forced to pack their own blankets from camp to camp and live in overcrowded under-ventilated bunkhouses. Indoor plumbing was unknown. Outhouses were allowed to overflow and foul drinking water... Miners complained of contaminated food served by uncaring cooks in unhealthy kitchens..."

Some mine operators deducted a dollar a month from wages for sanitary facilities never completed. Canmore had twenty cases of typhoid. Fever was common at Frank. At Taber the washhouse was so steamy that miners' clothes were too wet to put on. Hillcrest bragged of its

A bunkhouse card game is depicted in an undated photograph (above left). Railway construction camps were repeatedly investigated and deplored, though the fare awaiting a Canadian Northern construction crew at an Athabasca Landing camp about 1910 (above) at least looks hearty. However, the flowers on the table, the two women, and the photographer, suggest it was a special occasion.

Canmore had twenty cases of typhoid. Fever was common at Frank. At Taber the washhouse was so steamy that miners' clothes were too wet to put on. Hillcrest bragged of its 'crystallized stream,' which in fact was polluted with horse manure and mine effluent.

"crystallized stream," which in fact was polluted with horse manure and mine effluent.

Not surprisingly, one of Alberta's biggest strikes before the Great War was in the mines[5]. The United Mine Workers (UMW) wanted a closed shop and wage increase of 12% (miners earned from $2 to $3.50 a day). Management offered 5 1/2%. On April 1, 1911, seven thousand men from sixteen mines in District 18 (including all Alberta's coal communities plus some in Saskatchewan and B.C.) walked out.

With backing from international headquarters in the U.S., it promised to be a long strike. Many miners went home to Europe or to the homesteads they ran on the side. Their payroll of about $20,000 a day was a serious loss to surrounding communities. The nation ran on coal; it was the main winter fuel; railways depended on it; it generated steam for boilers and even for farmers' tractors.

By October domestic coal was running low all over southern Alberta, with a savage winter near. The strike finally ended in mid-November (the miners won a 6% raise) but not before Lethbridge had ordered U.S. coal at $7 a ton (roughly $2.50 above local prices) to keep its citizens from freezing.

Alberta was slipping into the pre-war bust, fertile ground for radical action[6], particularly from the Industrial Workers of the World (IWW). Unlike other unions, the "Wobblies," as they were

[4]As late as 1919 an Edmonton railway machinist told a royal commission on industrial relations that after catching the flu, he was laid off for a couple of weeks. 'That meant I went $100 behind. Probably it will be two or three years before I could catch up.'

[5]Many other Alberta workers struck during the pre-war years: freight handlers, bricklayers, plasterers, teamsters, house painters, carpenters, railway steamfitters, to name a few.

[6]In October 1912 Lethbridge even had a police strike, perhaps Canada's first, when a Torontonian won the job of inspector over local contenders. The chief hired strikebreakers from Calgary, inducted new special constables, got help from the Mounties and broke the strike.

The German gentleman who created a model town

HIS BACKERS TOLD MARTIN NORDEGG TO SINK $60,000 IN THAT PLACE
CALLED CANADA; ALL WENT WELL UNTIL WAR MADE HIM INTO AN ENEMY

Martin Nordegg was 39 when he reached Alberta in 1907 — a bit long in the tooth for starting life anew — but the pioneer West and the exuberant German were made for each other. Nordegg had boundless energy, vision, flair for planning and an extraordinary talent for ingratiating himself with the rich, famous and influential. This last skill helped make his fortune and kept him out of an internment camp during the Great War. Years later he described his Alberta odyssey in memoirs which, with typical élan, he titled *The Possibilities of Canada Are Truly Great.*

Born Martin Cohen in Silesia in 1868, he studied photo-chemistry and engineering, served in the German army, and later travelled in England and Ireland. He was a photo technician in Charlottenburg in 1906 when French Canadian Onésiphore Talbot, a visiting Liberal MP, piqued his interest in Canada. Nordegg (who had changed his name legally from Cohen in 1909) went to his boss, wealthy publisher George W. Buexenstein, for backing. A half-day later Buexenstein called Nordegg in, gave him a fat cigar, and said, "That place Canada is just now in great fashion." He advanced him $60,000 from a hastily formed syndicate of well-heeled Germans. Go and make us all rich, Buexenstein said.

After a stint in Ontario, where he met Prime Minister Wilfrid Laurier, assorted cabinet ministers and Guglielmo Marconi, the pioneer of radio, the gregarious Nordegg went west of Red Deer in search of coal. With the railway boom, it seemed to him the mineral of choice. An expert geologist helped him discover what would become the Nordegg Coal Basin. His high-level contacts enabled him to hook up with William Mackenzie and Donald Mann, who were pushing their Canadian Northern

Railway through the West. Soon Mackenzie was president and Nordegg vice-president of Brazeau Collieries, backed by an international consortium of bankers and financiers with a bond issue of $5.5 million (see Sect. 5, ch. 1).

Nordegg now launched into "the most important work of my life" — the creation of a community from scratch. "It was my intention to build a modern and pretty town; I insisted on having every cottage fitted with a bath..." His builders talked him out of it; in the end, five-room cottages had bathrooms; four-room places had none[a]. He insisted on having the best-equipped hospital west of Calgary and Edmonton. He filled a sketch book with drawings of company store, butcher and baker shops, poolroom, miners' club, church and RNWMP detachment[b].

When the buildings went up Nordegg selected the

Martin Nordegg in one of the few pictures taken of him sports the tailored quasi-military khaki gabardine suit, Boy Scout-style hat and bandit moustache that some said proved him a showoff. However his humour and genuine fondness for people made him popular everywhere.

colours, "soft pastels which proved very pleasing to the eye." For the water tower, thrusting its ugly head into the bucolic landscape, Nordegg experimented with shades of green until he found one that "hid it so completely one could not see the tower at all..."

Nordegg was a bit of a showoff. Everyone in the district knew the German horseman in tailored quasi-military khaki gabardine suit, Boy Scout-style hat and bandit moustache. But his irrepressible humour and genuine fondness for people were infectious and his town was a labour of love. When Mackenzie (by now Sir William) came to see it in 1914, he paid Nordegg the supreme compliment. He named the place Nordegg, which by the 1990s would be the only major centre on the David Thompson Highway west of Rocky Mountain House.

That year Nordegg's mines produced 155,322 tons of coal; in 1915, 261,000 tons — only 6% of Alberta production[c] but a boon to the Canadian Northern and to surrounding settlers. Nordegg's dream was paying off. Then came the repercussions of the Great War.

Nordegg's model town in 1914. He chose everything from the pastel colours for the houses to the shade of green for the water tower.

contacts. In the end he lost his coal company to Mackenzie, Mann and the financiers. He managed to sell his original backers' shares without loss but was barred from further participation.

Nordegg was financially comfortable, thanks to new connections in the United States and special assignments for various prime ministers whom he'd befriended. Between the world wars, his Ottawa home was a focal point for refugees

---

When the buildings went up Nordegg selected the colours: 'soft pastels which proved very pleasing to the eye.' For the water tower, Nordegg experimented with shades of green that 'hid it so completely one could not see the tower at all.'

Nordegg automatically became an enemy alien. He could have taken out Canadian citizenship but felt that, in wartime, it would seem like deserting his fatherland. His banker refused to advance more credit. In Toronto his fair-weather friend Sir Donald Mann kept him waiting two hours, then treated him with contempt. Another erstwhile colleague, Sir William Mulock, who had been Laurier's postmaster-general, wouldn't see him at all. Mackenzie remained at least superficially friendly and let Nordegg return west with credit to pay the bills. But in 1915 Canadian authorities confiscated his firearms and correspondence, then summoned him to Ottawa for an official inquisition. After that his few true friends urged him to leave quickly for the United States.

There he waited out the war, making more influential

from afar. His enemies in the West tried to strip Nordegg's name from his town, but failed. It remained dear to his heart until his death in 1948.   — *R.C.*

[a]Nordegg gave up on bathrooms after he discovered that miners' families from Poland, Italy and Romania were storing coal in the bathtub and bathing babies in the toilet. About fifty of these houses were built in 1914. Others were built later that looked the same but had no bathroom. Most were torn down for a provincial corrections camp opened late in the century. About seven or eight houses were preserved and remodelled, but municipal officials do not believe they were among Nordegg's originals.

[b]Local women were appalled when an itinerant madam established a tent-brothel a mile from town. But since not one local man (including the police) found fault with it, the business remained and prospered.

[c]By 1915 increased use of imported fuel oil was beginning to hurt the coal industry. Alberta and British Columbia producers petitioned the federal government to levy a heavier duty on oil.

nicknamed[7], embraced all ethnic groups with little of the usual Anglo-Saxon hostility toward "wops" and "bohunks." Its lower dues and policy of direct radical action (strikes, fisticuffs, sabotage) also attracted the itinerant "blanket stiffs" who travelled from job to job, bedrolls slung over their shoulders.

In Alberta the Wobblies focused their efforts on unemployed unskilled workers[8]. In 1912 they called out 250 Edmonton sewer workers on strike but won no appreciable gains. Then fifty IWW agitators got into a fight trying to enlist some city workmen. Edmonton called out its entire police force and the chief warned that any Wobblies parading or holding street corner meetings would be arrested. Subsequently their local secretary was.

After the bust began in 1914 Calgary and Edmonton had up to 7,000 and 5,000 jobless men

[7]Another derisive IWW nickname: 'I Won't Work.'

[8]The Wobblies were no friends of craft unions, such as the Trades and Labour Councils, accusing them of being in league with the bosses.

Coal mining — dirty, tough and dangerous

The Leitch collieries at Passburg (above) shut down with fifteen others in the big 1911 UMW walkout. Clockwise: the tipple at Bellevue c. 1911; a miners' group at Coleman c. 1923; an Edmonton collier crouches to his work in 1907 (the young man at right is probably a visitor accompanying the photographer); a 1910 group demonstrates the latest safety lamps; and workers in the McGillivray Creek tipple yard at Coleman, c. 1915.

respectively. IWW organizer Big Bill Haywood — six-foot-two and 225 pounds with a belly to match, a fast man with his fists or a bottle — told them: "Food, clothing, shelter are essential to life. Let the message of the IWW be: GET THEM! If you have to, take pickaxes and crowbars and go to the granaries and warehouses and help yourselves..."

They wanted work at 30 cents an hour; failing that, they demanded free lodging and three meals a day. They organized parades along Jasper Avenue with marching bands, banners shouting "WE WANT WORK AND FOOD" and Wobbly songs. They held sit-ins in downtown churches. One of their supporters was Fighting Joe Clarke, then an Edmonton alderman and later mayor, sometime lawyer, and former athlete. Fearing violence, civic officials acted. Edmonton's relief department doled out thousands of meals and hundreds of beds and assigned more than 3,400 men to

273

winter make-work (cleaning lanes and working on parks and sewers) at thirty cents an hour.

Calgary was less compassionate. Its police broke up demonstrations and occasionally arrested bearers of such "dangerous-looking" banners as "IF WE DON'T GET WORK WE WILL BEG AND STEAL." William McConnell, secretary of the Calgary branch of the IWW, was arrested and convicted of sedition for inciting a street corner crowd to steal.

In May 1914, six hundred men again paraded in Edmonton, but there was no more free food and lodging. The Wobblies threatened to call every unemployed man in Alberta to the city. It frightened a few merchants into forming a "vigilance committee," but the mass invasion didn't materialize. The Wobblies tried a new tactic: telling members to order big meals in restaurants, then refuse to pay. Thirteen did, and were jailed. Wobbly leader Jim Rowan was arrested and imprisoned for six months on a trumped-up murder charge.

With the end of the railway boom and the outbreak of the Great War, the IWW in Alberta began petering out. Many of the itinerant jobless were in uniform. But in fighting for and, to some extent, winning respect for the basic rights of unskilled foreign workers, the Wobblies were ahead of their time.

Although the Socialist Party of Canada denied affinity with the IWW and deplored its endorsement of sabotage, it shared the Wobblies' love of militant unionism. The SPC was small but well organized. Its members were steeped in Marxist doctrine. It would spearhead the formation, later in the decade, of what came to be called the One Big Union. For a time, it won the support of the District 18 miners of the UMW.

The SPC's Alberta membership included such colourful characters as Joseph Knight, who once moved to have preachers expelled from the Edmonton Trades and Labour Council. He said they belonged to the employers' class and had joined the TLC only to get support in suppressing Sunday band concerts and movies which were cutting down on their collections. Knight also

---

IWW organizer Big Bill Haywood — six-foot-two and 225 pounds with a belly to match, a fast man with his fists or a bottle — told them: 'Food, clothing, shelter are essential to life. Let the message of the IWW be: GET THEM!'

---

[9]The previous record-holder, at 5 1/2 hours, was R.B. Bennett, with the speech that sealed the fate of Premier A.C. Rutherford (Vol. 2, p. 428).

[10]Foreign workers didn't have to look far to find hostility. In June 1915, three hundred Hillcrest miners quit work because their employers would not kick 100 Austrian and German 'aliens' off the job. In Calgary in 1917, CPR freight handlers walked out when a German (later believed to be a Doukhobor) was hired.

[11]In 1911 the Calgary Labour Council even castigated the Boy Scouts as a movement that 'tends toward infusing the spirit of militarism.'

[12]Irvine co-founded a twice-monthly paper, *The Nut Cracker*, later renamed the *Alberta Non-Partisan*, then the *Western Independent*. It was a lively, well-edited showcase for independent writers and thinkers. The paper reached 10,000 circulation before it folded in 1920.

acquired modest fame for calling Edmonton an "exaggerated farm village."

Flamboyant Charlie O'Brien, Socialist MLA for Rocky Mountain, who after his election in 1909 had set off a book-hurling mêlée in the Alberta Legislature (Vol. 2, p. 222), lost his seat in 1913. However by then he had set a record for the Legislature's longest speech: six hours (censuring the government for not prosecuting after the 1910 Bellevue mine disaster) and still going strong when the House adjourned at 12:30 a.m.[9] Later that year the garrulous O'Brien was arrested in Calgary for haranguing a crowd and charged with "obstruction of the street."

Calgary Socialist John Reid also spoke his mind, and was sentenced to fifteen months for sedition. He said publicly that German wartime atrocities were no worse than Britain's; that he was British but not proud of it; that it was "a capitalist war; men are enlisting in the British army simply for meal tickets." Given the fervour of the times and the fact that thousands of Alberta men were killed in the war, it's a wonder he wasn't lynched.

The war, for many hitherto unemployed, meant three square meals a day and a new pair of boots. For those who didn't enlist, war industry jobs opened up at home. But it was still a sore point for most of the working class. The federal Wartime Election Act of 1917 disfranchised all German- and Austrian-born Canadians (naturalized or not), including many Alberta workers[10]. The anti-militarism of labour activists outraged patriotic Albertans[11]. On the first day of war Edmonton's Joseph Knight told a local meeting that the working class would as usual "bear the burden of misery and privation" from the conflict. District 18 of the UMW also opposed the war; members sometimes sang the *Red Flag* to show where their hearts were. Labour's loathing of capitalists increased when some Alberta businessmen paid workers in scrip to be exchanged for goods, thus supposedly freeing up cash for the war effort.

Conscription was the thorniest issue. Labour argued that if men were conscripted, the wealth of war profiteers should likewise be commandeered. In 1916 every worker was asked to fill out a

---

　　THE SOCIAL UPHEAVALS

registration card for a manpower inventory. Alberta workers correctly surmised that it was the prelude to conscription. Many refused to sign. Some Drumheller miners struck. The director-general of National Service, R.B. Bennett, shooting from the lip, said this opposition was probably instigated by German agents — earning him an official raspberry from the Alberta Federation.

Conscription came anyway, in June 1917. That autumn the Trades and Labour Congress of Canada decided to fight Prime Minister Borden and conscription at the ballot box and, in a landmark move, enlisted the support of the Socialist Party of Canada. But in the December election, with conscription the major issue, labour's force was fractured. Some candidates were Socialist, others were straight labour backed by Sir Wilfrid Laurier's Liberals.

One of the latter was the admirable William Irvine, called by his biographer, University of Alberta professor emeritus of philosophy Anthony Mardiros, "the founding father of the radical democratic socialist movement in Alberta." Scottish-born Irvine was trained in theology (in Calgary he was pastor of First Unitarian Church) but soon ranged into politics and journalism[12]. He sparred with the Calgary *Eye Opener* (where it was always open season on socialists) but in time Irvine won a rare commendation from editor Bob Edwards as "a capable upright man who enjoys the respect of all who know him."

Unlike some of his fellows, Irvine was highly literate, reasonable, and could illuminate a cause with a felicitous phrase. He recommended that disfranchisement "begin with individuals who have exploited the patriotism and the resources of our country in its time of grave danger." During a Calgary celebration of the Hudson's Bay Company's 250th anniversary, he wrote in part: "How

William Irvine (below left), described by his biographer as 'the founding father of the radical democratic socialist movement in Alberta,' won the admiration and respect of many, his opponents included. Even Tory R.B. Bennett expressed admiration for him after the two debated on the hustings. Irvine's twice-monthly paper, The Nut Cracker, included the in-jokes of current politics, sarcastic comment, political poetry, kudos for the favoured and invective for the non-favoured.

Provincial Archives of Alberta, A-13634

Delegates to the United Mine Workers convention held in Lethbridge in 1911 (at right) could pass for a group of lawyers. Two months after this photo was taken the UMW struck sixteen mines in Alberta, and 7,000 UMW members walked off the job. The issue was a closed shop.

can we celebrate by gorgeous pageant that company which debauched and made slaves of the poor aborigines?" He was a moving force behind the Non-Partisan League (NPL): "We are not a socialistic organization because we are an organization of the people and the people have not given us any mandate to adopt pure unadulterated socialism... We are, however, a working-class movement... We can take as big a chunk of socialism as we can digest and if we develop an appetite we can go the limit."

Irvine ran for the NPL in the 1917 Alberta election and lost. As a federal candidate that year he was supported by the NPL, the Labour Representation League and Laurier's Liberals. But the country was in no mood for anti-conscription views or anything else that smacked of pacifism. Irvine's opponent, a wounded war veteran (supported by R.B. Bennett), won easily. But Bennett, like so many other non-socialists, became an Irvine admirer after the two debated on the hustings. Irvine returned to preaching but his glory years were still ahead. In 1921 he was elected to a fed-

---

Flamboyant Charlie O'Brien, Socialist MLA for Rocky Mountain, set a record for the Legislature's longest speech: six hours (censuring the government for not prosecuting after the 1910 Bellevue mine disaster) and still going strong when the House adjourned at 12:30 a.m.

---

eral seat and in the 1930s was a co-founder of the Co-operative Commonwealth Federation, later the New Democratic Party.

Alberta labour fared badly in the 1917 election[13] and was worse off at home. Since war's beginning the cost of living had soared a whopping 65% and workers bore its brunt. Yet manufacturers, particularly those producing war materials, were making enormous profits. Labour turned to strikes again after two fairly tranquil years. Nearly 4,000 District 18 miners walked out in the summer of 1916, in defiance of a two-year contract that hadn't expired. They were earning $2.47 to $3.30 a day and wanted 10% more.

The public was not supportive. The war effort needed coal. "Though labour conditions are such that the present looks like a good time to drive a hard bargain," editorialized the *Lethbridge Herald*, "the public remembers every minute that we are at war and is not very sympathetic toward those who try to make selfish use of the fact."

[13]Across Canada, all 38 Labour candidates lost. Candidate Joe Knight, running for the Socialists, was characterized by the *Red Deer News* as 'a German soldier doing military work' for the enemy.

They settled for a 7 1/2% increase, but by fall 5,000 were back on strike demanding 25% more. They returned to work when the federal government promised a commission to see if the cost of living justified the 25% raise. In Alberta the commission found some higher food prices (in six months, for instance, canned salmon had soared by 37% and canned peaches by 17%) but many items were unchanged or cheaper.

Fretting at the inaction, the miners went back on strike in early 1917. Coal ran low. On January 30 Lethbridge's temperature hit -37 F, people burned their limited wood supplies and considered raiding the coal banks along the river. The miners returned to work with a raise of $1.75 a week, but in spring wanted a new contract.

Another strike followed with all 7,500 men of District 18 demanding 30%, twice as much as they were offered. It lasted three months but this time governments, public, their employers and their own international union stood against them. In June the federal government put a director of coal operations in charge of the district's mines. The miners got their 15% plus 7 1/2% more, plus a cost-of-living clause.

Everywhere, labour was chafing under the escalating cost of living. Edmonton's street railway employees struck; city council locked them out. A marauding gang of women, kin of the deposed strikers, did minor damage to the car barns[14]. Within eleven days the transit men accepted the city's offer (about half of what the union wanted).

Mining continued to be a hotbed of dissent. Near the end of 1917, six hundred Lethbridge miners struck over a closed-shop dispute and contravention of the latest agreement. They were quickly back at work; the country's temper was running short, with hints that able-bodied miners, previously exempt, might be drafted into the army.

However, the most vicious of all these disputes flared up at Drumheller. In February 1918, 2,000 of its miners walked out because one operator was hiring non-union men. The RNWMP sent twenty men to the scene. When a mob of 350 threatened the mine, two Mounties held them off. In Calgary, the *Albertan* was ecstatic:

...the RNWMP on Saturday added another record to their long list of magnificent deeds. The two policemen did not draw their guns but with that power which the force has spent years of accomplishment in establishing, they held back the immense crowd, the majority of whom were aliens; all were greatly excited and some half crazed with bad whiskey...

Meanwhile the Calgary Trades and Labour Council threatened a general strike, partly a bluff to win a hotel and restaurant workers' dispute. It worked, and a spate of other strikes followed in 1918: carpenters, teamsters, letter carriers, painters, retail clerks, civil servants, laundry workers, telephone linemen, freight handlers.

By autumn the federal government had seen enough. On October 11 an order-in-council forbade strikes or lockouts for the duration of the war (which would end exactly one month later), providing a fine of $1,000 and/or six months in prison. In addition, any male employee or employer of military age who broke the rule would be put in the army. Calgary labour unions defied the order; Ottawa

[14]Non-union street railway worker Alexander Harris was charged in magistrate's court for 'using grossly insulting and obscene language' against union man Charles Williamson. Harris had called Williamson 'a good-for-nothing,' among other things. Harris was fined $2 without costs.

'Organize!' was the rallying cry. Here Local No. 488 (Edmonton) of the United Association of Journeyman Plumbers, Gas & Steam Fitters & Steam Fitters' Helpers of the United States & Canada poses in full regalia c. 1911-12.

Provincial Archives of Alberta, A-19669

Not everybody was enthused when teachers first proposed the ATA

BAD PAY AND CANTANKEROUS BOARDS CAUSED SCHOOL STAFFS TO ORGANIZE

In 1916 the average annual salary of teachers in Alberta was $828.69, compared to the $800 the Edmonton Public School Board had paid its first teacher more than thirty years before. A high school principal could earn up to $3,000 a year but few of the province's 3,963 teachers were in that exalted class. Beginners got as little as $450.

This was the major reason the Alberta Education Association that year had before it a resolution to set up a provincial teachers' association. The AEA itself didn't fill the bill: it included university professors, high-ranking clergymen, officers of the Department of Education, trustees of the larger urban school systems and various MLAs. Many were members of the education establishment that was stifling teachers' progress.

That 1916 resolution failed, but at the next annual convention the teachers seized the floor (despite outcries from the old guard) and swept into being the Alberta Teachers' Alliance (ultimately the Alberta Teachers' Association).

Salaries were but one grievance. School boards were another. Teachers could be fired on thirty days' notice without cause. The boards negotiated all salaries, and teachers' wellbeing was often the least of their concerns. Some boards arbitrarily deducted donations to the war effort from teachers' salaries. Calgary ordered all single male teachers to enlist or be fired.

School boards, pressed for funding, sometimes balanced their budgets by cutting teachers' salaries, or by not paying them at all. Others hired people with provisional certificates (no teacher training). Almost half of the 1,184 teachers' licences issued in 1916 were provisional[a].

When all else failed the trustees simply closed the schools. About half — 48,000 — of Alberta's pupils in 1916 attended one-room schools, but on average only for 165 days a year (nearly thirty days less than in larger school dis-

tricts). Teachers were paid according to a formula based on number of days taught[b].

The new alliance decreed that there be only one teaching organization in the province, to include all — and *only* — persons with valid Alberta teaching credentials and employment in a public or separate school system. Preachers, professors, permit-holders and bureaucrats were not welcome. The ATA hired Edmonton high school teacher John W. Barnett, a former local president of the National Union of Teachers in Britain, as its secretary-treasurer. Among its aims: to "advance and safeguard the cause of education"; to "raise the status of the teaching profession in Alberta"; and to "unite members for their mutual improvement, protection and general welfare."

By 1920 Barnett was on a full-time salary of $325 a month (20% more than a school principal). The ATA had its own publication, to combat the anti-ATA stance of all newspapers except the Calgary *Albertan*, and membership of 1,763, representing about a third of the employed teachers in Alberta. Roughly half of them were in Edmonton, Calgary, Medicine Hat, Lethbridge and Wetaskiwin.

The ATA called for a minimum salary of $1,200 a year. It demanded the right of collective bargaining (which would remove the negotiating power of school boards that, in multi-room schools, liked to haggle with teachers individually). It asked job security, better working conditions, right of appeal against firings, and cumulative sick leave. In 1918 it demanded that teachers, if dismissed at the end of a term, must receive notice by the first of June or of December, and could not be fired at any other date except by permission of the Department of Education. The teachers also wanted the full school year to be deemed 200 days, for the purposes of calculating partial salaries.

All of these objectives, though far from realized, never-

Alberta Teachers' Association

John W. Barnett, an Edmonton high school teacher and former local president of the National Union of Teachers in Britain, was the ATA's first secretary-treasurer. This photo of him, one of the few to survive, was taken in the 1940s.

theless irritated or enraged the education establishment. But the fledgling association discovered it wasn't entirely toothless. A blacklist was devised for obdurate school boards: a notice in the press, and later in the *ATA Magazine*, advised teachers to check with the ATA office before seeking employment with the unyielding boards. It didn't prevent those boards from hiring, but greatly reduced their options[c].

By 1921 the ATA had established itself as a feisty union deeply committed to teachers' rights. Its motto, *Magistri Neque Servi* (masters not servants), said it all. It was reflected in a drive for more professionalism within its own ranks. By then its members occupied more than half the province's classrooms.

A minimum salary of $840 was about to become formalized in legislation (a scant victory but higher than the minimum in any other province). Alberta's median that year was $1,180. Many battles and much discouragement lay ahead, but Alberta teachers had a toe in the doorway to a better working life.   — *R.C.*

[a]The quality of teacher training accounted in part for the fact that only 5.5% of Alberta's 99,000 schoolchildren in 1916 were above Grade 8. Only 541 students reached Grade 12.

[b]Anyone teaching less than 210 days (which, for the purposes of the formula, was a full year) was paid for the number of days taught, divided by 210, multiplied by the agreed-upon annual salary. A teacher ostensibly earning $840 a year but teaching only 165 days (common in rural schools) received $660.

[c]In 1919 Edmonton separate school teachers struck for better wages and won some concessions, but their leaders lost their teaching jobs.

Alberta Teachers' Association

The A.T.A Magazine
Official Organ of the Alberta Teachers' Alliance
MAGISTRI NEQUE SERVI

Vol. I.   EDMONTON, ALBERTA, JUNE, 1920   No. 1.

FELLOW TEACHERS

Are you a member of the A. T. A.?

If not, do you know that you are a *clog* on the efforts of three-fourths of your fellow-workers in this Province.

Are you indifferent about the $1,200 minimum?

If you are, you are *betraying* the hand that supports you, and no amount of empty drivel about "the missionary spirit," or pious humbug about "patriotism," can disguise the fact.

Do you meet persons who express doubts about the propriety of teachers' organizations, and who advise you to keep clear of anything so banal or "common" as a "union?"

Mark those persons.   They are your *enemies*.   They fear organization, much preferring that you remain what you are, an individual powerless to resist domination.   *Magistri neque servi.*

This photo of a teachers' convention in Edmonton in 1917, preserved in the National Archives of Canada, is probably the first formal photograph of the ATA's founding members. The young man, third from right in the back row, bears a strong resemblance to John Barnett, but there are no identifications with the photograph. Volume I, Number I of the ATA Magazine (below left) came out in June 1920, with a severe indictment of teachers who resisted the unionizing movement.

The One Big Union flexes its muscle

One of the few extant pictures of the 1919 strike at Drumheller shows a determined group wielding tree limbs as weapons (above). Only one man is identified: Nick Gill, second from left in the back row. Squads sent to break up the strike included war veterans armed with rifles. These homes belonging to the miners at Drumheller (at right) were attacked by strike-breakers in 1919. After hurling rocks at their attackers the inhabitants fled to the hills, spent a cold, sleepless night, and were hunted by a posse the following day. Soon they gave up.

warned that the RNWMP would enforce it.

By then the Mounties were deeply into labour surveillance. Following the Russian Revolution of 1917 and its enthusiastic acceptance by Canadian labour[15], many Canadians began seeing Bolsheviks and Reds under every bed. The most successful RNWMP spy was Detective Constable F.W. Zaneth (born Zanetti in Italy and raised in Moose Jaw). In the spring of 1918 Zaneth was sent to check out the radicals behind the Drumheller strike. He had no special training; just quick wits, nerve, and a fluency in languages. He infiltrated the union so adeptly that he was sent back in September, posing as Harry Blask, a Wobbly from the U.S.

"Blask" rose rapidly in union circles, became an organizer for the Socialist Party in Calgary, attended labour conferences and knew all Alberta's radicals. Calgary's Wobblies suspected a stoolpigeon in their midst, so Zaneth (or Blask) loudly agreed that they should find and dispose of the "son of a bitch." Then, to cover his tracks, Zaneth went to Regina, contrived to get himself arrested as an alien travelling without a permit, was fined and released. When the news reached Calgary his stock rose ever higher in the unions.

"By April 1919 the RNWMP had organized a highly successful covert intelligence operation in western Canada," writes RCMP historian S.W. Horrall. "Secret agents or detectives had managed to penetrate every important radical organization, some of them occupying executive positions in which they had the confidence of the leadership[16]. Their reports gave a detailed account of the activities of these radicals as well as a verbatim record of their public speeches."

There was plenty to report; the decade of dissent peaked in 1919: a "volcanic crater" with "rumblings of internal disturb-

[15]In 1919 the Alberta Federation of Labour announced 'full accord and sympathy with the aims and purposes of the Russian and German revolutions.'

[16]Partly because of the Bolshevik scare, the RNWMP and Dominion Police merged in 1919, officially becoming the RCMP in 1920.

ances," one observer called it. RCMP intelligence teemed with reports on the newly formed One Big Union. It sprang to life in March at the Western Labour Conference, born of irritation with the Trades and Labour Congress of Canada (with its alleged Ontario favouritism, American domination and wishy-washy stance on political issues). The OBU was to be all-embracing, rallying the faithful behind demands for a six-hour day and five-day week[17].

Alberta supported it half-heartedly. In the cities, only Medicine Hat's unionists fully endorsed it. But elsewhere in the West most trade unionists rallied behind the OBU. So did most of the 5,100 miners in District 18, partly because of their appalling work and living conditions. The new union was a key factor in the Drumheller strike of 1919, nastiest in the decade.

The Drumheller miners broke away from the UMW to join the OBU and struck on May 24, demanding that the mineowners recognize the OBU as their legal bargaining agent. The mine-

'I kept tapping, tapping...'

TRAPPED IN A CUBIC-YARD POCKET, A MINER IS SAVED AFTER THREE DAYS

In April 1917, a cave-in trapped miner Henry Trenham of Champion at the bottom of Thigh Hill Mine, 56 miles north of Lethbridge. For three days and nights he crouched in a space 22 by 36 by 36 inches. After his rescue he told his story to the *Calgary Herald*:

"I made myself as comfortable as possible in the cramped space. The dust nearly choked me to death at first and for four hours I suffered agonies gasping for air. Then the atmosphere became more settled and I was able to endure it.

"I knew my greatest need was to save my air. My lamp went out and I tried to light it again. As it was a carbon lamp it would use no air. My matches merely sputtered and went out.

"I could hear my rescuers from the minute they started work at the mouth of the cave. I kept tapping, tapping with coal and earth lumps, but this was not forceful enough. I remembered a stone I had put into the wall. For a long time I was afraid to remove this in fear that the whole thing would come down and crush the life out of me. Finally I decided to risk it and I eased out the rock and put coal in its place.

"I gave up hope only once in that awful vigil. That was when I heard the rescuers begin to dig the tunnel at the foot of the shaft, away from me instead of towards me. Frantically I tried to make them understand through that wall of rock, but still they dug farther and farther away. As the sound of their picks grew fainter I felt that everything was over. [The rescuers dug a 43-foot shaft but missed Trenham's tomb by twenty feet. Rather than dig toward it and risk another cave-in, they dug around a further 23 feet.] "Presently I heard them coming back, and then I realized what they were doing. I resumed my tapping, and that gave them the exact directions, and soon I was out under the skies again."

John Zacharias

owners regarded the OBU leaders as wackos and revolutionaries, a view shared by Coal Commissioner W.H. Armstrong, who had been appointed by the federal government in 1917 with special powers to arbitrate wages, prices and production in the coal industry for the duration of the war.

The strike dragged into July. Winter coal orders began piling up. The operators hired from the widening pool of unemployed war veterans at $10 a day. Union men said the operators poured liquor into the veterans and turned them loose with pick handles, crowbars and brass knuckles to corral the strikers. The options were simple: come back to work or get beaten up.

The strikers travelled in packs for safety. One August morning a crowd of them gathered outside a mine to block entry to the strikebreakers. Two hundred veterans chased them off. In subsequent days, hundreds of strikers stalked Drumheller's streets, exchanging taunts and threats with the veterans. One Sunday morning the strikers marched to the Miners' Hall, made speeches and telegraphed the union head office for instructions. The OBU promised to send a representative from Calgary for a Monday meeting. But that day, gangs of ex-servicemen — goon squads, as the strikers called them — attacked miners' homes. Strikers and their families fought back with rocks and chunks of firewood. The squads brought up reinforcements with rifles.

Some strikers escaped into the hills, but after a cold, hungry and sleepless night, with a police posse now looking for them, many returned. The company warned that all men must sign up again with the UMW or get out of town, and that job preference would be given "first to returned soldiers, next, white men who had mining experience and last, the alien element."

Soon they all gave up. Five OBU leaders were caught, beaten up and shipped out of town; two were tarred and feathered. In time all of District 18 returned to the UMW[18]. This reversal began the steady decline of the OBU in the West.

The most vicious of all these disputes flared up at Drumheller. In February 1918, two thousand of its miners walked out. The RNWMP sent twenty men to the scene. When a mob of 350 threatened the mine, two Mounties held them off.

Meanwhile, with Winnipeg's historic General Strike of May-June 1919 under way, Alberta unions mounted sympathy strikes. But in Calgary only 1,500 walked out. Railway clerks, barbers, bakers, teamsters and the crucial transit electrical workers stayed on the job[19].

Edmonton unions weren't much more supportive (although Joe Clarke, now the city's mayor, was). In essence, the sympathy strike failed in Alberta and was over by mid-June[20]. Meanwhile, the federal government rammed through an amendment to the Immigration Act, allowing for the deportation of naturalized citizens charged with sedition. The Criminal Code was broadened to provide for arrest on suspicions. Then the RNWMP threw the main strike leaders (all OBU men) in jail. Police also raided labour temples and the homes of other suspected "radicals," seizing "Red" literature forbidden in Canada.

Meanwhile in June of 1919 the provincial government had appointed a royal commission on the coal industry, which submitted its report at the end of the year. Its recommendations were high-minded (improved living conditions, better education facilities, a better coal marketing system, a permanent commission comprising labour, owners, consumers and provincial government to regulate the industry and settle disputes). But virtually nothing came of this, chiefly because the federal government controlled Alberta's resources as a term of its entry into Confederation[21].

By the end of 1920 the OBU was for all practical purposes dead (although Joseph Knight represented it at a meeting in Moscow in July). The Wobblies had moved to greener pastures. Alberta miners received a 27% pay increase and the closed shop, and coal went up 45 cents a ton. But thereafter radical activity began shifting to central Canada.

"The causes of solidarity, labour and resistance would live on throughout the 1920s and 1930s," writes Queen's University history professor Bryan D. Palmer in *Working-Class Experience*. "But as new assaults on the surviving remnants of working-class oppositions and organizations were being mounted, labour faced an increasingly uphill battle."

[17] Long hours weren't the only Dickensian aspect of Alberta working conditions. In 1919 the Dominion Glass Company in Redcliff was caught employing children under the age of fifteen. The manager was fined $5 and costs.

[18] Mine operators strongly supported the UMW, fearing the OBU's radical and militant tendencies.

[19] Calgary postal workers struck in sympathy, were immediately fired by the federal government and never got their jobs back.

[20] The *Calgary Herald* maintained that enemies of the sympathy strike were not enemies of trade unions but of 'Bolshevism and the Russian Soviet government.'

[21] Ottawa was seen as catering to Ontario and Quebec, as it would be seen throughout the century. Alberta historian David Jay Bercuson writes, 'The federal government was never willing to drive the price of fuel in central Canada up, for heating or for industrial production, simply to sustain the Alberta coal industry.'

When the fire reached the coal dust, 189 men perished in the blast

ONLY 46 MINERS MADE IT OUT
AS THE 'BEST-RUN MINE'
IN THE CROWSNEST BLEW UP
AND THE HILLCREST BECAME
CANADA'S WORST MINING DISASTER

The worst mining disaster in Canadian history began, as most catastrophes do, without warning. Just after 9:30 that morning of June 19, 1914 — somewhere in the labyrinth of shafts, corridors and coal "rooms" that comprised Hillcrest Collieries' two mines in the Crowsnest Pass — rocks fell, sparks flew and the ever-lurking methane gas caught fire. Flames skipped through the tunnels to a pocket of coal dust. Then...

Two, maybe three, split-second explosions melded into one thunderous blast that shook the earth. It raced through the mines, and stripped oxygen from the air. For the 235 men underground it seemed like the end of the world. For 189 of them it was.

At the surface, concussion slammed one man to the ground and tossed two others against the walls of the hoist houses at the entrance to each mine. One man died instantly, the other minutes later. The blast shattered one hoist house's eight-foot concrete wall and tore the roof from the other. An ugly cloud of smoke poured into the sunny sky. The mine whistle began shrilling in bursts of three: *Emergency! Emergency! Emergency!*

One of two huge surface fans that, respectively, blew clean air into the mines — directing it with a series of brattices (screens) — and drew out bad air, had stopped. An electrician raced to restart and set it on exhaust. Both were now sucking carbon dioxide from below, which probably saved a few lives. Rock, timbers and smashed mine cars completely blocked the entrance to Mine 1. After a stunned moment — the mines had just been pronounced safe[a] — two would-be rescuers rushed into Mine 2 but staggered back choking. A call went out for the rescue unit from Blairmore, a mile to the north. Three Mounties galloped up on horseback from Burmis Mines, 2 1/2 miles east. Their first

Rescue workers use a coal car to bring bodies down from the mine. Two RNWMP corporals worked for many hours in the company washhouse at the grisly job of sorting and assembling shattered bodies and limbs — thereby earning a reluctant tribute from a UMW official who had no love for police.

grim task was to hold back crowds of weeping, terrified women and children from the village, whose blackest nightmare, the one that haunts all miners' families, had come true.

Survivors, only eighteen at first, began trickling to the surface, gasping for breath. They told of the panic below, the cries of pain and "HELP ME!"; of men lying in their own vomit; of piles of bodies, including horses that also worked the mines. One escaper, David Murray, looked around for his three sons, William, Robert and David Jr. They were still below. He plunged back in. All four died.

Again rescuers without oxygen masks went into Mine 2, this time getting down about 400 feet to Level 1. Just then Blairmore's rescue car arrived, legacy of an earlier disaster. In 1910 a mine explosion at Blairmore had killed 31 men. None would have died if there had been proper rescue facilities. For once government had moved promptly, establishing rescue stations at Blairmore, Lethbridge and Coalhurst.

Each station had seventeen portable breathing units, thirty tanks of oxygen, two compression pumps, pulmotors (for helping stricken men breathe when they were brought to the surface), electric hand lamps and quantities of caustic soda (for the chest pouches on rescuers' breathing units; it purified the air by absorbing carbon dioxide and carbon monoxide). Each station had trained scores of hand-picked men. Nearly a hundred of them now converged on Hillcrest. Special trains hurried in from Lethbridge, Fernie, Calgary

and Macleod with doctors, nurses and supplies. But most of Hillcrest's miners were beyond medical help.

By 11:30 a.m. 28 more were helped out, some barely alive. All told, 46 survived. The rest were lost. The oldest was 54, the youngest seventeen. One man died instantly with his pick still clenched in upraised hands. Another was sitting upright, head in hands. Another was found with a wet cloth halfway to his mouth, in a desperate effort to filter clean air into his lungs. Many lay prone, hands reaching out. A teenage boy had died with a smile on his face.

One of the dead, Tom Corkill, was working his last shift before going to his new homestead near Lethbridge. Rod Wallis and brother-in-law William Neath had planned to quit the mines in three days and return to farming in their native Nova Scotia. They went home in coffins. Charles Elick had survived thirteen hours underground in 1903, trapped by the Frank Slide, but this day his luck ran out. Brothers Alex, James and Robert Petrie died leaving two sisters and a widowed mother.

Another fire broke out below and with it fear of another explosion. Firefighting teams risked their lives — as did all the rescuers — to put it out. Now came the grisly job of retrieving corpses, some so badly burned or mangled that rescuers spirited them out at night so the stunned wives and children, still roaming pitifully at the surface, wouldn't see their state. Many had missing limbs; one was decapitated. RCMP Constable William Hancock was assigned to identify

As hope steadily wanes, families wait at the pithead of the Hillcrest Mine at the Crowsnest on the fatal morning of June 19, 1914, after explosions stripped the mine of oxygen and wiped out more than 80% of the day shift. The toll was 189 in the worst mine disaster of Canadian history which left 130 widows and 400 fatherless children.

On the cold grey Sunday of June 21, two days after the disaster, the bodies of 150 miners were interred in a common grave at Turtle Mountain. The funerals went on until nightfall.

them. Often his only clue was the brass ID tag that each man carried underground. Nova Scotian Sidney Bainbridge's body was never found; just one extra leg, which was surreptitiously buried in another man's coffin.

Corporals Frederick Mead and Arthur Grant had the ghastly task of assembling and cleaning bodies and limbs in the company wash-house, shrouding them in white cotton cloth and sending them under escort to the Miner's Hall. Hour after hour they worked without relief until even an

should inspect mines not less than once a month (which hadn't been happening) and that every company keep safety equipment at mine entrances (Hillcrest had not). Still, how could this calamity have happened in the so-called "safest and best-run mine" in the Pass? A formal inquiry posed theories but found no definitive answers. Veteran miner Harry White, first to tour the ravaged underground after the accident, concluded that falling rock in Tunnel 33 set sparks that started the explosion. The inquiry ignored him.

In consequence of the frightful Hillcrest disaster, both employers and government worked hard to introduce safer methods into the chaotically hazardous coal mining industry. This mine rescue team, photographed in the Crowsnest Pass c. 1920, is one early example.

official of the United Mine Workers union, which hated police, grudgingly paid them tribute.

On June 21, a cold grey Sunday, 150 men were buried in a common grave at the foot of Turtle Mountain. The funerals went on almost to nightfall. Other men were buried in private ceremonies or sent to distant homes. They left behind an estimated 130 widows and 400 fatherless children. Ultimately Hillcrest Collieries paid $1,800 to each family but, while claims were being processed, donations of food and money flooded in from all over Canada. Ottawa sent $50,000; the Alberta government, $20,000.

In July a coroner's jury ruled that the tragedy resulted from an explosion of gas and dust; that the government

But in September 1926, an even more devastating blast ripped through Hillcrest mines. This time only two men were underground. So it could not be blamed on sparks from a pick, a fallen lamp or an errant charge of dynamite. Harry White had been right.

Hillcrest kept going until 1949 when coal as a fuel gave way to oil and natural gas. Then, finally, the killer mine closed forever.

— *R.C.*

[a]Two fire-bosses, whose duties included checking the mines for danger, had successively toured them the evening and night before the accident, found methane gas pockets (common in Crowsnest Pass mines), posted warnings but reported that ventilation was good and the air was sufficiently moist to dampen explosive coal dust.

CHAPTER THREE

Furious at reciprocity's defeat, the farmers explode in revolt

A DEVOUT MISSOURI MULE-DRIVER BECOMES ALBERTA'S UNCROWNED KING BUT HENRY WISE WOOD SHUNS POLITICS IN FAVOUR OF CLASS ACTION

by **COURTNEY TOWER**

The only beast more balky, more cantankerous than the ordinary mule was the famous mule of Missouri. That is how the saying went — "stubborn as a Missouri mule" — when Henry Wise Wood was learning to be an accomplished teamster on his father's thousand acres in Ralls County, Missouri. He had a special talent for handling the obstinate but sure-footed and hard-working animals, and when he was fourteen, in 1874, he overheard his father say: "I have 300 men on this place, but no teamster like Henry." Young Henry later confided: "After hearing what my father said then, I was always more confident in his judgement."

It was a step from handling balky mules, each one preferring to go his own way, to welding individualistic Alberta farmers into a united team with Henry Wise Wood very much at the reins. Through a commanding presence and Christian fervour, he mobilized the farmers of a farming province into a powerful social, educational, economic and eventually political force. The United Farmers of Alberta were just that, united.

The UFA rose up in 1909 like a prairie storm, part of the great Canadian agrarian revolt against unequal tariffs, flint-hearted bankers, far-off manufacturers and local hard times. Starting with $1.67 in the central till, but with 5,000 fired-up farmer members in scores of communities, it soon was entrenched in library lending, social gatherings, adult education, political lobbying and co-operative elevators throughout Alberta. It rapidly became the effective power behind weak Liberal governments in Edmonton. Then, dumbfounding itself, in 1921 it *was* the government in Edmonton — and a force within the new

Henry Wise Wood, the man who developed the United Farmers of Alberta into the most powerful populist force the province had ever seen, fought hard to prevent it from 'going political.' When it did, he refused to become leader although the premiership was his for the asking. Christian before all else, he refused to compromise, and went into the history of the province as 'the uncrowned king of Alberta.'

Glenbow Archives, NA-627-1

Progressive movement that was shaking up remote Ottawa. The UFA ruled in Alberta from 1921 to 1935, and Henry Wise Wood ruled the UFA for its most powerful years, from 1916 to 1931. He was president of the Alberta Wheat Pool from its founding on Oct. 29, 1923, until 1937. Throughout his tenure, says author T.C. Byrne in *Alberta's Revolutionary Leaders*, "the UFA controlled provincial affairs. In reality, during this period Wood played the role of Alberta's uncrowned king."

Henry Wise Wood — a tall, spare man with beetling eyebrows under a high, bald pate, his steady brown eyes set deep and fervent in a calm face — was already a middle-aged man of means when he emigrated with his wife and four children to Carstairs in 1905. He was a radical, some at a later day might say left-wing. But he was also cautious and conservative, and others might say right-wing. He could be considered a prairie populist, but in a rather restrictive way — farmer-power was his whole concern. He fought successfully for years for his farmers to stay out of direct politics, preferring their organized influence instead — but then, after the die was cast to "go political," he helped them gain power.

This conflict within Wood's nature was the same kind of contradiction that roiled within western Canada. They were good times and bad, encompassing the birth of new settlement and bounding optimism, the ferment and horror of war, the anguish of drought and debt, and the resented distance from the centres of power where the pivotal decisions were made. Many groups and nostrums flowered and faded. In Alberta, all these melded into the UFA. When its cycle was over, true to its nature, it gave rise to two opposing political forces — the socialist Co-operative Commonwealth Federation (CCF), which later would become the New Democratic Party, and William Aberhart's Social Credit League (see sidebar).

Henry Wood — "HW" he was called — is described by his biographer W.K. Rolph[1] as "the most striking personality in the Canadian farmers' movement." He was repeatedly acclaimed head of the UFA because none would contest the office against him, and he ranked much higher in popular esteem in Alberta than the later Aberhart ever achieved. One typical reason: when he became head of the Alberta Wheat Pool he refused thereafter to take his modest $2,000-a-year pay as UFA president (when other farm leaders were taking $20,000 a year and more).

Beyond the farming community, however, his popularity was far less universal. Opponents called him names — "Bolshevik" or "alien demagogue" — for his message that a "farmer class" had to unite to compete equally with the established manufacturing class. They said his conviction that co-operation rather than competition was "the true social law" of a just and Christian world

The UFA was very fond of posing for photographs that demonstrated its numerical strength, among which this one, taken at the tenth annual convention in Calgary in January 1918, was particularly notable. The Liberal government looked on in horror.

THE SOCIAL UPHEAVALS

was "weird." Yet, says Rolph, "his influence over both the political and economic aspects of the provincial farmers' movement was unrivalled," and he became a power in the Canadian Council of Agriculture and the Canadian Wheat Board as well.

Wood was born into a prosperous farm family, the fifth child of a slave-holder who raised cattle and mules. Henry spent two years at a liberal arts college, read widely in the Bible, literature and lyric poetry. He studied political philosophy and, later, the geology of Alberta. At eighteen he and another boy had driven a team of mules from Missouri to his father's other place, a cattle ranch in Texas, through territory in which Indians still raided settlers. Marriage to Etta Leora Cook ended his college days and he became a successful Missouri cattleman, managing his father's farm.

He was a convinced and practising Christian, active in the church called the Disciples of Christ, which emphasized fellowship and faithful adherence to "the character and teachings of Jesus."

They believed themselves at the mercy of railway barons, gouging banks, and inefficient tariff-protected farm implement manufacturers from 'down east.'

Like many Christians in the early century he believed in the "social gospel." Jesus had taught that people are social beings, and religion must develop the true social spirit that is the goal and destiny of humanity. Social co-operation among farmers as a group, then, was as much a way of bringing about a regeneration of humanity's spirit as it was a way to secure political reform. The true law of life was co-operation. The false law of life was competition. And the true law of co-operation was the only way in the long run — a long run with no quick fixes — to remedy social and economic injustice. Services in his Missouri church could be conducted by lay people as well as ministers, and by women as well as men. This fact doubtless influenced the key role played by the UFA in winning the vote for women.

As a young Missouri farmer, Wood established a mutual telephone company to compete with the Bell Telephone Company and force better service and rates. He won. A company within the Bell system took over Wood's company and provided the lower rates farmers had demanded. That early experience as agrarian organizer he would later put to use in Alberta. He would also bring with him a distaste for farmer groups diluting their strength, as he saw it, by entering party politics.

[1] The definitive biography on Wood, *Henry Wise Wood of Alberta*, was written by William Kirby Rolph (1917-1953) of the University of Saskatchewan history department, and published in 1950 by the University of Toronto Press. Rolph died in Australia in 1953 at the age of 36, while on a fellowship to study the history of the Country Party in Australia.

Sudden death claimed two of the first three leaders of the Alberta farm movement. The first president, James Bower (left) bred Percheron horses near Red Deer, and developed a reputation as a formidable debater, but he soon resigned. The second (centre), W.J. Tregillus, a devout Anglican and reformist, died of typhoid fever in 1914. The third, James Speakman, a farmer at Penhold, was paid $100 a month to recruit members, run the UFA, write for the Grain Growers' Guide *and conduct research. Within a year he came down with pneumonia and died.*

Agrarian unrest in the U.S. was already some decades old, American farmers being agitated by the same sense of voicelessness against grain companies and "eastern powers" that Canadians felt. Wood admired in particular the ideas of Uriel S. Hall, who headed the powerful Farmers' Alliance in Missouri and believed in controlling state politics through candidates pledged to support farmers. But then Hall himself was elected to Congress as an agrarian Democrat and soon abandoned the farmers. The apostasy of his hero, and the consequent breakup of the Alliance in internal squabbles over politics, left a lasting impression.

However prosperous and successful on his father's farm in Missouri, Wood wanted land to pass on to his own sons. Like perhaps a million other Americans, he was enticed by the cheap land in the Canadian West. He acquired a section at Carstairs in the year that Alberta became a province, took up wheat production and enrolled himself as a member of the Canadian Society of Equity.

Edmonton area farmers had formed the first Canadian offshoot of the new American Society of Equity in 1902. Like so many other farm organizations of the day — Farmers' Alliance, Populists, Progressivists in the United States, the Dominion Grange in Ontario, various co-operators from Britain — the Society of Equity was an attempt to wrest a better share of wealth and voice from monopolists and middlemen.

Alberta and other prairie farmers were developing world-scale production. During the Great

War Canada was exporting 56% of the world's wheat sales. Yet wheat prices were set in Winnipeg and Minneapolis, and they responded to the world price established in Liverpool, England. At home, middlemen, meaning the elevator companies, were widely felt to be cheating the farmers by underweighing, undergrading and excessively docking.

Canadian farmers had other grievances. They knew that Canadian wheat production had required an enormous capital investment, in railways, the never-enough boxcars and elevator systems. But they railed against the high interest rates levied on them to pay off these investments. They believed themselves at the mercy of railway barons, gouging banks, and inefficient tariff-protected farm implement manufacturers from "down east" who could charge far more for farm

The federal government talked, studied, promised, but did not act. Well then, farmers must take control of the market, said the Society of Equity. They will set the prices.

machinery than American farmers must pay. As historian Paul F. Sharp summarized in his 1948 book, *Agrarian Revolt in Western Canada*: "The prairie farmer, Canadian and American, was at the mercy of forces which he keenly resented but could control only slightly."

Wheat prices had risen steadily since the late 1890s. However, in 1909 they faltered, and by 1912 and 1913 they had collapsed. The Great War forced them higher than ever, but even then they failed to rise as fast and as far as did freight rates, farm equipment and bank rates. A Dominion board of inquiry found in 1915: "It was doubtful whether during these years the wheat growers were making much more than good wages." Though they had won a fixed freight rate in the famous Crow's Nest Pass Agreement of 1897 (Vol. I, pp. 168-9), they still believed themselves unfairly charged. They especially resented high rates on farm equipment coming in. The federal government talked, studied, promised, but did not act.

Well then, farmers must take control of the market, said the Society of Equity. They will set the prices, together, and will stick to them. The Edmonton group even published in the *Edmonton Bulletin* a list of the prices they would accept — and nothing less — for hay, oats, barley, hogs, beef, butter and eggs. But this price cartel never worked. For the main product, grains, consumption was outside Alberta and local syndicates could not control the prices. The society launched co-operative enterprises to build elevators and other projects, which collapsed. The plans were too

The semi-monthly meeting of the Lakeview Branch of the UFA was held at Lakeview on Saturday, November 23, and was fairly well attended. It was unanimously agreed that the resolutions recently passed re: parcels post and binder twine be submitted to the annual convention. A resolution was also unanimously passed that we, the members of the Lakeview Branch of the UFA, do hereby request the members of the Provincial Legislature to have a measure passed at the next session whereby a system of government by direct legislation will be put on the statutes of this province.
–*Donald Cameron, Secretary-Treasurer reporting in the UFA section of the Jan. 8, 1913,* **Grain Growers' Guide.**

The board of the United Farm Women of Alberta, 1919. Irene Parlby (third from left, front row) warned them: 'Keep the larger community values before you, so that you will not run the danger of becoming a purely commercial machine, a fault from which so many men's locals suffer.' *

*Shown in this historic photograph are: (L to R, back row) Mrs. J.W. Field, Mrs. J. Dowler, Mrs. M.J. Sears, Mrs. O.S. Welch, Mrs. Macquire, Mrs. Charles Henderson; (front row) Mrs. A.M. Postans, Mrs. J.F. Ross, Mrs. W.H. Parlby, Mrs. Paul Carr, Miss Mary W. Spiller.

grandiose and the society was torn by internal dissension. Among those who had to swallow the loss of $7.50 on each $10 share they had bought was wheat farmer Henry Wise Wood of Carstairs.

Meanwhile, other farmers had similar ideas. In Lacombe in 1902 the Farmers' Association of Alberta was formed. It was "built on the ruins of an 1899 co-operative purchasing association modelled on the Rochdale Pioneers of Britain," recounts author Tom Monto in his history of the UFA, published in 1989. They formed branches, they ran a federal election candidate in the 1904 election (he came third), and they collapsed. Some surviving members went into the Society of Equity, some into a new Alberta Farmers' Association (AFA) formed in Strathcona in 1905. The

Henry Wise Wood's message to war-weary Albertans

Henry Wise Wood, the man called the "Uncrowned King of Alberta," was accused of everything from religious fanaticism to Bolshevism, and was unswerving in his Christian convictions.

He therefore surprised many, and alienated some of his more radical supporters, by vigorously supporting Canada's war effort and urging farmers to the maximum possible production.

The following was taken from his "Call to Arms" to western farmers, as carried in the Calgary Herald *on Jan. 22, 1918, when Russia had made peace with Germany and, for the Allies, the war had reached a point of crisis:*

"Simple duty calls to each and every farmer of Alberta to produce all he can till this war is over. The war — the actual conflict — has reached our farms...

"If we spend our time quibbling over the wrongs others are doing, quibbling over the prices which are already reasonable and profitable, while multitudes of helpless women and children are starving to death and our military efforts are in danger of breaking down for want of the things we should be producing, how will we ever justify ourselves before the world or before unborn generations of our own children?

"The farmers of western Canada are building an economic and political force. We possess the elements of a mighty power. The only safe foundation upon which we can erect this force is the true principle, the divine law, that right makes right. If we build on this foundation we have nothing to fear, for all other forces built on the same basis will harmonize and co-operate with us, and forces built on false basic principles will not be able to stand before us.

"We have nothing to fear from false charges [that farmers were profiteering from the war]. The only thing we have to fear is ourselves. We are face to face with responsibilities which will not give us a chance to be profiteers [since farmers did not set the prices of their wheat or meat], but they will force us to uncover our souls and show to the world whether we have the mean spirit of the profiteers or the spirit of true men."

AFA quickly became the strongest farmers' group, concentrating on educating its members and lobbying politicians.

On Jan. 15, 1909, in an historic meeting in Edmonton, came the development that would set the course of Alberta economic and political history for the next quarter-century. The Society of Equity and the AFA merged. Then, reported the *Edmonton Bulletin*, the 100 delegates braved the thirty-below weather (i.e. -22 C°) and "marched down the snowy Sixth Street hill...in line, four abreast" to meet Premier A.C. Rutherford at the opening of the final session of the first Legislature

Provincial Archives of Alberta, A-14708

The UFA worked hard, and played hard too

Debates, whist drives, box and basket socials, livestock and farm fairs — the UFA sponsored all sorts of social affairs. But picnics were the favourites, and could go on for days. Pictured above is one at 25 Ranch, near Nanton, in 1915. Opposite page, top, shows singing at a picnic at Hutton, on the Red Deer River forty miles southeast of Drumheller, on Victoria Day 1913; below it is a 1916 picnic at Dupont's Bottom, near Lethbridge. (For many years the Sunday nearest May 24 was celebrated as UFA Sunday.) At the immediate right, revellers pose at a masque ball held in Calgary by the United Grain Growers on New Year's Eve 1917.

of the new province. They represented 5,000 members from 122 locals, mostly in northern Alberta. Farmers, added the *Bulletin*, are "a most powerful factor in the upbuilding of the province." The new organization was to be called the United Farmers of Alberta. Its motto: "Equity!"

Thus too began the UFA's intimacy with the provincial Liberal government, a link that would last twelve years. It soon won from the government legislation establishing hail insurance, new regional railroads and the Alberta Farmers' Co-operative Elevator Company. Later it would extract promises of female suffrage and Prohibition.

The UFA Convention at Central Methodist Church, Calgary, 1916, the convention that elected Henry Wise Wood president for the first of fifteen times. Already the movement was gravely split on the question of 'going political.'

The UFA's first purpose, it announced, was "to educate [farmers] in collective action, a knowledge of the legal and political rights, and an appreciation of their calling." That the farmer should be considered a member of a "class" did not denote Marxism, the founding statement explained, and was not intended to promote class warfare, but rather to promote self-respect. Henry Wise Wood's ideas of the farmer class were anticipated here, though he was not a founder of the UFA.

The goal of the UFA was co-operative effort, so that "the moral, intellectual and financial status of the farmer may be improved thereby." The UFA would "watch, influence and promote legislation..." but never be a party or endorse any politician. Another objective was "to encourage the establishment of an equitable banking system," a principle the descendant CCF and Social Credit would embrace in different ways.

No sooner had it been founded than the UFA began proliferating all over the province. By April 1911 the number of locals had doubled to 270. The membership jumped from 5,000 to 13,000. It was member-controlled. Local meetings became a vehicle to educate young people "on their rights, duties and responsibilities so that they may understand the evil effects of vicious legislation upon their calling." They were to press for new markets and a better marketing system. Locals brought policy proposals to annual conventions.

From their first convention, at Red Deer in January 1910, the UFA supported the devices of initiative, referendum and recall. Initiative meant that voters by petition could force the calling of a voter referendum on proposed legislation. Referendum meant that the vote of the electorate would bind the Legislature. Recall meant that on petition of a given percentage of voters, a member could be forced to resign and face another election. Thus it was possible for an electoral

The doughty journal that fuelled the crusade

WITH RADICAL EDITORIALS, PUNGENT ARGUMENT AND CAUSTIC CARTOONS THE *GRAIN GROWERS' GUIDE* BECAME OTTAWA'S BANE IN THE WEST

by George Oake

When Conservative leader Robert Borden journeyed west in the summer of 1910 he referred to his venture in "G-G Country," or Grain Growers' country, as though he was travelling to some exotic and dangerous land where the natives waited in ambush.

But the appellation G-G might better have read G-G-G because Borden's western nemesis was the *Grain Growers' Guide*, a monthly newspaper with the cutting edge of a scythe and the power of a two-bottom plough in the political hardpan of the prairies of 1910 to 1920.

While the *Guide* contained erudite and prolix articles on such essentials as fertilizers and farm machinery, it was also a journal of political and philosophical ideas, laid out by a dazzling array of thinkers like the Rev. J.S. Woodsworth, later founder of the Co-operative Commonwealth Federation, the political ancestor of the New Democratic Party. Woodsworth wrote a column entitled "Sermons for the Unsatisfied," a term that described virtually every western farmer.

The leavening was supplied by Arch Dale, a cartoonist whose caustic pen-and-ink caricatures of the politicians of the time would make him a legend. His finely detailed style was forty years ahead of its time in both wit and artistry.

Add to that Gustavus Myers' trenchant views on Canadian wealth, the feminist polemics of Nellie McClung and Emily Murphy, and the pacifist pronouncements of Francis Beynon, and readers had a manual for reform[a]. But women's rights, pacifism and socialism were mere footnotes to the *Guide*'s major crusade of a co-operative movement among the country's farmers.

The lofty principles proclaimed on its masthead declared: "The *Guide* is designed to give uncoloured views from the world of thought and action and honest opinions thereon, with the object of aiding our people to form correct views upon economic, social and moral questions, so that the growth of society may continually be in the direction of more equitable, kinder and wiser relations between the members, resulting in the widest possible increase and diffusion of material prosperity, intellectual development, right living, health and happiness."

But not all the *Guide*'s views were uncoloured, and it often saw red in its rant against corporate wealth and high protective Canadian tariffs that lined the pockets of Ontario manufacturers at the expense of western farmers. "Always bear in mind that the good old patriotic slogan of the Canadian Manufacturers' Association — 'Canada for the Canadians' — means Canada for 2,500 Canadians," snarled the *Guide* in a 1910 thrust at Ontario's rich and elite.

In fact, as Henri Bourassa's *Le Devoir* became the rallying cry for French Canadian nationalism, the *Grain Growers' Guide* established itself as the voice of the farm movement, which would create a political revolution in the 1920s. In the 1911 campaign, however, its

Western Canada Pictorial Index, 1977-61909

Edward Partridge, the extraordinary farmer from Sintaluta, Saskatchewan, who accomplished much but suffered a sad personal fate.

In one of the Guide's first Christmas issues, it was not above providing a child's prayer with a political message.

Glenbow Archives, NA-4407-1

THE MILCH COW

' artist has here attempted to portray the idea which the Big Interests of Eastern Canada seem to have of the proper function of the Western Provinces. The Bankers, Railway Corporations and the Manufacturers rejoice to see a big crop in the West because it will increase their own profits, but when the farmers of the West ask for er rates of interest, lower freight rates and Free Trade, so that they can get the full value of the crops they produce, Big Business, with the aid of the Party Politicians, ays succeeds in having their demands refused.

Arch Dale's most famous cartoon, entitled `The Milch Cow,' expressed the Guide's view of Canadian economics. Below, cartoonist Dale at work in his later years.

editors opposed the formation of a third party as a "hazardous undertaking." But by 1916, it had become disgusted by Ottawa's inaction on agricultural issues such as tariffs and supported the efforts of those in the farm movement who wanted to "go political."

"More and more it becomes evident that the West should declare a western policy in western interests and send to Ottawa members who will support that policy regardless of the two political parties," the *Guide* declared. Like the Reform Party movement that took hold in western Canada eighty years later, it supported "recall," the device that empowered electors on petition to force a sitting member to resign, thereby causing a by-election. "To put a man in office and leave him there for five years, so that he is absolute in his power, makes a farce of representative government," the *Guide* editorialized in 1910.

Yet for all its faith in raw democracy the *Guide* later deplored anarchy or the communism that was embraced by so many "progressive" North American periodicals in the wake of the Russian Revolution. When the 1919 Winnipeg General Strike occurred the *Guide* did not approve. The strike leaders, it declared, were preaching "the doctrines of Bolshevism, confiscation and rule by force." This served to increase the schism between farmers and organized labour in Canada's burgeoning industrial cities, it said.

Like so many other things on the prairies, the *Guide*

answered a need. The western news media did not adequately voice the discontent of radical Ontario reform Liberals who had moved west or the thousands of American farmers who had migrated north bringing the message of agrarian populism with them. To this mix was added a surge of trade unionists from Great Britain, some of whom became farmers, still brooding over the injustices of class, privilege and monopoly. These formed the readership of the *Guide*.

The man who pulled it all together was Edward Alexander Partridge, a veteran of the Northwest Rebellion from Sintaluta, Saskatchewan, who in 1906, appalled at the machinations of the Winnipeg Grain Exchange, organized the Grain Growers' Grain Company, a co-operative, and gained for it a seat on the grain exchange. His fulminations against the grain trade soon saw him expelled from the exchange. But his opponents didn't reckon with his Messianic skill as a farm organizer and the political muscle of the farmers when aroused. Manitoba Premier Rodmond Roblin forced the exchange to reinstate the Grain Growers' Grain Company.

Partridge never resumed his seat on the exchange, though, because he was already off and running on new schemes. Chief among them was something called the Partridge Plan, or the public ownership of all grain elevators. The federal government rejected such socialistic ideas, but the three prairie provincial governments established a co-operative elevator system with public financing. Meanwhile, Partridge had already moved on to his next project — the establishment of a regular agrarian newspaper. The Manitoba and Saskatchewan Grain Growers' Association and the United Farmers of Alberta formed an interprovincial council in 1907 and endorsed the idea. Thus the *Guide* was born.

The first issue appeared in June 1908, and characteristically Partridge was already attempting a new idea — an alliance of the *Guide* with the labour movement. But the farmers mistrusted labour, and the irrepressible Partridge was replaced after the first issue by Roderick McKenzie, secretary of the Manitoba Grain Growers' Association. He was succeeded in 1911 by George F. Chipman, a reporter for the *Manitoba Free Press*, who remained editor of the *Guide* until 1930.

Chipman was instrumental in promoting a farmers' march on Ottawa in 1910, histrionically known as "the Siege of Ottawa." Nevertheless, it was the largest demonstration on Parliament Hill up to that point. Five hundred western grain growers were joined by 300 others from Ontario, Quebec and the Maritimes.

Despite the paper's influence — circulation rose from a few thousand in 1908 to more than 110,000 in the late 1920s — the *Guide* was never financially secure and its fortunes seemed to rise and fall with that of the Progressive movement, which was eventually absorbed by the national parties.

By the standards of the day, the *Guide* was a handsome publication, with cover drawings and photographs carefully thought out. Early editions featured a woman on a pedestal holding the scales of justice. The plinth bore a single word, Equity. By 1921 there were photo covers, one of them showing a farmer on snowshoes carrying a rifle. A frozen-stiff timber wolf was slung over his shoulder, and the caption read, "The Trophy." The animal-rightists of a later generation would have been appalled.

Partridge, meanwhile, had eventually exhausted himself. He organized the Square Deal Grain Company. After it folded in 1913, he returned to become the "Sage of Sintaluta," revered by many in the farm movement. His

Provincial Archives of Manitoba, N-13687

Western Canada Pictorial Index, 1977-61917

Canada's Prosperity—and Its Foundation

Editor George Chipman (bottom right) promoted the 1910 march on Ottawa by 800 grain growers. Women's editor Francis Beynon (top right) was a fiercely militant pacifist. A 1910 Guide *cartoon by Dick Hartley (above left) succinctly expresses the paper's core conviction: The farmers were carrying the nation on their backs.*

1926 book, *A War on Poverty*, was described by one reviewer as "a strange mixture of Ruskinian socialism, old Ontario Toryism, western Utopianism and religious fervour." It advocated that western Canada separate and create a new state called Coalsamao[b]. Partridge himself was a depressive. He died in 1931, probably by suicide.

By 1928 the *Guide* had lost its original fervour and had become in effect a magazine of advice for farmers and rural entertainment. It was then taken over by the United Grain Growers who published it as a magazine for the rest of the century under the title *Country Guide*.

[a]Francis Beynon was the *Guide's* feisty women's editor who spelled her name with the masculine form, rather than the feminine Frances. An advertising writer for Eaton's in Winnipeg, one of the first women in such a profession, she became a journalist and women's editor of the *Guide*. At the outbreak of the Great War, she called upon women to refuse to send their sons 'to be shot down in order to settle a dispute between nations or to gratify the greed of gun-making corporations.' Her pacifism became so militant that by 1917 even the *Guide* couldn't live with her and she was forced to resign. She moved to the U.S., later returned to Canada and died in Winnipeg in 1951 aged 68.

[b]Coalsamao (pronounced *Co-al-sa-ma-o*) was derived from the first letters of the provinces that would make it up (British) COlumbia, ALberta, SAskatchewan, MAnitoba, and part of Ontario. It was to be a self-constituted co-operative commonwealth with the motto, 'Each for all and all for each.'

majority to force the Legislature to take up a proposal and (by recalling him) they could oust any MLA who attempted to stop it.

Many locals made an early start at co-operative buying of supplies in bulk and the selling of produce and insurance. They became the centres of community organizing. They built "co-operative halls," then gathered in them for lectures and discussions, followed by hearty meals and lively square dances. They held picnics — "the highlight of many a farm family's summer for they attracted people from far and near," says one history. They sponsored debates, whist drives, box and basket socials, livestock and farm fairs. They held working bees, and organized travelling libraries. All of this built what one writer calls "a sense of agrarian kinship." Even more, they inculcated a cast of mind that went deep, an outlook on the far-off big interests and big parties that for decades remained assertively Albertan.

Free or freer trade with the United States was pursued more assiduously by the UFA than by other western Canada farm organizations. Prime Minister Sir Wilfrid Laurier, on his famous 1910 tour of the West, was met at Red Deer by the first UFA president, James Bower. Bower presented a resolution that said the protective tariff against U.S. goods "is but the levying of tribute upon the people, not for the legitimate expenses of the government, but for a private and privileged class...and to the prejudice of agricultural interests." The UFA wanted Canada to negotiate reciprocal reduction of U.S. duties on livestock — cattle, horses, swine, sheep and poultry. Laurier, impressed, persuaded his Liberal party to accept American overtures for a reciprocity agreement, leading his government into destruction as a result (Sect. 2, ch. 1).

But in the course of that campaign the victorious Conservative leader, Robert Borden, put the Tory party definitively on the line. The Grain Growers are powerful "in this western country," he

---

Alberta farmers drew a lasting lesson. 'The rest of Canada must bow to Ontario,' the *Grain Growers' Guide* observed bitterly. That was a fact never forgotten.

---

told a farmers' delegation in Brandon. "But if it were ten times what it is, and if you were able and prepared to make me prime minister tomorrow on condition that I would support this [reciprocity] pact, I would not do it."

That doomed reciprocity. But it also helped doom the Tory party in Alberta for the next half-century. For that was the tone the farmers heard — obdurate, sententious and harsh. Some 200 locals of the UFA's 270 in April of 1911 forwarded resolutions to Ottawa supporting reciprocity. Said the *Lethbridge Herald:* "...the representatives of the agricultural sections of Alberta in the Dominion House will take note of the resolutions passed." The UFA was alone among prairie farm organizations in officially endorsing reciprocity, though all campaigned for it. And all were crushed. Laurier and reciprocity suffered a smashing defeat (Sect. 2, ch. 1). But in Alberta his Liberals took every constituency but one. From this, Alberta farmers drew a lasting lesson. "The rest of Canada must bow to Ontario," the *Grain Growers' Guide* observed bitterly. That was a fact never forgotten.

But political defeat far from discouraged Alberta and western farmers. Rather, it made them fighting mad. Before the election, when 800 farmers demonstrated in what was grandly called "the Siege of Ottawa," Laurier had promised the action that resulted in the Reciprocity Agreement. The *Lethbridge Herald* noted that westerners "predominated" in the delegation, and enthused: "It will not be long before Canada will speak as the West speaks." Alas, after the election the same newspaper was left to comment: "The flag-waving period is passed; the farmers see for themselves that it was merely the ruse of the interests to catch them in the high-tariff net." The *Herald*'s publisher, W.A. Buchanan, now a member of parliament, in his maiden speech to the Commons tackled eastern Conservative allegations that Alberta's pro-reciprocity vote demonstrated an anti-Dominion sense pervasive in western Canada:

"There is no desire on their [westerners'] part for any tariff which would wreck any legitimate industry in this country. But, Sir, we think we are entitled to consideration, and we believe that reciprocity with the United States is in the best interests of western Canada and in the best interests of eastern Canada."

The Alberta Non Partisan, June 19, 1919

UFA resentment over the power of eastern banks and manufacturers (below right) had been boiling since the defeat of Reciprocity in 1911; it would continue to boil for decades to come. In the cartoon at right, Non-Partisan League stalwarts eye the advancing army of UFA locals with interest, and some dismay.

Glenbow Archives, NA-3055-27

The farmers' response to the 1911 election result was thunderous. They joined the UFA in waves, many urging repeal of the clause forbidding the UFA from running political candidates. After a hot fight in the 1912 convention in Edmonton, the UFA voted strongly for the third consecutive year not to form its own party. One delegate identified as G. Lively of Islay had the convention "in an uproar a number of times," said the *Edmonton Journal*. "He arraigned the trusts and special interests in scathing terms and declared they controlled both the existing parties." Henry Wise Wood was a delegate to that convention but played no prominent part in a debate that was going his own way anyway. The UFA threatened to boycott high-priced Canadian farm machinery. And it called on the Edmonton government to take over all railways in the province. But it did not vote to "go political."

By now the UFA was clearly the prime agricultural force in the province. The government of Arthur L. Sifton, who replaced the scandal-tainted Rutherford in 1910 (Vol. II, Sect. 6, ch. 2), deferred to it quickly and

Spying Out the Land

often[2]. In effect, a UFA-Liberal alliance was in force. The UFA executive helped write the act establishing the Alberta Farmers' Co-operative Elevator Company as a 1913 answer to years of complaints that the corporately owned elevators shortchanged farmers. To provide competition with the 2,000 private elevators in Alberta, the government advanced 85% of the $8,000 to $13,000 cost of each elevator, with the farmer-owners raising the rest. In the first year, 46 elevators were built. The Alberta co-op merged with its Manitoba counterpart, the Grain Growers' Grain Company, in September 1917 to form United Grain Growers Ltd.

Alberta farmers flocked to their own elevators. In 1914 they brought them 3.8 million bushels, and 16.4 million bushels by 1917. The company, a financial success from the start, handled the marketing of farmers' livestock as well as grain, and the co-operative purchasing of their coal, flour, binder twine and other supplies.

In return for the elevator and other legislation passed at the request of the UFA — hail insurance, support for provincial railroads, a bill to permit "direct legislation" — the UFA made it clear to members that Sifton should be supported. Accordingly, he won 38 of the 56 seats in the 1913 election (Sect. 2, ch. 2).

The direct legislation bill was in response to the UFA's goal of initiative, referendum and recall. The act would permit a plebiscite to be held if 20% of the electorate signed a petition favouring a piece of legislation. If the public then voted for it, the Legislative Assembly would make it law.

[2]Not all in the Sifton cabinet were enchanted by the UFA. Rolph says that one angry minister told UFA members to 'go home and slop the hogs.' Rolph does not identify the minister.

Financing and credit became a central concern of both the future Social Credit and CCF parties. It was the abiding problem for farmers and of the UFA from its inception. In frustration, the UFA adopted the following resolution at its annual convention at Red Deer in 1910, with which both future parties would toy:

WHEREAS the banking system is a mystery to most of the rank and file of people and

WHEREAS there exists a grave suspicion that the financial institutions are taking a very unjust toll of real values from the people who produce real wealth in return for fictitious values and service and

WHEREAS it is our duty to prevent exploitation and spread education on these matters

THEREFORE BE IT RESOLVED that this convention go on record as in favour of the nationalization of our banking and credit system.

This conflict with the banks would become a battlecry of the Social Credit movement in the 1930s, and even find an echo decades later in the oil boom, when repeated efforts were made to establish western-based banks and free the province of Toronto- or Montreal-based financial control. Meanwhile, the eastern-based ones lost tens of millions of dollars when the Alberta oil boom collapsed, then determinedly cut off most credit to Alberta business, further exacerbating the ancient distrust and animosity.

[3]A year later, announcing the date of the second UFA Sunday (May 27, 1917), Wood said that Jesus was the philosopher for whom people were searching to answer 'all the great problems of a confused and perplexed civilization.' Through Christ the 'true civilization' had to be built 'in the most practical intercourse of everyday life.'

Arthur Sifton reluctantly brought in Prohibition after 58,295 Albertans voted for it, and 37,209 against, on July 21, 1915 (see ch. 1, this section). Local UFA groups organized, held rallies, sponsored hundreds of local projects, not only assuring the outcome of the Prohibition vote but also training activists for later popular campaigns, including the ones that brought it to power.

Indeed, such moral crusades were dear to the agrarian reformer. Political corruption was deeply felt, not only in far-away Ottawa, but right at home, as was demonstrated in the Alberta & Great Waterways scandal that had destroyed the Rutherford government. The UFA shared the conviction of the women's movement that such corruption would be purged if women took part in politics. Hence the formation of the United Farm Women of Alberta in 1916, and the strong UFA support for female suffrage. Irene Parlby, first UFWA president, endorsed this sentiment. It was the duty of the UFWA, Mrs. Parlby told a UFA convention in 1919, "to keep the larger community values before you, so that you will not run the danger of becoming a purely commercial machine, a fault from which so many men's locals suffer."

It was the UFA's convention of January 1916 that elected Henry Wise Wood president for the first of fifteen times. Wood, by now active in the UFA, had been defeated in a run for the presidency in 1915 by James Speakman of Penhold. A 66-year-old Englishman who spoke German "and several other European languages," Speakman had been a founding director. He was persuaded to move from his farm to Calgary, and was paid $100 a month to conduct a membership drive, run the UFA's affairs, be the Alberta contributor to the *Grain Growers' Guide*, and conduct research into and advocate cheaper loan capital for farmers. However, he came down with pneumonia and died in December 1915, a month before the next convention.

A similar fate had befallen his predecessor, the second president, W.J. Tregillus, who supplied Calgary with milk from a herd of Holsteins and drove a spirited team of hackneys through the streets of the city. Tregillus, a man of strong reformist conviction, a devout Anglican, and an advocate of political party involvement against the theories of Henry Wood, was president of the UFA and the co-operative elevator company when he died of typhoid fever on Nov. 12, 1914, at 56.

On January 15, 1909, in an historic meeting in Edmonton, came the development that would set the course of Alberta economic and political history for the next quarter-century.

The first president, James Bower, had come out from Ontario and made a name as a breeder of Percheron horses with his three sons near Red Deer. He had been active in farm organizations before and developed a national reputation as a formidable debater. He declined to stand in 1912.

Thus it was that Henry Wood assumed the leadership of a movement that had been led by skilful reformists. His own first action as president was to take up Resolution 63, tabled by the Roseview Union, and to personally move it: "That the Sunday nearest May 24th, Empire Day, be officially declared UFA Sunday, to be set apart for the discussion of UFA affairs from a religious viewpoint."[3] Years later, Norman F. Priestly, a Methodist minister who became a farm and co-operative leader through to the 1950s, was to write of UFA Sunday:

> In subsequent years at many points throughout the province from the Dunvegan Crossing of the Peace River to the national park Writing On Stone near the International Boundary at Milk River, UFA Sunday was held in the open air with the service conducted by local clergymen, or officers of the organization. Denominational differences were temporarily forgotten, and public worship held in God's great out-of-doors, sometimes with the aid of a public address system or of a piano atop a large farm truck. It is a sad fact that the disunity brought about by political action in later years caused the abandonment of this excellent form of community effort.

The UFA eased some problems, though it could never entirely solve them. One was the shortage of railway boxcars to move grain. The *Lethbridge Herald* in January of 1912 reported that southern Alberta had shipped fewer than four million bushels of an eleven-million-bushel crop. If the car shortage were not soon solved, said the *Herald*, it would "cause an untold loss to the farmers of the south, and cause a financial depression." The boxcar problem would continue well into the century, but judicious applications of public heat and anger moved Ottawa to help the railway companies provide more cars from time to time, usually at the taxpayers' expense.

The failure to gain reciprocity in the 1911 election by no means silenced Alberta's demand for it. But the Borden government seemed set against the western interest. It raised tariffs, rather than lowering them. The outbreak of war in 1914, if anything, made things worse. While eastern industry flourished through war production, its profits rising and largely untaxed, the farm economy declined. The great immigration influx was cut off. The land boom stopped abruptly. A shortage of labour developed, increasing the cost of producing wheat and meat in soaring quantities to

---

Henry Wise Wood therefore had to bend, or break, as the UFA met in annual convention in January 1919, to adopt the New National Policy. He bent — in part.

Direct legislation by the initiative and referendum is not a tool or machine for turning things upside down, but a political tool by which the people may turn their public business right side up. Where politicians rule we find public affairs in private hands; where the people rule we find public affairs in the hands of the people. It does not interfere with any legitimate or constitutional function of the Legislature, nor does it substitute legislation by the 'ignorant masses' for legislation by 'experts.' Mere election to a legislative body does not make a man an expert. Anyone who knows anything of legislative bodies knows that experts are very rare in Legislatures.
–from 'People's Power in Oregon' by W.G. Eggleston of Portland, Oregon, in the Jan. 1, 1913, Grain Growers' Guide.

feed the Allied nations. True, wheat prices — which hit a low for the decade of 67 cents a bushel in 1913 — began rising again[4]. And western farm acreage increased nearly 80% from 1913 to 1919 under appeals to patriotism and profit. But the cost of everything the farmer used began to rise more sharply. Though wheat prices rose, high interest rates and debt charges continued, and the costs of farm equipment and transportation rose faster. "By 1917 most farmers were less well off than they had been in 1914," wrote Wood's biographer Rolph. "The action of the government in raising the tariff and controlling agricultural prices while leaving war profits largely untaxed convinced thousands of western farmers that the federal political parties were run for the benefit of the privileged few."

Acreage yields rose and then fell. Bumper crops in 1915 and 1916 briefly raised farm optimism. In 1915 Alberta wheat growers averaged 31 bushels to the acre, best in the country. Then came devastating crop failures in 1918 and 1919, at averages of just over seven bushels to the acre, the worst yield on the prairies. One effect was to drive farmers deeper into debt.

Labour costs were particularly irksome. Henry Wood told the UFA in January 1918 that the federal government had given "unmistakable instructions...to exempt all bona fide farmers" from conscription into the military services because farming was "just as vital to the carrying on of the war as the service being rendered in the trenches." Those "unmistakable instructions" fell apart just three months later and a new farm uproar developed when exemptions for farmers aged 20 to 22 were removed.

This created a crisis in the farm movement itself. After an angry debate, the UFA telegraphed its support of the federal decision. The front line, after all, must come first. Ontario farmers had marched on Ottawa to protest against it. Borden read the Ontarians the Alberta telegram. Wood hurried to Toronto and apologized to an angry mass meeting of 2,000 Ontario farmers because the Alberta telegram had been "used against you." He said it had not been worded quite correctly, although it did in fact largely mirror his own sentiments. The rift was soon resolved, but Alberta farmers became more convinced than ever that the traditional parties simply could not be trusted. Even so, they did not slack in producing food: Canadian wheat exports grew from 114.9 million bushels in 1913 to 139.9 million bushels in 1920.

As the war progressed, the Borden government seemed increasingly ill-disposed towards the West. In 1917 the railways were allowed to increase their freight rates. Ottawa refused frequent requests for free trade with the United States in wheat and agricultural implements. Indeed, in 1915 general tariffs were raised 7 1/2% but controls on wheat export prices were imposed in 1917 (albeit at $2.21 per bushel for No. 1 Northern in storage at Fort William, a price seen by Wood and many others as fair). Many western dissenters nonetheless felt farmers should be able to cash in on wartime prices. There were certainly no price controls on manufactured goods.

In this spreading sense of unfair treatment, the Canadian Council of Agriculture (the CCA) of which Wood was an active director[5] produced a December 1916 "Farmers' Platform" that became rural Canada's political rallying cry. At bedrock was the belief that "Parliament is becoming more and more under the direct influence of industrial, financial and transportation interests, represented by men of wealth in financial and industrial centres."

[4]Wheat prices in Alberta: 1913, $0.67 a bushel; 1914, $0.91; 1915, $0.88; 1916, $1.33. Wheat prices at Winnipeg: 1913, average $0.87 a bushel; 1917, average $2.20.

[5]The Canadian Council of Agriculture would later become the Canadian Federation of Agriculture.

[6]The term 'New National Policy' was an allusion to the National Policy of Sir John A. Macdonald's Tories which envisioned the West as primary producers required to buy from tariff-protected industries in Ontario and Quebec (Vol. I, p. 236). Hence the New National Policy was the reverse of the old National Policy.

The Farmers' Platform called for free trade. To replace tariff revenues, it wanted a graduated income tax, taxes on corporate profits, an inheritance tax and a tax on unimproved land (to discourage speculation and encourage production). Railways would be nationalized, along with express and telegraph companies. Political reforms would include abolition of patronage, and the use of initiative, referendum and recall. None of the demands was new, or by later world standards particularly radical, but they came together in one coherent package, born of frustration. "The persistent neglect of the farmers' problems and the refusal of the government to make any serious effort to meet their demands had finally led to this political outburst," writes biographer Rolph. The following month the UFA's annual convention endorsed the platform and declared that politicians had to support it if they wanted agrarian backing.

Two years later the CCA produced a New National Policy[6] consisting of the Farmers' Platform with post-war additions such as reform of the Senate, admission of women to Parliament, and a far greater degree of autonomy for Canada. The key clause was that farmers' associations would only back candidates who supported the New National Policy. That came closer still to direct political action, an issue the UFA had to face at the next annual convention, in Edmonton in January 1919.

Henry Wise Wood and his adherents wanted "group government." They saw classes or groups competing on even terms with each other to pressure governments, not themselves *be* governments. But ever since the reciprocity election in 1911, this ideal had been meeting growing internal opposition. Now, with the Great War ended, the idea of direct political action began spreading like a fever through the local UFA unions, Wood's views notwithstanding. If the businessmen and lawyers sent to the Legislative Assembly and Parliament ignore the farmers, so ran the argument, then the farmers must go there and represent themselves. The movement was fanned by executive members within the UFA who also belonged to the Non-Partisan League, a political phenomenon of the times that was both influential and brief.

The Non-Partisan League had originated in the agrarian discontent of North Dakota where it had been swept to power in state elections. From there its ideas migrated north into Saskatchewan and thence, early in 1917, into Alberta. The policy of the league took the Farmers' Platform and New National Policy a step further to the left, requiring even more nationalization — of terminal elevators and flour mills, of banking and credit systems and public utilities. Organized farmers would enter politics, and would take political action together with labour. Both moves were directly contrary to Wood's doctrine.

Much as they respected Wood, people like Ontario-born UFA vice-president James Weir of Parkland often opposed Wood's support of the federal Union government, a Conservative-Liberal coalition formed to enact conscription for military service. They likewise opposed his stand against direct political action. Weir conspicuously spoke for, and became a leader of, the NPL. So did other

UFA executive members, such as J.W. Leedy, former Populist governor of Kansas[7], and W.D. Trego[8]. Its most effective public speaker and writer was the Rev. William Irvine, the Presbyterian-turned-Unitarian minister and editor who became a leading figure in the socialist movement in Canada. In the League's first newspaper, *The Nut Cracker*, Irvine wrote that the party system "with its hollow sham and hypocrisy, special privilege in legislation, a rotten civil service, narrow-minded nationalism and pretended patriotism, has got to go." That cry had been uttered many times before within the UFA and found resonance with farmers. The difference was that this time it came with a call to direct action.

Within months of its inception, the NPL ran four candidates in the 1917 Alberta election and elected two — Weir himself for Nanton and Louise C. McKinney for Claresholm. In her first crack at provincial politics, the temperance leader became the first woman elected to a legislative seat in the British Empire. A spate of farmer activism ensued across the province. UFA locals in increasing numbers endorsed the league in 1918 and 1919, forcing the UFA's executive to fight back or perhaps perish.

Henry Wood therefore had to bend, or break, as the UFA met in annual convention in January 1919, to adopt the New National Policy. He bent — in part, engineering the position that direct political action would be up to local UFA unions to decide, on local merits. The result of this was a showdown with the NPL in each local. Would the farmers be represented by the NPL, or by a candidate running directly on a UFA ticket? In hard-fought meetings in towns across Alberta, the NPL sought to be the UFA's semi-autonomous political wing and Wood adherents fought against any splitting of UFA authority.

In bruising battles, with Wood stubbornly resisting all suggested compromises, the older, larger and wealthier organization gradually began to prevail. The idea of a "political action committee" within the UFA was defeated. Peacemakers within the NPL, especially Weir himself, began to yield, fearing a mortal split within Alberta's premier farmer organization between Wood adherents and a political action body. Thus it was Weir, more than Wood, who made possible the union of 6,000 NPL members and 19,000 UFA members at the 1919 convention. However, the following year, the UFA convention overwhelmingly returned Wood as president.

It was now a new, united and formidable organization, and it looked forward eagerly to its first test of strength in the provincial election that would occur the following year (Sect. 7, ch. 3). There was, however, a grave difficulty. Wood might compromise the UFA, but he would not compromise himself. This left the political aspirations of the UFA leaderless. It had everything a party needed: poll by poll organization at the constituency level, overwhelming grassroots support, clear policy objectives, but no leader. If it won, who would be premier? In 1920, nobody had an answer.

[7]Leedy had a curious political history that culminated in Alberta. He was elected to the Kansas State Senate in 1892, became 30th governor of Kansas from 1897 to 1899, moved to the Alaska territory in 1901 for health reasons and became mayor of Valdez, emigrated to Canada in 1910 and took up farming at Whitecourt. He ran unsuccessfully in the 1917 provincial election as an independent.

[8]W.D. Trego had been in the implement business in Iowa. He moved to Gleichen in 1906. He was elected fourth vice-president of the UFA in 1915 and first vice-president in 1916.

Section Five

THE BIG BUST OF 1914-15

The economic downturn of 1914-15 struck hard at every business and every community in Alberta, but for Edmonton there was a double calamity. The North Saskatchewan River rose 48 feet above normal level in 1915, driving 2,000 from their homes and blacking out the city. Edmontonians feared — with good reason — it would wash out the Low Level Bridge. The Canadian Northern Railway stationed two locomotives and fourteen gravel-loaded boxcars on the bridge, to stabilize it. This saved the structure.

Glenbow Archives, NC-6-1432

Construction crews muscle the ties into position as the Canadian Northern pushes forward to Athabasca Landing where service was opened in 1912. Behind them comes the tracklayer. The scene was being duplicated at points all over the province in the great rail-building frenzy of 1910 to 1914.

Glenbow Archives, NA-1712-1

CHAPTER ONE

Five railways plunge into ruin and the Canadian National is born

MACKENZIE & MANN'S VISIONARY ROAD REACHES THE COAST AND DIES; THE BRITISH LOSE MILLIONS WHEN OTTAWA GRABS THE GRAND TRUNK

by TED BYFIELD

It was a party to remember, that celebration in January 1911 at the Toronto offices of the Canadian Northern Railway — a spontaneous eruption of singing, dancing, drinking and finally a torchlight procession down King Street. Thus did employees and friends of Messrs. Mackenzie and Mann greet the announcement, in the New Year's Day Honours List from London, that the founders of the Canadian Northern had been made knights bachelor of the realm. So much for the soreheads who called them crooks and profiteering scoundrels! William Mackenzie was now Sir William. Donald Mann was now Sir Donald. The Canadian Northern Railway, the system patched together by the two Ontario-born western

railroad contractors, had gained imperial recognition.

And so it surely should, said the celebrators. After all, the Canadian Northern was the centre-piece of a gigantic conglomerate of some thirty corporations, developed by Mackenzie or Mann or both, in the fifteen years since they started with a stretch of track near Gladstone, Manitoba (Vol. I, Sect. 4, ch. 4). The railway itself consisted of two networks, one in the West, one in the East. The western system, webbed through the three prairie provinces and feeding traffic to the Great Lakes at Port Arthur (later Thunder Bay), had 3,325 miles of track in operation, and as many under construction. Nine thousand men would be at work on Canadian Northern track gangs the next summer. In Alberta alone it embraced a main line running east from Edmonton with nine branches (built, under construction or planned), one of which would soon connect Edmonton with Calgary via Camrose and Drumheller. Construction had begun on the main line west from Edmonton to Vancouver. A daring plan was being advanced to create a second main line from Kamloops, B.C., through the Crowsnest Pass to Lethbridge and east, a direct challenge to the Canadian Pacific.

The eastern network was only a fifth as extensive but similarly complex, threading through scores of towns and cities in southern Ontario and Quebec. Financing was being arranged for a connecting line east from Port Arthur through the bushland of northern Ontario. A three-mile tunnel into downtown Montreal was under construction. A similar tunnel was proposed under Burnaby Mountain to downtown Vancouver. The railway also operated express and telegraph services.

By mid-decade two railways were competing with the Canadian Pacific in offering service between Edmonton and Calgary. Below, an official party welcomes the arrival of the first Grand Trunk Pacific train into Calgary in February 1914. Prominent among them is Mayor Herbert Sinnott, standing between the rails, hands in pockets. At right, onlookers await the departure from Calgary of one of the first Edmonton-bound Canadian Northern trains.

Provincial Archives of Alberta, P-4097

THE BIG BUST OF 1914-15

Nor were Mackenzie and Mann holdings restricted to railways. Mackenzie controlled the streetcar systems and much of the municipal power supply in Toronto and Winnipeg. He was the principal figure behind mighty Brazilian Traction, the biggest utility in the biggest country in South America. With a German syndicate, the partners held extensive coal interests at Drumheller and on the eastern slopes of the Rockies. They had taken over the Dunsmuir coal properties on Vancouver Island, and were mining coal in Cape Breton. They were into whaling and fisheries and, extensively, lumbering. Two Canadian Northern liners plied the Atlantic on scheduled runs, and the partners had promised British Columbia to develop shipping between Victoria and the Orient. In remote northwestern B.C. they owned a nine-mile railroad in connection with a mining property they were developing.

Like most other railway magnates, they were deep into real estate. The Canadian Northern, says its historian T.D. Regehr, was directly responsible for the establishment of 550 prairie cities, towns and villages[1]. By 1911 the railway had sold off 2.7 million acres of its land grant to settlers, but still held 1.8 million acres. It also owned extensive real estate in downtown Edmonton, and a railway yard and right-of-way in Calgary, and was negotiating a big landfill project with Vancouver for the marshland east of False Creek.

All this activity significantly spurred western Canadian optimism. A few days after the New Year's party, the *Medicine Hat News* confidently front-paged an announcement that a Canadian Northern feeder line would soon reach the Hat. (It never did.) In April the Calgary *Albertan* declared: "One hundred and seventy new towns will be born in western Canada this year. This

will be an advance of practically one every two days, which is very rapid even in these days of rapid developments." The Grand Trunk Pacific would create 24 of these towns, it said, the Canadian Pacific fifty, and the Canadian Northern a resounding 96. Mann in particular fervidly fanned such optimism, enchanting one reporter with speculation about a line into northern B.C. as soon as the problem of tunnelling through glaciers could be solved.

So high honours were surely indicated, and the question was why they had not come sooner. The chief explanation was that Mackenzie and Mann were not approved in respectable Toronto and Montreal business circles, where they were seen as a couple of fast-talking railway contractors on the make — dishonest, conniving and unscrupulous — whose success was entirely attributable to good luck and good times. So said Sir Thomas Shaughnessy (soon to become Lord Shaughnessy), the American railroader brought to Canada 29 years earlier to rescue the CPR from imminent bankruptcy. This view, understandably enough, was shared and voiced by one of the CPR's top lawyers in the West, the powerful Tory, R.B. Bennett of Calgary.

To the Liberal establishment they were equally suspect, especially to Charles Melville Hays, another American, brought in to rescue the old Grand Trunk. Hays had conceived the idea of extending it across the continent as the Grand Trunk Pacific, a second Canadian transcontinental line. His crews were even now building west from Edmonton through Yellowhead Pass and east

[1]T.D. Regehr, in *The Canadian Northern Railway* (Macmillan, Toronto, 1976), says that the Canadian Northern hauled out 31% of the bumper Canadian wheat crops of 1915 and 1916. The CPR carried 56%. The Grand Trunk Pacific and several American roads carried the remaining 13%.

In an early demonstration of what would one day be called 'sexist' advertising, Grand Trunk Pacific Telegraph stenographers line up for a publicity photo in front of their downtown Edmonton office.

from Prince Rupert up the Skeena valley. The GTP would be one of the highest-quality, highest-cost railways in the world, most of it underwritten by the Liberal government. Hays had spurned appeals to collaborate with the Canadian Northern and its two (in his opinion) nefarious promoters (Vol. II, Sect. 2, ch. 2). Thus Canada, earlier considered too unpopulated to support one transcontinental railway, would now have three. The further irony was that "respectable" Canadian railroading was represented by two Americans, while disreputable Canadian railroading was represented by the Canadian-born Mackenzie and Mann[2].

Jealousy and suspicion aside, however, even defenders of Sir William and Sir Donald recognized them as extremely tough negotiators, not above subterfuge. Constantly expanding in advance of their capitalization, and short of cash, they paid few debts they could put off. In Edmonton in 1901, for instance, they bought land from the city for $5,000 for a station at First Street and Mackenzie Avenue (101 St. and 104 Ave.) and downtown yards. Characteristically, they did not produce the $5,000. The presence of the station shifted downtown Edmonton westward, the city boomed, and by 1916 the Canadian Northern land was worth $2.5 million. The city,

Mackenzie and Mann were not approved in respectable Toronto and Montreal business circles, where they were seen as a couple of fast-talking railway contractors on the make — dishonest, conniving and unscrupulous.

[2]As a further irony still, the wonder-worker of American railroading in this era was a Canadian. James Jerome Hill, creator of the Great Northern, whose encounter years before with Donald Smith, later Lord Strathcona, one of the founders of the CPR, is recounted in an earlier volume (Vol. I, p. 121). By 1911, Hill's Great Northern had absorbed the Northern Pacific and the Chicago, Burlington & Quincy and was the principal carrier for the northwestern United States. He published his memoirs, *Highways of Progress*, in 1910, and died in 1916 at the age of 87. Lord Strathcona, his keen competitor and lifelong friend, predeceased him by two years, at 93.

still unpaid, now demanded a higher price. Even so, only under threat of legal action did the railway finally pay up — the original $5,000, no more.

"Mackenzie," says historian Regehr, "was a rather humourless, domineering character with almost unbounded energy, tenacity and enthusiasm. He loved to intimidate people and attempted to do it whenever he could. Often he was not particularly careful about the means he adopted to achieve his objectives, and those who felt aggrieved by his actions were not likely to take the matter lightly." Many years later, for example, a federal arbitration board disclosed that one railway speculator, badly hammered by Mackenzie and Mann's acquisition of a major north-south spur in Saskatchewan, was so enraged he became permanently "unbalanced."

From an account left by the German investor Martin Nordegg, Mackenzie biographer R.B. Fleming reconstructs the way the Mackenzie-Mann team alternately beguiled, bamboozled and bludgeoned Nordegg into a deal that led to development of Alberta's eastern slopes coal fields, northwest of the town that bears Nordegg's name[3]. Fleming's reconstruction, in *The Railway King of Canada* (UBC Press, Vancouver, 1991), depicts the unsuspecting Nordegg as the victim of a "sting" operation. The partners lay a trap for him, then feign outrage and indignation at his proposals and

(Above) The thrilling roar of the steam engine enthrals these two Edmonton youngsters as a Canadian Northern locomotive hauls a freight train up the north bank of the North Saskatchewan River below Victoria Drive. Le Marchand Mansion apartments, which would survive the century, peek over the hilltop. The old Canadian Northern line would one day become a paved bicycle path. (Right) crowds line up to board a Grand Trunk Pacific transcontinental bound eastward about 1913, at the Edmonton Canadian Northern and GTP station on the northwest corner of First and Mackenzie, soon to become 101 Street and 104 Avenue.

Coal production in the Nordegg-Brazeau area continued until the 1950s when the last of the mines there closed. Few trains ran west of Rocky Mountain House after 1962. However, the line to the Brazeau was not officially abandoned until 1992, though by then trees with trunks up to eight inches in diameter were growing between the rails.
– from rail historian Les Kozma

[4]Between 1910 and 1920, the Canadian Northern built branchlines from Vegreville to Calgary through Stettler and Drumheller (completed in 1912); from Warden, south of Stettler, west to Nordegg (1914); from Edmonton north to Athabasca Landing (1912); from Edmonton to Camrose (1914); from Edmonton to Sangudo (1914); from Saskatoon to Drumheller through Alsask, Oyen and Hanna (1912); from Camrose to Alliance (1916); from St. Paul Junction (near Oliver) to St. Paul (1917-20); from Hanna to Steveville (1920). The main line was constructed from Edmonton to Yellowhead Pass through St. Albert, Villeneuve, Calahoo, Onoway, Lac Ste. Anne, Entwistle, then paralleling the Grand Trunk Pacific.

[5]Some Canadian Northern additions to the western map were: Fenn, probably after a particularly zealous construction gang waterboy; Scollard, after an otherwise unidentified railway official; Morrin (formerly Blooming Prairie), after the locomotive engineer who drove the first train into town; and Rochester (previously Ideal Flat), after Herbert Rochester, secretary to Malcolm MacLeod, general manager of western lines.

accuse him of attempting to swindle them, finally settling with him on joint development of their coal properties in "the West." Canadian National historian G.R. Stevens, in *The Canadian National Railways* (Clarke Irwin, Toronto, 1962), says this arrangement nearly "led to blows" at a subsequent meeting in London, after Mackenzie and Mann acquired the Dunsmuir coal properties on Vancouver Island. Nordegg's German syndicate claimed an interest in the Dunsmuir mines as well. The duo argued — successfully — that Vancouver Island was not in "the West," a term they insisted applied to the prairies only.

"As high-pressure operators they sometimes implemented their courage with cunning which may not have stopped this side of knavery," Stevens writes. "Like the Elizabethan adventurers whom they so closely resembled, one day they would be honest seamen and on the next privateers if not outright pirates." Sir Wilfrid Laurier's biographer, O.D. Skelton, had trouble making up his mind about Mackenzie and Mann. In his history of Canadian railways, *The Railway Builders* (Glasgow & Brook, Toronto, 1916), he commends their "mastery of political diplomacy" and their "untiring persistence and great financial resourcefulness." In *The Life and Letters of Sir Wilfrid Laurier* (Gundy, Toronto, 1921), he deplores them as "the most corrupting single factor since Confederation times, apparent in campaign contributions, advance information as to the location of land deals, free passes for members and their families, the buying of newspapers — the whole long trail of parliamentary corruption, of degradation of parliamentary institutions, of the lowering of the morals of public life."

Certainly the partners proved adept at manipulating western provincial governments, though here they clearly held the advantage. Settlers often located on the promise of railway service; otherwise they could not market their crop. Since provincial governments guaranteed branch-line construction bonds, voters expected them to make the railways perform. This put the politicians at the mercy of the railway. Beginning in 1910, the Alberta government launched a massive loan-guarantee program, much of it to finance Canadian Northern branch lines[4]. As usual, the names of railway officials or favourites dotted the countryside[5], though sometimes this influence is disputed[6]. And a very strange story lies behind the naming of one Canadian Northern town[7].

In 1911 relations with the three prairie provinces could hardly have been better. Saskatchewan Premier Walter Scott referred to the Canadian Northern as the government's "partner." In 1909 Manitoba's minister of Public Works, Robert Rogers, had effusively recommended it in a telegram to Premier Richard McBride of British Columbia, thereby helping gain a B.C. guarantee on an enormous bond issue to finance the main line from the Yellowhead Pass to Vancouver.

This was an impressive coup. McBride was a Tory and a populist who in a later day would probably have been called a B.C. separatist. He began as a foe of Mackenzie and Mann; in 1902 he had resigned from the Dunsmuir cabinet in protest against his premier's plan to back their pro-

---

To Laurier's biographer, Mackenzie and Mann were 'the most corrupting single factor since Confederation times, apparent in campaign contributions, advance information as to the location of land deals, the buying of newspapers — the whole long trail of parliamentary corruption.'

---

jected Edmonton, Yukon & Pacific line from Edmonton to the northern B.C. coast. He then became leader of the opposition and defeated Dunsmuir. Pursuing a policy of strict frugality, McBride and his treasurer, R.G. Tatlow, thereupon pulled the province out of bankruptcy.

As the decade unfolded McBride was being wooed both by the federally bankrolled Grand Trunk Pacific, whose arrogance soon alienated him, and the ever-ingratiating Canadian Northern. In the end, with the reassurance from Manitoba, he backed Mackenzie and Mann. He waited for the Legislature to adjourn in 1909, then announced a $21-million bond guarantee to a Canadian Northern subsidiary. Tatlow and another minister, Fred Fulton, promptly quit, but McBride called an election for November and won it handily. The deal, however, had an unusual clause. The province had right of approval over the line's freight rates, with no interference from Ottawa.

Three transcontinental lines were now to cross B.C. The original CPR line came from Calgary through Kicking Horse, Rogers, and Eagle passes to Kamloops, then descended the Thompson and

Fraser rivers to Vancouver. The Grand Trunk Pacific set its route from Edmonton through Yellowhead Pass, then north and west through the Fraser, Nechako, Bulkley, and Skeena river systems to Prince Rupert. Finally, the Canadian Northern was paralleling the GTP from Edmonton through Yellowhead Pass, then heading southwest through the North Thompson valley to Kamloops and paralleling the CPR down the Thompson and Fraser canyons to the Lower Mainland and Vancouver[8].

To ease negotiations Mackenzie and Mann were naturally ready with passes for politicians, and other such amiable gestures. But their election contributions were actually far from lavish, and when politically connected applicants were given jobs they were expected to earn their pay, and fired if they didn't. What angered and alarmed their foes was not so much the manner of their government financing as the scale of it. Their entire empire had been erected on borrowed money, nearly all of it government-guaranteed. By 1917 they had borrowed $116 million on federal guarantees and $108 million on provincial ones. Alberta had guaranteed them just under $19 million, Saskatchewan $14.8 million, and B.C. $40.1 million. They had been deeded four million acres of Manitoba and two million acres of Ontario, as a reward for mileage built. (Alberta made them no land grant.)

For capital borrowing they had a much-practised formula. Government guarantee in hand, they would create a bond issue (or several separate issues), which they sold to a London financial house for immediate cash. In 1911 they could collect as much as 98 cents for every dollar bond issued, in tough times as little as 60 cents. The financial house would then sell the bonds to investors, usually retired British professionals, civil servants or army officers. The Canadian Northern's reputation was so high in 1911 that it was able to sell some securities with no guarantee at all. The bonds were offered on different time terms, interest rates and other conditions — a sort of smorgasbord of investment paper, one historian observed, with something designed to appeal to just about any investor.

The most damaging accusation against Mackenzie and Mann concerned construction. They usually acted as the Canadian Northern's construction contractors. It was assumed that they vastly overcharged and pocketed the proceeds, thereby greatly enriching themselves while the taxpayer, through the bond guarantees, took the risks. No amount of pep-talk promotion was able to rid them of this widely-held suspicion.

William Mackenzie did not lack the appurtenances of respectability, however. His vast home, Benvenuto, atop the hill on Toronto's Avenue Road, loomed as a lordly presence above the city[9]. He and his Catholic wife, Margaret, to whom he was deeply devoted and upon whom he depended psychologically, produced six daughters and three sons (Vol. I, p. 177). In their earlier years, she matched him in enterprise; children notwithstanding, she found time to run a tavern. The very January of that New Year's party their daughter Grace married a dashing French airman, Count Jacques de Lesseps, son of the builder of the Suez Canal, who during their courtship made Grace the first woman to fly over New York City. The family future had been centred on son Alex, but in 1907 he had died of a heart attack after minor surgery. This left Joe, who had become a Paris playboy, and Roderick, a great construction camp boss who built the main line through B.C. But Joe Mackenzie's interest in California racehorses and, among other things, a Winnipeg bordello did not suit him to inherit the kingdom.

Much less is recorded about Sir Donald Mann, who in 1994 still lacked a biographer. It was he who planned the fruitful deals with prairie governments, "ran the business," and took direct charge of the mining activities (Mackenzie handled the more social and diplomatic side). Mann spent much time in Montreal, though his home was in Toronto and he had a summer estate called Fallingbrook, just east of Toronto. He comes through as more hard-boiled than Mackenzie, although he was a spiritualist who did not shrink from urging people to pray. His physical strength was said to be prodigious; his appearance on construction sites left the men awestruck. His only son, Donald, appears to have taken no part in the business.

It seemed in 1911 that all doors lay open to the two partners, whatever their reputation. They were about to build both east and west from the prairies. The money was available. What could possibly go wrong? Said David B. Hanna, second vice-president and the railroad genius behind the whole Canadian Northern operation: "There was no cloud in the sky."

Indeed, politically speaking, things improved. Mackenzie, although a Conservative, is believed

[6]One dispute concerns the naming of Camrose. Eric and Patricia M. Holmgren in their book *Over 2000 Place Names of Alberta* (Western Producer Prairie Books, Saskatoon, 1976) suggest it was taken from the Welsh words for 'crooked moor,' *cam rhos*. Mackenzie biographer Fleming says it was originally called Sparling and changed to honour Cameron and Rose McKenzie, the children of A.C. 'Big Archie' McKenzie, who ran a store in Sir William's home town of Kirkfield, Ontario, and married Sir William's niece. McKenzie and Sir Donald Mann's brother, Alexander 'Sandy' Mann, were the contractors who built the line south from Vegreville, but by that time the town was already named. The City of Camrose takes the position that both theories are viable, but records the 'Cam' and the 'Rose' as coming from Camille and Rose, wife and daughter of Big Archie.

[7]In *Over 2000 Place Names of Alberta* the Holmgrens tell how the railway asked the settlers to name the original terminal town on its projected line to the Peace River. The settlers decided on Deep Creek, which the post office rejected because there was already a Deep Creek. So they combined their own names in the following curious way: Sutton (or possibly Sides), Albers, Nanton (the Alberta town where Mrs. Albers had previously lived), Gaskell, United (for the fact they'd put their names together), Deep Creek, and Orangeville, from the name of the local school district. Hence Sangudo.

[8]In later years the CPR in fact created most of a fourth, extending its Crowsnest line from Kootenay Lake westward to Midway, then via its Kettle Valley system to Merritt and finally through the Coquihalla Pass to Hope on its main line 25 miles from the beginning of the Fraser's estuary at Chilliwack. The Coquihalla section, however, was rendered so undependable by avalanches that the CPR abandoned it. Later the Coquihalla Highway followed the Coquihalla stretch of the route.

As power and speed improved so did railroading's hazards

(Top left) When a flood washed out a roadbed, into the river crashed this Canadian Northern locomotive on the Grand Trunk Pacific Coal Branch southwest of Edson. The temporary trackage has already been laid around the spot. (Below) Hauling a load of coal east from Nordegg, this Canadian Northern locomotive spread the rails apart and plunged off them. (Lower left corner) A Canadian Pacific wreck at Leduc in 1914. (Left) A CPR locomotive appears to have ploughed into a freight at Bellevue.

A head-on crash kills five, and injures 41 people in Alberta's worst wreck

They called it the Canadian Northern's 'Moonlight Express' and it left Edmonton's downtown station at 6:45 Saturday evenings, headed for Alberta Beach. Midway between Villeneuve and Calahoo, about fifteen miles northwest of Edmonton, the line jogs first right then left. As the Moonlight Express locomotive crew came round the second bend, they saw to their horror a coal train headed straight for them on the single track. Brakes screamed and sparks flew from the steel wheels, but when stopping the trains became hopeless both crews jumped and saved themselves. However, the second passenger car of the express hurtled over the first, then smashed down into it. Five died and at least forty were injured. A dispatcher's error was blamed.

[9]Mackenzie purchased his magnificent limestone mansion, built in the baronial style with a tower at each corner, for $100,000 in 1897. It had been built six years earlier by S.H. Janes, property speculator, lawyer and ex-seaman, who named it with the Italian word for 'welcome.' On the same hill, about a mile to the west, Sir Henry Pellatt built Casa Loma, even more imposingly medieval, which survives. Mackenzie helped Pellatt finance it and was probably never repaid; Pellatt was bankrupt by the time his castle was completed. Benvenuto was torn down in the 1930s.

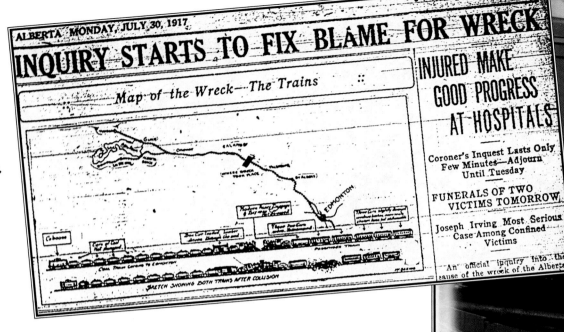

ALBERTA MONDAY, JULY 30, 1917

INQUIRY STARTS TO FIX BLAME FOR WRECK

Map of the Wreck—The Trains

SKETCH SHOWING BOTH TRAINS AFTER COLLISION

INJURED MAKE GOOD PROGRESS AT HOSPITALS

Coroner's Inquest Lasts Only Few Minutes—Adjourn Until Tuesday

FUNERALS OF TWO VICTIMS TOMORROW

Joseph Irving Most Serious Case Among Confined Victims

An official inquiry into the cause of the wreck of the Alberta

to have been the man centrally responsible for organizing eighteen senior Toronto businessmen, all Liberals, to sign a manifesto against Laurier's proposal for Reciprocity with the United States (Sect. 2, ch. 1). This helped doom the Laurier government. In the fall of 1911 Conservative leader Robert Borden, much in Mackenzie's debt politically, defeated the Liberals. And in December the entire $35-million federally guaranteed bond issue, floated to finance the Northern Ontario project, was swallowed immediately by the London market.

There was the odd cloud, however, even in 1911. A Toronto newspaper, the *Financial News*, cried alarm at the scale of the Ontario bond issue: "Sir William Mackenzie's issue of a loan of such a magnitude, at such a time, is destined to act very unfavourably upon Canadian financial interests in London." Also, the Canadian Northern was unable to meet a small interest payment on a debenture issue. The federal government for the first time had to make it good.

But the worst news was seen at the time as fortuitous. William Thomas White, a Toronto financier, a close friend of Mackenzie's and one of his eighteen Liberals, had left the Liberal party over reciprocity and run as a Tory. Borden named him Finance minister. White saw, probably before anyone else in the government, that the two new Canadian railways were wildly over-extended and could bring on the financial collapse of the government. Therefore, he reasoned, there must be no more government-backed railway loans.

The next year, 1912, brought one bad break after another. Construction costs of the main line in B.C. and in Yellowhead Pass soared to as much as triple the original estimate. This made the bonds harder to sell; Mackenzie had to persuade McBride (by now Sir Richard McBride) to authorize a higher interest rate to make them more attractive. McBride agreed, over the objections of his cabinet colleagues. Worse still, Alberta and Saskatchewan successfully argued before a federal board that the Canadian Northern freight rates charged against their shippers far exceeded those charged in Manitoba. Instantly Canadian Northern revenues in two prairie provinces dropped by 7 1/2%. Then the *Royal George*,

Premier Richard McBride of British Columbia whose support of the Canadian Northern eventually saw his own political career dependent on that railway's success.

GENERAL NOTICE

The following rules and instructions are issued for the government of all employees whose duties bring them in contact with the maintenance or operation of the **Westinghouse** air brake and air train signal. Such employees will be examined from time to time as to their qualifications for such duties by an inspector of air brakes, or such other person as may be appointed. Every such employee will be required to pass a satisfactory examination, in which intelligent practical understanding of the mechanism of the brakes and knowledge of his duty will be required, rather than ability to satisfactorily answer questions. Any employee whose work indicates an apparent absence of the requisite brake knowledge may be required to pass an examination at any time following such indication.

one of the two transatlantic liners, hit a rock in the St. Lawrence and almost sank. No lives were lost, but the publicity was bad and the disruption of service worse.

That May a Canadian Northern bond issue proved exceedingly hard to sell. R.M. "Monty" Horne-Payne, the wheelchair-bound debenture-pedlar so integral to the success of Canadian Northern bonds in Britain, urgently warned the partners that the London market was getting soft. They must seek investors on the continent.

By fall it seemed everything was going wrong. Cash was tighter than ever; contractors' bills could not be met. Mackenzie called on Borden. All Canadian railways deemed to serve the "general interest of Canada" (as distinct from mere branch lines) qualified for an outright federal cash subsidy. Although obviously qualified, the Canadian Northern's B.C. line had not received it because that would place its freight rates under federal control, a situation precluded by the terms of the B.C. bond guarantee. Would Borden make the grant but waive federal control? Borden did, with surprisingly little opposition objection. But the additional $5.35 million on the 512-mile line from the Yellowhead to Vancouver still didn't cover its huge costs.

By the end of 1912 disaster loomed. Canadian bonds of all kinds were not selling, for a variety of reasons. Some economic "cyclicists" saw the boom at an end. Canadians must compete with other rapidly developing countries like Argentina and Brazil, and with one another. The bonds of western municipalities were everywhere being offered, as were those of other Canadian railways. In 1912, the CPR floated a £100-million issue to finance mainline improvements and new prairie branch lines, and the Grand Trunk Pacific a £32-million offering. Talk of war was increasing too; investment capital might be needed at home.

More desperate than ever now, Mackenzie went back to Borden with an urgent request for a direct government loan of $25 million. The projected Ontario lines, once completed, would qualify for a $12-million federal cash subsidy, he argued, with which the railway could repay almost half the loan. The CPR, after all, had been given $60 million in cash grants plus a 25-million-acre land

---

A federal arbitration board disclosed that one railway speculator, badly hammered by Mackenzie and Mann's acquisition of a major north-south spur in Saskatchewan, was so enraged he became permanently 'unbalanced.'

---

grant. If you counted the cost of the National Transcontinental, of which the Grand Trunk Pacific had full use, government grants to the GTP could be calculated at $243 million. By comparison the Canadian Northern had received practically nothing but bond guarantees.

His reasoning impressed Borden, but not the entrenched Canadian financial community; the CPR's Shaughnessy particularly deplored the proposal. He cited Mackenzie and Mann's allegedly "large profits" on railway construction contracts. He suggested the government demand 51% of the Canadian Northern common stock for doing the deal. Toronto financier E.B. Osler confidentially advised R.B. Bennett that Mackenzie himself was personally worth "somewhere between $15 million and $100 million." Why not make him put up his own money? So Borden turned Mackenzie down. Then, said Mackenzie, would the government advance the cash subsidy due on main lines already constructed, other than those in B.C.? Again Borden refused, but he pitied Mackenzie. "He has aged greatly in the last two years," he noted in his diary. Later relenting, he advanced the cash subsidy over strong objections from Finance Minister White.

Along with short-term loans that Mackenzie arranged through the Bank of Commerce, this enabled work on the main line to continue through 1913. Prairie branch-line construction had to be halted, however. Protests from settlers streamed in; confrontations with politicians sometimes became desperate. At one point twelve angry men from St. Paul, Alberta, camped in Premier Sifton's office. They called him a liar, a crook and a lunatic because work had been cancelled on a promised branch line, and refused to leave until he agreed to increase the provincial bond guaran-

The birth, life and death of Alberta's 'Peanut Line'

THE CROWN OF LACOMBE'S DREAMS DIED WITH THE ELECTRIC RAILWAY

by Courtney Tower

Soon after the construction of the Canadian Pacific's Edmonton-to-Calgary line, settlers east and west of Lacombe began campaigning for rail connections to this important transportation link, and on Feb. 25, 1909, they felt they had won the battle. An act of the Legislative Assembly incorporated the Lacombe and Blindman Valley Electric Railway, whose sponsors were farmers and merchants from Bentley and Rimbey. Another statute incorporated the Lacombe, Bullocksville and Alix Electric Railway, sponsored by a patrician trio, Senator Peter Talbot, Henry Morehouse Trimble and William R. Wilson.

The Hon. Peter Talbot and friends never got to laying tracks, and let the franchise lapse. They were perhaps deterred by the fact that there already was a CPR branch line from Lacombe to Bullocksville and Alix, and the Grand Trunk was building another one north and south through Alix. But the Lacombe and Blindman Valley line did go ahead.

The Great War and shortage of money may have delayed it, but the line — renamed the Lacombe and North Western Railway in 1919 — reached Bentley in 1917, and Rimbey in 1921. By 1917, however, the "electric" component no longer applied. Resident Bert DeGraff later recalled: "The railroad first ran an oil turbine kind of trolley car, made in England. It was a Jonah. The next was a gasoline car. It was some better. Then came the Peanut steam locomotive... I may have these down wrong but we had them all and the steam engine was the best of them all."

The Peanut and the Peanut Line are local lore, told in the community history *Lacombe: The First Century*: "The Peanut itself was akin to a donkey engine and as described by Pete Danner 'had the water tanks slung over the boiler like saddle-bags on a horse.' The crew was sometimes referred to as the Outlaws, a number of them having been previously fired from the CPR."

The fine hand of the CPR was seen in the scuttling of great plans for Lacombe and the Canadian Northern to thrive in a happy partnership based on coal. The Canadian Northern had claim to part of the coalfields discovered north of Nordegg in the Brazeau River valley, which could amply fuel its steam engines. Lacombe provided the best access to the fields. And the town, claiming 1,800 souls in 1911, laid plans for many more in subdivisions called Fairview Heights and Hyde Park.

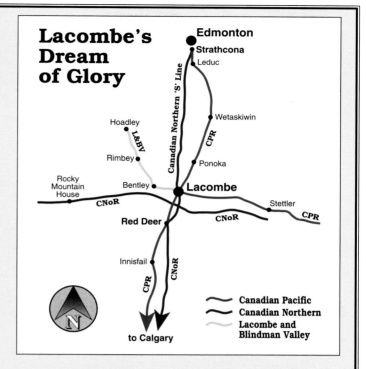

Lacombe's Dream of Glory

"...Divisional point for the Brazeau and Calgary-Strathcona lines of the CNR (Canadian Northern Railway) to be located at Lacombe," Calgary's *Albertan* reported on May 18, 1912.[a] "...the coal supply for the entire system will be distributed from this point... [It is] expected that trains will be running into Lacombe within a month and fuel from the great Brazeau coalfield before freeze-up."

The *Albertan* was more than a bit premature. The Canadian Northern did acquire a right-of-way through Lacombe. It planned underpasses on main streets. It petitioned the federal government for permission to cross the CPR's Calgary-Edmonton right-of-way. But nothing was imminent in 1912. Then came the war, and furthermore the CPR refused to let the new line cross over or under its tracks.

As the episode is recounted in *Lacombe: The First Century*, "Thus the balloon burst, the concrete footings and foundations laid by the Canadian Northern at the site of Jackson siding (a mile south of Lacombe) receded under a growth of weeds, and this early vision of town development faded into oblivion."

[a]The *Albertan* story was about half right. Lacombe was to be the divisional point on the Canadian Northern's 'S-Line,' a fast line between Strathcona and Calgary, to shorten the Canadian Northern's freight route that ran from Edmonton to Vegreville, then south to Calgary. Grading was commenced on the S-Line in 1912 and discontinued the following year. By then 11.9 miles had been graded and 1.3 miles of steel laid south from Strathcona, 1.9 miles graded south from Lacombe and 6.1 miles north from Red Deer. No further work was done on these lines until 1910 when the grade into Red Deer was rehabilitated and the steel laid. The balance of the right-of-way was sold off in 1938. However, Lacombe was never intended to be on the Canadian Northern's Brazeau branch.   — from Les Kozma, railway historian.

THE BIG BUST OF 1914-15

ll over the province the rail builders were at work

(top left) The new Canadian Northern line heads through a rock cut in the scrub bush west of Edmonton, about 1912. (Above) An earth-moving machine known as an elevator loader is at work on the Grand Trunk Pacific near Irricana, 1910. Horse-drawn wagons circle the rig hauling away the dirt. (Right) An elevator-loader operator perches high above the equipment to guide the grading of the Canadian Northern's Saskatoon-Calgary line, 1912. (Below) A CPR extra gang takes a break at Crossfield. (Far left lower) The Grand Trunk Pacific pushes through Yellowhead Pass west of Jasper, 1911.

[10]Apart from its horrendous interest payments, the Canadian Northern had been a profitable railroad. Canadian National historian G.R. Stevens points out that in the four operating years 1910 to 1913 its gross revenues had risen from $13.8 million to $23.8 million, with operating expenses consistently running at about 66% to 70% of that. However by 1913 its funded debt stood at $300 million. This would expand to $400 million before its transcontinental lines were completed: thus only the continued expansion of western Canada could have made it viable.

tee from $2,000 a mile to $3,000. From before noon until 9:30 p.m., the northern deputation "camped continuously on the track of the luckless premier," the *Calgary Herald* reported, "and at one time held him hostage in his own office." Little Arthur finally gave in. The rails, however, did not reach St. Paul until 1920.

By December, in order to move bonds for the B.C. work, Mann was pressuring the McBride government for another rise in the interest rate. Although the line was one of the best in the country, he wrote, it required sixteen major bridges and the construction costs were "even worse than I thought." Despite a cabinet rebellion, McBride agreed. His political fate now depended on the completion of the Canadian Northern's main line. But meanwhile work was stopped on the False Creek project and Vancouver city council threatened to sue.

By the end of 1913 White foresaw that the Canadian Northern could not be completed without some kind of reorganization. The government could not keep lending money. Neither could it put the company into receivership, because both Ottawa and the provinces would immediately become responsible for all the loans. The railway now owed Mackenzie and Mann $20 million for construction work; if it went into receivership, they would sue the government. And the Bank of Commerce had been steadily lending money to the Canadian Northern on the strength of the guarantees on the unsold bonds. If the railway went down, so would the Commerce. Borden noted in his diary that of late his Finance minister had become "excited...nervous...up in the air."

Meanwhile, following Shaughnessy's advice, the government investigated Mackenzie and Mann's various other interests, and above all how much they had raked off the construction jobs. The report, prepared and sworn by the partners' lawyer, Zebulon A. Lash, hit the cabinet like a thunderbolt. In their entire careers, they had never made a single cent on a Canadian Northern contract. They had never claimed expenses from the railway, nor drawn a salary. Their only earnings came in the form of company dividends[10]. Moreover, while they were worth a great deal on paper, their other enterprises were as ill-disposed as the railway. They were, to all intents and purposes, broke. Subsequent audits, taken when the railway was nationalized, would verify all this.

William Mackenzie did not lack the appurtenances of respectability. His vast home, Benvenuto, atop the hill on Toronto's Avenue Road, loomed as a lordly presence above the city. His Catholic wife, Margaret, to whom he was deeply devoted, matched him in enterprise. Their six daughters and three sons notwithstanding, she early on found time to run a tavern.

But if money hadn't motivated them, demanded one cabinet minister of another, what had? The only answer seemed to be an almost insane determination to finish building the railroad.

This knowledge softened the cabinet members, but the proposal they produced did not look very soft to Mackenzie and Mann. The government would advance $40 million in loan guarantees. But the partners must place in the Canadian Northern all the assets of the assorted subsidiary companies, must cancel the $20 million the railway owed them, and must surrender to the federal government 40% of the common stock. By now, of course, they had no alternative.

A bill writing this agreement into law went to the Commons in May 1914. Then came another shock. While the Liberal opposition to it was not severe, and Liberal premiers in the West supported it, a young lawyer from the government's own benches rose to denounce it, even threatening to join the Liberals over the issue. This was none other than CPR counsel Bennett, who eloquently deplored both the legislation and the men it would rescue, their "boundless ambition," their "greed for wealth," their "falsification and subterfuge." The Canadian Northern was "unworthy to be called a railroad," he charged; it was "a trail of corruption extending from Halifax to Victoria." But the bill went through.

July 1914 therefore found Sir William once again in London, gaunt and exhausted, furnished with a new federally guaranteed bond issue and beckoning an increasingly icy market. Then, on August 4, Britain declared war on Germany. "That's it," said Sir William. "I'm finished." In a family photograph taken in England at the time he appears as an old man. "In two years he had aged twenty," says biographer Fleming.

Railway politics were fair game for cartoonists

(Below, top left) The Eye Opener delivers its opinion on railway nationalization, with Canada howling for help while the CPR looks on and laughs. (Lower left) The Brooklyn Eagle blames anti-American sentiment for futilely trying to derail American investment in Canadian railways. (Above right) The Montreal Star shows Canadians struggling to solve the shortage of investment capital before it wrecks Canadian railroads. (Below right) The Eye Opener in 1915 sees Sir William Mackenzie as the very thing needed to bankrupt Germany.

CLEARING THE TRACK

The passengers on the "delayed progress express" work together to clear the line of a heavy obstruction. —Montreal Star.

Tough on the Lady

A FUTILE ATTEMPT
—Harding, in Brooklyn Eagle.

Sir William Mackenzie at Berlin

With little of the fanfare that attended the driving of the last spike on the Canadian Pacific thirty years before, Sir William Mackenzie hammers home the last spike on the Canadian Northern transcontinental line at Basque, B.C., west of Kamloops, in January 1915. Admiring workmen look on.

[11] Regehr recounts the damage to the salmon run in his history of the Canadian Northern. Complaints from the provincial fisheries inspectors had been coming in since 1913. 'In a number of places they have literally shot the whole side of the mountain into the river,' said a provincial report, 'filling up numerous bays where the fish used to rest, and as at Skuzzi new points projecting far out into the stream have been formed, so congesting the waterway as to make it next to impossible for the fish to get through.' Exasperated, the government hired a dredging contractor to clear the stream, and sent a $90,000 bill to the Canadian Northern. Head office passed it on to its B.C. subsidiary, which sent it to the contractor. The sum was finally deducted from a bill the province owed the railway. Mackenzie and Mann owned all three corporations involved, and also had an interest in the fishery.

And finished he was, although his ruin took another three years to accomplish. The war instantly froze British investments overseas and closed the continent. Mackenzie ordered work stopped on all Canadian Northern construction projects, and returned to Canada. The Borden government countermanded the halt order, however, instructing the banks to advance money on government credit notes. The main line was needed for the war effort.

In the fall of 1914 crews worked all night in the Fraser Canyon, rushing the line to completion and, in the process, blasting so much rock into the river as to gravely damage the salmon run[11]. By Jan. 23, 1915, the eastward-building crews met the westward at a point beside the Thompson River named Basque. Mackenzie rushed west to drive in a very plain last spike. A formal spike-driving, set for February, was cancelled when a tunnel near Basque collapsed.

The war proved no bonanza for the Canadian Northern. Labour and fuel costs rose. Equipment was scarce and expensive. Huge interest costs began to show on the balance sheet, and in December 1914 the Canadian Northern showed its first operating loss. Again it defaulted on interest payments, and again the government had to make them. Curiously enough, in the spring of 1915 Canadian Northern bonds began selling well in New York. Historian Stevens explains that the valour of the Canadian troops who stopped the German gas attack at Ypres provoked a "deep response" in Americans, whose interest in their hitherto undistinguished northern neighbour suddenly soared.

An October 1915 trip for the press and members of Parliament, from Montreal to Vancouver on the new transcontinental line through Edmonton, also seemed to be a tremendous publicity coup. But the operational losses on the system were now creating a new crisis, set off by the banks' refusal to extend further credit on any terms. In April 1916 Borden ruefully wrote in his diary, "I would personally prefer to resign and let the Grits clean up their own mess." In May he decided to act, naming a three-man royal commission to find a solution. It consisted of a lawyer, Sir Henry Drayton, chairman of the Board of Railway Commissioners and later federal minister of Finance; a British economist, W.M. Acworth; and A.H. Smith, president of the New York Central.

At the same time, at the behest of Mackenzie and Mann, the New York investment house of Kuhn, Loeb & Company was hired to assess the viability of the Canadian Northern. The Kuhn, Loeb study, presented in March 1917, found the railway economically viable. So too did Smith of the New York Central, who filed a minority report for the royal commission. Drayton and Acworth thought otherwise. Declaring its stock value-less, they recommended the railroad be nationalized. This finding was instantly challenged by Mackenzie and Mann. Borden ordered a review, which upheld their criticism: many of the assets had not been taken into account. Drayton conceded he had erred, but still favoured nationalization. This left the decision to Borden.

By late spring of 1917 his mind was made up. On June 14 he called Mackenzie to his office so that he would be the first to know. The Canadian Northern, he said, would be taken over by the government. Borden's diary records what then happened: "Sir William," he wrote, "was a man of iron nerve and this was one of only two occasions on which I saw self-control desert him. Knowing my decision was final, he was silent for a moment and then completely broke down, with audible sobs that were most distressing." What the Borden diary does not record is that Mackenzie had just learned as well that his wife's illness was terminal.

Sir William Mackenzie (left) shows age fast creeping upon him in this photo taken on the steps of the B.C. Legislature after the Canadian Northern line was completed in 1915. With him is Premier Sir Richard McBride.

Events now moved swiftly. A bill introduced in November authorized the government to acquire the remaining 60% of the company stock. An arbitration board began hearings in Toronto to determine how much Mackenzie and Mann should be paid. They asked $30 million, then came down to $20 million. The board set the figure at $10.8 million, most of which went to the Bank of Commerce. Mackenzie attended the hearings but did not testify, and towards the end of the month he was absent. He was at his wife's bedside. On Nov. 29, he left her to take a brief nap. Suddenly aroused, he sped to her room and clutched her hand. Margaret Mackenzie was dead.

On Sept. 6, 1918, Sir William Mackenzie and Sir Donald Mann resigned as president and vice-president of the Canadian Northern, which thereafter ceased to be. Something called the Canadian Government Railways came into being instead, embracing the Canadian Northern and the Intercolonial Railway. The first president was David Blythe Hanna. In 1923 it would become Canadian National Railways.

Meanwhile, Canada's other new western railway, the Grand Trunk Pacific, had fallen into an even worse case than the Canadian Northern. From the time it began building its superb line west through Yellowhead Pass (Vol. II, Sect. 2, ch. 2), troubles mounted. In the construction season of

---

The government investigated Mackenzie and Mann's various interests. The report hit the cabinet like a thunderbolt. They had never made a cent on a Canadian Northern contract, never claimed expenses, nor drawn a salary. While they were worth a great deal on paper, they were broke.

1912, repeated accidents on the upper Fraser River are said to have cost the lives of fifty men. More lives were lost as the eastward-building contractors encountered unforeseen hazards on the Skeena. All this further soured relations between the railway and the McBride government[12].

Other relations had long gone sour too. When a federal arbitration board had recommended a pay raise for Canadian railwaymen, the CPR immediately accepted it. The Grand Trunk's hard-headed Charles Melville Hays did not, and the consequent strike shut down the whole Grand Trunk system. Pushed by Laurier's labour minister, Mackenzie King, Hays settled, but then fired 250 of the strikers and terminated the pensions of the rest. The Laurier government was furious; even other Grand Trunk executives were appalled.

THE USE OF SAND

19. The use of sand increases the stopping power of brakes considerably, and must always be used in cases of emergency; its proper use in a service stop when rail is bad or slippery is also a benefit. The proper method is to commence its use before the brakes are applied, and continue up to the time of stop. Commencing to use it when near stopping point to prevent going by is very likely to result in flat spots on wheels, because of their having commenced to skid before sand was used.
–*from 'Rules for the Operation and Inspection of the Air Brake and Air Train Signal,' Canadian Pacific Railway Company, December 1917.*

Something else inflamed the Ottawa government even more. Hays had pledged to use the new National Transcontinental line to ship western grain to the Atlantic through Moncton. But then he began acquiring property for a line into Providence, Rhode Island, which would have opened the Canadian West to New England manufactured goods. These things helped defeat Laurier in 1911, but did not endear Hays to the Tories, who neither believed nor trusted him.

Therefore Hays's sudden death on the *Titanic* in April 1912 (see sidebar) might be thought to have improved his railway's prospects. In fact, it contributed to the destruction of both the Grand Trunk Pacific and its parent, the Grand Trunk Railway. The reason, says Canadian National historian Stevens, was the utter incompetence of Hays's two successors: Sir Alfred Smithers, a London financier who became chairman of the board, and Edson J. Chamberlin, who became president.

Both men, says Stevens, were reasonably competent railroad operators. But their new jobs required far more than that; they demanded diplomacy, cause-pleading skill, aptitude at negotiations. Hays had some of these attributes, Smithers and Chamberlin had none. They were entirely incapable of dealing with the consequences of the colossal political boondoggle of the previous decade known as the National Transcontinental Railway.

The NTR was a bizarre attempt to provide Quebec with a French-speaking hinterland development, such as the West afforded English-speaking Canada. Therefore a line had been built from Moncton to Quebec City, then through more than 1,300 miles of non-farmable wilderness from Quebec City to Winnipeg, bypassing southern Quebec and Ontario (Vol. II, p. 110-111) and generating almost no traffic whatever[13]. Its construction occasioned "knaveries unequalled in the history of railway construction in Canada," says Stevens. A 1912 royal commission found that the construction estimate of $30,000 a mile had ballooned to $100,000 — of which at least $20,000 went to "utter waste and theft."

The Grand Trunk was committed by contract to lease and operate the NTR at 3% of its construction cost per annum, and the NTR was already losing $6 million a year. When the commis-

---

On August 4, Britain declared war on Germany. 'That's it,' said Sir William, 'I'm finished.' In a family photograph taken in England at the time, he appears an old man. 'In two years he had aged twenty,' says his biographer.

---

sion revealed the NTR's actual cost, it behoved Smithers and Chamberlin to get the Grand Trunk out of the deal as soon as possible. Instead, they seemed at first to insist upon fulfilling it. "It is our intention to live up to our obligation within the strict letter of the matter," said Chamberlin in an August 1913 interview. At one meeting with Borden, Smithers said he thought the government should operate the National Transcontinental. In that case, Borden replied, it would also have to take over the Grand Trunk Pacific. It was Smithers' opportunity to rid the Grand Trunk of both white elephants. He didn't take it.

He and Chamberlin did resolutely postpone the GTR takeover of the NTR, for the sufficient reason that the war was already crippling the whole Grand Trunk system. As with the Canadian Northern, material costs spiralled upward. Locomotives priced at $20,000 in 1914 cost $50,000 in 1917. The price of freight cars tripled. Wages rose by 25%. Everything was in short supply. Immigration traffic stopped. Indeed, railways were the only major Canadian industry not to profit from the war. In January 1915 the Grand Trunk met the government's urgent request that it now take on the National Transcontinental with the flat reply that it would go under if it did. Borden offered interim help, another out for Smithers and Chamberlin. They rejected it. By January 1916, Finance Minister White reported (after an inquiry) that the position of the Grand Trunk Pacific was "hopeless." The same royal commission that studied the Canadian Northern therefore studied the Grand Trunk system as well.

The commission gave Chamberlin yet another opportunity to free the Grand Trunk of its commitments to the NTR and the burden imposed by the GTP. Instead, he fired off an abusive letter, accusing the government of perpetrating a "crime" against the Grand Trunk and of seeking the "confiscation" of GTR assets. The subsequent commission report staggered the British financial community, by recommending nationalization not only of the Canadian Northern and the Grand

[12]The Grand Trunk Pacific doubtless attempted to improve relations with B.C. Premier Richard McBride and his government by bestowing his name on its biggest centre between Yellowhead Pass and Prince George.

[13]Agronomists of the time were much taken with the potential of the Great Clay Belt, an area of several thousand square miles west of the Quebec-Ontario border and mainly in the James Bay watershed, which many saw as capable of rivalling the prairies. However, agricultural endeavours in the Great Clay Belt disappointed all expectations and have never been marked with great success.

A great ship takes a great railroader to his death

THE *TITANIC* DISASTER SAVES HAYS FROM THE GTP'S IGNOBLE RUIN, BUT A CALGARIAN WHO DID SURVIVE SPENT HIS LIFE EXPLAINING WHY

"The White Star, the Cunard and the Hamburg-America lines are devoting their attention and ingenuity in vying with one another to attain the supremacy in luxurious ships and in making speed records. The time will come soon when this will be checked by some appalling disaster."

The man who said that was Charles Melville Hays, president of the Grand Trunk Railway, and he had cause to be concerned. He made the observation about 9 o'clock on the evening of April 14, 1912, and he and his wife and other members of his family were at that moment passengers on the largest and most luxurious of the liners he was talking about. It was said to be "unsinkable," it was on its maiden voyage, and it was called *Titanic*[a].

About three hours later, as Hays and his wife lay in their berths in cabin B-79 on the promenade deck, the great ship suddenly shuddered. Obviously the hull had hit something.

Artist Ken Marschall's 1974 conception of the sinking of the Titanic.

Hays and the rest of his party made their way to the deck and found the ship had hit an iceberg. At first the passengers assumed there was no real emergency. As the deck tilted, however, they gradually realized *Titanic* was doomed, and that there was nowhere near enough room in the lifeboats for all the passengers. Hays put his wife and daughter in a lifeboat, wrapped fur coats around them and bade them farewell. He was confident, he told them, he would escape because the *Titanic* could last a further ten hours. In fact her great stern heaved in the air three hours later and she slid to the bottom, the band still playing as she went down. With her went Hays, his son-in-law and his male secretary. More than 1,500 passengers and crew perished.

One Calgary couple escaped. A.A. "Bert" Dick, who owned the Dick Block and the Alexandra Hotel, found a place in one of the lifeboats with his wife. He spent the rest of his life explaining how it was he got in that boat, since nearly all the survivors were women and children. His wife, he said, had dragged him in with her when all the women and children had been given places.

Another Albertan involved told a terrible story. Ole K. Norman had been farming near Edmonton and returned to his native Norway for the winter. He booked steerage on the *Titanic* to return to Canada. Steerage passengers, he said, were "packed like rats" far below decks. After the ship began to pitch toward the bow, they panicked and rushed up the companionways to the deck. The crew ordered them to return, firing several revolver shots into the air. These were heard by those in the lifeboats. Most obeyed, including women and children. All were drowned. Norman refused to budge, and eventually found a seat in one of the last boats lowered.

Hays was returning to Canada in time for the opening ceremonies of the Grand Trunk's Chateau Laurier Hotel in Ottawa. The ceremonies were cancelled and the hotel never did have an official opening. As a memorial all Grand Trunk trains halted for five minutes at 11:35 a.m. EST, April 25.

On how pivotal to Canadian railroading was the loss of Hays, historians are not agreed. G.R. Stevens, who wrote the official history of the Canadian National, says Hays was saved from ignominy by a timely death. He blames Hays in particular for the catastrophe that befell Canadian railways.

However, he adds, Hays' survival might have saved the parent Grand Trunk from nationalization. His successors, Stevens contends, were incompetent and unwise. Hays at least would have put up a far better case to save the railway.

— *T.B.*

[a]A superb article on the life and death of Charles Melville Hays appeared in the December 1993 edition of the magazine *The Beaver*, written by Gavin Murphy, an Ottawa lawyer, described as 'a longstanding *Titanic* enthusiast.'

Canadian National Archives, 33459

Charles Melville Hays

Millions to lay the track, millions more to rip it up

NO SOONER WERE ALBERTA'S PARALLEL TRANSCONTINENTALS OPENED
THAN WARTIME RAIL NEEDS SENT THE WRECKERS TO TEAR THEM OUT

by Courtney Tower

They ripped up and shipped away 192 miles of western railway track in 1917, and that was bizarre enough. More bizarre still was the fact that the track, taken from the rival Canadian Northern and Grand Trunk Pacific, was never really missed by railroaders, although some townsfolk were sadly affected.

The first call from the British government for steel rails, to be sent overseas and relaid in order to pursue the fighting in France, came in December 1916. The Dominion govern-

Alberta, and Red Pass, B.C., which is 25 miles east of Tête Jaune. GTP rails had to be used, Ottawa decreed, because they were the same as the ones already sent. Canadian Northern rails would have to be rebored or reslotted to match, which would weaken them.

Communities along the way were horrified. Edson residents, bombarding Dominion parliamentarians with telegrams, lobbied to particularly good effect. Frank Cochrane, minister of Railways and Canals, replied that he would tear up every railroad in Canada if necessary to win the war. But

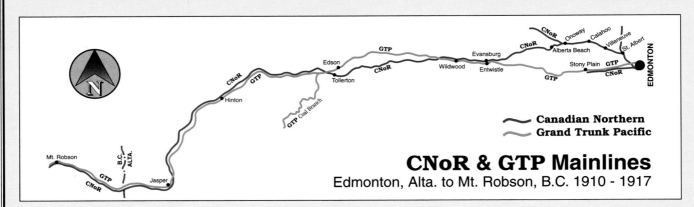

Canadian Northern
Grand Trunk Pacific

CNoR & GTP Mainlines
Edmonton, Alta. to Mt. Robson, B.C. 1910 - 1917

ment answered "Ready, ay, ready" the very next day. Between Winnipeg and Moncton, New Brunswick, according to railroad historian Leslie S. Kozma, 800 miles of rail "were removed from sidings and yards," mostly those of the government-owned National Transcontinental line.

In May 1917 the British called for more. This time the track was to be found in the parallel lines of the GTP and the Canadian Northern west from Edmonton. Up to near Mount Robson, British Columbia, the lines ran five miles apart at the most and sometimes almost on top of each other, a calamitous duplication through areas that never would be more than sparsely settled.

The GTP mainline to Prince Rupert went through Stony Plain, on to Edson, thence through Yellowhead Pass and fifty miles on to Tête Jaune Cache in B.C. The Canadian Northern went northwest to Onoway and on to Evansburg, actually crossing over the GTP at their respective stations of Chip Lake and Leaman. Its route lay just two miles south of Edson, where a divisional point called Tollerton was located, then skirted Brulé Lake to Jasper and the Yellowhead summit.

Apparently unaware of the greater settlement along much of the GTP line, the Dominion government issued orders May 21 to begin lifting the GTP track between Imrie,

he would look after Edson and its industries, he declared. Compromise was reached: 102 miles of the Canadian Northern and ninety miles of the GTP were taken up. The portions of the GTP to be retained for service were then relaid with Canadian Northern steel. Edson was saved, ending up as promised "on the main line of the new composite railway." (The loser, the Canadian Northern's Tollerton, died.)

Composite was the right word. On May 29 construction crews began connecting the two chopped-up lines to create one temporary wartime track. Abandonment of one caused little inconvenience when the other was nearby. The GTP stretch paralleling the Canadian Northern between Lobstick Junction and Chip Lake was abandoned, for instance, but trains ran on the Canadian Northern line just to the north. Within five months, 23,784 tonnes of rails and 1,128 tonnes of angle bars were sent to Trois Rivières, Quebec, for shipment abroad, although no one seems to know whether they got to the front.

After the war the temporary trackage of the consolidated line became permanent, when the GTP and the Canadian Northern both became part of Canadian National Railways. The abandoned lines can still be traced in aerial photographs, or sometimes seen from the Yellowhead Highway.

Trunk Pacific but of the GTP's parent Grand Trunk too.

This was exceedingly controversial. Like the Canadian Northern, the GTP constituted a financial adventure with government putting up most of the money. Not so the Grand Trunk, the major railway between Quebec City and the southwestern Ontario cities of Sarnia and Windsor, founded in 1851. Private British investors had put up 93% of its capital. Where the Canadian Northern had two shareholders, the Grand Trunk had 100,000. Why had the commission recommended nationalizing it? The answer — because its London head office was too far away from Canada — seemed absurd. And how much was Canada prepared to pay for it? The commission didn't say; it made no estimate of the Grand Trunk's value.

Then began a raucous and tumultuous brawl that would remain in the courts for seventeen years, and bitterly sour British investors on Canada. Britons had financed 113 railways outside the United Kingdom; this was the first time any one of them had been threatened with nationalization. Smithers and Chamberlin vehemently protested, citing again and again the unpayable debt that Canada historically owed the Grand Trunk, its first important railway. Borden's government, and particularly Arthur Meighen, replied that during the boom the Grand Trunk had falsified its accounts in order to pay dividends to its shareholders, and had let the system fall into disrepair. Smithers demanded Canada pay a lump sum for the railway plus an interminable annuity of $8 million a year. Meighen offered no lump sum and a rental of $3 million a year, which was derided as "a beggarly dole." At an uproarious shareholder meeting in 1918, cries of "Shame! Shame!" greeted Smithers' reference to Canada's ingratitude.

Edson J. Chamberlin, after whom Edson, Alberta, was named. CN historians blame his fumbling for the failure and nationalization of the Grand Trunk. He was its last president.

The British press swarmed to the cause of the aggrieved shareholders, castigating Canada for robbery. When Borden presented legislation appointing an arbitration board to fix the price, wild scenes followed in the Commons. "There is nothing right about it [the bill]," shouted one member. "The object is wrong, the method is wrong, the plan is wrong and the timing is wrong!" In an all-night sitting Nov. 4, 1919, however, it passed the Commons, and survived in the Senate by a margin of four votes. Meighen, who followed Borden as prime minister in July 1920, told a meeting of the Canadian Club in Montreal, "We are at the penalty stage of railway developments in this country. A price of some form has to be paid by the people of Canada. We are now at the point where an awakening bitterness follows a night of intoxication; an ebb of retribution now follows in the wake of a floodtide of railway construction." It was a fitting epitaph for Canada's wild western railway orgy, but Meighen was heckled repeatedly.

Two members of the three-man arbitration board declared the Grand Trunk common stock and three classes of preference shares to be worthless. The books had indeed been falsified to justify dividends, they found, and therefore only the bonds were redeemable. William Howard Taft, former president of the United States, who served as third member of the board, vehemently disagreed. He valued the railway at $64 million, urging Canada to be generous in the settlement. Canada was not, and $180-million worth of Grand Trunk stock became waste paper. Protests and lawsuits went on until 1934. On Jan. 8, 1920, Canadian National Railways assumed control of the Grand Trunk trackage. In July the CNR took over the Grand Trunk Pacific.

Three other dates in the story remain significant:

Oct. 5, 1922: David Blythe Hanna's career as president of the Canadian Government Railways came to an end because he refused to countenance interference by the Mackenzie King government in the operation of the system. The whole board resigned, and with the appointment of the new board the properties came under the name Canadian National Railways. Hanna died Dec. 1, 1938, nineteen days short of his 80th birthday.

Dec. 5, 1923: Sir William Mackenzie died at Benvenuto, several weeks after collapsing from a heart attack on the golf course. He was virtually insolvent. His son Roderick had died on March 1 that year in Los Angeles.

Nov. 9, 1934: Sir Donald Mann, 81, died at his Toronto home, his wife at his side. Although he was undoubtedly one of Canada's greatest railway builders, the *Globe* reporter assigned to write his obituary could find only 200 words about him in the files. Right to the end he had continued to travel daily on the streetcar to his small downtown office, muttering to himself as he stared out the window[14]. The neighbourhood talk was that Sir Donald had become quite senile.

[14]A little boy about five years old got on the Queen Street streetcar with his grandmother one day about 1933. 'That's Sir Donald Mann,' she whispered. The little boy had no idea who Sir Donald Mann might be. Neither did he know that many years later he would be writing this chapter in this book.

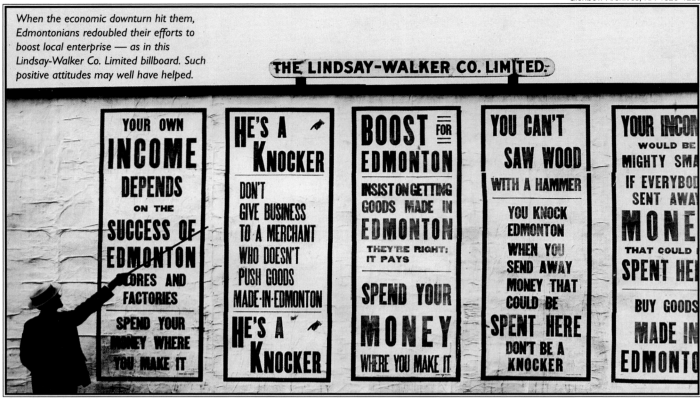

When the economic downturn hit them, Edmontonians redoubled their efforts to boost local enterprise — as in this Lindsay-Walker Co. Limited billboard. Such positive attitudes may well have helped.

THE LINDSAY-WALKER CO. LIMITED.

YOUR OWN **INCOME** DEPENDS ON THE **SUCCESS OF EDMONTON** STORES AND FACTORIES — SPEND YOUR MONEY WHERE YOU MAKE IT

HE'S A **KNOCKER** DON'T GIVE BUSINESS TO A MERCHANT WHO DOESN'T PUSH GOODS MADE-IN-EDMONTON HE'S A **KNOCKER**

BOOST FOR **EDMONTON** INSIST ON GETTING GOODS MADE IN **EDMONTON** THEY'RE RIGHT; IT PAYS SPEND YOUR **MONEY** WHERE YOU MAKE IT

YOU CAN'T SAW WOOD WITH A HAMMER YOU KNOCK EDMONTON WHEN YOU SEND AWAY MONEY THAT COULD BE **SPENT HERE** DON'T BE A KNOCKER

YOUR INCOME WOULD BE MIGHTY SMALL IF EVERYBODY SENT AWAY **MONEY** THAT COULD SPENT HERE BUY GOODS MADE IN EDMONTON

CHAPTER TWO

As the boom becomes a bust Edmonton politics turn violent

THE CITY'S POPULATION DROPS BY NEARLY A QUARTER, TEACHER PAY IS SLASHED, THE POLICE BUDGET HALVED, AND ALDERMEN DESCEND INTO FISTFIGHTING

by VIRGINIA BYFIELD

The period from 1914 to 1920 was emphatically not the best of times for Edmonton. It brought not only the bloodbath of the Great War and the deadly terrors of the influenza scourge, but also one of the worst economic calamities in the city's history, rivalling even the Great Depression that lay a decade and a half ahead.

Population declined by nearly one-fourth between 1914 and 1918. Cash was short and credit shrinking. The civic administration, continually skirting bankruptcy, took drastic economic measures. The police budget, for example, was halved. For three years the municipal power plant was leased to a private company. Construction of new school buildings was abruptly halted and they stood derelict and unfinished. Unemployment soared, and rising prices exacerbated the distress it caused. The city council, far from relieving the problems, descended instead into long-standing vendettas that simmered and exploded, culminating on one memorable occasion in a council chamber fistfight, and on another in the arrest of an alderman for criminal conspiracy.

Occupying the mayor's chair for 1914 was flamboyant realtor William J. McNamara, who had

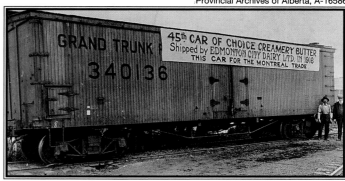

Nero Fiddled While Rome Burned!

Are We Sleeping While Edmonton Is Going Into Bankruptcy?

Edmonton to be the graveyard of all our hopes and ambitions? Can we continue to pay our taxes on property which is steadily depreciating in value? Shall we continue scaring away CAPITAL and BIG ENTERPRISE while we watch our property being sold for taxes? Let every ratepayer and every citizen answer these questions for himself in a business-like manner!

Natural Gas and What It Means to Our Fair City.

Gentlemen—On Monday, November 8th, we shall be asked to decide this question. This is not a time to look at things in a small way—what we want is a broad perspective of our city's future.

Are We Being Used to Avenge the Personal Spite of Individuals?

The Coal Men's Opposition

Naturally the coal interests are opposed to Natural Gas.

Avenging a Personal Grudge!

There are certain individuals in our city putting forth every effort to discredit the gas company to avenge personal spite.

Vote for Natural Gas on Monday

VOTE FOR NATURAL GAS!—It Means a Heavy Construction Program and Work for Every Man Under a Fair Wage Clause—Not to be paid for with the Ratepayers' Money but by Outside Capital!

THE GAS AGREEMENT:

Edmonton Firm Believes in Using Edmonton-Made Products

The above illustrations are reduced reproductions of a set of five hanger cards in four colors that are just completed for the Great Western Garment Company, Ltd. The order comprises 10,000 cards, 13x17 inches, and they are reproduced in what is known, technically, as the four color process. This is the largest exclusive color job ever placed in the city of Edmonton.

It might be interesting to note that the G.W.G. overalls have the largest sale, in Western Canada, of any overalls, and the extensive and aggressive advertising campaign promoted by the Great Western Garment Company is largely responsible for this volume of sales.

The color drawings and color plates are the work of the McDermid Engraving Company, Ltd., and the color printing was done by Esdale Press, Ltd. Both are Edmonton firms.

The Great Western Garment Company are to be complimented for their confidence in local firms and their loyalty to Edmonton-made products in placing this large order locally instead of sending it East.

If the going gets tough...

As the prosperity faded, Edmonton tried harder on both the promotional and personal level. A 1915 Journal ad (top left) pushes natural gas. The group at top right is publicizing a trainload of goods for Athabasca. Struggling firms from Nakamun Asphalt to Great West Garment (at left) hawked their wares locally.

[1] Fighting Joe Clarke (1869-1941) would maintain his presence on Edmonton's political scene through to 1937 when he wound up a final term as mayor, his third. Ontario-born and an Osgoode Hall law graduate, he had come to Edmonton in 1908 after a ten-year sojourn in the Klondike. Clarke was an accomplished amateur athlete (boxing, rugby football, track and field) and determined patron of amateur sport. Although he was more out of office than in — and despite several tries never successful above the municipal level — he was also a loud and constant patron of the underdog, and was never known to back down from a political scrap.

[2] The Alberta experience of IWW organizer James Rowan included one strange and never explained episode, writes labour historian David Schulze. With a colleague named Barrett he travelled to Lac la Biche to see Hiram Johnson, another Wobbly who was homesteading there, and found Johnson murdered. When they reported this, the police arrested both of them for murder and vagrancy. They served six months' hard labour for vagrancy, but the murder charges were dropped and the crime was never solved. Labour men concluded the murder charges were trumped up.

[3] Westmount School, under principal Gordon S. Harman, became the scene in 1918 of Edmonton's first experimental junior high, largely to take the pressure off the city's few and crowded high schools. A strict disciplinarian, principal Harman always carried a strap in his hip pocket. He called it his 'harmanizer.'

defeated his predecessor, lawyer William Short, by a mere 236 votes. That McNamara won at all was due to the support he received from one of the most colourful and controversial characters ever to adorn Edmonton city politics. Alderman Joseph Andrew Clarke, a man beloved of labourers, the unions, the unemployed, the ethnic minorities and just about anyone with a beef against the city's burgeoning bureaucracy, delivered for McNamara the crucial East Side[1]. "Fighting Joe" Clarke looms large in Edmonton municipal politics in these years and later, but the McNamara-Clarke coalition was an uneasy one — so uneasy that within seven months it would explode, loudly and with large headlines.

Meanwhile, there was no escaping the fact that the boom on which the city had been riding so high had unquestionably become a bust. Had it not been for the worldwide financial anxiety that preceded the outbreak of the Great War in 1914, writes John C. Weaver in the *Urban Historical Review* (Vol. 2, 1977), Edmonton might have kept jogging along without serious trouble, despite its habit of enriching various insider interests, its lavish borrowing to extend development, and its infatuation with deficit-prone utilities. By 1914, however, the over-extended city was known in the all-important bond market as "a negligible commodity," Weaver notes.

Upon taking office, Mayor McNamara soon found himself forced to give thousand-dollar golden handshakes to ten senior employees, to cut back civic wages across the board, and to repudiate sewer construction contracts. One of his first official acts that winter was to talk with jobless

---

IWW organizer James Rowan led 600 men in a march on City Hall and another on the Legislature, but the province only advised them to look for farm jobs. Many did, but as the IWW pointed out, most farmers were also as 'poor as Lazarus and up to their ears in debt.'

---

men at the city's Industrial Workers of the World (IWW) headquarters. They asked for municipal jobs at thirty cents an hour, or else three meal tickets daily and a decent place to sleep. Sympathetic, the mayor offered two meals, straw mattresses in a building on the exhibition grounds, and part-time street-cleaning jobs for sixty or so men. But by January, writes David Schulze in *Labour* (Vol. 25, 1990), a fifth of the city's $25,000 relief budget had been spent.

The IWW, which had been organizing railway construction gangs since 1911, had moved into the cities as tracks were completed and crews laid off. Popularly known as the Wobblies (and by contemptuous newsmen as the "I-Won't-Works"), the IWW was the only union that represented unskilled and migrant workers and made no ethnic distinctions. IWW organizer James Rowan led 600 men in a march on City Hall and another on the Legislature, but the province only advised them to look for farm jobs[2]. Many did so, especially at harvest time when the city subsidized their rail transport. As the IWW pointed out, however, most farmers were also as "poor as Lazarus and up to their ears in debt."

The public schools were similarly afflicted. Teachers' salaries were reduced by 10% in 1914, with a further cut of 5% later for anyone making more than $1,250 annually. No new school buildings would be planned for a decade. Lack of money for sewer connections delayed for two years the opening of seventeen-classroom Westmount School on 31st Street (131 St.) at Muskoka Avenue (111th)[3]. Construction of sixteen-room Highlands School was stalled amidst legal threats from contractors. Its second-floor and utilities hookups would not be completed until 1920.

The best solution to all their problems, Edmontonians thought in 1914, would be an oil bonanza like the one that galvanized Calgary that spring. And why not? Standard Oil and several local consortiums were exploring north to Athabasca, east to Wainwright and west to Rocky Mountain House. The *Bulletin* reported in July that samples from the Nakamun field north of Edmonton were on display in the city. The Nakamun manager pronounced himself "elated" at the public interest. For the past several years his company had been working "under the most adverse circumstances through a period when there was no oil fever."

For oil speculation, as for real estate, fever was the operative word. Promoters naturally did their best to work it up, while reassuring possible investors of the soundness of their prospects. "OIL! OIL! OIL!" shouted one advertisement, quickly adding: "We have organized one of the most conservative oil companies in Canada, namely, the Mirror Oils Limited." Another local company,

TODAY'S THE DAY—EMPIRE DAY

What Alberta's capital needed, many residents believed, was a nearby oil strike as big as Calgary's. And why, with exploration crews busy on all sides, shouldn't it have one? The American Canadian Oil Company, here drilling near Morinville c. 1914, was only one of many hopefuls. Inset, an Edmonton Journal cartoon urges the British navy to switch from coal to oil, thus causing Alberta to dance for joy.

the *Eldorado*, listed three MLAs among its principals. Maritime Petroleum reported a strike that December on Henry Dredner's farm, seven miles east of Leduc, and brought a pint of the stuff to the *Bulletin* office. "Even a layman realizes it is the real thing," the newspaper wrote. "There is the unmistakable oily odour, and when a quantity was poured on a piece of paper, it ignited instantly and flared fiercely."

The *Bulletin* quoted O.T. Ross, described as an American geologist and oil expert, as saying that Edmonton would "soon be the centre of activity in oil explorations, with numerous refineries fed by pipelines from the North." Oil brokers opened scores of instant offices in Edmonton to cash in on Calgary's Turner Valley strike. Mayor McNamara headed south to buy some likely property there, saying he would soon start drilling on his own account. The prospectors and promoters were right, of course — but a half-century premature.

So the economy continued downward, and the mayoralty was no sinecure. One thing, however, McNamara did accomplish. Ever since Edmonton and Strathcona amalgamated in 1912, argument had been raging among their citizens as to how their street names and/or numbers should be coordinated. Mail went astray; streetcar route planners tore their hair; renaming was actually begun at one point, then stopped. Not until April 1914 was a new street-naming plan agreed upon by plebiscite (see sidebar).

There would be no further triumphs for Mayor McNamara, however — and all on account of what was known as "social vice," namely prostitution, drunkenness and gambling, more or less in that order. Popular historian James H. Gray in *Red Lights on the Prairies* maintains that most Edmontonians "wanted a wide-open town, so long as the worst excesses of being wide open were prevented." That was certainly Alderman Joe Clarke's view (openly stated), and probably the mayor's too (not openly stated).

In any event, it didn't work. The mayor was scarcely in office before the town seethed with allegation and acrimony. One obvious obstacle to the "wide-open town" was Police Chief Silas H. Carpenter. A tough-minded Montreal cop, Carpenter had been hired to replace Chief A.C. Lancey after Lancey's second resignation in late 1912 (see Sect. 2, ch. 5). He had begun an immediate crackdown, both in the department and on the streets. Some 2,500 drunks were arrested in 1913, along with the keepers of four dozen brothels, their inmates and habitués, plus myriad gamblers, opium smokers and vagrants. Carpenter also purged the department of what he considered corrupt and incompetent officers. Since none of this evidenced a "wide-open town," within a month of taking office Mayor McNamara fired Chief Carpenter.

Three thousand Edmontonians who did *not* want a "wide-open town" immediately signed a petition on Carpenter's behalf, organized by several former mayors. The Temperance and Moral

I am writing you this letter to let you know of the nature of an attempted perversion of justice by the Police Magistrate, and also that inasmuch as Heaton is now under sentence in the Lethbridge Jail for one year, in view of the fact that he will be tried upon this perjury charge at the next court of competent criminal jurisdiction, you may decide whether it is advisable to go to the expense of sending him to Lethbridge in the meanwhile or not, and that inasmuch as certain officials of the Department of the Attorney-General have secured absolute statements and confessions from Heaton that his whole story connecting the writer with any conspiracy with Pierson and McMillan was concocted, framed up and induced by certain promises made by Chief of Police George Hill on the representation that he was acting for the Department of the Attorney-General, I am asking that copies of these statements and the names of the witnesses be furnished me forthwith, in order that at the trial of this case no further miscarriage of justice in connection with the judicial farce now being conducted in the City of Edmonton may take place.

– from a letter of Joseph A. Clarke to the Department of the Attorney-General, April 28, 1915.

Edmonton Daily Bulletin

Morning Edition · *Morning Edition*

VOL. IV., NO. 244. · EDMONTON, ALBERTA, SATURDAY, MAY 23, 1914 · TWENTY PAGES TODAY · PRICE FIVE CENTS

CHIEF LANCEY IS DISMISSED

Deputy Chief May Go---Wholesale Dismissals Predicted

ALARMING GROWTH OF VICE IN THE CITY

Investigation by The Bulletin Has Revealed Conditions of Worst Kind

POLICEMEN AWARE OF LAW VIOLATION

Disorderly Houses Have Been Conducted With no Attempt at Concealment

CHARGES ARE MADE OF AN ORGANIZED GRAFT SYSTEM

Air is Full of Rumors of Protection Money Being Ladled Out in Unlimited Quantities—Women Claim That They Paid Money For Protection

Say Were Paying For Protection

City of Edmonton Archives, EA-267-180

City of Edmonton Archives, EA-267-159

Silas H. Carpenter (above left), police chief in 1912-13, cracked down on 'social vice,' got rid of officers he considered incompetent or corrupt, and was himself summarily sacked. His replacement: none other than ex-chief A.C. Lancey (right) whose firing the year before had occasioned resounding headlines.

[4] The Temperance and Moral Reform League was as adamantly opposed to gambling as it was to prostitution, and therefore considered the city's many licensed 'clubs' a blot on the urban landscape. 'I don't know what you know about these clubs,' said league president T.H. Miller at the league's January 1914 protest meeting, 'but I know men who've gone to financial and every other ruin that way.'

Reform League met at McDougall Methodist Church, deplored the firing as a "triumph for lawlessness," and demanded an inquiry by the provincial attorney-general[4]. City council stood fast, however. The aldermen knew just the man to replace Carpenter. Back for the third time came the resignation-prone Lancey.

This time Chief Lancey barely lasted three months, but that brief period destroyed the McNamara administration. Lancey promptly reinstated officers purged by Carpenter, and got back to business as usual. The word spread among "ladies of the night" across the West that Edmonton was "open" again. Dubious characters like William Wheeler, who ran the Dominion Club on First Street (101 St.), allegedly competed to sell these women police protection, or at any rate claim to. "Disorderly houses" and streetwalkers proliferated alarmingly, causing reputable citizens to bitterly complain. Lancey ordered some purely symbolic raids on the larger "disorderly houses" and gambling clubs, much to the scorn of his critics who saw that vice continued to thrive.

One such raid in May, however, blew up the town. Detective Ernest Seymour, a rehired Carpenter reject, raided Wheeler's Dominion Club. As Seymour's cohorts battered down the front door, the gamblers escaped out the windows. Did Seymour seize the gaming equipment, angry citizens later asked. He did not, replied Seymour, because club manager Wheeler had offered to look after it for him. As soon as the police left, the gamblers returned.

When word of the Dominion Club raid leaked out, hundreds jammed McDougall Church in an even bigger protest rally than the January one. The mayor and council could stall no longer. Lancey was canned again, and in a resolution introduced by Clarke, and passed unanimously, council requested a judicial inquiry to determine: (a) whether the growth of Edmonton crime and vice had been such as to "indicate a failure on the part of the civic authorities to enforce the law," and (b) whether any alderman or civic servant had profited by protecting any "illicit or illegal undertaking."

The inquiry began in mid-June 1914 under Mr. Justice D.C. Scott, and for the next five weeks provided the best show in town, crowding out the alarming financial news, even the looming war. Before the commission, Mayor McNamara emerged a transformed man. Overnight he had become a tireless crusader against vice. He had fired Carpenter because he believed the chief was doing a rotten job, he said. Furthermore, he had been much offended by rampant Edmonton vice long before he decided to run for mayor. Having thus declared himself, he left for Toronto on business.

Ex-chief Lancey told a different story. He swore that at a meeting with the mayor and several aldermen he had been instructed to get rid of the street prostitutes but leave the brothels alone.

His problem, he said, was that the citizenry kept insisting he raid the brothels. What was the hapless chief to do? He was "between the devil and the deep sea." But then came Detective Seymour. McNamara had told him the previous fall he was angry with Carpenter for hauling him into court on traffic charges. "He said he would get rid of Chief Carpenter no matter what they would say."

There was other incriminating testimony. Charles Gill, manager of the Pantages Theatre, testified that he had paid $25, in cash when a cheque was refused, to deputy chief Sam Wright (another Carpenter reject) for arranging to get a banned "vice sketch" called *Truth* back on stage. Mrs. Jessie Bell, former proprietor of a large men's rooming house on Kinistino Avenue (96 St.),

The explosive 1914 council of Mayor W.J. McNamara (centre rear). City archivists identify the aldermen as: (back left) A.B. Campbell, J.A. Kinney; (back right) G.H. May, J.M. MacDonald, H.A. Calder; (front row) H.R. Smith, Rice Sheppard, J. Driscoll, James East. The empty chair may belong to McNamara's erstwhile ally, Alderman Joe Clarke.

The mayor was scarcely in office before the town seethed with allegation and acrimony. One obvious obstacle to the 'wide-open town' was Police Chief Silas H. Carpenter. A tough-minded Montreal cop, he had begun an immediate crackdown, both in the department and on the streets.

near the Savoy Hotel, said Chief Lancey had advised her against selling her furniture to the new lessee, one Billie Morton, a well-known madam. But when she mentioned that Alderman Joe Clarke was Billie Morton's solicitor, Mrs. Bell said, the chief quickly changed his mind, exclaiming, "Here's where I keep my nose out of it!"

Past and present city policemen swore that certain prostitutes had complained to them about having to pay protection money, which they thought was going to the police. Other witnesses

Detective Ernest Seymour's curiously conducted raid on the Dominion Club (below) blew up the town. Below left, an earlier photo depicts Seymour as a uniformed officer.

City of Edmonton Archives, EA-29-1

A Bulletin *headline and a* Journal *cartoon announce the result of Mr. Justice D.C. Scott's inquiry into the Edmonton Police Department. No one emerged very creditably, except for Silas Carpenter, the police chief Mayor McNamara had fired.*

implicated William Wheeler of the Dominion Club as a self-proclaimed police "fixer." Someone referred to as "Joe with the big mitt" was also said to be in on the protection racket. Could that be Joe Clarke? To assume so was not justified, the judge later observed.

Dick Fryant, another Edmonton detective, said that when he asked Seymour why he would not raid known brothels, Seymour replied "I can't, for I take my orders from other persons the same as you take them from me." Several prostitutes were called as witnesses. They agreed that "everyone knew" the welcome mat was out in Edmonton, but developed faulty memories as to specific details[5].

Mr. Justice Scott, after hearing voluminous evidence — much of it conflicting, hearsay and quite probably perjured — concluded that police policy under Lancey was to ignore brothels unless there were complaints, and even then merely order them to relocate. The firing of Carpenter was not justified, he declared. He appeared to have run a well-disciplined police force.

Mrs. Jessie Bell, former proprietor of a large men's rooming house near the Savoy Hotel, said Chief Lancey had advised her against selling her furniture to the new lessee, one Billie Morton, a well-known madam. But when she mentioned that Alderman Joe Clarke was Billie Morton's solicitor, Mrs. Bell said, the chief quickly changed his mind.

---

[5]Alderman Clarke, chairman of the council's safety and health committee, took an active part in the questioning, employing a term that would soon disappear from popular usage. A prostitute was a 'sporting woman' who would 'sport' with her clients. Among pages of testimony the Journal published from the 1914 Scott Inquiry, for instance, is the following: 'When did you start to be a sporting woman in Edmonton?' demanded Clarke of witness May Smith. 'I came here as a sporting girl,' she replied. 'And have you been sporting ever since?' 'Yes, off and on,' said the witness.

Lancey and Seymour were guilty of "grave misconduct." Deputy chief Wright was "not to be believed." And obviously some sort of protection racket was operating, although no evidence had convincingly implicated Alderman Joe Clarke in it.

The Scott investigation drove a rift between McNamara and Clarke that burst into the open at the August 6 council meeting. During a discussion of economic retrenchment measures, Clarke remarked that the mayor had a habit of "betraying his trust." Furious, McNamara demanded what he meant by that. "When you tried to gain control of the police department I opposed you," roared the mayor, "if that's what you're on about."

"That's a deliberate lie," Clarke shouted back. "You can't climb into the bandwagon with the moral reformers at this late date and try to make out you've been with them all along — you cheapskate!" Other aldermen calmed the pair sufficiently to finish the meeting. But the instant it ended McNamara yelled, "I repeat now everything I said during the meeting, and I add that you are a coward and a liar!" whereupon they began slugging each other. The fight raged out of the council chamber, through the hall and into the street, while they blacked each other's eyes and bloodied faces. Had they been two ordinary individuals, the *Bulletin* remarked, they would have spent the night in the police cells.

There were calls for the mayor's resignation, which he ignored. But then Alexander

The resolute gentlemen above, according to the archive record, constituted Edmonton's Morality Squad when Police Chief Silas Carpenter took over. Their job: to keep the lid on gambling clubs and 'disorderly houses' — more or less. The uniform of Edmonton's finest (upper left), like most Canadian police forces up into the 1930s, followed the style of Britain's 'bobbies.' At bottom, the force in 1914 was becoming motorized.

Livingstone, a former alderman, launched a legal action on quite another matter. That spring the mayor and Alderman James East had helped finance exploration of a possible gas well at Viking, 75 miles southeast of Edmonton. They had also voted on a council resolution authorizing the city to take the well over at cost if they were successful. Mr. Justice W.C. Ives, who heard the case, commented that these actions appeared to him commendable and public-spirited. Nevertheless, the terms of the city charter compelled him to rule that since April 28 both men had been technically disqualified for municipal office.

This late October ruling unseated both McNamara and East, leaving Edmonton temporarily mayor-less. By December McNamara's one-time ally, Alderman Clarke, was in a worse predicament — namely in a city jail cell, having considerable difficulty getting bail. The new police chief, George Hill, a veteran of the Edinburgh constabulary, had arrested him on charges of inciting and abetting criminal offences in a conspiracy to discredit Chief Hill himself.

At the trial in January 1915 a recently convicted safecracker, Frank Heaton, testified that Alderman Clarke had written a letter to a Saskatoon detective named Springer, suggesting he send along some crooks to start an Edmonton crime wave, the idea being to make the chief look bad. When Detective Springer told Heaton and two other Saskatoon "yeggs" about this, the trio decided to try their luck. Unfortunately, they all got caught and were currently in jail. Franklin Haddock, a private detective whom Chief Hill had invited in from Winnipeg immediately after his own appointment the previous June, said Alderman Clarke had admitted as much to him in private conversation — unaware, of course, that Haddock was working for Hill.

Mr. Justice James D. Hyndman found this tale too much to swallow. Convict Heaton was not the most credible of witnesses, he observed. Both Alderman Clarke and Detective Springer would have to be complete fools to act as they were alleged to have done. Describing the case as "peculiar in many ways," he briskly delivered a verdict of not guilty. There were no immediate political implications, either; Clarke's two-year aldermanic term had another year to go.

But by then a stiff new broom had swept into Edmonton municipal politics. In October a delegation of influential citizens had tried to persuade former mayor John A. McDougall to return to politics and sort things out as he had done in 1908 (Vol. II, Sect. 2, ch. 1), but McDougall was unwilling to repeat his rescue mission. The Moral Reform League then spearheaded a campaign to elect William Thomas Henry, a furniture dealer (co-founder of Blowey, Henry Ltd.) and a

City of Edmonton Archives, EA-362-32 • City of Edmonton Archives, EA-160-205

'That's a deliberate lie!' shouted Joseph Clarke (right). Thereupon Clarke — alderman, lawyer, and friend of labouring men and 'sporting women' — began slugging it out with Mayor McNamara (left), right there in the council chamber. But Clarke would remain an Edmonton municipal politician for a long time to come.

City of Edmonton Archives, EA-10-1061

Despite the dire prophecies, Edmonton did not go under; but by 1920 it was a quiet, backwater little city. This view of 102 Avenue, looking east toward 124 Street, is typical of the times. Not for nearly half a century would the city begin to fulfil the grandiose plans of those optimistic boom years, and actually need all the municipal infrastructure installed then. Also notably absent here are the trees that would later distinguish it.

Police Chief George Hill (at right) got threats like this letter (below) published in the Bulletin *in December 1914. The town clearly harboured 'a nest of bad characters' who counted on 'influential backing,' the* Bulletin *commented. But Chief Hill remained healthy, and kept his job until Joe Clarke fired him in 1920.*

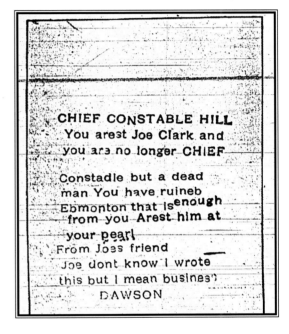

Methodist, along with a "clean city" aldermanic slate. Opposing Henry was lino-type operator and inveterate political activist Joseph Woods Adair.

"I stand by Alderman Clarke," was Adair's forthright declaration, "for I have known him for years and he is a soldier of the common good. I will stand sponsor for the 1914 administration." The *Journal* was equally forthright. "There you have it," the newspaper commented. "If you wish not only to have the evils which prevailed during 1914 continued, but aggravated...you know how to vote on Monday... To turn down Mr. Henry and put Mr. Adair in the mayor's chair would be nothing less than inviting bankruptcy." Edmontonians agreed. In an unprecedented turnout of 10,000 voters they endorsed the whole clean city slate, and made Henry mayor by a margin of 6,000.

Dick Fryant, another Edmonton detective, said that when he asked Seymour why he would not raid known brothels, Seymour replied, 'I can't, for I take my orders from other persons the same as you take them from me.' Several prostitutes were called as witnesses. They agreed that 'everyone knew' the welcome mat was out in Edmonton.

Mayor Henry did not disappoint them, but his three-year administration (1915-18) would encompass the very worst of the economic bust. The war was providing some relief to the local economy, it is true. Coal production increased and new mines opened. Wheat acreage doubled in two years, the price per bushel rose by 50%, and the 1915 harvest was phenomenally good. But the sprawling city, with its interior gaps, overbuilt infrastructure and heavy debt, was simply not viable. Moreover, its very population was shrinking, from 72,561 at the 1914 peak to 54,846 in 1918. Between January and April 1914 the records show the streetcars carrying nearly five million passengers. In the same period in 1915 the total dropped by more than a million.

The unemployment situation continued to worsen into the winter of 1914-15. The Edmonton Board of Public Welfare, as reported in the *Bulletin*, estimated the number of Edmonton jobless at 5,000. Even so, the newspapers published no more stories about threats of violence. (There never had been any actual violence.) With funds provided by the province, the city was able to hire 500 men to build sewers that winter — three days a week and twenty cents an hour paid in groceries or meals and lodging.

Single men could turn to the Salvation Army at a pinch, and many had likely drifted away by now to more

William T. Henry (at left), supported by a 'reform' coalition, was elected mayor for the 1915 term by a landslide vote, at the head of a 'clean city' slate. He did not disappoint his supporters and, although beset by the worst of the bust, was twice re-elected.

The year the North Saskatchewan went on a rampage

EDMONTON'S RIVER JUMPED TEN FEET IN TEN HOURS AND THEN CRESTED 48 FEET ABOVE NORMAL, DARKENING THE CITY AND DRIVING OUT 2,000

The worst natural catastrophe to befall Edmonton in the early 20th century struck just as the economic bust was tightening its grip on the city. The North Saskatchewan River rose ten feet in ten hours on June 28, 1915, in an angry brown torrent that threatened every building on Ross's and Walter's flats. At their crest, on June 29, the waters reached an estimated 48 feet above normal level, several feet higher than the great flood of 1899 and the flood of 1907 that wiped out much of the city's lumber industry (Vol. II, p. 260). The flood of 1915 drove 2,000 people from their homes, demolished many houses and most of the industries on the flats. All told it caused damage of at least $750,000.

The *Bulletin* reported on June 29 that tons of debris were battering the Low Level Bridge, while the water swirled furiously around it. Fourteen ballasted freight cars and two Canadian Northern locomotives, with steam up, had been kept standing on the bridge all night to stabilize it, however, and it was holding. The debris included whole houses and barns, along with logs and thousands of feet of dressed lumber from John Walter's two sawmills. The *Bulletin* described the mills themselves as "a mass of ruins."

Edmontonians thronged McDougall Hill and the High Level Bridge, watching aghast as scores of houses below them were swept away and hundreds flooded. Refugees fled to a relief centre hastily established at Bennett School on Gallagher Flats in the Cloverdale district. On the second day, however, when the flood reached there too, they had to be moved to higher ground: Alex Taylor School, the Edmonton City Dairy, church halls and private homes.

The *Bulletin*, which never missed a

political angle, credited the leadership of Mayor William Henry — at least in part — with the fact that no lives were lost and morale remained high. Volunteers worked steadily on rescue missions, along with the city police, carrying marooned families and their possessions to safety. The city's new Board of Public Welfare got one of its first tryouts, and volunteers were much involved in relief efforts as well. The *Journal* appealed for donations of clothing and bedding, to be delivered to the former real estate offices of York & McNamara.

Civic employees tried desperately to keep the power and water plants operating, but failed. At the pumping plant the chief engineer reportedly worked for hours in water up to his armpits. By noon on June 29 the flywheel was revolving in water and sending a stream of it up to the roof. The last of

the municipal utilities had to be shut down. The city was without electricity (including, of course, streetcars), water or telephones. The *Bulletin* staff kept on publishing, working by gasoline lamplight and running the presses with an emergency gasoline engine.

As soon as the waters receded, Edmonton got busy putting things to rights. But the sawmills, brickyard and tannery on the flats never did reopen. They just couldn't raise the money.

— *V.L.B.*

The spectacular panorama above, shot from the south bank, shows the river in full flood. At right, wrecked houses and other debris surge against the Low Level Bridge, which was ballasted with Canadian Northern freight cars. Below, the inundated power and water plants can be seen in the background, steam flowing from their stacks. Opposite, a boatman with a load of household goods poles northward along 100th Street on Ross Flats.

promising places. Others were doubtless among the 25,000 Albertans who enlisted. Civic relief officer Thomas R. Turnbull, who had 300 families on his list, appealed for offers of cheap housing. Although many landlords were understanding, he said, he often had to intercede on behalf of penniless families. What's more, Turnbull told the *Bulletin* reporter, the names of some of the welfare applicants would surprise him: people who once earned a good living. With jobs lost as firms cut staff or folded, they were reduced to porridge and dry bread before they could bring themselves to ask for help.

Nevertheless, however bad things get, there is always some money around. At the July 5, 1915, opening of the Grand Trunk Pacific's magnificent 175-room Macdonald Hotel, on the southeast corner of McDougall Avenue (100 St.) and Jasper, 500 Edmontonians attended a gala dinner and dance. It was, said the *Journal*, "perhaps the most brilliant social event in the city's history. The chateau-style hotel, sheathed in Indiana limestone and roofed with copper, had been three years under construction at a cost of $2.2 million. In the two-storey Confederation Room, artist

One problem the amalgamators of the two cities didn't foresee: how would they identify the streets?

MAIL CHAOS FOLLOWS THE UNION DUE TO THE DUPLICATION OF NAMES; THE NUMBER SYSTEM SOLVES IT, BUT ONLY AFTER THE USUAL BRAWL

Time was when many thoroughfares in Edmonton and Strathcona had names: Abernethy Avenue and Cristabelle Street, Coot Avenue and Picard Street, Brackman Street and Bertha Avenue, Ottawa Avenue and Griesbach Street. Some of these (the last two among them) were duplicated on both sides of the river. Each town also possessed a substantial area of numbered streets, organized on two incompatible systems.

No sooner had the amalgamation of the two cities been proclaimed in February 1912 than complaints began about postal mix-ups. "It can easily be imagined that serious loss and inconvenience may arise from letters wandering aimlessly round," the *Edmonton Journal* observed. Everyone agreed that something must be done; it took two years of wrangling, however, to agree on precisely what.

The chief cause of confusion was probably the similarly numbered streets, although it is hard to see why even they should have caused all the trouble that allegedly was occurring. In old Edmonton (i.e., north of the river), the north-south streets from the city centre westward bore numbers that began at First Street. Strathcona by contrast had established a quadrant system for its central core. Streets ran north-south

City of Edmonton Archives, EA-267-159

City engineer Arthur J. Latornel, designer of the 'one comprehensive system.'

and avenues east-west, with Whyte Avenue and Main Street (later 104th) serving as dividing lines. North of Whyte Avenue, for example, First Street NE paralleled Main Street one block east; south of Whyte Avenue it became First Street SE.

In addition, however, Strathcona had many named streets: older ones like University Avenue, a diagonal along the south border of the university, and Walter and St. Placide Streets on the flats; newer ones like Riverview Avenue and Highlands Street in later developments. North of the river, all the old east-end thoroughfares were named, not numbered (and were on a slight diagonal too). All the east-west roads also had names, as did most of those in burgeoning subdivisions.

Adding to the patchwork effect, rapid development was creating instances in which one street often boasted two or three names. What later became 107 Avenue, for example, was called Nelson Avenue between First and 21st Streets, Heiminck Street east of First, and Short Avenue west of 21st. And the east end had a Short Street as well. Such arrangements might be all very well for the locals, critics complained, but are bad for befuddled

Frederick S. Challener himself supervised the installation of a full-sized copy of his painting of the 1864 Charlottetown conference that launched Canada[6]. For the next half-century the Macdonald's imposing Empire Ballroom would be the centre for Edmonton high society.

But city finances were becoming ever more troublesome. In 1915 the Henry administration

---

The sprawling city, with its interior gaps, overbuilt infrastructure and heavy debt, was simply not viable. Moreover, its very population was shrinking, from 72,516 at the 1914 peak to 54,846 in 1918.

---

reduced departmental expenditures by a further 25%, and one of the first jobs to go was that of assistant building inspector. As the *Journal* observed, "not much of a rush" for building permits was expected. Similar heroic measures put four of the five city utilities into the black[7]. By

[7]The infatuation of Edmonton civic politicians with municipal ownership of utilities, says urban historian John C. Weaver, was due more to business strategy and boosterism than to socialist tendencies. They also believed, however, that public ownership would provide a higher moral tone and superior service. But 'neither claim stood the test of experience in early Edmonton,' Weaver writes. 'The streetcar department served realty interests, and the telephone department functioned like any private utility company.'

strangers, delivery men and postal employees.

They are also extremely uncongenial to the tidy engineering mind. There was an urgent need, declared city engineer Arthur J. Latornel, for "one comprehensive system" whereby street names and house numbers "should immediately signify their location." At the behest of city council he produced a number of proposals, variously combing different elements.

A 1912 plan, affecting only the south side, had east-west avenues numbered from the river southward. Streets would run north-south and have names arranged alphabetically, east of Main for noted citizens (Anderson, Bennett, Calder) and west of Main for universities (Aberdeen, Berkeley, Cambridge). But the residents voted "No."

As Latornel and a council committee argued their way through a succession of subsequent proposals in 1913, one constant survived, notably that avenues should run east-west and streets north-south. Another was the proviso, spelled out in the amalgamation agreement between the two cities, that Strathcona's Saskatchewan Avenue was sacrosanct. (The Edmonton equivalent would later become 97th Ave.). So Latornel hammered out several quadrilateral plans for the entire city, combining numbers and names in various ways. The committee balked at them all.

What they finally agreed upon by July 1913 was the comprehensive number system that would ultimately prevail, but not without first being adopted and then cancelled.

City of Edmonton Archives, EA-10-184

Perhaps the only surviving photo of a pre-numerical Edmonton street sign is this 1914 shot of a desolate marker at Jasper and Hastings (which became 87 Street). The photographer was facing east on Jasper.

Council gave Latornel the go-ahead for this system. Eight thousand street signs were ordered. Work began. But then the anti-number opposition organized rallies and got a court injunction that halted the entire project. It was all a plot against Mayor William Short, the *Journal* claimed. Even after the injunction was removed, the aldermen were reluctant to proceed.

Not until March 1914 did the next mayor, W.J. McNamara, tackle the street controversy by proclaiming a public competition for the best plan, with a $100 prize. Entries ranging from a postcard to a six-foot-by-six-foot map poured in. City council picked the best of them, which became known as the Edmonscona Plan and involved numbers plus names of cities, counties, provinces, rivers, lakes, seas, historical characters, authors, poets, mountains and trees — all arranged in selected districts.

Then the city's voters were asked to choose by plebiscite between Edmonscona and the 1913 "all-numerical system," on which considerable work had already been completed. They chose the numbers. Another seven decades would go by before Edmontonians, increasingly conscious of their history, would begin to try to retrieve some of their historic street names.

— *V.L.B.*

The Macdonald Hotel rises regardle[ss]

Bust or no bust, the Grand Trunk Railway dug the Macdonald's McDougall Hill site in 1912 (below) and completed the limestone sheathed hotel (above) by 1915. For elegant dining, indoors or al fresco, the hotel set a new standard in the Alberta capital (opposite page).

Historically-minded citizens were shocked in mid-October 1915 to find that workmen were demolishing old Fort Edmonton, which for three-quarters of a century had stood on the North Saskatchewan's north bank. The public works department assured them, however, that the components would be carefully preserved and the fort rebuilt somewhere else, as a museum. Meanwhile, it was in the way of the legislative landscaping.

September all but the street railway were paying their way. But more was to come. In 1916 the *Bulletin* would report further budget reductions throughout City Hall, from halving the engineering department to providing no new coats for firemen. Meanwhile Henry painfully whittled away at the $22-million debenture debt that weighed heavy on Edmonton's slender revenues, and would long continue to do so.

Not that considerations like these prevented the 1915 aldermen from asking to be paid. They produced a bylaw giving themselves a $1,000 annual salary. The ratepayers turned them down flat. Another money bylaw would have enabled the city to pursue the Viking gas proposal (the one that got McNamara in trouble). Mayor Henry favoured it, as did many other people eager to ensure a municipal natural gas supply. Some hundred Edmontonians travelled to Viking by Grand Trunk Pacific special train the week before the gas plebiscite, and were much impressed by the mass of flame spouting from the well's four-inch pipe. The bylaw was defeated nonetheless — for the time being[8].

Meanwhile, the *Journal* reported on Oct. 13, 1915, "something resembling panic reigned among citizens who value the historic" when they suddenly discovered that old Fort Edmonton, on the slope just below the Legislature, was being torn down. The rough, 75-year-old log building was very dilapidated, and was in the way of the landscaping planned for the legislative grounds. However, the Public Works department promised, the components would be carefully stored and the fort rebuilt, perhaps on the high south bank of the river just west of the High Level Bridge. As things turned out, half a century would pass before this promised reconstruction would begin, several miles to the west. But it would be a thorough one, and include the chief factor's house that had previously been destroyed by fire, and much more besides.

Henry stood for the mayoralty again in December 1915 and went in by acclamation. At the end of his second term in 1916 he tried to retire, but when five men declared their candidacies leading citizens were so alarmed that they persuaded him to change his mind. As the *Journal* put it, "The good qualities of some of the five are recognized, as well as the undesirable qualities of some of the others." Who could tell what might happen in a five-man race? Ultimately four of the aspirants for the 1917 term dropped out and the only contender left to oppose Henry was Joe Clarke, who had lost his aldermanic seat the previous year. But Fighting Joe was also soundly beaten in this first bid at the mayor's job.

Perhaps Clarke was lucky at that. The 1917 civic financial situation proved even more parlous. In August Mayor Henry had to write to the school trustees that he "very much regretted" they would be getting no money whatsoever for the balance of the calendar year. "I might say, however," he added, "that in the event of the market improving between now and the end of the year (which is hardly likely) we may be enabled to borrow the issue against the arrears of taxes, in which case we will be very pleased to pay the School Board the full balance due."

The frantic trustees didn't wait for the market, writes Michael A. Kostek in *A Century and Ten: The History of Edmonton's Public Schools*. They appealed to Education Minister J.R. Boyle, who proposed an ingenious scheme. The board should use its remaining capital funds to buy City of Edmonton bonds, he suggested, thus enhancing the city's credit rating so it could borrow operating funds to keep the schools running. This was not strictly legal, but the minister promised to enact legislation to correct that problem, which he did.

The "social vice" issue had not vanished either, although the emphasis shifted from prostitution. Edmonton was assuredly still home to "sporting women," but much less was heard of them. After Prohibition began in 1916 the police were largely occupied, one way or another, with the illegal liquor trade. And although policemen had clearly not become incorruptible, Mayor Henry and Chief Hill seemingly maintained discipline. When Constable No. 62 was discovered in 1917 to be bootlegging — while in uniform, which made it worse — the chief summarily fired him, and was instructed by the police commission to charge him as well.

By the end of his third term Henry definitely felt he had done his share; he would not run again. Five candidates, Fighting Joe among them, contested the mayoralty. The newspapers backed Harry Marshall Erskine Evans (1876-1973), an Ontario geologist who came west in 1906 to prospect for coal on the Pembina River. He had settled in Edmonton to deal in bonds, insurance and real estate — along with volunteer work for the Red Cross, Edmonton Board of Public Welfare and the wartime Canadian Patriotic Fund. (In 1946 he would be made an officer of the Order of the British Empire for his work in two world wars.)

Going into 1918, Evans noted, Edmonton had a million dollars in debt past due and three million about to come due, besides the ongoing financial requirements of the city. This was the major concern. Other matters were important, but the main thing was to somehow stay solvent. He handily won the election. "I hope Mr. Evans will have as pleasant a time in office as I have had," Henry commented with no trace of sarcasm.

For H.M.E. Evans, mayor in 1918, collecting tax arrears was a daunting challenge. At one point he appealed to Edmonton Rotarians to urge their neighbours to pay up and save the city from bankruptcy. Many owners just could not pay, however; over a three-year period the city became the reluctant owner of 44,348 forfeited lots.

Cutting costs was only half the solvency battle; the other half was revenue. The city's chief source of it was property taxes, and collecting them in the post-bust years ranged from difficult to impossible. At one point Mayor Henry, addressing the Rotary Club, had appealed to the Rotarians to induce their neighbours to pay up so the city could survive. But many, including speculators who had failed to market their holdings during the boom, simply could not pay up[9]. As tax arrears mounted, their land reverted to the city. Between 1918 and 1921, Weaver notes, the City of Edmonton would fall reluctant heir to no fewer than 44,348 forfeited parcels of land[10].

Mayor Evans applied new incentives and penalties in 1918 to reduce tax arrears, and by June this brought in nearly half a million dollars on past due accounts. The same could not be said of that year's auctions of city-seized lots,

[8]Many Edmontonians yearned for a natural gas supply such as Medicine Hat and Calgary enjoyed, but it was seen as an expensive proposition and was contentious. Mayor William Short's defeat by W.J. McNamara in late 1913 may have been due in part to Short's interest in the Pelican gas strike on the Athabasca River. In July 1915 an aldermanic party journeyed up the Athabasca to see the Pelican wells (stoving in their boat en route) and jubilantly reported that 'there's enough gas there to blow up the whole of North America.' But not for another eight years would Edmonton actually manage to complete a deal for natural gas.

When new fire chief R.G. Davidson walked in, seventy firemen walked out. Mayor Evans and the council backed the chief, authorizing him to hire a whole new complement of men.

The chief could handle a bad fire but the union beat him in the end

Fire Chief R.G. Davidson's new crew managed to contain the gasoline-fuelled 1918 blaze at the Lines-Brake Automobile Company, although not before it had gutted the Maryland Hotel (below). Little better could be expected, as evidenced by the earlier Cockshutt Plow fire on Eighth Street (opposite page, top), the 1913 blaze at Reed's Tea and Bazaar at 10004 Jasper (opposite, bottom), and the destruction of Douglas Brothers department store at 2 Whyte Avenue (above), also in 1913. It was labour politics, not poor job performance, that beat the chief.

For sightseers boarding a tour bus on 102 Street north of Jasper Avenue, there was plenty to look at in the amalgamated Edmonton of 1914. The bus ride itself would be a thrilling novelty for many — if a somewhat jolting one, in view of those solid rubber tires.

[9]Among Edmonton's hard-pressed businesses was the Grand Trunk Pacific's showpiece Macdonald Hotel. When it opened in 1915, the GTP negotiated a deal for twenty years of reduced taxes. But in 1918 the railway's legal representative was back asking for further reductions. 'We are not now running it so much as a hotel but more or less as a philanthropic institution,' he said, citing loss figures. In fact, the railway was thinking of closing both its Winnipeg hotel (the Fort Garry) and the Macdonald — not that this was to be taken as a threat, he added meaningfully.

however. One Thomas W. Brown set a new low when he acquired four Highlands lots for $21. The Evans council even considered taxing churches, then thought better of the idea. Other innovations would prove just about as unpopular, however. The mayor and council asked the provincial Legislature for authority to levy (for two years) a personal income tax, and also a graduated business tax. The province refused to let the city loose on the railways, banks and trust companies. Something, after all, must be left for them to tax.

Another big headache during the Evans regime was the growth of labour militancy, which began with the firemen. The fire chief, William G. Henderson, had resigned in December 1917, reportedly advising the mayor and commissioners that no member of the 76-man force was competent to replace him. But when they reappointed R.G. Davidson, who had been chief from 1906 to 1911, the Firefighters' Federal Labour Union objected. On February 2, when the new chief walked in, seventy firemen walked out. According to their recent agreement with the city, said the union local, all appointments must be from within the department and in strict seniority.

All except the chief, argued council. It authorized Chief Davidson to hire a new complement of men, who got their baptism of fire, more than figuratively, in the early hours of Sunday, Feb. 24. Black smoke was seen emerging from Monarch Billiard Hall, in the basement of the Lines-Brake Automobile Company at 10031 - 102 Street. The new brigade, aided by volunteers, fought hard amidst the exploding gas tanks of some 120 automobiles stored there, but the flames spread to the Maryland Hotel next door. Although there was no loss of life, both buildings were gutted[11].

The customary inquiry heard allegations that (a) the equipment was in bad shape, (b) the new brigade was inadequate and (c) one of the strikers had interfered with the hose pressure. No startling conclusions were reached, but still the strikers refused to work for the new chief. So the mayor and council made a bid for public support. They asked the citizens by plebiscite whether they favoured council's stand in the firemen's dispute. "No," came the answer, 6,539 to 2,330. Chief Davidson and all the new men had to go; the "old brigade" returned on a shorter work week, with one of their former captains as chief.

Fire was a minor disaster, however, when compared with the terrible Spanish influenza epidemic that struck that fall, causing immense suffering in Edmonton, as elsewhere (see Vol. IV).

One businessman who prospered in hard times was John (Mike) Michaels, shown here with two customers. Michaels began his career at age ten as a New York newsboy, arrived in Edmonton in 1912, and set up this stand at Jasper and 101 Street. In 1916 Mike's Newsstand moved to the store on Jasper Avenue west of 100A Street which it would occupy for decades to come. Soon it was selling newspapers in seventeen foreign languages along with the English ones, thus mightily appealing to the city's increasingly articulate ethnic component. Michaels would later found the Provincial News Company.

So terrified were civic authorities (and the populace, for that matter) that all the schools were closed from October 18 to January 2.

Shortage of money notwithstanding, in mid-decade the public school board did begin providing pupils with free supplies — penhandles, rulers, paintboxes, writing and drawing books and so on. This was tightly budgeted, however, at $1.06 per pupil. No names or "disfiguring marks" were to be made on items that would be reissued to youngsters, and any reissues had to be fumigated at the end of term "in view of the danger of the spread of disease."

Meanwhile the cost of living was estimated to have risen nearly 60% since 1914. Pressure for wage hikes was coming from the Civic Service Union, from Local 30 of the Trades and Labour Council, and from the firemen — which covered most civic employees. By July council capitulated, authorizing pay increases of 8% to 16%. Even so, the Evans administration managed to reduce the city's debenture debt by a million dollars and ended the year with a reasonable surplus in general revenue account and even (overall) on the utilities.

At the same time, Edmonton businesses had been conducting a frantic campaign to persuade people to patronize locally-produced products. Great Western Garment spread the creed that to wear any other kind of work clothes was something close to treasonous while boxcars carried streamers advertising the fact the goods they carried came from Edmonton, Alberta.

Despite his successes, by mid-1918 Mayor Evans had nevertheless had enough; he did not run again. Competing for the mayoralty for 1919 were businessman Charles E. Wilson, finance committee chairman under Evans, and the irrepressible Joseph Andrew Clarke. There could be no question of the superior qualifications of Mr. Wilson, the *Journal* editorialized. A Clarke victory, Wilson supporters predicted, would bring financial ruin to Edmonton. But for Fighting Joe, it was to be third-time lucky. Barely had the campaign begun when poor Wilson was laid low by the flu. No wonder so many citizens were ill, commented Clarke, who as usual was throwing accusations in all directions; Edmonton sanitary conditions were worse than those of any other place north of the Mexican border.

Perhaps the people were getting tired of financial stringency. Joe Clarke became mayor for 1919 by a narrow 487 votes (4,762 to 4,275). He had made it at last. Moreover, he would repeat his triumph, winning the mayoralty again for 1920 by a more comfortable margin. Civic politics consequently became livelier once again, and more acrimonious.

By now elections right down to school board level were being fought on a party basis: Clarke and the Dominion Labour Party (chiefly east end) versus the Citizens' Progressive League (chiefly

[10]Trying hard to squeeze some revenue from all the land seized for tax arrears, the city for many years leased outlying parcels to farmers. Some of the hopeful new developments the curbers had been flogging on Jasper Avenue in 1913 literally became cow pastures and long remained so, causing the medical health officer in 1927 to lament 'the large number of private cows scattered from one end of the city to the other.' Vacant lots were also leased cheaply as garden plots, and to hard-up citizens who built shacks on them. These shacks were equally distressing to municipal health officials, who could hardly complain to the landlord.

[11]Fire was a constant hazard, but the decade's most notable loss was the Thistle Rink at 629 Second Street, the locale since 1905 for important public functions from hockey games to the first session of the Alberta Legislature. When the Thistle burned to the ground in 1913, the new Livestock Pavilion on the Exhibition grounds was adapted to replace it, and functioned through much of the century as the Edmonton Gardens. Another significant fire in the decade was at All Saints Anglican Pro-Cathedral on Third Street in 1919. The church and parish hall were destroyed; all that remained was the bell.

[12]Opposing Joe Clarke for the 1920 mayoralty was city council's 1919 finance chairman, print shop owner Matthew Esdale, who accused him of both financial irresponsibility and of fostering dangerous labour elements. No sooner had Clarke taken office in 1919, Esdale charged, 'than the corridors of the Civic Block became a seething mass of disgruntled radicals.'

west end). The "ethnic" voters of the east side were beginning to see the possibilities of politics. Since there were few actual ethnic candidates as yet, they sought and found a sympathetic ear in men like Joe Clarke. So did working men and women of all kinds. They knew their man. In May 1919, when many Edmonton workers walked out in sympathy with the general strikers in Winnipeg, Mayor Clarke told one of their delegations: "Well, I think you would have been a bunch of suckers if you had not struck, and a bunch of suckers if you come back."

This was something Clarke detractors did not soon forget, although the mayor protested he was only trying to promote harmony[12]. The sympathy strike lasted barely five days and was quite good-humoured, Mayor Clarke pointed out. The streetcar operators, for example, did their best to minimize any inconvenience. True, replied the detractors, but that was due to the good sense of Edmonton workmen — no thanks to the mayor.

There was also the matter of law enforcement, always a Clarke obsession. In January 1919, Moral Reform League secretary A.W. Coone in a newspaper letter charged the police with "laxity, inefficiency and graft." Delegations from the league and the Woman's Christian Temperance Union descended upon the three-man police commission (Judge Hedley C. Taylor, Magistrate Philip Primrose and Mayor Clarke). Liquor was being freely sold in downtown hotels, they asserted, with particular reference to the Macdonald. In the interests of all citizens, but particularly of the returned soldiers, this sorry state of affairs must be corrected. Chief George Hill must be dismissed and the police force entirely reorganized.

Judge Taylor mildly replied that in his opinion the police were doing quite a good job. Magistrate Primrose noted that the returned men seemed well able to look out for themselves.

The decline and ruin of the short-lived boom's tycoons

MAGRATH AND HOLGATE LOST THEIR MANSIONS, THE GARDINERS WOUND UP SELLING CABBAGES, AND THE BRANDERS CREATED A SPECTACULAR GARDEN

A few of the men who grew rich in the Edmonton boom emerged with their fortunes more or less intact, but most were ruined by the bust. It depended largely on the timing. Real estate promoters who piled up huge paper profits between 1911 and 1913 watched them vanish in 1914, typically ending up rich in land but too cash-poor to pay the taxes necessary to keep it.

Such was the fate of W.J. Magrath and B.A. Holgate, the partners who developed Highlands as a fashionable district

City of Edmonton Archives, EA-500-273

on the city's east side, centred on their own fine mansions high above the river (Sect. 2, ch. 5). Holgate lost his home to the city in 1921 when the tax arrears on it reached $5,000. Magrath managed to hold onto his for a further ten years, then he too had to let it go.

Meanwhile, on Edmonton's west side, the story of John B. Gardiner of Capital Hill was unfolding. Gardiner, an insurance executive, bought a quarter-section in 1906 on a height above the junction of the MacKinnon Ravine and the North Saskatchewan River. Although it was even beyond the Glenora district, then considered remote, he subdivided nonetheless. By 1913, despite the distance, he had sold a number of lots and built himself a handsome home on the cliff, with a grand view of the city to eastward.

At that stage, writes Edmonton historian Tony Cashman, Gardiner was thought to be worth $3.5 million. He and his wife used to drive downtown in dignified style, in an electric brougham with flowers from their gardens and greenhouses arranged inside in cut-glass vases.

John B. Gardiner, developer of Capital Hill, was reputedly worth $3.5 million when he established his landscaped estate where the MacKinnon Ravine meets the North Saskatchewan River west of the city. By the 1930s it was a picturesque ruin.

Mayor Clarke said it was all the fault of his political opponents three years earlier. In any event, he added, the mayor and not an appointed commission should have entire authority over the police and he intended to see that this happened. Fine with him, commented Judge Taylor; he'd been doing his best, but he hadn't asked for the job.

No admirer of Chief Hill either, Mayor Clarke publicly described the man who had jailed him in 1914 as "not a proper man for the position." And in his second term he achieved two long-desired objectives. The province passed a city charter amendment transferring police authority to the mayor alone. Henceforward, Clarke declared with obvious satisfaction, a police representative would report daily to the mayor's office. Furthermore, at about the same time, Chief Hill unmysteriously became ex-chief Hill[13].

In financial matters, Mayor Clarke was a determined optimist — one of the several attributes that made sober-minded Edmontonians anxious about him. The good times would return, he insisted. With $70 million worth of real estate and $77 million worth of civic infrastructure on hand, how could Edmonton be in economic danger? And true enough, Edmonton did not go into bankruptcy during his two terms, possibly because the ratepayers kept voting down the Clarke council's money bylaws. (The mayor alleged all sorts of sinister influences in this, from coal companies to the federal government.)

By 1920 Edmonton had survived the painful transition from plenty to penury, the wind-down from its mighty economic binge, and was levelling off. But Alberta's capital would struggle for decades with the debt incurred in the halcyon days, and not for nearly half a century would the gaps fill in between all those ambitious real estate developments.

[13]Police Chief George Hill's final encounter with the city of Edmonton was to sue it for $400 in an attempt to collect sick leave pay he said was owing to him. And just where, demanded Mayor Joe Clarke, was the proof he really was sick? But Hill was not the only civic official to clash with the mayor. In 1919, for example, Clarke threatened to withhold the salary of the medical health officer, Dr. T.H. Whitelaw, over the handling of a scarlet fever case. The doctor should have reported this controversial case to the mayor's office, not just routinely to the board of health. 'He openly defied me,' Mayor Clarke indignantly informed the *Journal*. He said Whitelaw had declared he'd do the same 'on every occasion that the opportunity offered.'

Then came the bust; few other houses would be built in the Gardiners' Capital Hill development for decades to come. But they themselves stayed on in their home on Gardiner Point (later renamed Summit Point). When the house burned down, they moved into the coach house, and kept on working on their extensive flower gardens, where they had always taken a hand even in the days when they had servants.

As they became more and more hard up, Cashman writes, the solution came naturally: Gardiner grew cabbages and sold them to local stores. After he and his wife died, the property went to ruin. Nevertheless it made a marvellously romantic ruin: gateway, stone terraces and fountains, and the remains of hedges, lawns and gardens gone wild among the undergrowth.

Another Cashman tale, of a garden that owed its very existence to the real estate crash, is in its way equally typical of the times. Dr. James Brander had invested in 54 lots in Silver Heights, east of Mill Creek. At the boom's end, he was left with all 54. He paid the taxes and kept title, but the lots remained empty.

Empty, that is, until 1921 when the doctor's 76-year-old father, George Brander, decided to plant peonies and kept right on until he had five acres in bloom: 17,000 plants of eight different kinds. George Brander himself maintained his Silver Heights peony gardens until 1933, and his family kept them going until the Second World War. And every summer thousands of Edmontonians came to admire them.

— V.L.B.

W.J. Magrath's columned Ada Boulevard mansion (top) makes a fine background for lawn bowling. Below it is the home of Magrath's partner and neighbour, B.A. Holgate, under construction in 1913. The Magrath and Holgate fortunes did not long survive, but their houses did.

CHAPTER THREE

As the bust paralyzes Calgary one word reignites the city: oil

A SIXTY-FOOT COLUMN OF AMBER LIQUID AT THE DINGMAN DRILL SITE
SETS OFF A POPULAR ORGY OF STOCK-BUYING AND UNBRIDLED GREED

by **BRIAN HUTCHINSON**

Glenbow Archives, NA-2119-4

By the fall of 1913, the great boom was plainly over — vanished, as it were, within a matter of months. Nearly all the 400 real estate outfits lining the downtown streets were boarded up. Not only had Calgarians abandoned the dream of quick wealth, but many had to struggle to survive. Hundreds of tradesmen were abruptly out of work. As the men searched for jobs among the scores of half-finished buildings that stood stark and dormant throughout the suddenly slackened city, the autumn winds blew cold, a grim reminder of a boom gone bust.

Yet on October 6 came a ray of hope. That was the day William Elder drove in from Turner Valley. No time to stop and chat, he told a group of surprised acquaintances standing on a street corner. He had to get over to the office, and fast. Elder, head driller for Calgary Petroleum Products Company Ltd., had some big news to share with his boss. He raced over to company headquarters on First Street E., charged up three flights of stairs, flung open a door, and stumbled into the arms of Archibald Wayne Dingman, managing director. "We've done it," Elder shouted. "We've struck oil."

Thus began the most furious ten months of money-changing in the city's history to that point. Calgarians had long suspected that pools of black gold lay underneath the hard-scrubbed prairie soil, but until then had little proof of it. In 1888, the Negro cowboy John Ware was riding through the grassland west of Okotoks when he came upon a small pond. He stopped for a drink, and noticed a light film of oil covering the water and emitting a strong sulphurous odour. He tossed a lit match into the bog, and the resulting explosion sent his horse scampering into the brush. Other local ranchers occasionally noticed strange smells wafting through the foothills, but none made any serious attempt to understand the phenomenon, much less exploit it. To them, it was just some smelly swamp vapour.

Then came William Herron, an Ontarian who settled on a 960-acre farm 25 miles south of Calgary near the town of Okotoks, who supplemented his income hauling coal from the beds along Sheep Creek. Some time in 1911 Herron recognized the odour leaking from a rocky outcrop as that which he had

When Dingman No. 1 blew in, on May 14, 1914 (and thereafter blew twice daily until the crew got it capped), Calgarians were certain that their prosperity was once again assured. Beside the spigot, his hand on the pipe, is A.W. Dingman. Alderman T.A.P. (Tappy) Frost, who conducted a one-man oil trade mission to Toronto and Winnipeg, is holding out a mug.

known during his younger days in the Pennsylvania oil-fields. He captured samples of the vapour in a couple of gallon stone jugs, sent them to the U.S. for analysis, and found it was petroleum gas. Herron gambled. He paid $33,000 for a section of land alongside the creek bed and for mineral rights to another nearby section. Then he convinced Dingman, founder of the Calgary Natural Gas Company, and R.B. Bennett, Calgary's Tory member of Parliament, to visit the site.

Dingman, a descendant of United Empire Loyalists from Ontario, came west in 1902 at the age of 52. His Calgary Natural Gas was formed shortly thereafter, piping the product into the city from a well on the Sarcee Indian Reserve, supplying hundreds of homes and fuelling the Calgary Brewing and Malting plant.[1]

Dingman assembled four other well-known Calgary

The crucial moment came when the drillers of Dingman Well No. I reached 2,700 feet. With a hiss and a roar, a geyser of naphtha-laced, light-grade oil spouted sixty feet into the air. (Reports in New York City made it 200 feet.) Within hours, it is said, 200 automobiles were hurtling down the road to Turner Valley. Here interested onlookers are given a small demonstration.

businessmen — Senator James Lougheed, rancher-brewer A.E. Cross, broker-entrepreneur T.J.S. Skinner, and A. Judson Sayre, an American-born developer — and together they formed Calgary Petroleum Products Company Ltd. and committed $50,000 in development capital. If a survey turned up nothing but gas, they could still pipe it into Calgary and turn a tidy profit. But if it was oil, that meant real money.

Ironically and perhaps prophetically, the agreement that was to give birth to Alberta's oil

---

Herron found himself in with big players and was soon squeezed out of the enterprise. His partners bought 55% of his holdings, then forced him to hand over half of his remaining stake to Dingman as a 'service charge' for organizing the new company. He was also refused a seat on the board of directors.

---

industry also planted the seeds of a feud that was to destroy the partnership between Herron and Dingman before the end of the decade. Herron found himself with big players and was soon squeezed out of the enterprise. His partners bought 55% of his holdings, then forced him to hand over half of his remaining stake to Dingman as a "service charge" for organizing the new company. He was also refused a seat on the board of directors.

From the surviving records, it seems Dingman started the fight. In 1914, he claimed that the syndicate had overpaid Herron for the properties he had transferred in the initial agreement. Herron, still bitter and resentful at not being given a director's seat seven years earlier, responded in 1919 with a counterclaim that he had been underpaid on his 25% interest in the company and began to prepare documentation for litigation. Nine months later Dingman fuelled the fire by contending Herron had agreed to file on several sections for the syndicate but had instead filed in his own name. Herron indignantly defended himself against this latest slur in a letter to William Pearce, another director, rather triumphantly detailing how he (Herron) had run to his house and dragged his gasping wife back to the Dominion Lands Office to prevent David McDougall and Ira

Provincial Archives of Alberta, P-1883

Segur of the McDougall-Segur Oil Company from filing on lands which he believed contained part of an oilfield. "Was I doing that for the Calgary Petroleum Products Company, as Dingman afterwards made you believe?" he demanded of Pearce. "Not on your life. Neither did he think at that time that I was." By now, however, the rift was already well beyond repair.

But Herron was far from defeated. He used his proceeds to launch another venture, this time with Bill Elder. Herron-Elder Gas and Oil Development Company Ltd. was followed by a series of new companies, all founded by Herron.[2]

The syndicate started drilling in January 1913, two miles southwest of Black Diamond. Work was slow and exhausting. Elder and his crew pulled twelve-hour shifts alongside their cable rig, a primitive system that pounded heavy iron bits through the earth. Across the industry, it averaged about five feet a day. But six months later, news reached town that the "Dingman" well had hit a large pocket of gas. It was a significant discovery, producing two million cubic feet a day. More intriguing was Dingman's claim that a stream of clear "gasoline" was pouring from the well. "The gasoline is an indication of an oil base," he told the *Calgary Herald*. "We feel sure it is only a matter of drilling until we strike the oil." What was in fact coming out was neither gasoline nor oil, but naphtha.

In the soft prairie substrata the Dingman drillers exceeded six feet a day and three months later they broke through a layer of sandstone at 1,562 feet. A few gallons of straw-coloured liquid bubbled to the surface, and Elder made his hurried trip to town. Dingman had a quick look at the samples and called Bennett, who quickly assembled the rest of the company's directors. Dingman was instructed not to breathe a word about the discovery until it was determined how much oil lay at the bottom of the hole, but the orders came too late; rumours of a major strike out Turner Valley way reached Calgary just behind Elder, and the city seemed to go berserk.

"Knots of men collected on the street corners and talked petroleum," the Calgary *Albertan* reported. "John D. Rockefeller certainly would have felt himself in a sympathetic atmosphere could he have been here to breathe the oil-impregnated air of Calgary." The Dominion Lands Office was immediately over-run with "prospective oil barons" clamouring for maps of the Turner Valley region, and organizing exploration parties.

Leaseholds changed hands at an astonishing clip, netting sellers huge profits. Harold Harvie was one of the first to cash in and the timing couldn't have been better, since the company for which the young man worked had recently gone bankrupt. Harvie was wandering about the city, muttering about his bad luck, when he ran into an old chum, Billy DeGraves, a reporter with the *Albertan*. DeGraves was in an excited state, having just heard the rumours of an oil strike. He was broke, as usual, but convinced Harvie to gamble his last $40 on a piece of land near the Calgary Petroleum Products well. "I didn't know whether to go for it," said Harvie, "but Billy talked so hard and so

[2]Herron organized Prudential Oil and Gas Company Ltd., Alberta Consolidated Ltd., Sheep River Oil Company Ltd., Macleod Oil Company Ltd., Canada Southern Oil and Refining Company Ltd., and Okalta Oils Ltd. Of these, Okalta was the most successful, becoming Turner Valley's biggest crude producer by 1926. Herron died thirteen years later, but Okalta continued to dominate Alberta's oil patch well into the 1940s. In 1970, its name changed to Oakwood Petroleums Ltd., which became a subsidiary of Calgary-based Sceptre Resources Ltd.

This composite picture places William Stewart Herron against the Dingman Discovery Well No. 1.

Provincial Archives of Alberta, P-1839

fast that I decided to take a chance." Three hours later, he sold half his holdings for $3,350. "It was the quickest money I ever made in Calgary," smiled Harvie. When asked to describe his occupation, he replied "retired businessman."

By the week's end, twenty new "oil" companies had been incorporated. It was easy to jump into the business. Historian James Gray notes in his book *Talk to My Lawyer* that title to Alberta's natural resources was still vested in the federal government. "All that one needed to obtain a 21-year lease on petroleum and natural gas rights underlying a quarter-section of land was $85 — $5 for a filing fee to be paid to a clerk in the government land office along with $80 for the rental at fifty cents per acre per year." Once they had that business attended to, fledgling oil barons could offer as many as 500,000 shares to the public.

Hundreds of lease applications were filed, covering a strip of land fifty miles long and twenty-five wide, 800,000 acres in all, even though there was still no word regarding the true nature of the Calgary Petroleum strike. Dingman finally admitted that "oil of a very high specific gravity has been struck in the company's No. 1 well, and the quality is equal, if it does not excel, the finest grades found in any oil territory." While Dingman warned it could be months before the well produced enough to merit production, his words went unheeded; the buying and selling of drilling

---

Rumours of a major strike out Turner Valley way reached Calgary just behind Elder, and the city seemed to go berserk. 'Knots of men collected on the street corners and talked petroleum,' the Calgary *Albertan* reported. The Dominion Lands Office was immediately overrun with 'prospective oil barons' clamouring for maps of the Turner Valley region.

---

rights and stock continued unabated. Calgarians who missed the land boom seemed determined not to lose out on this one.

Few Calgarians realized the stuff coming out of the Dingman well was not oil. Naphtha is a flammable liquid sometimes referred to as "natural gasoline." The fact that Dingman demonstrated its unique properties by using it as car fuel seemed even more impressive. Since the newspapers freely interchanged the words "oil" and "gasoline," oil it was. In fact, commercial-grade oil wouldn't appear at Turner Valley in any significant quantity (more than ten barrels a day) until

Glenbow Archives, NA-67-51

after 1920, when drilling techniques improved and companies could afford to bore through the cretaceous sandstone sealing the petroleum reservoir.[3]

The press joined in the fever unrestrained, the *Albertan* relaying even the wildest claims to its readers with a confident authority and calling Dingman's modest prognostications "painfully conservative." The *Herald*, meanwhile, preached caution. "The day of the oil company promoter is with us," it moaned. "It is the duty of every good citizen of Calgary to nip the floating of fake oil companies in the bud... There are a hundred men in Calgary today whose sole endeavour is to pinch off some easy money... They are looking for suckers. Don't be one of them. IF YOU WANT SOMETHING THAT GLITTERS, BUY A REAL GOLD BRICK."

The paper's dire warnings would soon be vindicated, though the bogus barons would not arrive for another few months. In the meantime, temperatures dropped below freezing and snow started falling. As Christmas approached, reports from Turner Valley dried up; "oil" was still trickling out of the casing pipe at the Calgary Petroleum well, but not in any great quantity, and Dingman was talking about drilling another hole. The newspapers turned their attention to other matters, and Calgarians settled back into the bust.

For many, the winter of 1913-14 was a season of hardship and misery. By December the city was unmistakably in an economic depression. The city's finances evidenced it. A series of bond

[3]Turner's biggest crude strike did not occur until 1936. That 6,828-foot well, owned by Turner Valley Royalties Ltd., produced 850 barrels a day.

Business-suited promoters look speculatively upon a boxed-in spring in the Turner Valley (below), which is showing an encouraging oil seepage. It was on land leased by the Independent Oil Company. Opposite page, the main street of Turner Valley about 1918.

Glenbow Archives, NA-952-9

issues sold out, buoyed no doubt by the city's boom-time reputation, but the council was forced to cancel municipal improvement projects nonetheless. Students in Ogden shivered as the temperature dipped to 46° Fahrenheit (8°C) inside their school because there was no money to fix the broken furnace. Ratepayers in Capitol Hill complained that the streetcars serving their neighbourhood were "frightfully cold." The once-profitable system was losing money, "principally due to the fact that many men have been laid off," noted the *Herald*, and coal was being rationed.

One group prospered — the slum landlords. Living conditions were worst in Riverside, also known as the "foreign section," on the north side of the Bow River next to the General Hospital. W.L. Ross, a medical health inspector, discovered one tiny house with twenty beds shoved together upstairs. Six beds lined a room on the ground floor, and seven more in the basement. "The bedding was stiff with dirt," reported the *Herald*. "The floors were caked with crud half an inch thick, and all the garbage was being dumped at the back door or into the river." Around the corner in Ykow Sloboday's rented shack, "a young baby was lying almost naked on the filthy floor when the inspector called. Eighteen men, one woman, and two small children live here. They eat and sleep in the same room."4

Blowouts, fires and injuries were all part of the job on those first cable rigs

THEY DIDN'T DRILL, THEY POUNDED — IF WIND DIDN'T BLOW THEM DOWN

Provincial Archives of Alberta P-1303

While Calgary's first oil barons built impressive brick mansions and drove opulent motor cars, life out in the oilfields was in sharp contrast. Rig workers pulled twelve-hour shifts, seven days a week, with a break every fortnight. Wages ranged from $3 to $7 a day, depending on experience and position. Crewmen slept in makeshift shacks, 12 by 22 feet, ate tinned food, and drank home brew. The chief entertainment was the weekly poker game. Turner Valley and Black Diamond held few attractions aside from a brothel placed strategically between the two tiny settlements.

Work on the original cable rigs was difficult and tedious. Derricks were about 85 feet high, made of rough lumber, and had consumed $50,000 by the time they hit a depth of 3,500 feet, a process that took about two years. Three steel cables were connected to the top of the structure by block pulleys, and ran back down to the floor. One was connected to the drilling line, the second to the bailer, and the third used to pull or lower the 8 1/2-inch-diameter casing pipes. The whole contraption was powered by coal-fed steam engines.

Holes were not so much drilled as pounded. Heavy iron bits were raised to the top of the derrick and then dropped, pushing farther and farther into the ground. When the "driller" started his shift, he lowered the bit to the bottom of the existing hole like a weighted fishing line. Then he marked the line to measure its depth, started raising and dropping the bit, and slowly let out more slack. As the bit

The ranks of the unemployed swelled to more than 2,000, a circumstance few could have imagined a year earlier. Something was desperately wrong, and "the politicians," as usual, suffered the blame. Agitators started calling for reforms. In January 1914 the Socialist party held an impromptu meeting in Victoria Park, where 200 homeless men had gathered. Six police officers surveyed the scene as James Fisher, one of Edmonton's leading "Reds," showed up and implored the crowd to join his cause. "It's cold. Some of you have not got a bed to sleep in. It's time for action," he cried.

Then a local school teacher, identified as Miss Muskitt, stepped forward and delivered a rousing speech to the shivering throng. "All you see around you today, everything that is beautiful and substantial, has been created by you men, the toilers, the producers, and yet you are not permitted to enjoy it. It is humiliating to beg for a job. If you beg, you are arrested. If you steal, you are arrested. The only thing left seems to be for you to quietly starve if you will submit to the inhuman dictates of your masters. Until you are organized you will never be respected or heeded." Miss Muskitt then launched a scathing attack on the Rev. D.A. McKillop, superintendent of Associated Charities, a church-funded organization that provided shelter and hot meals to those

gradually pounded its way through the earth, a casing pipe was lowered into the hole.

The process was exceedingly dangerous. There was, for instance, nothing to prevent a blowout. If a crew unexpectedly hit a pocket of gas, the sudden release of pressure underground could launch the drill bit up through the casing and into the hovering crowd of workers at the top of the hole. With nothing left to weigh it down, the gas could blast out of the wellhead with tremendous force, destroying the casing and nearly impossible to cap.

There were other dangers. Winds could blow the derrick down. Arms and legs could get caught in the machinery. W.J. Thompson, a rig captain with Herron-Elder, was making repairs at the top of one derrick and fell, hitting his head on the wooden beams on the way down and breaking both his ankles. Fires were not uncommon. One night in November 1915 workers on the Southern Alberta Oil Company rig near Black Diamond found themselves trying to stem a heavy flow of naphtha pouring from the well. A farmer wandered over to inspect the scene, and got no closer than 500 yards when the burning lantern he was carrying ignited the fumes. The derrick exploded into flames. Two men were trapped in the fire and suffered serious burns to their torsos and faces before managing to escape. William Livingston, president of the company, fled the inferno and ran smack into a barbed-wire fence. "The grass and vapour were burning around him," reported the *Herald*. "Half stunned, he gasped for breath and inhaled some of the fumes and finally made

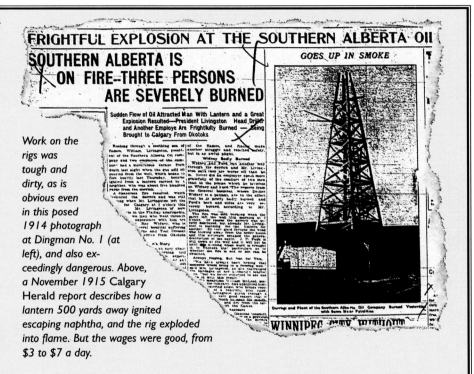

Work on the rigs was tough and dirty, as is obvious even in this posed 1914 photograph at Dingman No. 1 (at left), and also exceedingly dangerous. Above, a November 1915 Calgary Herald report describes how a lantern 500 yards away ignited escaping naphtha, and the rig exploded into flame. But the wages were good, from $3 to $7 a day.

another struggle and reached safety, but in an awful plight."

Conditions and technology improved as the years wore on. By the end of the decade, most new derricks were made of steel. In 1925, Royalite Oil introduced the first pair of rotary drilling rigs to the area. The new rigs were expensive, around $150,000, but could drill deeper and faster. They were also considered safer. Buckets of mud were forced down the drill hole, putting pressure on the seam, and thus reducing the odds of a blowout. As the 1920s came to a close, the old cable rigs had largely disappeared. Few mourned their passing.

— *B.H.*

In a melee of utterly unregulated trading, Alberta's oil patch is launched into history

Calgary photographer Harry Pollard, a youthful immigrant from Ontario in 1898, was on hand to record the 1914 Turner Valley discovery and the ensuing stock promotion frenzy, depicted on the next four pages. Every available downtown space was taken up by brokers, agents and curb traders. Shares were traded night and day, six days a week. (Police Chief Al Cuddy personally patrolled the streets to prevent trading on the Lord's Day.) Fistfights sometimes erupted as men struggled to put down their money. Nevertheless, it was this chaotic activity which established Calgary as the financial capital of Canada's oil industry.

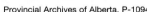

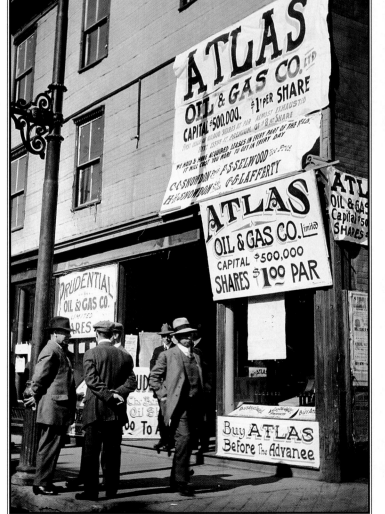

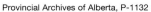

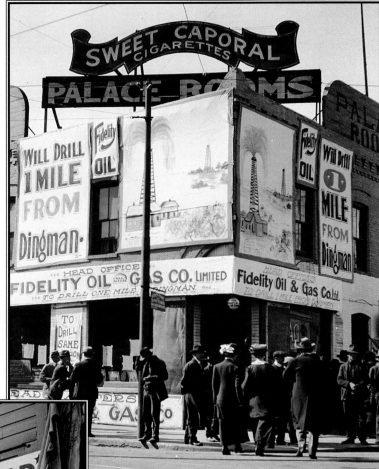

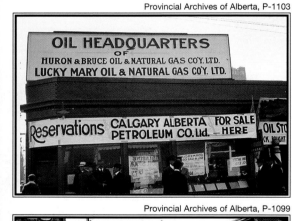

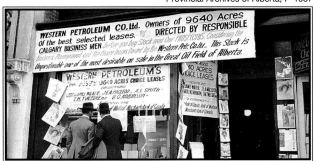

[5]Lowes tried to reverse his luck with a series of semi-successful forays in the oil patch, but he could barely support himself and his family, thanks to poor health and a serious drinking problem. In 1931, he was admitted to the Ponoka mental hospital, suffering from alcoholic psychosis. He died there nineteen years later.

out of work. "He rolls you out of bed, even if it is thirty below zero. If you do not roll out," she added, "he'll roll you up."

A week later, Fisher interrupted a council meeting and demanded that the city build a shelter large enough to house 500 homeless men and provide them with blankets and two square meals a day. The aldermen were outraged, charging that Fisher wanted to turn Calgary into another Edmonton, a place that "on account of its liberality was in danger of being swamped with unemployed men from all over the province." Everyone knew Edmonton was lax on drifters. According to the *Albertan*, "unwelcome guests of that city are allowed to loiter around a building in the fair-

The press joined in the fever unrestrained, the *Albertan* relaying even the wildest claims to its readers with a confident authority and calling Dingman's modest prognostications 'painfully conservative.' The *Herald*, meanwhile, preached caution. 'The day of the oil company promoter is with us,' it moaned.

grounds where they smoke and play cards and put in time in other leisurely and pleasurable ways. It's just like a long happy holiday for the fortunate floaters." Fisher was thrown out of city hall and council passed a motion to leave the charity work to the churches.

Goodwill went only so far. McKillop reported his association was caring for 125 families and hundreds more single men. "Our treasury is entirely exhausted," he reported, adding that disbursements for the month of February totalled $2,339, while donations added up to less than $2,000. Some large companies did their bit; P. Burns and Co., for instance, delivered 1,000 pounds of fish to Associated Charities. But some of those in a position to help turned a blind eye. Clifford

The fumed oak panelling, candelabra and marble columns of the Palliser Hotel, opened during the oil boom, provided a fine setting for big oil deals. The hotel cafe, with a private telephone on every table, became a popular trading locale — until the bartering got so abrasive that the management had to remove some of the barterers.

Provincial Archives of Alberta, P-4122

Sifton, minister of the Interior in the old Liberal government, seemed oblivious to the unemployment problem when he toured Calgary in February. Things didn't look so bad, he said. "It is nothing like what it was when I was a boy. That was when they had the real 'hard times.' I remember when they had soup kitchens and bread lines."

Though some fared better than others, few escaped the Depression's grim effects. Freddie Lowes, Calgary's flashy real estate magnate, saw his considerable fortune begin to fade by the end of the year. He responded to the sluggish economy with typical, if misguided, optimism, insisting the thirst for land would never wane. But when property values plummeted, notes Max Foran in an article on Lowes published in *Alberta History*, he "was left with substantial, unsaleable holdings secured on lines of credit...His subsequent plunge into bankruptcy was dramatically swift."[5]

Meanwhile, drilling activity slowed at Turner Valley. Only well financed companies like Calgary Petroleum Products and Herron-Elder could afford to run crews. Over the winter and deep into spring, intermittent rumours that Dingman's discovery well had finally hit oil invariably proved false. Then one morning in May, workers at the Dingman well hit 2,700 feet. Suddenly, they heard a hiss, and then a roar. Seconds later, a bolt of clear, amber liquid blasted sixty feet in the air, soaking several astonished onlookers with light-grade oil, again laced with a heavy concentration of naphtha. The geyser collapsed after a minute, but the brief, unexpected explosion marked the second round in the oil boom. Within hours, 200 motor cars were hurtling down the road to Turner Valley. This time, Calgarians wanted to see the purported discovery for themselves. They weren't disappointed. The Dingman well blew like clockwork — twice a day before workers managed to cap the well and direct the flow into a metal storage tank[6].

Once again the city went on a rampage, astonishing even the *Albertan*. "If a visitor from the planet Mars had dropped off a CPR train at any time yesterday," wrote one reporter, "he would have doubtless recorded in his notebook the interesting fact that Calgary had a population of 80,000 people, mostly lunatics."

A local bandit known as Ponoka Pete robbed a gentleman of his silverware and carved glass, but overlooked a nice fat bunch of oil stock certificates sitting near his bed. Ponoka was ridiculed in the press for missing the real find. Everyone was after oil stock — doctors, lawyers, shopkeepers, janitors, even children. The *Albertan* reported that a seven-year-old delivery boy was seen sobbing outside the office of one suddenly important petroleum company. He had his nickel and wanted a share, but was told the outfit did not sell in blocks of less than 100. Robert Campbell, member of the Legislature for Rocky Mountain, happened by and gave the youngster $5. The investment doubled before nightfall.

Nearly every city employee, from Mayor Herbert A. Sinnott to the nightwatchman, either held stock or wanted some. Calgary's police force was swept up in the frenzy. Joe Carruthers, the city's "fingerprint wizard, is retaining only one set of shoes, one suit of underwear, and one suit of clothes," reported the *Albertan*, "having pawned all the rest of his personal effects to invest in leases and oil stocks." George Miller, the city jailer, had "the undesirable distinction of being the only man on the force, so far as it is known, who has no oil stock."

When they weren't busy speculating, the police had their arms full keeping order. Officers were regularly dispatched to First Street, where huge crowds gathered on the sidewalk in front of the large oil company offices. Fistfights were common as men struggled to get inside and put down their money. Every available space downtown was taken up by curb traders, agents and brokers. They set up vending stands in "hotel lobbies, barber shops, cigar stores, drugstores, and on the street," the *Herald* marvelled. Cotton banners and makeshift signs festooned the downtown core, promoting the latest surefire winner. "A blackboard is all that is necessary to put one in business as a broker. First comes the inspiration, then the blackboard, then the money." There was even a special trading office for "lady investors," safely removed from the hurly-burly of the street trade.

Shares changed hands day and night, six days a week, with only occasional interruptions. Sundays were set aside for sermonizing. Clergymen had to remind Calgarians that greed was still a sin. Police Chief Al Cuddy vowed to crack down on traders selling stock on the Lord's Day, even stalking the streets himself in plainclothes to hunt them down. "His policeman's mentality could countenance the perpetuation of fraud, on a wide scale," notes John Schmidt, author of *Growing Up in the Oil Patch*, "only so long as it wasn't done on Sunday."

Real attempts were made to control the fledgling industry but for the most part the buying and selling continued unfettered by law. Curb sellers ignored requests to apply for licences. When the

[6]Bill Herron made regular deliveries of naphtha to Okotoks, hauling the heavy steel drums on horse-drawn wagons. Roy Flieger, a tool-pusher on a local well, remembers filling his Model T with naphtha for nine cents a gallon. "It was pretty wild stuff," he wrote in a 1979 history of the Turner Valley oilfields. "It smelled something like rotten eggs and when you stopped in Calgary at a filling station, the attendant would invariably say as he removed the cap from the gas tank, 'Whew, Turner Valley, eh?' "

The cigar-chomping pastor and his oilfield scam

REV. GEORGE EDWARD BUCK LOOKED MORE CONMAN THAN CLERGYMAN
BUT HE COULD PREACH ALL RIGHT, AND DO OTHER THINGS LESS EDIFYING

Of all the high-pitching hucksters and scam artists infesting Calgary in the spring of 1914, none could match the Rev. George Edward Buck for sheer boldness and temerity. An insurance salesman turned fire-breathing preacher, Buck lied, cheated, and stole his way into oilpatch infamy.

In 1907, he left his native Ontario for Calgary, where he formed a congregation of the Church of Christ (Disciples). He looked decidedly unclerical, striding around town in his trademark broadcloth coat and soft dark hat. He was rarely seen without a pipe or cigar wedged in his mouth, and when he drove to church in his bright red Dodge motor car, his waxed moustache flapped in the breeze. But Buck was a spectacular orator; people flocked to hear his weekly effusion on socialists, suffragettes, and other godless wretches.

Avarice, however, was not on his list of denunciations. He profited handsomely, it was said, from the real estate boom, and was one of the first to buy property in the Turner Valley area when the Dingman well hit gas. He created his own company, Black Diamond Oil Fields Ltd., sold 5,000 shares for a dollar each, and started drilling in late January 1914. His ads in the newspapers claimed his company was drilling "on the absolutely best oil land in the whole fields... Black Diamond stock, par value $1 per share, is going UP in price and is being eagerly bought up by intelligent, wide-awake people."

Three months later, having found not a drop of oil, Buck ran out of cash. His drill crew was threatening to move the rig unless he paid them $12,000 in outstanding bills. Desperate for capital, Buck tried to borrow money. He implored his congregation to buy shares, and persuaded his office staff to flog stock to family members. Finally, he resorted to fraud.

One morning in May, Buck assembled his office staff in Calgary. "I'm a little late this morning because I've been lying awake and I have thought up a little scheme," he told them, something that would save the company from bankruptcy. "Leave everything up to me. If you go along, you'll be looked after. I'm going to go through with it," he added, "even if it leads me to jail."

That evening, working under the cloak of darkness, Norman Fletcher, Roy Minue and L.L. Tyrrell dumped several gallons of crude oil and gasoline into Buck's Black Diamond well. Then they poured water into the sluice, churned the noxious mixture with a hand pump, brought it up in the bailer, and poured some into a barrel. The following day, Buck escorted Bill Cheely of the Calgary *Albertan*[a],

Rev. George Edward Buck, he of the resounding oratory, waxed moustache and bright red Dodge car, was unmatched among oilpatch hucksters for sheer fraudulent boldness. When his Black Diamond Oil Fields struck no oil and ran out of cash, he simply poured some oil down the hole, pumped it up before witnesses, and issued more stock.

Charles Tyron of the *Calgary News-Telegram*, and two aldermen out to the well and ordered his men to open the container. Whatever it was, it certainly looked and smelled like oil.

Both newspapers carried detailed stories of the Black

Diamond "strike." Hungry for any good news after three months in the doldrums, Calgary's oil speculators sprang into action. Tiny Phillips, Buck's rig captain, recalled encountering a huge crowd of people inside the Black Diamond office on First Street East. He warned them that Buck had "salted" the well but found his words "did not seem to have any effect on the investing public," Phillips recalled. "They were buying up stock like mad." Speculation of an impending gusher spread from mouth to mouth "with mysterious rapidity," noted the *Albertan*, "and the price of the stock leapt up wildly in the broker-age offices. Sales were made at $7 and even higher."

Buck paid his bills and gave each of his loyal office workers shares for keeping their mouths shut. But he faced another dilemma. If the well didn't start producing, what would he tell his new investors? Fortunately, his timing had been perfect; a week later, the Dingman well came in with an historic roar, and attention shifted to the new discovery.

Having won a brief reprieve, Buck plotted his next move amid constant rumours his company was sitting on a major find. He refused to confirm the stories, but hinted that something "big" was in the works. He kept up the charade by inviting carefully selected guests to inspect his Black Diamond operation. It was like visiting a baronial castle, recalled Tiny Phillips, in John Schmidt's book *Growing Up in the Oil Patch*. "The well was surrounded by a ditch full of water and the river, and only after Buck gave a password was the drawbridge let down and the visitor was given safe conduct across the moat. The derricks in those days were built of wood and enclosed, so it was impossible to see what was going on inside." A beefy guard named Ernest Budge would hoist his rifle and fire "four or five rounds when visitors approached from the opposite bank of the Sheep River. This gave an air of mystery to the whole outfit. Buck encouraged this activity."

However, Buck's luck expired that summer with the onset of war and the collapse of the oil boom. Word soon spread that the Black Diamond well had been fixed and Buck found himself enmeshed in scores of lawsuits. When the Alberta government launched a judicial inquiry into phony oil companies, Black Diamond Oil Fields Ltd. topped the list. The commission was derailed on constitutional grounds, but the province's attorney-general, C.W. Cross, was determined to expose the bogus oil barons, and Buck was charged with conspiracy to commit fraud.

During a preliminary hearing in November 1915, his chagrined investors provided the court with every detail of the swindle. "It was a dramatic tale and would make a corking good moving picture scenario," observed the *Albertan*. "All the auxiliary 'stuff' was there. The derrick in the grey of the dawn. The conspirators furtively pouring in the 'dope.' The mad rush of the automobiles with aldermen and newspaper reporters from town; the excitement in the city following the strike." Roy Minue, his head bowed, testified that he knew what he did was "wrong, but I was liable to lose my job if I didn't go ahead."

Buck's trial was scheduled for the following January, but after posting bail he fled across the American border, leaving his wife and five children to fend for themselves. The erstwhile preacher trundled up and down the United States for a few months in his distinctive red Dodge before finally settling in Wichita, Kansas, where he assumed a new identity and formed another oil company. Soon he was "booming along in characteristic Black Diamond style, making a big splash and figuring in the 'Who's Who' of Wichita," said the *Albertan*.

By March 1916, the Royal North-West Mounted Police were on the case, and Inspector John Nicholson was dispatched to apprehend the fugitive and extradite him back to Canada. Nicholson had no trouble tracking him down. He arrived in Kansas in April, and after a complicated legal battle with the fugitive's new lawyers, managed to gain Buck's extradition. In the fall of 1917 Buck was found guilty of fraud for salting his Black Diamond well, and sentenced to four years in jail.

But even that reversal he overcame. He appealed and won on a technicality; in exchange for the Crown's promise not to lay any more charges, he agreed to leave Canada for good. He moved his family to Wichita, and was never heard from again in Calgary.

— *B.H.*

Glenbow Archives, NA-1072-2

Rig captain at Buck's Black Diamond site, A.P. (Tiny) Phillips encountered an eager crowd of investors at the company's First Street office. He told them Buck had 'salted' the well, he later claimed, but they kept right on 'buying up stock like mad.'

aCheely's name is connected with two salting incidents, this one and the one at Olds described in the main chapter. Though it was rumoured Cheely knew in advance of the Olds case, he was never accused of involvement in this one.

Glenbow Archives, NA-2442-5

Calgary Stock Exchange opened in June, only a fraction of registered companies bothered to buy a listing. Investors were advised to ensure they were supplied with official stock certificates when buying shares, but this proved no guarantee of a company's soundness. "Printing houses worked overtime turning out share certificates in non-existent and unlocated wells," notes D.I. Istanffy, in his 1950 thesis *Turner Valley: Its Relationship to the Development of Alberta's Oil Industry*. "If the crest on one company's bonds showed one 'gusher,' that of its competitor was certain to show two."

While some investors certainly were being cheated, they didn't seem concerned. At the height of the oil rush, more than $500,000 changed hands every 24 hours. Shares in Calgary Petroleum Products jumped from $12.50 to $200 in three days. One man, desperate for a stake in the discovery well, laid down $1,000 for two shares while a lucky curb dealer netted a cool $1,460 for a sin-

The discovery defied the geological wisdom of 1914

BUT DINGMAN'S DRILLERS MISSED A BILLION BARRELS OF OIL THAT LAY BELOW THEM, MOST OF WHICH WOULD LATER BE MADE UNRECOVERABLE

By Tom McFeely

The discovery of the Turner Valley oilfield occurred largely in spite of the geological knowledge of the day, not because of it. Indeed, from both a geological and production standpoint, the entire history of Turner Valley is marked by ignorance, missed opportunity, and profligate waste.

Little was known about the western Canadian sedimentary basin in the second decade of the 20th century. For example, Eugene Coste, the man responsible for bringing the Bow Island natural gas field into production in 1909, believed in the now-discredited notion that ancient volcanic rocks were the source of the hydrocarbons that secured his fortune. And while contemporary experts with the Geological Survey of Canada may have had a clearer notion about the sedimentary origins of the oil and gas being discovered in the province, they too were guilty of glaring mistakes. Virtually everyone believed that no oil would be found in the deeper, older Mississippian limestones that underlay the Cretaceous formations in which the Bow Island and other early gas fields had been located.

That mistaken conception meant that almost none of the vast deposit of gas and oil underneath Turner Valley, a reservoir estimated at a billion barrels of oil and three trillion cubic feet of gas, was tapped by the Dingman No. 1 discovery well or by other wells drilled in the following decade. The great "discovery" of May 14, 1914, actually drained only a relatively insignificant Cretaceous sandstone, subsequently dubbed the Home sand. Ten years later, that formation had yielded a paltry 66,000 barrels of petroleum condensates, mainly naphtha, from the little-valued natural gas that flowed to the surface.

Not until the drilling of the famous Royalite No. 4 well in 1924 was the massive Mississippian reservoir, located only a few hundred feet beneath the Home sand, finally discovered. Even then, according to some accounts, the limestone was only penetrated because Royalite No. 4's drillers, having

nothing better to do after encountering no significant reserves of hydrocarbons higher up in the hole, continued to bore downward while geologists debated what should be done. In October of 1924, as the crew was finally preparing to abandon the seemingly doomed venture after drilling almost 300 feet into the Mississippian limestone, a whiff of "sour" hydrogen sulphide gas was detected. Soon afterward,

gle share in McDougall-Segur, a promising new company rumoured to be sitting on oil-bearing property. Florence Henderson sold a 480-acre lease two miles northwest of the McDougall-Segur well for $54,000 and a new dress. Miss Henderson, a CPR clerk, acquired the rights a year earlier for $165[7].

The old booster spirit was revived when Alderman T.A.P. (Tappy) Frost set out on a one-man trade mission. He ended up in downtown Toronto, ladling spoonfuls of Turner Valley oil from a wooden bucket, "publicizing the discovery like a carnival barker," according to George de Mille, in his book *Oil in Canada West*. When rumours surfaced in Winnipeg that the Dingman well had been salted, a nefarious practice whereby oil and gasoline were poured down a well and later drawn to the surface in front of a few gullible pigeons, Alderman Frost rushed off to the Manitoba capital,

[7]Of the 500 and more oil companies that opened in the weeks after the Dingman gusher, only nineteen actually drilled, and of those just six completed wells, at an average cost of $50,000. Since it took two years to drill 3,500 feet, it can be safely assumed that most of the oil barons had no intention of breaking ground.

the well blew in at a tremendous rate. By 1932, condensate production from the Mississippian reservoir had reached nearly 4,000 barrels a day, while up to 600 million cubic feet of unwanted gas was being flared off daily.

But notwithstanding the new knowledge that the limestone contained an immense pool of gas, most geologists still misinterpreted the structure of the Turner Valley field. The prevailing belief remained that it was a relatively simple "anticline," or dome, within which natural gas rested atop salt water. In reality, experts subsequently concluded, the ancient Mississippian reservoir had been distorted by the later upthrust of the Rocky Mountains. The folding and eastward push caused by the mountain-building had left a huge

Glenbow Archives, ND-8-419

oil deposit trapped on the western flank of the field, inaccessible to holes drilled at the more easterly sites of the earlier Turner Valley discoveries. Those had penetrated the field's crest, which contained only natural gas and condensate.

Only in 1936 was this structure finally confirmed, when Robert A. Brown (whose son of the same name was later to head Home Oil) and Calgary *Albertan* publisher George Melrose Bell (whose son went on to be the oilman and publisher G. Max Bell) scraped together enough money to drill a discovery well to the west. At a depth of 8,282 feet, the gusher blew in at a rate of 960 barrels of oil a day. That triggered a renewed burst of Turner Valley production, peaking at 27,000 barrels of oil a day in 1942.

By then, though, the vast majority of Turner Valley's oil had become unrecoverable, due to the massive loss of reservoir pressure caused by the flaring off of enormous volumes of unwanted natural gas while producing more marketable condensates during the field's earlier years. Of the billion barrels thought to lie in the original field, only about 140 million have been produced. Had the reservoir not been depressurized, it might have yielded nearly four times as much. As well, an estimated 1.8 trillion cubic feet of gas was flared off. Together, at the price levels of the 1990s, the lost oil reserves and wasted gas would be worth more than $10 billion. The epic waste, in fact, was the goad that led to the establishment of Alberta's oil and gas regulatory agency.

One final irony of the entire Turner Valley affair is that Alberta's first major discovery occurred there, in the geologically complicated and difficult-to-drill foothills region. Eight decades later, much of the area's estimated hydrocarbon reserves would remain unproven simply because the expense of searching for oil and gas would continue to daunt even the later era's more geologically sophisticated and technologically adept explorers. Meanwhile, larger and more easily tapped fields, such as Leduc and Redwater, would not be located for more than three decades after the Dingman No. 1 discovery.

Dingman wells Nos. 1 and 2, at the Turner Valley site in 1914, looking west. Like the industry's geologists, the government's experts also cherished what would prove to be a glaring misunderstanding of the geology.

J'EVER SEE SUCH LUCK?'

—From The Regina Leader.

'No abatement of oil fever in Calgary,' the Albertan headlined when it ran this front-page cartoon May 23, 1914. Spokane money was 'present in great amounts' and 'considerable New York and Chicago capital was wired in.' The cartoonist depicts Arthur Sifton, the supposedly pro-Edmonton premier, as a reluctant passenger on the back seat of Calgary Prosperity.

[8] In 1915, a reporter from Utica, New York, toured western Canada and described the Palliser as 'the only thing in Calgary worth looking at or being interested in...its ten magnificent storeys [it had eight] rise above the surrounding hovels and shacks and homely frontier town like a Grecian statue on a clam flat... A hotel with kerosene lamps, boiled pork and potatoes for dinner, tin washbasins, and yellow soaps would fit Calgary. Instead they have a palace.'

[9] Whether Cheely knew the Monarch well was salted remains a mystery. John Schmidt, in his book *Growing Up In The Oil Patch*, suggests the newspaperman was in on the scheme, but adds the public was left in the dark for years. In any event, Monarch's sudden prosperity lasted only a few months. The company went broke in 1916.

samples of genuine Dingman "crude" in hand. The *Manitoba Free Press* called the visit a success: "The conflicting reports which have been in circulation over the oil situation in Alberta have brought the subject very much in the limelight. As a result, many answered the call of Alderman Frost to investigate the facts. They came, they saw, and were convinced. The city of Calgary has been vindicated."

Money poured in from eastern Canada, Spokane, Chicago, Boston and New York. Oil fever hit Edmonton too. The daily CPR train to Calgary was crammed with residents "anxious to do a little gambling." However, while shares might trade freely in the Alberta capital, the enthusiasm was lacking. Calgarians had gone "stark raving mad," noted one New York investor on a swing through the province. "You people are puritanical by comparison," he told the *Edmonton Bulletin*.

Perhaps enticed by erroneous reports that Dingman had shot a stream of oil 200 feet into the air, wealthy investors from London were said to be on their way to Calgary via New York. They would have no trouble finding suitable accommodation. The opening of the eight-storey Palliser Hotel coincided with the boom. It was the grandest, most luxurious resting place in the province, a fitting monument to Calgary's new status as Canada's oil capital. (Edmontonians, cherishing the Grand Trunk Pacific's equally magnificent Macdonald, presiding majestically above the river valley, would of course disagree.) The Palliser's dining rooms and salons were fitted with fumed oak panelling, candelabra lighting, marble columns and floors, and handmade rugs. Employees were ordered to follow certain rules of decorum set out in an official hotel handbook: "No chewing gum or tobacco, no reading, no talking louder than in a soft undertone on guests' floors." Bellboys were not allowed to talk to female help in corridors, "except on matters of duty," nor were any staff members permitted to receive visits from relatives or friends, "unless in case of sickness or death."[8]

Would-be oil lords swarmed the hotel, transforming it into a sort of opulent trading floor. The first-floor cafe was a popular place to do business, thanks to the presence of private telephones on every table. The bartering became so abrasive that management was forced to remove them. Amused at the speculative frenzy going on inside the hotel, one wag posted the following list of house rules:

1. No well shall be drilled before 6 a.m. or after 3 p.m. Operations at that time are liable to disturb paying guests while in the midst of beautiful dreams of vast wealth and permanent gushers.

2. No more than one well shall be drilled in each leather chair or sofa during one time interval. It is exhausting to the furniture.

3. No well shall be drilled in a tone of voice which is audible within the three-mile zone and causes the skylight to flutter.

And so on.

By mid-June, a dozen derricks dotted the landscape around Turner Valley, but Calgary Petroleum's discovery well was still the only one producing anything remotely similar to oil. "Give them a few more weeks, we'll all hit pay dirt," was the phrase commonly heard around the brokerage houses on First Street while Calgarians waited with rising desperation for the next big strike. Bill Cheely, managing editor of the *Albertan*, created another round of hysteria when he reported that a vast reservoir of oil, probably the "largest in the world," had been tapped by the Monarch Oil Company, 35 miles north of Olds. "This is the real thing," he quoted the company's geologist as saying. "It is what the oil operators of Alberta have been looking for all these years. It is black petroleum." It was nothing of the kind. The well had been salted, a fact that Cheely may have known when he splashed news of the "awesome discovery" in bold print all over his newspaper. The headlines had the desired effect. Monarch shares jumped to $40 from $8 overnight and sparked yet another round of frantic speculation[9].

The patch received another blast of publicity a month later when the Duke and Duchess of Connaught and their daughter, Princess Patricia, paid a visit to the discovery well. After an elaborate outdoor luncheon, the governor-general's party toured the drill site. In his excitement, one of the drillers threw open the well, treating everyone in the immediate vicinity to an unexpected petroleum shower. "The royal party took their immersions of the spray with frank merriment," reported the *Albertan*. "The ladies, fully alive to the cleansing properties of gasoline, successfully washed their dust-stained gloves in it [while] the Duke expressed his amazement at the power exhibited by the well."

The episode made headlines across the Empire, but by then the "European situation" had consumed everyone's attention. On Aug. 4, 1914, Great Britain declared war on Germany, and interest in Alberta's fledgling oil industry waned. "At first there seemed reason to believe that the wartime need for oil would lead to accelerated development," note Turner Valley historians David Breen and R.C. Macleod. "[But] as mobilization commenced in Canada and the mother country, the prospect of attracting significant external capital soon withered... By the spring of 1915, the flow of outside capital had almost ceased." Rigs sat idle. The 160 Calgary brokerages of 1914 had dwindled to three by June of 1915. Drill teams had moved on, and leases were allowed to expire. Calgary's streets emptied, as most of the city's brokers, oilmen, hucksters and speculators sought greener pastures or found themselves on the battlefields of Europe[10].

The Great War also had the effect of paralyzing Calgary municipal politics. In July 1914, Mayor H.A. Sinnott announced he wouldn't be running again, and that December a Calgary doctor, M.C. Costello, defeated two other aldermen to become mayor. Costello was Calgary's wartime mayor and was returned for three more one-year terms, once by acclamation, twice by election. Trying for a fifth term in 1918, a month after the war ended, he was defeated by Alderman R.C. Marshall who served through 1919 and resigned in 1920. His successor was Mayor Samuel H. Adams, a lawyer who had paid his way through university by selling country newspaper subscriptions all over the prairies on a bicycle. The colourful Adams would carry Calgary's municipal politics into the 1920s.

[10]**Calgary Petroleum Products continued to operate in Turner Valley through the war years but with poor results. When its absorption plant burned down in 1920, leaving the company on the brink of bankruptcy, the directors voted to refinance with the help of Imperial Oil Ltd., a subsidiary of Standard Oil of New Jersey, and Royalite Oil Company Ltd. was born. It made its first major gas discovery in 1922, and built a refinery in Calgary, connected by pipeline. Two years later, Royalite #4 hit a huge pocket of naphtha that yielded a million barrels before running dry in 1929. Royalite was absorbed into Gulf Canada in 1969.**

Bob Edwards' Eye Opener in this prescient 1915 cartoon pinpointed the central import of the Turner Valley development. The province had a new industry that would compete with agriculture. But if anyone at the time had suggested that seventy years later the cash flow from oil would be five times that of farming, even Edwards would have dismissed such a notion as lunacy. Ironically, many of the oil industry's big players would be raised on prairie farms.

Index